T0373104

In this remarkable book, Bartlett begins where any scholar and thinker should begin: in humility. He wisely stresses the biblical importance of unity amongst believers. He then follows the path of sound biblical exegesis, appropriate attention to the existing literature and a fresh non-biased perspective, to arrive at sound conclusions with strong supporting evidence. He admits where there are difficulties in interpretation (whether historical or textual), but also helps to 'hack through' some of these biblical and theological 'thickets'. This book is an excellent addition to the canon of literature on what the Bible says about men and women. The summaries and guiding questions at the end of each chapter make the text both accessible to the average reader and a great resource for group or academic discussion.

The Rt Revd Dr Mouneer Hanna Anis, Bishop of the Episcopal/Anglican Diocese of Egypt with North Africa and the Horn of Africa

An important contribution to a debate on which all sides need to listen carefully to each other with humility and a shared commitment to Scripture.

Peter Baker, Senior Minister, Lansdowne Church, Bournemouth, UK

If, like me, you thought there was very little new to say on this topic, here's a book to make us think again. If, like me, you've become somewhat jaded by the sterile trading of arguments back and forth between the two main sides, here's a book that invites both parties to reassess where they stand, and why. If, like me, you thought you'd pretty much settled your views on the main biblical passages, here's a book to remind us that the Lord always has 'fresh light to break forth' from his word. As befitting a scholar and writer who is concerned for unity in our witness to the good news of Jesus, Andrew Bartlett's treatment of this most crucial of issues is elegant, clear, winsome and gracious. Even where I disagree with him, I'm profoundly grateful for the challenge to look more closely at the Scriptures. I'd encourage you to do the same. Read it. Read it with an open Bible. Read it with others. Read it with a Berean-like curiosity to see if these things are so.

Antony Billington, Theology Advisor, London Institute for Contemporary Christianity, and Senior Pastor, Beacon Church, Ashton-in-Makerfield

The treatment of 1 Corinthians 7 is the best I've come across. Very sound arguments.

Revd Kuruvilla Chandy, Trivandrum, Kerala, India

Books on this topic can often be accompanied by the sound of an author steadily grinding their axe in the background. This work is refreshingly different. Meticulous research, careful argument, objective assessment and judicious evaluation make this a significant scholarly contribution to the discussion on the role of men and women in Christ's church. It is essential reading for all in leadership.

Ian Coffey, Vice-Principal and Director of Leadership Training, Moorlands College, Dorset, UK

Andrew Bartlett offers an enriching and generous engagement with a difficult but important issue. He provides the reader with a clear understanding of the breadth of the debate and the various shortcomings of different positions. He doesn't merely present the extremes of the discussion but instead helpfully offers insightful development of the arguments and clear conclusions on each relevant passage. He has a commitment to close reading of the text, alongside intelligent and articulate interaction with biblical scholarship and a gift for enabling readers to examine their own presuppositions. These all contribute to making a book which is both intellectually stimulating and spiritually rich. This is sure to be a significant and helpful addition to the conversation, and will be a must-read for those who are already familiar with the issues, as well as those new to the debate.
Ellie Cook, Staff Worker, UCCF: The Christian Unions, blogger and speaker

This is an excellent introduction to, and review of, the biblical teaching concerning men and women in marriage and ministry. The author is a judge and international arbitrator with theological training and he has produced a judicious, thorough and well-argued *eirenicon*, to be taken seriously by both complementarian and egalitarian alike. His careful analysis of the biblical evidence results in the description of strengths and weaknesses in the arguments for both positions. This leads him to call for a reframing of the debate with a greater mutual understanding. I particularly valued his discussion of the textual position of 1 Cor. 14:34–35 and the review of the meaning of *authentein* in 1 Tim. 2:12. I would not like to be the attorney that appears before him with a poorly argued brief, such is his precision! This should become one of the major texts on the topic.
Revd Richard Crocker, General Secretary, Evangelical Fellowship in the Anglican Communion, Fairfax, VA, USA

In over forty-five years of involvement in Bible translation I have frequently grappled with the interpretive issues dealt with in this book. Faithful translation should be accurate and unbiased, allowing the original text to speak for itself. This is the ideal, but translators are human. Cultural biases have affected English translations of texts concerning women. The author's professional background helps him take a clear and refreshingly new look at the key texts. With careful scholarship and sound reasoning he resolves some important translation issues. I would recommend that Bible translators take note of this book.
G. J. Dannenberg, Bible translation consultant for Turkic languages

As an arbitrator I look for careful assessment of evidence and contextually sensitive reasoning. This book has both.
Dr Robert Gaitskell QC, international arbitrator

No matter what your current opinion on the topic is, this thoroughly researched book will make you think. It looks at all the important biblical passages as well as the historical context and the current debate and brings a fresh perspective to it.
Julia Garschagen, speaker and apologist, Zacharias Institut für Wissenschaft, Kultur und Glaube (Zacharias Institute for Science, Culture and Faith), Germany

This is a major contribution to the debate on the place of men and women in Christian ministry. It breaks new ground and is an important read whatever view you hold.
Dr Michael Green, author and theologian

Global communications are driving social change in East and South Asia. This increases the danger of importing Western theories unchallenged. I hope the insightful exegesis in this book will help Asian theologians and church leaders to engage with the Scripture without getting caught in the tramlines of the complementarian/egalitarian debate.
Anthony Harrop, former Publishing Consultant for the Asia-Pacific region, United Bible Societies

This is a landmark book on this key topic. It is an extremely readable yet in-depth study. Unexpectedly, I found it to be a page-turner because I really wanted to know what was on the next page. Andrew Bartlett has a profound understanding of Scripture. This book has changed and clarified my own thinking. It should be read by all Christians, from new converts to archbishops. Wives, buy it for your husbands! Husbands, buy it for your wives!
Professor Sir Colin Humphreys CBE FRS FREng, author of The Mystery of the Last Supper *and* The Miracles of Exodus

If we as evangelicals are sometimes tempted to do our theology (and preach our sermons!) by proof-texting, I know of no better antidote than this book: Bartlett's close attention to context transformed my understanding of several passages I thought I knew well. Drawing on his legal background and wide reading, and with absolute respect for the authority of Scripture, his careful scholarship has produced an analysis which is comprehensive, meticulous and clearly expressed. What's more, it is totally accessible to the interested layman, as it avoids technical terms and does not require knowledge of Greek – he explains what you need to know as you go along.
Revd Charles Mason, Priest-in-Charge, Waltham St Lawrence, Diocese of Oxford, UK

This book is rigorous, fair-minded, cautious, exegetical, analytical, logical, and dispassionately presented. I predict this will become **the** textbook used in colleges and seminaries that want to discuss women in ministry afresh. Every pastor, every elder board, every deacon board – anyone needing to sort through this topic must read this book.
Revd Canon Dr Scot McKnight, Professor of New Testament, Northern Seminary, Illinois, USA

Although I lean more towards a fully complementarian position, I want to commend this book because of its recognition of the importance of Scripture in Christian belief and practice, its desire to explain Scripture in its biblical context, its scholarly quality and its promotion of good relationships between Christians who have divergent views, with objective assessment and without personal criticism.
Andrew Muwowo, founder, Proclamation Institute Zambia

This is a must-read for anyone considering the Bible's teaching on the roles of men and women. It has changed some of my thinking. Using his skills as an international arbitrator and his deep theological understanding, Andrew weighs up the biblical teaching on this often contentious issue. His conclusions are fresh, illuminating and challenging to both egalitarian and complementarian alike. Every Christian leader and serious Bible student should read and digest this book. It will go a long way to bringing more humility and unity on the subject, which is a great need in today's church.
Michael Ots, evangelist, international speaker and author

Many dedicated and talented Christian women look for creative and honest ways to follow their calling in a way that is consistent with the teaching of the Bible. This can be a painful and confusing struggle. Some go to work in secular fields because they feel they are not welcome to use their gifts in the church. This book is analytical, dialogical and honest. It helps spiritually gifted women to find their place. But the issues that it addresses are important not only for individual women. They have to do with the presence of God's kingdom, missional effectiveness and – last but not least – godly attitudes among all believers.
Dr Einike Pilli, Principal, Tartu Theological Seminary, Estonia

An enjoyable and fascinating read. Andrew Bartlett writes in an engaging, highly readable style. He does not press his own views home but models a gracious openness; he ends each section with questions that are focused on biblical interpretation, personal reflection and practical application to church life. The book benefits from clear summary sections which ensure that, despite the complexity of some of its detail, the reader does not lose the main focus of the argument. This book is stronger for the fact that it does not pretend to have all the answers, but by reading it you will accompany a writer on his quest for understanding and you will encounter with him the twists and turns of his journey of discovery.
Dr Debra Reid, Director of Undergraduate Studies, Spurgeon's College, London, UK

Andrew Bartlett's magisterial study should be required reading for anyone exercising a teaching or leading ministry in any church. Every Bible student and ordinand should have it on their shelves as it is not just a book to read once, but a resource showing how to rightly handle the word. With devastating thoroughness, he subjects some of the most challenging passages in Scripture to rigorous scrutiny to establish

their true intent. He gives light to views from some illustrious predecessors in the faith which may make you wince in shame. He did not expect to arrive at some of his conclusions when he set out to write, and not everyone will necessarily agree with all of them, but as we spur one another on in our desire as men and women to be obedient as God's redeemed image bearers, we will have our eyes opened and our lives blessed by yet more truth that shines from God's holy word.
The Rt Revd Keith Sinclair, Bishop of Birkenhead, UK

Whether you hold a complementarian or an egalitarian viewpoint, this book challenges you to read the Bible with fresh eyes. It is hard not to read the Bible through our frameworks, thus backing up our personal positions and prejudices while writing off others who hold a contrary opinion. Andrew Bartlett is seeking to reframe this contentious debate, which requires his readers to take careful note and read familiar passages again. He writes with both humility and meticulousness, pointing out inconsistencies with both frameworks. You may not agree with all of his conclusions but his reasoning should be carefully considered. At the very least, this book gives us much food for thought as we seek continually to reform our understanding in the light of God's word.
Karen Soole, blogger, speaker and author of Unleash the Word

This thought-provoking and masterly analysis is also a thoroughly enjoyable read.
Marcus Taverner QC, London, UK

This is a stunning contribution to the debate about men and women in the church, for which I'm deeply grateful. The author's determination to follow the evidence wherever it leads, based above all else on meticulous handling of the Bible, has blown apart my assumptions, resolved my uncertainties, transformed my thinking and built new convictions. I pray that the Lord will use it to help evangelical churches align themselves more faithfully with Scripture.
Tony Watkins, speaker and writer on media and the Bible, recently an elder of Above Bar Church, Southampton (FIEC), now studying for a doctorate in practical theology

This book is very thorough, leaving no stone unturned. Some of the 'stones' certainly needed to be turned!
Mike Wheate, formerly International Personnel Officer, Operation Mobilisation

This is a superb, cogent, precisely written and enjoyable book. Its author has endeavoured with considerable success to draw together a huge amount of material on a topic which all too easily leads to more heat than light. His qualifications in law perhaps lend themselves to a more objective reading of Scripture as he seeks to apply a judicial perspective to evaluating the material. His willingness to criticize both sides' reasoning is noteworthy. Another real advantage of this book is that its key focus is 'the biblical texts, in their context'. Ruthlessly centring on this focus results in a detailed

exegesis of key texts, which helps the reader to keep an eye on the ball, in what is a very large discussion. The book makes a real contribution to the debate. It also suggests some valuable new approaches to the evidence, not least on 1 Timothy 2. And chapter 16 ('Taking stock and moving closer together') should be required reading for anyone approaching this topic. Whether you consider yourself egalitarian or complementarian, this book will challenge, provoke and deepen your understanding of Scripture.
Paul Woodbridge, Secretary of the Tyndale Fellowship and former Tutor in New Testament, Oak Hill College, London, UK

Andrew Bartlett has carefully studied Scripture to offer a sound assessment of both the complementarian and egalitarian positions. Without advocating one over the other, he has presented very helpful principles to discern how men and women may best witness and serve together for God's glory in each ministry context.
Ven. Wong Tak Meng, Archdeacon, Diocese of Singapore, and Dean of Cambodia

This book's consideration of male and female relations according to Scripture is a model of clarity, scholarship and summary. It is in every sense a judicious work, which helps to resolve some contentious issues of biblical interpretation. Its aim is thoroughly constructive: to promote mutual understanding and unity among those who believe in Holy Scripture and wish to be faithful to it.
Dr Nigel G. Wright, Principal Emeritus, Spurgeon's College, London, UK, and former President, Baptist Union of Great Britain

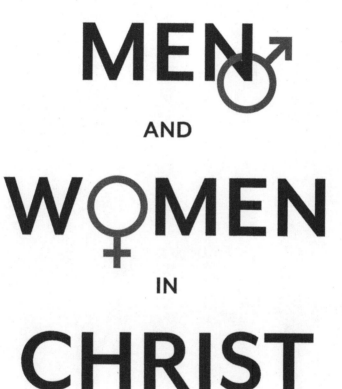

MEN ♂

AND

WOMEN ♀

IN

CHRIST

ANDREW
BARTLETT

MEN

AND

WOMEN

IN

CHRIST

FRESH **LIGHT** FROM
THE **BIBLICAL TEXTS**

INTER-VARSITY PRESS
36 Causton Street, London SW1P 4ST, England
Email: ivp@ivpbooks.com
Website: www.ivpbooks.com

Bible acknowledgments can be found on p. xxix.

First published 2019
Reprinted with corrections 2020

British Library Cataloguing-in-Publication Data
A catalogue record for this book is available from the British Library.

ISBN: 978-1-78359-917-2
ebook ISBN: 978-1-78359-918-9

Set in Monotype Garamond 11/13pt
Typeset in Great Britain by CRB Associates, Potterhanworth, Lincolnshire
Printed and bound in Great Britain by Clays Ltd, Bungay, Suffolk

Inter-Varsity Press publishes Christian books that are true to the Bible and that communicate the gospel, develop discipleship and strengthen the church for its mission in the world.

IVP originated within the Inter-Varsity Fellowship, now the Universities and Colleges Christian Fellowship, a student movement connecting Christian Unions in universities and colleges throughout Great Britain, and a member movement of the International Fellowship of Evangelical Students. Website: www.uccf.org.uk. That historic association is maintained, and all senior IVP staff and committee members subscribe to the UCCF Basis of Faith.

*To all scholars, whether complementarian, egalitarian or unaligned,
who with sincere hearts and true faith have laboured to understand and explain
God's word concerning men and women*

CONTENTS

PREFACE

This book is for scholars, pastors, Bible teachers, and anyone with a serious interest in how we should understand the Christian scriptures concerning relations between men and women in marriage and in church life. Because of the sharp divide between so-called egalitarian and complementarian viewpoints, this topic has vital implications for the unity and witness of the church.[1]

I have been in churches of both persuasions, to my benefit, and I have good friends who hold opinions on each side with strong and sincere conviction. While I have served as an elder or in similar roles, I am not currently doing so. This means I am not under obligation to support a particular viewpoint.

Although I have a degree in theology, I work in the law. My career as an English barrister is largely behind me and I now work as a judge and international arbitrator. Impartially adjudicating a dispute requires a different mindset from advocating for one side. As a judge or arbitrator, I have no prior commitment to a particular result but am required to go wherever the evidence and reasoned arguments lead. I have sought to adopt the same dispassionate

---

1. I explain and critique the labels 'egalitarian' and 'complementarian' in chapter 1. This book is not about whether women may be 'ordained' as 'priests' or 'bishops' in holy orders, as understood in some parts of the church. That raises a different set of questions about church tradition and order, which the New Testament does not directly address.

approach to the issues covered in this book. When I started writing, I was unsure what conclusions I would arrive at.

Everyone agrees in theory that attention to context is vital for understanding what someone has written. Adjudication of a legal dispute often requires an understanding of commercial correspondence which takes into account both the written words themselves and the real-life context within which they were written. In my work I often have the experience of interacting with people who wrote the letters which are being interpreted, and who therefore correct my misunderstandings. Time after time this provides sobering practical lessons in seeing how radically context can affect the meaning of what is written, and also how important it is to attend to the precise details of the words used if we are to understand correctly. This book tries to apply those lessons to reading letters written by Peter and Paul.

To support his warning that not many should become teachers, James says that we all make many mistakes (Jas 3:1–2). I was reminded of these words recently, when I diligently checked which days an art exhibition was open and then, in true Homer Simpson style, booked non-refundable train tickets for the only day when it was closed. Doubtless I have also made mistakes in this book. But I hope they are not enough to affect my overall conclusion, which is that each side makes important contributions towards understanding what the Bible teaches on these topics and, in order to be closer to Scripture, each needs to move beyond the confines of the existing debate and closer to each other. I hope and pray that this book will make a positive contribution.

My profession requires me to assess arguments which are presented persuasively, by capable and intelligent people. Within the broader discussion, I have made particular use of two major works: Wayne Grudem's *Evangelical Feminism and Biblical Truth* (*EFBT*) and Philip Payne's *Man and Woman, One in Christ: An Exegetical and Theological Study of Paul's Letters* (*M&W*). I have chosen these because of their thoroughness and because they are among the best-reasoned presentations on each side. The length of Grudem's major work is largely driven by the range and number of arguments advanced by a wide variety of egalitarian writers; where he has rebutted weak or speculative arguments, I do not go over old ground again. The published literature is too vast for interaction with all of it. My central focus is the biblical texts, in their context.

Paul writes: 'All Scripture is inspired by God and useful for teaching, for reproof, for correction, for training in righteousness' (2 Tim. 3:16). This is my starting point. Some readers may not share it. This is not the place for defending it. To Christian readers I would simply say, the Bible is our anchor. If we set ourselves adrift from it, we are severing our connection with God's revelation of himself in Jesus Christ. To any non-Christian readers I would say that there is no-one like Jesus, and nothing that makes sense of life like Christian faith. If any readers are sceptical of the very idea of revelation, they may like to consider how odd it would be if God created people in order to love them and relate to them, and then did not communicate with them.

My discussions of the biblical texts do not address any questions about authorship: I accept that Paul and Peter wrote the letters attributed to them in the New Testament, with the assistance of others where indicated.[2]

The arguments from Genesis 1 – 3 in chapters 5, 8, 9 and 13 are all presented on the basis of reading the text at face value. For contemporary readers, especially those interested in scientific theories of human origins, this approach may raise some questions. It is not necessary to address those questions in this book, because we do not need to take prior interpretive decisions about what is literal and what is figurative or symbolic in order to hear what the Genesis writer intends to convey which is relevant to our topic.[3] Paul's points in 1 Corinthians 11:2–16 and 1 Timothy 2:12–15 are taken from the way the Genesis story is presented, because he believes that the Old Testament scriptures constitute revelation from God in the precise form in which they are given (1 Cor. 10:11; 2 Tim. 3:16–17; see also Matt. 19:4–5; 22:31). To what extent Paul himself understood the accounts literally or in other ways is a question which need not detain us, because it does not affect the nature of his reasoning. Wherever I refer to the fall, I am referring to the biblical account, not to one particular theological understanding of it rather than another.

Translations from the New Testament are my own, except where otherwise stated. On the spectrum of possible translations they are markedly literal. They

---

2. In particular, I proceed on the basis of Paul's authorship of Ephesians, 1 and 2 Timothy and Titus. In my view the arguments against authenticity depend upon mistaken presuppositions and faulty reasoning. The experience of writing the present book has strengthened my conviction that the same voice speaks in 1 Corinthians, Colossians, Ephesians and the three Pastoral Epistles.

3. For a more comprehensive understanding of Gen. 1 – 3 it would be necessary to take such decisions. At a minimum, the church has usually understood the serpent not literally but as a figure for the evil one; this is reinforced by Luke 10:18–19; 2 Cor. 11:3, 14; Rev. 12:9; 20:2; and see Rom. 16:20. If the narrative should be understood as largely symbolic, this would make no difference for our purposes, since the purpose of such symbols would be to convey truth about God and mankind. We also do not need to consider the debate over whether Moses was the writer.

are not meant as substitutes for published versions, which aim to provide functional or optimal equivalence to the original. My purpose is to help readers get a reasonable idea of what individual words or phrases are being discussed, without needing a Greek New Testament or lexicon open beside them.

When I render a Greek word in English letters I identify it by giving the form of the word that would be given in a dictionary (nominative singular for nouns, first person singular present indicative active for verbs, and so on). I have departed from this practice where necessary (for example, where words in a phrase need to be in grammatical agreement). Such departures should be clear from the context.

In this book I express various disagreements with what scholars and Bible translators have written. I wish to emphasize that, however strongly expressed, my criticisms are solely of their reasoning or of the accuracy of their interpretation. In no instance do I intend any personal criticisms.

Wayne Grudem's *EFBT* and Phil Payne's *M&W* are both the result of prodigious effort over many years. I owe an enormous debt to them. Phil Payne was also kind enough to provide detailed comments on several draft chapters; unfortunately, circumstances prevented Wayne Grudem from doing the same. Additionally, in the chapters on 1 Timothy 2 I have particularly interacted, with profit, with *Women in the Church* (*WITC*).

As regards New Testament Greek I have received invaluable aid from widely available reference resources, particularly the fine websites at Bible Hub (<biblehub.com>) and Step Bible (<stepbible.org>). Bible Gateway (<biblegateway.com>) has provided access to a wide range of English versions. I have also been helped by *The New Greek–English Interlinear New Testament: A New Interlinear Translation of the Greek New Testament*, United Bible Societies' 4th, corrected edition with the New Revised Standard Version, translators Robert K. Brown and Philip W. Comfort (Carol Stream, IL: Tyndale House, 1990).

Where the References list does not provide bibliographical details for older works in English or for translations of ancient texts, this is because I have used published versions which are in the public domain and quickly accessible by an online search.

I am very grateful to those who somehow found time in their busy lives to provide comments on one or more draft chapters, even when they disagreed with what they were reading, including Nigel Atkinson, Antony Billington, Brian Capper, Bobbie Cole, Ian Coffey, James Dannenberg, Charles de Lacy, Charles Mason, Michael Ots, Rosemary Pepper, Richard Rogers, John Stevens and my wife, Elisabeth, who was pleased to help with any task that may bring her fellow American believers closer together. Their thoughtful and gracious comments saved me from many mistakes, infelicities and obscurities. Those which remain are entirely my own. My thanks go also to my ever-helpful editors at IVP/SPCK, Philip Duce and Rima Devereaux, and copy-editor Suzanne Mitchell.

To God be glory.

Andrew Bartlett
London

ABBREVIATIONS

BDAG   *A Greek–English Lexicon of the New Testament and Other Early Christian Literature*, ed. W. Bauer, F. W. Danker, W. F. Arndt and F. W. Gingrich, 3rd ed. (Chicago: University of Chicago Press, 2000)

BNTC   Black's New Testament Commentaries

BST   The Bible Speaks Today

BT   *The Bible Translator*

CBE   Christians for Biblical Equality

CBMW   Council on Biblical Manhood and Womanhood

DBE   Ronald W. Pierce and Rebecca Merrill Groothuis (eds.), *Discovering Biblical Equality: Complementarity without Hierarchy*, 2nd ed. (Downers Grove, IL: InterVarsity Press, 2005)

EFBT   Wayne Grudem, *Evangelical Feminism and Biblical Truth: An Analysis of 118 Disputed Questions* (Leicester: Inter-Varsity Press, 2004)

EvQ   *Evangelical Quarterly*

FIEC   Fellowship of Independent Evangelical Churches

JBMW   *Journal for Biblical Manhood and Womanhood*

JETS   *Journal of the Evangelical Theological Society*

JGRChJ   *Journal of Greco-Roman Christianity and Judaism*

JSNT   *Journal for the Study of the New Testament*

LSJ   *A Greek–English Lexicon*, ed. Henry George Liddell, Robert Scott and Henry Stuart Jones, 9th ed., with rev. supplement by P. G. W. Glare (Oxford: Oxford University Press, 1996), electronic edition under CC-BY-SA by the Perseus Project of Tufts University

M&W	Philip B. Payne, *Man and Woman, One in Christ: An Exegetical and Theological Study of Paul's Letters* (Grand Rapids: Zondervan, 2009)
NCBC	New Century Bible Commentary
NICNT	New International Commentary on the New Testament
NIGTC	New International Greek Testament Commentary
NTS	*New Testament Studies*
PNTC	Pillar New Testament Commentary
RBMW	John Piper and Wayne Grudem (eds.), *Recovering Biblical Manhood and Womanhood: A Response to Evangelical Feminism* (Wheaton: Crossway, 1991)
TGC	The Gospel Coalition
ThZ	*Theologische Zeitschrift*
TNTC	Tyndale New Testament Commentary
TrinJ	*Trinity Journal*
TynBul	*Tyndale Bulletin*
UBS	*The New Greek–English Interlinear New Testament: A New Interlinear Translation of the Greek New Testament,* trans. Robert K. Brown and Philip W. Comfort, United Bible Societies' 4th, corrected ed. with the New Revised Standard Version (Carol Stream, IL: Tyndale House, 1990)
WBC	Word Biblical Commentary
WITC	Andreas J. Köstenberger and Thomas R. Schreiner (eds.), *Women in the Church: An Interpretation and Application of 1 Timothy 2:9–15,* 3rd ed. (Wheaton: Crossway, 2016)

Bible versions

AMP	Amplified Bible, 2015
ASV	American Standard Version
BRG	BRG Bible, 2012
CEB	Common English Bible, 2011
CEV	Contemporary English Version, 1995
CJB	Complete Jewish Bible, 1998
DARBY	Darby Translation
DLNT	Disciples' Literal New Testament, 2011
DRA	Douay-Rheims 1899 American Edition
EHV	Evangelical Heritage Version, New Testament & Psalms, 2017
ESV	English Standard Version (Anglicized), 2001
GNT	Good News Translation, 1992

GNV	Geneva Bible, 1599
GW	God's Word Translation, 1995
ISV	International Standard Version, 1995–2014
KJV	King James Version
MOUNCE	Mounce Reverse-Interlinear New Testament, 2011
NABRE	New American Bible (Revised Edition), 2010
NASB	New American Standard Bible, 1995
NET	New English Translation, 1996–2006
NIV	New International Version (Anglicized), 2011
NIV 1984	New International Version, 1984
NKJV	New King James Version, 1982
NLV	New Life Version, 1969
NMB	New Matthew Bible, 2016
NOG	Names of God Bible, 2011
NRSV	New Revised Standard Version, 1989
NTE	New Testament for Everyone, 2011
OJB	Orthodox Jewish Bible, 2011
PHILLIPS	J. B. Phillips New Testament, 1972
RSV	Revised Standard Version, 1971
RV	Revised Version, 1881
TLB	The Living Bible, 1971
TLV	Tree of Life Version, 2015
TPT	The Passion Translation, 2017
VOICE	The Voice, 2012
WE	Worldwide English (New Testament), 1998
WYC	Wycliffe Bible, 2001
YLT	Young's Literal Translation

BIBLE ACKNOWLEDGMENTS

1. REVISING TRADITION, SEEKING UNITY

> How good and pleasant it is
> when God's people live together in unity!
> (Ps. 133:1, NIV)

What is this book about?

Bible-based Christianity is threatened with a needless schism. Devout believers line up under rival banners emblazoned 'complementarian' and 'egalitarian'. The champions of each group claim that they alone are being faithful to God's word as given in the Bible. They are passionate about the cause of Jesus Christ; they are also passionate about the dangers of the competing opinion.

Some complementarians say that their rivals are disobeying God's design, undermining both family and society, and giving encouragement to sexual confusion and immorality. Some egalitarians say that complementarians are opposing God's purposes, damaging Christian witness, and pouring fuel on the fires of domestic abuse, pornography and the denigration of women.

These far-reaching claims may seem out of proportion with the actual points of divergence. The debate is over the place of men and women in marriage and in church leadership, as portrayed in the Bible. Complementarians say that men must be leaders of their wives and that church roles involving authoritative teaching are reserved for men. Egalitarians disagree on both points. The purpose of this book is to encourage progress towards reducing and resolving these disagreements.

How did these issues become so divisive?

The loudest voices have been raised in the USA. Despite the vigorous life and growth of the church in South America, Africa and the Far East, the USA remains dominant as regards publications and resources. The discussion reached a turning point in 1986, after the winter meeting of the Evangelical Theological Society. Since that time the division has become more firmly entrenched.[1] The Council on Biblical Manhood and Womanhood (CBMW) was set up in 1987 to promote the complementarian teachings of what became known as the Danvers Statement (because it was adopted in Danvers, Massachusetts).[2] The CBMW soon published a book called *Recovering Biblical Manhood and Womanhood: A Response to Evangelical Feminism (RBMW)*.[3] In 1988 Christians for Biblical Equality (CBE) was begun (based in Minneapolis), in opposition to what it called 'the shallow biblical premise used by churches, organizations, and mission groups to exclude the gifts of women'. It adopted its own, firmly egalitarian, statement in 1989.[4]

A process of polarization has ensued. Organizations which had previously allowed liberty of opinion started drawing red lines. For example, the Southern Baptist Convention, which had previously allowed women pastors, revised its statement of faith in 2000 to add the words 'While both men and women are gifted for service in the church, the office of pastor is limited to men as qualified by Scripture.' When The Gospel Coalition[5] was set up in 2005, it included an explicitly complementarian position in its Confessional Statement.[6] In 2012 a team leader in a campus ministry refused to allow female staff to teach Bible studies to mixed-gender audiences, and was demoted as a result.[7]

An insistence on adopting one view or the other is not, or not yet, reflected widely across the world. Four thousand Christian leaders from 198 countries

1. *DBE*, 61, 64 (Pierce).
2. Available from the website <cbmw.org>.
3. This book was re-issued in 2006 with an additional preface.
4. CBE International, 'Statement on Men, Women, and Biblical Equality', <https://www.cbeinternational.org/content/statement-men-women-and-biblical-equality>. The quoted words are from elsewhere on the CBE International website.
5. An influential cross-denominational Reformed evangelical fellowship of churches.
6. TGC, 'Confessional Statement', <https://www.thegospelcoalition.org/about/foundation-documents/#confessional-statement>.
7. Kidd 2012.

gathered in Cape Town, South Africa, in 2010 at the Third Lausanne Congress on World Evangelization. They stated in the Cape Town Commitment:

> We recognize that there are different views sincerely held by those who seek to be faithful and obedient to Scripture. Some interpret apostolic teaching to imply that women should not teach or preach, or that they may do so but not in sole authority over men. Others interpret the spiritual equality of women, the exercise of the edifying gift of prophecy by women in the New Testament church, and their hosting of churches in their homes, as implying that the spiritual gifts of leading and teaching may be received and exercised in ministry by both women and men.[96] We call upon those on different sides of the argument to ... accept one another without condemnation in relation to matters of dispute, for while we may disagree, we have no grounds for division.[97][8]

But despite the Cape Town Commitment, the polarization is becoming more visible beyond the USA. For example, in the UK the Fellowship of Independent Evangelical Churches (FIEC) re-confirmed its prohibition on women pastors and elders in churches in 2011 by adopting a formal Women in Ministry Statement, expressing its understanding of Scripture.[9] Although less prescriptive than what it replaced, it took a firm position, which meant that some pastors and churches, which had not been acting in line with long-standing FIEC policy, had no option but to leave.[10]

The Vice Principal of a UK theological college commented in 2018: 'The tone of the debate has become more strident in the past couple of years. ... Women ... sit in a classroom with men who don't think they should be there!'[11]

---

8. Lausanne Movement 2011. The references given are: [96] 1 Tim. 2:12; 1 Cor. 14:33–35; Titus 2:3–5; Acts 18:26; 21:9; Rom. 16:1–5, 7; Phil. 4:2–3; Col. 4:15; 1 Cor. 11:5; 14:3–5; [97] Rom. 14:1–13.

9. FIEC, 'Women in Ministry Statement', updated November 2016, <https://fiec.org.uk/resources/article/women-in-ministry-statement>.

10. Stevens 2012: 'The result of this vote was that a very small number of churches left the Fellowship, either because they already had female leaders functioning as elders, wanted to have female leaders functioning as elders, or they did not wish to belong to an association of churches which was exclusively complementarian in practice.'

11. Personal communication to the author from Revd Ian Coffey, Vice Principal and Director of Leadership Training at Moorlands College, 10 February 2018.

The obligation to maintain unity

This polarization is disturbing. There is 'one body'. Through the apostle Paul, God commands the church to 'make every effort to keep the unity of the Spirit in the bond of peace' (Eph. 4:3–4, NIV). Jesus prayed for his followers 'that they may be one' (John 17:11). Some clear principles for handling disagreements are set out in Romans 14:1 – 15:13. It is no light matter to insist on a complementarian or egalitarian red line when fellow Christians, who are not ignoring Scripture but doing their utmost to follow it faithfully, are not of the same mind on it.

In practice, it is not always possible to maintain full unity. Some matters are so important (for example, whether a church holds to the full humanity and deity of Jesus Christ) that boundaries must be drawn. There can also be practical reasons which make unity difficult to maintain. For example, considerable graciousness and ingenuity would be needed to enable churches which believe that they should be governed by monarchical bishops (single leaders over each geographical area) to be in the same organized grouping as churches which reject that belief. Nevertheless, if a church or other Christian association ties membership to a particular interpretation of Scripture which is not generally shared, this needs clear justification.

Organizations which have insisted on dividing over this issue have sometimes published explanations of their position. Such explanations do not always address the question of how such insistence is consistent with the command of Ephesians 4:3–4 to make every effort to maintain unity, or with the principles for handling disputed matters set out in Romans, both of which they regard as no less authoritative than the texts relied on in support of their interpretations of gender relations.

We will return to the topic of unity in the final chapter. Before then, we must examine the debated texts to see God's good purposes, and how far one or the other position can be supported. First of all, it is necessary to say something about the history of interpretation of a woman's place, and then about how biblical interpretation ought to be carried out.

The traditional 'Christian' view of a woman's place

The traditional majority Christian view was robustly patriarchal. Women were inferior to men, both in rank and in nature. Men were the leaders in all spheres of life. As compared with men, women were regarded as inherently defective, being less intelligent, more prone to sin and unfit for the kinds of leadership which men were able to provide. They were not in God's image in the same full sense as men. Some teachers believed that this was the way God originally created them, while others understood women's defective nature to be a result of the fall.

The traditional majority view is found in the writings of Christian teachers through the centuries, including some of the faith's best-known luminaries such as Augustine, Aquinas, Luther and Calvin:

Clement of Alexandria (about 190):

> The mark of the man, the beard, by which he is seen to be a man, is older than Eve, and is the token of the superior nature. (*The Instructor* 3.3[12])

Augustine of Hippo (about 418):

> The woman together with her own husband is the image of God, so that that whole substance may be one image; but when she is referred separately to her quality of help-meet, which regards the woman herself alone, then she is not the image of God; but as regards the man alone, he is the image of God as fully and completely as when the woman is joined with him in one. (*The Trinity* 12.7)

> That a man endowed with a spiritual mind could have believed this [the lie of the serpent] is astonishing. And just because it is impossible to believe it, woman was given to man, woman who was of small intelligence and who perhaps still lives more in accordance with the promptings of the inferior flesh than by the superior reason. (*Literal Commentary on Genesis* 11.42)[13]

Albertus Magnus (about 1258):

> For a woman is a flawed male and, in comparison to the male, has the nature of defect and privation, and this is why naturally she mistrusts herself. And this is why whatever she cannot acquire on her own she strives to acquire through mendacity and diabolical deceptions. Therefore, to speak briefly, one must be as mistrustful of every woman as of a venomous serpent and a horned devil. . . . the female is more prudent, that is, cleverer, than the male with respect to evil and perverse deeds. . . . In this way,

---

12. Locations of quotes from ancient sources are styled in the format '3.3', meaning 'Book 3, Chapter 3'.
13. Quoted by Clark 1983, 40.

the woman falls short in intellectual operations, which consist in the apprehension
of the good and in knowledge of truth and flight from evil. . . . sense moves the
female to every evil, just as intellect moves a man to every good.

> (*Questions concerning Aristotle's* On Animals, Book 15,
> Question 11: Whether the male is better suited
> for proper behaviour [mores] than the female)[14]

Thomas Aquinas (1273):

As regards the individual nature, woman is defective and misbegotten . . .

> (*Summa Theologica*, Part 1, Question 92, Article 1, Reply to Objection 1)

Woman is naturally subject to man, because in man the discretion of reason
predominates.   (*Summa Theologica*, Part 1, Question 92, Article 1, Reply to Objection 2)

Martin Luther (1535):

The woman, although she was a most beautiful work of God, nevertheless was not the
equal of the male in glory and prestige . . . this sex . . . is inferior to the male sex.

> (*Lectures on Genesis 1 – 5*, Gen. 1:27)[15]

John Calvin (1548):

There is no absurdity in the same person commanding and likewise obeying, when
viewed in different relations. But this does not apply to the case of woman, who by
nature (that is, by the ordinary law of God) is formed to obey; for *gunaikokratia* (the
government of women) has always been regarded by all wise persons as a monstrous
thing; and, therefore, so to speak, it will be a mingling of heaven and earth, if women
usurp the right to teach.

> (*Commentary on Timothy, Titus, Philemon*, 1 Tim. 2:12)

Now Moses shows that the woman was created afterwards, in order that she might
be a kind of appendage to the man; and that she was joined to the man on the express
condition, that she should be at hand to render obedience to him. (Genesis 2:21). . . .
God did not create two chiefs of equal power, but added to the man an inferior aid.

> (*Commentary on Timothy, Titus, Philemon*, 1 Tim. 2:13)

---

14. Resnick 2008, 454.
15. Pelikan 1958, 69.

Let the woman be satisfied with her state of subjection, and not take it amiss that
she is made inferior to the more distinguished sex.

(Commentary on 1 Corinthians, 1 Cor. 11:12)

Unquestionably, wherever even natural propriety has been maintained, women have
in all ages been excluded from the public management of affairs. It is the dictate
of common sense, that female government is improper and unseemly.

(Commentary on 1 Corinthians, 1 Cor. 14:34)

Richard Hooker (1597):

[T]hings equal in every respect are never willingly directed one by another: woman
therefore was even in her first estate framed by Nature, not only after in time, but
inferior in excellency also unto man . . . [I]n ancient times . . . women . . . were in
marriage delivered unto their husbands by others. Which custom retained hath still
this use, that it putteth women in mind of a duty whereunto the very imbecility
of their nature and sex doth bind them; namely to be always directed, guided and
ordered by others. *(Of the Laws of Ecclesiastical Polity 5.73)*

Adam Clarke (about 1831):

The structure of woman's body plainly proves that she was never designed for those
exertions required in public life. In this the chief part of the natural inferiority of
woman is to be sought. *(The Holy Bible with a Commentary and Critical Notes, 1 Tim. 2:13)*

Charles Hodge (1860):

The ground of the obligation [of wife's obedience] . . . is the eminency of the husband;
his superiority in those attributes which enable and entitle him to command. . . . This
superiority of the man . . . thus taught in Scripture, founded in nature, and proved
by all experience, cannot be denied. . . .

(A Commentary on the Epistle to the Ephesians, Eph. 5:23)

These views were not uniform. More positive notes were sometimes heard.[16]
But these kinds of remarks represented the predominant opinion concerning
women.

---

16. See the citation from Tertullian in chapter 2, 27. See also Chrysostom, *1 Corinthians*,
    Homily 26 (about 390): 'For what if the wife be under subjection to us? It is as a

Jesus Christ and women

The traditional view was held by the majority of Christians during most of church history. It is now generally recognized as a source of shame that the name of Christ was associated with it. It could not in truth be justified from his teaching and practice. While Jesus did not overthrow the patriarchal structure of the society in which he lived, and while he chose twelve male apostles (a choice which we will consider in chapter 14), nevertheless he broke with prevailing cultural conventions of hierarchical male–female relations at point after point:

- Against convention, he pointedly recognized women as his followers alongside men when he said, 'Whoever does God's will is my brother and sister and mother' (Mark 3:35, NIV).
- Against convention, he spoke alone with a Samaritan woman of dubious reputation and instructed her (John 4:1–30).
- Against convention, he approved of Mary of Bethany sitting at his feet to learn from him, like a male disciple, when custom would have had her helping her sister with the meal preparations (Luke 10:38–42).
- Against convention, he allowed many women who were not his relatives to travel with him in his band of male and female disciples (Luke 8:1–3).
- Against the convention that women's testimony was inferior to men's, he chose Mary Magdalene to be the first witness to his resurrection, and he sent her to tell his other disciples (John 20:14–18).

In his teaching he said nothing that designated women as inferior to men or that placed restrictions on how women might serve God, as compared with men. Women went on to fulfil prominent roles in the young churches, including

---

(note 16 *cont.*) wife, as free, as equal in honour.' But the same author said: 'If the more important, most beneficial concerns were turned over to the woman, she would go quite mad. Therefore God did not apportion both duties to one sex . . . Nor did God assign both to be equal in every way . . . But taking precautions at one and the same time for peace and for decency, God maintained the order of each sex by dividing the business of human life into two parts and assigned the more necessary and beneficial aspects to the man and the less important, inferior matters to the woman. God's plan was extremely desirable for us . . . so that a woman would not rebel against the husband due to the inferiority of her service' (*The Kind of Women Who Ought to Be Taken As Wives* 4).

as prophets (Acts 21:9; 1 Cor. 11:5) and as patrons, hosting assemblies of believers in their houses (Col. 4:15).

Paul vividly expressed the unity and equal standing shared by all Christian believers when he wrote in Galatians 3:26–29 (ESV):

> [I]n Christ Jesus you are all sons of God, through faith. For as many of you as were baptized into Christ have put on Christ. There is neither Jew nor Greek, there is neither slave nor free, there is no male and female, for you are all one in Christ Jesus. And if you are Christ's, then you are Abraham's offspring, heirs according to promise.

In Christ, women are 'sons'. In the context of first-century culture this figure of speech means that, instead of being second class, they have full status and full rights of inheritance. With men they are equal co-heirs of God's promise.

This New Testament picture of women and men stands in stark contrast to the traditional Christian majority view.

Readers may wonder: how did the commentators of the past deal with what is said about men and women in Galatians 3:28? The short answer is that they did not pay a great deal of attention to whether it should impact on their view of women. Chrysostom's commentary on this verse refers to 'Greek', 'Jew' and 'slave', but makes no mention of 'female'. Calvin's commentary on it says that Christ 'makes them all one', but he sees no particular implications in regard to the relations of men and women.[17]

Rejection of the traditional view – new terminology

The full history of protests against the traditional view would require another book. Here it is sufficient to say that, with changes in culture, this view became a source of increasing discomfort, especially in the latter part of the twentieth century. This prompted a fresh look at what the Bible says about a woman's place. How far was the traditional view really based on Scripture, and how far was it derived from cultural assumptions? The result of this reconsideration has been that few devout Christians, at least in Westernized countries, now hold the traditional view. Instead, two new interpretations of Scripture have come into circulation, which are conventionally termed 'complementarian' and 'egalitarian'.

---

17. Chrysostom, *Commentary on Galatians*; Calvin, *Commentary on Galatians*. There is a short historical survey in *RBMW*, 149–150 (S. Lewis Johnson).

It is difficult to imagine more unsuitable labels than these for identifying the differences between the new interpretations. The differences are neither over whether women and men are equal, nor over whether they are complementary. Nearly all complementarians believe in the equality of men and women. Nearly all egalitarians believe that men and women are complementary. And neither side believes in the philosophical basis underlying secular egalitarianism. In this philosophy, men and women are no longer people in community who owe obligations to God and neighbour. Instead, they are individual holders of equal rights, and therefore autonomous persons with the sovereign right to choose their own identities. The two labels also give the impression of monolithic groups at either end of a linear spectrum, whereas the reality is a constellation of overlapping opinions.

Egalitarians hold that all church roles are equally open to men and women and that marriage is a fully symmetrical partnership without any differentiation that makes the husband in any sense the leader. The essential points of difference are therefore (1) whether the leadership and teaching functions of pastors and elders in the church are reserved for men alone, and (2) whether husbands have any leadership role in marriage and/or have unilateral authority over their wives. (By 'unilateral', I mean that the authority is one-way only, the husband being in a superior position.)

General belief in the full, inherent equality of men and women is a recent and obvious novelty, compared with the traditional view.[18] Less obvious at first sight is the full novelty of the complementarian position. When complementarians claim that their position is 'historical', this is a misconception.[19] This novelty needs a little explaining. Formerly, male superiority and female inferiority were understood to be grounded in nature as created by God, or else in nature after the fall. Women should not take part in public life or perform any task involving government, since they lacked the necessary abilities. John Knox wrote in 1558:

18. Some writers call this 'ontological' equality. They mean that men and women are equal in their being, or equal as persons. This implies equality in value, in status before God and in the qualities that make us human.

19. Smith declares herself 'convinced' that '*the historical understanding is right*' (emphasis original) and 'frustrated and saddened' by the manner of its rejection. Yet she herself strongly rejects the view that women are 'less intelligent, less gifted, less useful, more gullible or somehow inferior', and that only men may 'lead a nation', which is in fact the majority historical understanding. See Smith 2012, 17, 37, 64, 226, 232.

Who can deny but it is repugnant to nature, that the blind shall be appointed to lead and conduct such as do see? And ... that the foolish, mad, and frenetic shall govern the discreet, and give counsel to such as be sober of mind? And such be all women, compared unto man in bearing of authority. For their sight in civil regiment [= government] is but blindness; their strength, weakness; their counsel, foolishness; and judgment, frenzy, if it be rightly considered.

(*First Blast of the Trumpet against the Monstrous Regiment of Women*)[20]

This limitation was understood to reach into every part of life, whether civil society or family, and therefore extended also into the church. However, most complementarians now argue for a position that is almost opposite to this: they affirm that women may take positions of leadership in wider society. The only definite restrictions for which they contend are in marriage and in church leadership.[21]

The competing stories

The egalitarian story goes something like this:

God created men and women to be truly equal. But, ever since humanity first fell into sin, women have been oppressed by men. Patriarchal culture unjustly kept women under male control, both in the family and in wider

---

20. Knox's *Blast* was against all rule ('regiment') by women in the civil sphere, from magistrates to monarchs, and in particular Henry VIII's daughter, Queen Mary. He argued that it was men's duty to enforce against women the curse of Gen. 3:16 ('he will rule over you'). I have modernized his spelling.

21. The reversal of the traditional understanding is explained more fully in Brown 2012. She writes: 'the true traditional interpretation says that, since male authority/ female subordination is grounded in creation, it is normative in the temporal kingdom. Because it is normative in the temporal kingdom, it is also observed in the church. The contemporary "traditional" interpretation says that, because male headship/female subordination is grounded in creation, it is normative in the church (but not applicable outside the church).' *RBMW* offers a 'new vision' (11). The Danvers Statement proposes no restriction on women's leadership in wider society. However, some strands of complementarian writing are equivocal on this. They suggest or hint that some occupations may be unsuitable for women because requiring personal exercise of authority over men, though usually without identifying firm examples. I refer to this again in chapter 11.

society, treating them as less than fully human. Jesus came to redeem this
world from sin and its effects. He intended his followers to be led by the
Spirit, living in full obedience to God's design. Among other things, this
should have meant that women were liberated from male domination and
were respected as equals, both in the home and outside. But, after a short-
lived good start, the church accommodated itself to patriarchal culture,
just as it did to the evils of slavery. Many centuries passed before the
church woke up to the need to take a stand against slavery. It was even
longer before the church woke up to the oppression of women. It is only
recently that churches have begun to treat women as the equals of men.
There is more work yet to be done. Complementarianism must be
opposed. It is a misguided attempt to cling on to misinterpretations
of the Bible which arose from the sinfulness of patriarchal culture.

Complementarians tell a different story:

> God created men and women to be truly equal. It is right to acknowledge
> men's bad behaviour towards women, which conflicts with God's design.
> Jesus came to redeem this world from sin and its effects. He intended his
> followers to be led by the Spirit, living in full obedience to God's design.
> Whenever the church has not regarded women as being of equal value
> with men, and as having equal standing before God, the church has been
> in error. The modern controversy over a woman's place has had the good
> effect of highlighting and correcting some wrong attitudes. But a concern
> for equality does not justify departing from the plain teaching of the
> Bible, which is for our good and for God's glory. There is an important
> distinction to be drawn between equality of worth and sameness of role.
> God has called men and women to different roles. The Bible shows that
> men are called to lead in the family and in the church. Egalitarianism must
> be opposed. It fails to distinguish correctly between God's Word and
> cultural misinterpretations of God's Word. It throws out the baby with
> the bathwater.

Methods of interpretation

Where these stories differ, how do we decide which one is correct?

The methods we use to interpret Scripture determine the results that we
obtain. Complementarian writers have expended much effort, and much ink,
criticizing methods of interpretation used by some egalitarian writers. The

principal complaint has been the use of methods which really amount to rejecting the authority of the Bible for Christian faith and life. In particular, they charge that egalitarians, in order to arrive at conclusions which are palatable in contemporary culture, have used arguments which are incompatible with evangelical beliefs.[22] These criticisms have sometimes been justified. But examples of poor methods can also be seen on the complementarian side of the discussion. Methods of interpretation are therefore a centrally important topic, and I owe readers an explanation of the approach I will take in this book.

In my view there are at least seven vitally important tools in the interpretive toolbox. I describe these as (1) primacy of Scripture over tradition, (2) paying appropriate attention to culture, (3) going back to the source language in context, (4) coherence, (5) a Christ-centred canonical approach, (6) spiritual openness, and (7) practical wisdom. I lay out my understanding of these in appendix 1.

Without these tools we cannot understand Scripture accurately. All of them help us to adopt a position of appropriate humility before the text.

The path ahead

On the surface, a legal dispute is simply a contest between two parties, each advancing a conflicting case. But beneath this appearance there is usually another debate going on. The underlying debate is between each side's case and the actual evidence, or between each side's interpretations and the actual words of the governing contract or correspondence, understood in their context. Something similar is going on here. The important, underlying debate is not between Grudem (and fellow complementarians) on one side and Payne (and fellow egalitarians) on the other side but between their proposed interpretations and the actual text of Scripture, understood in context. I therefore focus less on their disagreements with each other and more on whether their proposed interpretations accurately reflect the text. This is a necessary approach, since on some points both sides may turn out to be wrong.

---

22. The word 'evangelical' is used in many senses. My use of it in this book does not refer to the Religious Right. Nor does it have anything to do with whether worship songs are accompanied by guitars and drums. I use it to refer to the theological outlook which emphasizes the message of the gospel and regards the Bible as the church's primary authority for faith and practice.

Changing the metaphor from the courtroom to the jungle, finding Scripture's path will be like hacking our way through thickets. Some branches represent cherished interpretations which need to be laboriously cut away. Others, which seem at first to be obstructions, prove on closer inspection to be signposts, showing us where the path continues.

While we should always approach with humility the writings of those who preceded us in the faith, on this particular subject a substantially new start was needed because of the impact of traditional patriarchal culture upon biblical interpretation. When the waning of that culture made it possible to hear the teaching of Scripture more accurately, the rejection of the doctrine of women's innate inferiority required new thinking. Both sides in the current debate have arrived at their new positions through the efforts of capable, devout and conscientious scholars. It should be no surprise if we need to combine insights from each.

In chapter 2 we begin with the relations of husband and wife as depicted by Paul in 1 Corinthians 7 and find a surprising measure of agreement between egalitarians and complementarians. Chapters 3 and 4 build on this with a study of Paul's instructions in Colossians 3 and Ephesians 5, leading to a nuanced view of the marriage relationship and its attendant duties. We find a biblical concept of the husband's unique headship which is markedly different from what is presented in some complementarian writings and is also contrary to egalitarian tenets. Chapter 5 looks at the Old Testament, especially Genesis 1 – 3, and finds an emphatic differentiation of man and woman but insufficient support for hierarchical notions of male headship. In chapter 6, we conclude that Peter's view of the husband–wife relationship is substantially the same as Paul's.

Chapters 7 and 8 move on from marriage to church life and engage with 1 Corinthians 11. Despite the despair often expressed by commentators of all stripes about whether we can ever be sure what Paul meant, close attention to the text provides a satisfying solution to its puzzles. (If using *Men and Women in Christ* for group study, it would be possible to take a break after chapter 8.)

Continuing with church life, we look next for the answer to the enigma of the silencing of women in 1 Corinthians 14:34–35. In chapter 9 we see how commentators have struggled to find a satisfactory explanation of these two verses, and in chapter 10 we examine the debate over whether these two verses were contained in the letter that Paul originally wrote.

Chapters 11 to 13 address the most challenging part of our inquiry. What is the intended scope of the restrictions which Paul places on women in 1 Timothy 2? Considerations of context drive me to reject both Payne's egalitarian interpretation and Grudem's complementarian interpretation (including its recent restatement in *WITC*). I offer an understanding generated by Paul's train of reasoning and the information available from the letter as a whole and the wider context. However, this is not at all a case of 'a plague on both your houses'.[23] Rather, my hope is that this fresh perspective might prove to be a blessing to the warring houses and bring them closer together.

Chapters 14 and 15 survey the New Testament's portrayal of local church leadership, looking at roles that women fulfilled and at the qualifications for elders.

Chapter 16 takes stock and comes back to the vital topic of unity. Some appendices contain additional material.

Writing this book has been remarkably similar to the experience I have often had in the hearing of a legal dispute. I start from a position of uncertainty. As the forensic process continues, things fall into place more and more, until it seems that every newly emerging fact and every new insight points in the same direction, confirming and solidifying the conclusions which are gradually forming.

When I started writing I was unsure where I would end up. From previous knowledge of the debate, I thought that I might arrive at a fully egalitarian position on marriage. As regards women's ministry, I thought I might find reasonably strong and finely balanced arguments on both sides, meaning that any conclusion on that issue could only be tentative. I was wrong on both points.

The proverb warns us, 'To answer before listening – that is folly and shame' (Prov. 18:13, NIV). I therefore make one request to the reader. Although the discussion questions at the end of each chapter encourage the expression of views, do, please, suspend firm judgment on whether you agree with what I have written until you have read and understood the whole book. Time after time, while writing the book, further study of a passage has compelled me to go back, re-think, and re-write what I had already written about an earlier passage.

Does it really matter?

'How good and pleasant it is when God's people live together in unity!' (Ps. 133:1, NIV). Divisions can be healed when Christian scholars go back to Scripture with open and humble minds, filled with the Lord's love and joy, and desiring to regain unity in order to please him.

---

23. William Shakespeare, *Romeo and Juliet*, Act 3, Scene 1.

Superficially, a book on differing biblical interpretations affecting marriage and church life may seem irrelevant to wider society. But unity and witness are inseparably connected (John 17:23). We live in a confused and hurting world. While Christians are busy disagreeing among themselves, there is a culture war going on, a swirling debate about human identity, same-sex marriage and fluidity of gender. The Christian contribution to that debate needs to be the very best that it can be. To be salt and light to our utmost, Christians need to speak not from controversial positions on which we are unable to agree, but from a secure biblical understanding of the nature and relations of men and women.

Summary of chapter 1

1. Christian unity is being damaged by a polarizing schism between egalitarians and complementarians.
2. The traditional interpretation of the Bible, to the effect that women are innately inferior to men, has rightly been rejected as being based more on patriarchal culture than on the actual text. Both egalitarians and complementarians now regard women and men as inherently equal and now affirm that women may be leaders in wider society. But complementarians insist on male leadership in the church and in marriage.
3. Faithful interpretation of the Bible gives Scripture priority over tradition, pays attention to culture, goes back to the source language in context, looks for coherence and takes a Christ-centred canonical approach; and it does this with spiritual openness and practical wisdom (appendix 1).
4. Applying those methods will lead to the conclusions of this book, which will be that the complementarian and egalitarian positions are each partly correct and partly mistaken.
5. If Christian believers can move closer together on these issues, this will please the Lord and strengthen the church's service as salt and light in a confused and hurting world.

Questions to consider

1. In what ways and to what extent was Jesus' behaviour towards women in conflict with traditional views?
2. Do you find anything in appendix 1 particularly surprising or interesting? What and why?
3. Has the complementarian–egalitarian divide affected you? In what ways?

2. HUSBAND AND WIFE, MEN AND WOMEN: 1 CORINTHIANS 7

'Is not my word like fire,' declares the LORD, 'and like a hammer that breaks a rock in pieces?' (Jer. 23:29, NIV)

Marriage: hierarchy or not?

For centuries the church taught that women were inherently inferior to men and innately unsuitable to be leaders, whether in the home, in the church or in wider society. Most Christians now recognize that this viewpoint was not faithful to the Bible but instead was a product of fallen human culture.

If we reject women's inferiority, what are the implications for marriage? Should the husband no longer be in authority over his wife or are there still valid reasons for maintaining that authority?

Most egalitarians resist any kind of male leadership in marriage. Complementarians still argue for some kind of leadership (sometimes hierarchical, sometimes not). But they seldom now argue that men must lead because women are unfit to do so. Instead, they rely on the detailed contents of particular texts. The principal passages relied on are Paul's teaching in Ephesians 5:22–33 (with the parallel passage in Col. 3:18–19) and Peter's exposition in 1 Peter 3:1–7. These are buttressed by 1 Corinthians 11:3 and a hierarchical reading of Genesis 2 – 3. We will look at these in chapters 3 to 8.

Before going to these much-discussed texts, we will start somewhere else, which is 1 Corinthians 7.

Some recent history of 1 Corinthians 7

The church regards itself as under obligation to adhere to the teaching of the apostles (Acts 2:42; 2 Tim. 2:2). By far the longest and most detailed piece of writing in the New Testament on the subject of men, women and marriage is by the apostle Paul in 1 Corinthians 7. One might therefore expect it to have a prominent place in any serious survey of New Testament teaching about men and women. Moreover, this chapter of 1 Corinthians is the only place in the New Testament where there is an explicit statement about a husband's authority over his wife. So it would appear to be not merely a relevant passage but a rather obvious place to start.

In 1991 the Council on Biblical Manhood and Womanhood (CBMW) produced a book explaining and defending the complementarian position (*RBMW*). Twelve chapters of the book are presented as 'exegetical and theological studies'. However, none of these is focused on 1 Corinthians 7. And the chapter which is specifically about marriage proceeds as if Paul's teaching on marriage in 1 Corinthians 7 did not exist.[1]

Thirteen years later Wayne Grudem produced his major work, *EFBT*. His intention was to update and supplement *RBMW*. One might therefore expect that the absence of a chapter devoted to 1 Corinthians 7 would be remedied. Grudem begins with two foundational chapters presenting his understanding of the biblical vision of manhood and womanhood in creation and in the church. In order to identify the issues to be resolved, he cites the complementarian Danvers Statement and, as a contrast to it, the egalitarian CBE Statement. He quotes the actual words of the CBE Statement, with its reliance on 1 Corinthians 7:3–5 for the proposition that husbands and wives 'are bound together in a relationship of mutual submission and responsibility'. He then asks, 'which position is right?'[2] One might think, therefore, that he could not fail to address 1 Corinthians 7. He gives his answer over some seventy-seven pages, but does nothing to remedy the omission. His answer says nothing about 1 Corinthians 7 or about the CBE Statement's reliance on verses 3–5.

In 2009 Philip Payne produced the evangelical egalitarian's equivalent to Grudem's major work. Payne includes a chapter on 1 Corinthians 7, concluding

---

1. *RBMW*, 161–175 (Knight). The sole mention of 1 Cor. 7 in the chapter on marriage is a reference to the possibility that a slave could become free (1 Cor. 7:21). However 1 Cor. 7 is briefly mentioned in the book's introductory chapter, which I cite below.

2. *EFBT*, 17, 30.

that this scripture 'presents a remarkable picture of Paul's vision of the equality of man and woman in marriage and in spiritual Christ-centered ministry'. CBMW published in its journal a detailed scholarly review of Payne's book by Tom Schreiner. His stated purpose is to present Payne's ideas and to rebut them. But he omits to deal with Payne's chapter on 1 Corinthians 7. He does not mention its existence.[3]

To help me with the present book, I sought recommendations of recent, good-quality, complementarian writing and was pointed to two books published by women authors in 2012.

Claire Smith, who is Australian, is the author of *God's Good Design: What the Bible Really Says about Men and Women.* Her book has glowing endorsements from Don Carson and other prominent complementarians. She aims to deal with 'the key Bible texts' that 'should determine' the best model for marriage. She presents five chapters on marriage. But none is on 1 Corinthians 7. She does not tell the reader why she judges that it is not a key text on marriage. Suffering from the same blind spot, complementarian reviewers praise the book for being comprehensive.[4]

Carrie Sandom, who is British, is the author of *Different by Design: God's Blueprint for Men and Women.* Does she cover Genesis 1 – 3? Check. Ephesians 5? Check. 1 Peter 3? Check. 1 Corinthians 7? No. In 232 pages of discussion there is one footnote which refers to one verse of it.[5]

An unaligned observer cannot help noticing the marginalization and neglect of this passage of Scripture by complementarian writers. I do not suggest that these omissions by the authors of *RBMW*, or Grudem, or Schreiner, or Smith, or her reviewers or Sandom, represent a conscious strategy to evade an inconvenient text. It is routine that scholars with a strong commitment to a particular position struggle to give an adequate hearing to a conflicting point of view. In all walks of life, whether in courts of law or in New Testament scholarship, a partisan commitment makes it harder for us to be objective. In

---

3. *M&W*, 108. Schreiner 2010, 33–46.
4. Smith 2012, 9. In her chapters on marriage she makes incidental references to 1 Cor. 7 at 124, 132, 150, 206. See the pages inside the front cover: William Taylor: 'comprehensive'; Carmelina Read: 'comprehensive'; Andrew Heard: 'comprehensive'; Jonathan Fletcher: 'It is a *must* for egalitarians . . . Their frequent objections are faced and answered.' See also *WITC*, 249–251 (Yarbrough).
5. Sandom 2012, 62, refers to 1 Cor. 7:39, on the subject of marriage to an unbeliever. See also *WITC*, 247–249 (Yarbrough).

the course of this book we will see examples of the same difficulty on the other side of the debate.

Threefold relevance of 1 Corinthians 7

For the purposes of the present debate, 1 Corinthians 7 provides three important insights into Paul's thinking. We see (1) the end-time perspective that he brings to bear on relations between men and women; (2) how he views a husband's authority over his wife; and (3) his view of the equality of women with men.

1. Paul's end-time perspective: the world in its present form is passing away

Some people in the Corinthian church believed that they had arrived at a superior spiritual state (1 Cor. 4:8). They thought they had risen above the unspiritual and earthly things which preoccupied ignorant people. Since, as they saw it, marriage was an unspiritual and earthly thing, they were advocating complete sexual abstinence, and a question about this had been addressed to Paul (7:1). One of Paul's reasons for writing to them is to correct this wrong perspective.

How would Paul have responded to them if, as a Jew, he had not also been a follower of Jesus Christ? In 6:16 (quoting Gen. 2:24) he has referred to God's design of the sexual union of man and woman in marriage. He could have referred to this again, and to the creation mandate that humanity should be fruitful and increase in number (Gen. 1:28). He could have said that for this reason marriage, sexual union and procreation are God's will, and so the Corinthians should not abstain.

But he chooses not to express his reasoning in this way. Why? Because this would miss the most important consideration. Paul's view of the world is now Christ-centred. The Messiah has come. A different stage in God's plan has arrived, so a new perspective on life is needed. The truth of Genesis 2:24 is now overlaid by a new outlook. His key point in 1 Corinthians 7 is that the end of all things is now in sight. After setting out his practical instructions in verses 1–28, Paul both summarizes this new outlook and states the underlying reason for it. With an impressive rhetorical flourish, he writes:

> What I mean, brothers and sisters, is that *the time is short*. From now on those who have wives should live as if they do not; those who mourn, as if they did not; those who are happy, as if they were not; those who buy something, as if it were not theirs to keep; those who use the things of the world, as if not engrossed in them. *For this world in its present form is passing away*. (vv. 29–31, NIV; emphases added)

Spelled out more prosaically: because Christ has come, the end is already in view; this is so much more important than the world in its present and temporary form that it relativizes all the present circumstances of our lives.[6]

Many New Testament ideas feed into this perspective. Christ has been raised from death, therefore his people will also be raised from death (6:14). Paul knows that when all are raised, there will no longer be marriage between men and women (Luke 20:34–36). He knows that in Christ all are designated as 'sons' with equal rights of inheritance and there is no longer 'male and female' (Gal. 3:26–29). The phrase 'male and female' is an exact quotation from the Septuagint of Genesis 1:27; by boldly stating that in Christ it no longer applies, Paul signals unmistakably that a new era has dawned. In Christ, and therefore in the Christian, the new creation has begun (2 Cor. 5:17). Humanity's original calling to fill and subdue the earth (Gen. 1:27–28) is now to be fulfilled in a different way in and through Jesus Christ (1 Cor. 15:24–25; Eph. 1:23; 4:10).

Like most heresies, the one that Paul addresses here is a distorted or unbalanced truth. The present time is a mixture of 'now' (God's kingdom has arrived in Christ) and 'not yet' (believers remain part of the old creation and God's kingdom has not yet arrived in its fullness). Because the kingdom is now, marriage is no longer required for filling the earth, and singleness (which involves celibacy – 6:18; 7:8–9) has become commendable (7:7–8, 32–35). Marriage is not as important as it was before; it is a concession instead of a command (7:6–7).[7] But this is not the whole story. Because God's kingdom is not yet, marriage remains a part of God's purposes for this present life, and it

---

6. This is a general point about the time in which the Christian lives, between the first and second comings of Christ. It should not be confused with taking account of the 'present crisis' referred to in v. 26, which was a temporary event, not now identifiable with certainty, but probably food shortages following one or more failed harvests. Compare 1 Cor. 11:21–22; 16:1–4; Rom. 8:35 (written from Corinth two years later). See Blue 1993, 579; Ibita 2016, 33–53. Some say v. 26 indicates that Paul expects the second coming imminently, but this view creates unwarranted conflict with his outlook in other letters, especially 2 Thess. 2:1–8; 3:10–12.

7. In God's kingdom single people have spiritual descendants, in fulfilment of Isa. 56:3–8. On singleness see also Matt. 19:12; Acts 8:39. Some commentators have taken the concession of v. 6 to be the way husband and wife are told to relate in vv. 3–5, but this seems to miss the significance of v. 7, where Paul makes clear that the 'concession' is marriage itself (referring to the whole of vv. 2–5), as contrasted with singleness.

is better to marry than to burn with passion (7:8–9). While this present life continues, sexual relations in marriage are a remedy against the immorality which is rife in Corinth (5:1, 11; 6:9, 13, 15, 18–20; 7:2).[8]

In short, while creation is still in view, redemption and new creation are in the foreground. Paul therefore cannot satisfactorily deal with the promotion of sexual abstinence by simply telling his readers to give priority to the creation mandate, which requires procreation. This would not be a satisfactory answer, because a Christian perspective on marriage must now also take into account the advent of the new creation.

2. Marital relations and equal authority

It is in this context that Paul writes about the marital duties of spouses to each other:

> Let the husband render to the wife the debt, likewise also the wife to the husband. The wife does not have authority over her own body, but the husband (does); and likewise also the husband does not have authority over his own body but the wife (does). Do not deprive each other except perhaps by agreement for a season that you might give time to prayer. . . .   (7:3–5, as translated by Piper and Grudem)[9]

At first sight, these verses reveal in plain terms Paul's view of a husband's authority over his wife. The husband's authority is exactly paralleled by the wife's authority over her husband. In saying that each partner has authority over the other, Paul appears to envisage a situation of equality and mutual submission. He is saying each partner should yield to the other's authority.

But this is said in the specific context of discussing sexual relations and joint prayer. Some commentators interpret what Paul writes later in the letter (11:2–16) as showing a belief in the unique authority of men over women. So do these remarks in 7:3–5 truly reveal Paul's overall view of marriage, or is he advising only a special exception to the husband's unilateral authority? Does he mean that a married couple's sexual relationship and prayer life constitute a special case, where a general one-way authority of husband over wife does not apply?

This is how traditional commentators reconciled Paul's remarks with their belief in hierarchical male authority and the inferiority of women: the husband

---

8. This does not mean Paul considers that the only remaining purpose of marriage is to be a remedy against immorality. See the discussion in chapter 4.

9. *RBMW*, 79 (in the introductory chapter of questions and answers).

is head except in bed.[10] The idea that Paul must intend a special exception appeared to make good sense when viewed through the spectacles of traditional culture, where it was taken for granted that the husband was in charge.

When we look more closely at what Paul writes, we do not find a justification for regarding the marriage bed and joint prayers as a special exception. There is no trace in 1 Corinthians 7 that Paul means to state an exception to a general authority of the husband over the wife.[11]

If Paul had believed in unique male authority, then in order to pursue his objectives of disagreeing with sexual abstinence (v. 1) and combating sexual immorality (v. 2), he did not need to write what he did in verses 3–5. All that he needed to say was that the marriage relationship should include regular sexual relations. His statement that the wife has authority over the husband's body goes much further than is necessary for his objectives. Why go so far? It must reflect his view of marriage. The broad reason which he states in verse 4 (that each spouse has authority over the other's body) shows Paul's view of the nature of the relationship.

The idea that these areas of married life are a special exception makes little sense. Physically, a couple's sexual relationship is the most intimate aspect of their marriage. Within a Christian moral framework, it is a foundational element which distinguishes it from other close relationships. Spiritually, their prayers together are at the heart of their marriage. To make an exception in these two central matters would strike at the root of a hierarchical relationship. If there is equal authority and mutual submission at the physical and spiritual centres of the relationship, it would be strange indeed for there to be an overarching hierarchical relationship in less distinctive or less central matters.

This analysis is confirmed by what Paul says about decision-making. In a one-way relationship of authority and submission, decision-making is not joint, and the consent of the subordinate is not required when the person in authority makes a decision. But Paul here expressly instructs consensual decision-making concerning sexual intercourse and praying together. This is a rejection of the ascendancy of the husband. His teaching cannot justifiably be reconciled with

---

10. For example, Chrysostom, *1 Corinthians*, Homily 19; Calvin, *Commentary on 1 Corinthians* ('But it may be asked, why the Apostle here puts them on a level, instead of requiring from the wife obedience and subjection. I answer, that it was not his intention to treat of all their duties, but simply of the mutual obligation as to the marriage bed').

11. We will look at 11:2–16 in chapters 7 and 8.

a belief in a hierarchical one-way authority of husband over wife. He could not have contradicted more clearly the prevailing view of an unequal and hierarchical relationship.

This teaching is markedly different from the prevailing culture. While Plutarch commends mutual agreement in marriage, he makes clear that this is merely a decorous veneer over the husband's rule, for he adds that every activity carried on by mutual agreement should disclose the husband's leadership and preferences; if the husband prefers sexual misbehaviour with a paramour or maidservant, his wife should not be indignant; and while it is the wife's duty to respond to her husband's advances, she should not initiate intercourse herself.[12] In a society where men are usually in charge, and where in the worst cases wives are regarded as little more than their husbands' property, Paul's teaching is revolutionary. 'Paul offers a paradigm-shattering vision of marriage as a relationship in which the partners are bonded together in submission to one another, each committed to meet the other's needs.'[13]

This is so contrary to ingrained patriarchal culture that it has often been sidelined or ignored. Even today there are many who think of sexual intercourse in marriage not in this equal way but as a husband's right and a wife's duty. Some translators have thought that Paul could not have meant what he wrote, and have therefore blunted the force of his words. For example, NIV 1984 translated verse 4 rather obscurely as: 'The wife's body does not belong to her alone but

---

12. *Moralia*, 'Advice to Bride and Groom', 11, 16, 18. Plutarch was a Greek philosopher and essayist, writing a few decades after Paul. Unlike Plutarch, Paul places male sexual desire and female sexual desire on the same footing (vv. 3–5). Doubtless he was influenced in doing so by his knowledge of the Hebrew scriptures. See Song 4:1–5; 7:6–9 (male); 1:2–4; 4:16; 7:11–13 (female).

13. *M&W*, 107, citing Richard B. Hays, *First Corinthians* (Louisville: John Knox, 1997), 131. Corinth was a Roman colony, where Roman laws were in force. The power of the *paterfamilias* (male head of the household) was considerable, extending to the legal power of life and death over his children. Infants could be exposed and left to die or, after infancy, members of the family could be condemned to death by the *paterfamilias* under a formal domestic judgment: Buckland 1921, 103. Under Roman law there were various forms of marriage, with differing legal consequences. In the most formal version still current in Paul's time (marriage *cum manu*) the wife's legal status was the same as a female child of her husband: Gaius, *Institutes* 3.83; Buckland 1921, 118. However, by this time most Roman marriages took place *sine manu* (without full power transferred to the husband): Lincoln 1990, 369. For more information on first-century marriage, see chapter 3, 39–40.

also to her husband. In the same way, the husband's body does not belong to him alone but also to his wife.' But ESV, to its credit, here faithfully follows the Greek: 'For the wife does not have authority over her own body, but the husband does. Likewise the husband does not have authority over his own body, but the wife does.'

This equality in marriage could be seen as supported by the background of the created unity of husband and wife in Genesis 2:24 or by the foreground of the equality of men and women in God's new creation, or from both of these sources. However it is derived, there is no escape from the force of what Paul says here. For 'have authority' Paul uses the Greek verb *exousiazō*. This is related to the usual noun for 'authority', *exousia*, which Paul uses frequently (for example, see Rom. 13:1–3; 1 Cor. 15:24; 2 Cor. 10:8; 13:10; Eph. 1:21). He is unambiguously depicting husband and wife as having equal authority. If Paul had believed God's design was that a husband should have unilateral authority over his wife, he could not have written these remarkable words.

This understanding is confirmed by attention to 1 Corinthians 7 as a whole, as we shall see next.

3. Equality of men and women in personal relations

Contrary to the prevailing culture, Paul does not hold a view of male–female relations where men are in the ascendant. In this chapter he makes a series of twelve statements in which he carefully balances what he says about men and what he says about women, so that his view of the complete equality of relations between men and women is evident:

- each man, each woman (see v. 2 – equal access to sexual relations);
- the husband, the wife (see v. 3 – equal duties in the marriage bed);
- the wife, the husband (see v. 4 – equal authority over the other partner and equal submission to the other);
- the widowers, the widows (see v. 8 – same advice for both sexes);[14]
- a wife, a husband (see vv. 10–11 – same divorce restrictions for both);[15]
- brother with unbelieving wife, woman with unbelieving husband (see vv. 12–13 – same rule for men and women);

---

14. For explanation of how the context shows that the 'unmarried' (*agamois*) in v. 8 should be understood as meaning 'widowers', see Fee 1987, 287–288.

15. The words translated as 'separate' and 'divorce' should not be understood anachronistically, as if reflecting the modern legal distinction. See Fee 1987, 293–294; *M&W*, 106.

- wife, husband (see v. 14 – each is spiritually affected by the other in the same way);
- brother, sister (see v. 15 – same rule for men and women if the unbelieving partner leaves);
- wife, husband (see v. 16 – each partner has the same potential for saving the other);
- betrothed man, betrothed virgin (see vv. 25–28 – same advice for the engaged of both sexes);
- married or unmarried man, married or unmarried woman (see vv. 32–34 – singleness has the same spiritual advantage for both sexes).

Not one of these statements makes any assertion of male superiority or unique male rights.

Paul's only nod towards the patriarchalism of Corinthian culture is in his twelfth statement, where he gives some advice specifically for fiancés. As males, they are expected to make a decision about whether to convert an engagement into marriage (vv. 36–38). But the balance of equality is not disturbed, for he joins with this some advice specifically for widows, which makes clear his view that a woman is free to make her own decision about whether or whom to marry (vv. 39–40).

These twelve statements are inexplicable if Paul believed in unilateral male authority in personal relations between men and women.

Complementarian acceptance of the significance of 1 Corinthians 7

I have drawn attention to the absence of 1 Corinthians 7 from the exegetical and theological studies in *RBMW.* It does, however, receive a mention in the introductory chapter of questions and answers. After setting out their literal translation of verses 3–5, Piper and Grudem say:

> Doesn't this show that unilateral authority from the husband is wrong?
> *Yes.* But let's broaden our answer to get the most from this text and guard it from misuse. . . . This text is not a license for sexual exploitation. It is an application to the sexual life of the command, 'Honor one another above yourselves' (Romans 12:10). Or: 'In humility consider others better than yourselves' (Philippians 2:3). Or: '[D]o not use your freedom to indulge the sinful nature; rather, serve one another in love' (Galatians 5:13). . . . There is a *wonderful mutuality and reciprocity* running through this text from verse 2 to verse 5. Neither husband nor wife is given more rights over the body of the other. And when some suspension

of sexual activity is contemplated, *Paul repudiates unilateral decision making by the wife or the husband*.[16]

These prominent complementarians here expressly recognize that 1 Corinthians 7:3–5 is consistent with Paul's wider teaching about Christian relationships (Rom. 12:10; Gal. 5:13; Phil. 2:3) and that it is inconsistent with unilateral authority of the husband. Piper and Grudem even add: 'This text is one of the main reasons we prefer to use the term leadership for the man's special responsibility rather than authority.'

Unfortunately, this acknowledgment of the significance of 1 Corinthians 7 is not consistently carried through. Complementarian views of marriage often lack a proper integration of this insight with other passages of Scripture. Piper writes elsewhere in the same book that mature masculinity 'accepts the burden of the final say in disagreements between husband and wife'.[17] This assertion discards what he has called the 'wonderful mutuality and reciprocity' and Paul's repudiation of unilateral decision-making. These verses in 1 Corinthians 7 are the only explicit guidance in the Bible on how decisions should be made in the marriage relationship. Faithful Christians are not at liberty to disregard this guidance.

Some early Christian writings, before traditional patriarchalism largely recaptured the Christian imagination, reflect this biblical perspective. About 145 years after Paul had written to the Corinthians, Tertullian wrote of husband and wife:

> What kind of yoke is that of two believers, of one hope, one desire, one discipline, one and the same service? Both brethren, both fellow servants, no difference of spirit or of flesh; nay, truly 'two in one flesh'. Where the flesh is one, one is the spirit too. Together they pray, together prostrate themselves, together perform their fasts; mutually teaching, mutually exhorting, mutually sustaining. . . . Between the two echo psalms and hymns; and they mutually challenge each other which shall better chant to their Lord. . . . These are the things which that utterance of the apostle has, beneath its brevity, left to be understood by us.[18]

---

16. *RBMW*, 79–80; emphases added.
17. *RBMW*, 32.
18. Tertullian, *To His Wife* 2.8 (written about 200). The 'utterance of the apostle' is 1 Cor. 7:39 – marriage 'in the Lord' (see *To His Wife* 2.1), expounded with allusions to Eph. 4:4; 1 Cor. 12:5; Gal. 3:28; Eph. 5:31; Col. 3:16.

In chapters 3 to 8 we shall go on to see that 1 Corinthians 7:4 is the only explicit mention in the New Testament of a husband's authority over his wife. We have seen that this mention is coupled with a balancing statement of a wife's authority over her husband. Unless we have misunderstood, it follows that any leadership by a husband that is conceived as the exercise of unilateral authority in a hierarchy of husband over wife is in direct conflict with the apostle's teaching.

'"Is not my word like fire," declares the LORD, "and like a hammer that breaks a rock in pieces?"' (Jer. 23:29, NIV). With twelve blows, the hammer of 1 Corinthians 7 breaks into pieces the rock of marital hierarchy.

Is Paul an egalitarian?

In 1 Corinthians 7 Paul conveys a non-hierarchical view of marriage in which husband and wife are equal. But this does not mean that Paul is ideologically opposed to the existence of hierarchies where they are appropriate.[19] Nor is he an egalitarian in the modern sense. He is not proceeding from the modern secular position which views human persons as individual holders of equal rights which they should be able to exercise freely, without interference from others. We need to beware of the anachronism of imagining that his writing is addressed to our questions, rather than to the questions which his first readers had.

His words to husbands and wives in verses 3–5 commence with marital obligations ('Let the husband render to the wife the debt, likewise also the wife to the husband'). Thus his first emphasis here is on obligations, not on rights or entitlements.

He then switches to the language of rights in a way that to modern ears may sound like a licence for sexual exploitation: 'The wife does not have authority over her own body, but the husband does; and likewise also the husband does not have authority over his own body but the wife does.' But he is not encouraging exploitation, for he is using the language of rights with a negative emphasis, saying first what the wife is not entitled to ('does not have authority over her own body') and then what the husband is not entitled to ('does not have authority over his own body'). Thus he is not promoting the exercise of rights but, rather, calling each partner to yield to the other.

This is egalitarian in so far as it treats husband and wife as full equals. But Paul is not calling for the exercise of individual rights. Rather, where each partner has equal rights, each should submit to the other.

---

19. We come to this in chapter 3.

Where next?

Egalitarian readers may have found themselves nodding assent during this chapter. But we will find in the next two chapters that Paul's view of marriage does not coincide with the modern egalitarian view.

The reaction of complementarian readers to this present chapter may be: 'We can see that some complementarian writers have not paid full attention to 1 Corinthians 7, but aren't you placing on it more weight than it can properly bear? What about 1 Peter 3:1–7, Ephesians 5, and 1 Corinthians 11:2–16? Don't they show that Paul must have meant that sexual relations and joint prayer were a special exception to a husband's unilateral authority?' I will therefore be cautious in how I use 1 Corinthians 7 in support of understanding other passages. However, we will see that when those texts are carefully read they are fully consistent with what we have seen in 1 Corinthians 7.

Paul wrote this letter from Ephesus (1 Cor. 16:8). We will turn next to his letters to the Colossian and Ephesian believers, which he wrote probably some two to four years after his long stay at Ephesus had concluded.

Summary of chapter 2

1. Despite the prominence of 1 Corinthians 7 as the longest discussion of marriage in the New Testament, and despite its containing the only explicit New Testament mention of a husband's authority, complementarian analyses have tended to overlook it or downplay it.
2. Paul's view of the world is Christ-centred. Creation remains in view, but redemption and new creation are in the foreground. His perspective on marriage takes into account that the Messiah has come and the end is in sight. This relativizes all the present circumstances of believers' lives, which become unimportant in comparison with what is to come. In this light, he commends singleness and offers a strikingly equal view of marriage.
3. According to Paul in verses 3–5, husband and wife have equal authority. He repudiates unilateral decision-making. Leadership by a husband that is conceived in terms of one-way authority over his wife is in direct conflict with the apostle's teaching.
4. Verses 3–5 cannot justifiably be regarded as a special exception to a husband's unilateral authority, applicable only in the areas of sexual intercourse and joint prayer.
5. As far as can be determined from verses 1–16, 25–28, 32–40, Paul envisages complete equality of personal relations between men and women. If Paul

believed in a hierarchical, unilateral authority of husband over wife, it appears inexplicable that he wrote these words.

6. This does not mean that Paul is an egalitarian in the modern sense. He is not calling for individuals to exercise their rights within marriage; rather, he is calling each equal partner to yield in submission to the other, in line with Romans 12:10; Galatians 5:13; Philippians 2:3.

Questions to consider

1. What role has 1 Corinthians 7 had in your thinking about marriage?
2. Do you currently think the traditional view, that the equal authority of husband and wife applies only in the marriage bed, can be maintained on the basis of what Paul writes in 1 Corinthians 7? Why or why not?
3. What are your reactions to 1 Corinthians 7:29–31? Are there implications for the way you think or the way you live?

3. HIERARCHIES, SUBMISSION AND LOVE: COLOSSIANS 3 AND EPHESIANS 5

> ... to be subject to their husbands, so that no one will malign the
> word of God.   (Titus 2:5, NIV)

Three disputed questions

We saw in chapter 2 that human marriage is a temporary institution, which will not continue in the resurrection. The Messiah has come; the old creation is being replaced by the new. In this period of overlap Paul offers a counter-cultural view of marriage as an equal partnership in which husband and wife have equal authority. But is this understanding of 1 Corinthians 7 consistent with what we find in later letters, where Paul instructs wives to submit to their husbands (Eph. 5:22–33; Col. 3:18–19; Titus 2:4–5)?[1]

While commentators now generally agree that men and women are of equal value and dignity in God's sight,[2] they disagree over three questions which arise from these further letters:

1. Does Paul teach in these letters that marriage is a hierarchical relationship in which the husband is in a position of unilateral authority over the

---

1. For carefully reasoned accounts of the dates and circumstances of the writing of these letters, see Mosse 2007. He dates 1 Corinthians in 55, Colossians and Ephesians in 57–59, and Titus in 63–64.
2. For example, *EFBT*, 25–26.

wife? This involves deciding what Paul means when he says that the
husband is 'head' of the wife (Eph. 5:23).

2. The second question is closely related to the first. It concerns what
   kind of submission Paul has in mind. Is the wife's submission a one-
   way submission to a higher authority or does Paul envisage mutual
   submission of husbands and wives as in 1 Corinthians 7:3–5?

3. Does Paul teach a complementarian view of marriage in which
   husbands and wives have differentiated responsibilities, or is his view
   fully egalitarian, with no such distinction?

There is a wide range of differing interpretations. It is useful to identify four
possible combinations of answers to these questions, representing four positions A–D on a spectrum, as shown in Table 1.[3]

Table 1: Spectrum of interpretations

	Complementarian			Egalitarian
	A	B	C	D
1. Husband as authoritative leader of the wife?	yes	yes	no	no
2. What kind of submission?	one-way only, to a higher authority	partly one-way, partly mutual	mutual	mutual
3. Differentiated responsibilities?	yes	yes	yes	no

Wayne Grudem argues for position A. He prefers to speak mostly of leadership and headship rather than of hierarchy and authority, because of the danger
of over-emphasizing structured authority. Nonetheless, he writes in defence of
hierarchy and argues that the wife's submission to the husband is a one-way
submission to a higher authority.[4]

---

3. These four positions do not exhaustively represent the full range of commentators'
   differing opinions, but they are sufficient to provide a useful basis for our discussion.

4. *EFBT*, 41, 60, 188–214; *RBMW*, 11, 71–72, 75, 172–173 (Piper and Grudem),
   206–207 (Grudem), 422 (Piper and Grudem). It is not clear to me how Grudem
   reconciles position A with his understanding of 1 Cor. 7, as referred to in chapter 2
   above. Other contributors to *RBMW* also refer to hierarchy in the context of

Complementarian George Knight adopts position B: 'The mutual submission to which all are called . . . does not . . . rule out the specific and different roles and relationships to which husbands and wives are called in the verses addressed to them.'[5]

A number of other complementarian commentators agree, in distinction from Grudem, that Paul instructs mutual submission.[6]

Philip Payne takes position D, which is at the opposite end of the spectrum from Grudem. He holds a fully egalitarian interpretation of what Paul writes. Because the commands to submit and to love apply to all believers, he considers that there is no biblically mandated differentiation of husbands' and wives' responsibilities.[7]

However, position D is subject to a possible objection. To indicate the respective duties of husband and wife Paul uses a metaphor (head and body) and a comparison (Christ and the church). Each of these is asymmetrical and non-reversible. This objection leads to the intermediate position C, which is complementarian to the extent that it recognizes a differentiation in the responsibilities of husband and wife.

There are some preliminary topics which need to be elucidated before we address the disputed questions. These are (1) the relationship of Colossians and Ephesians; (2) Paul's view of submission as a Christian virtue and of hierarchies; (3) the ideas contained in the word which Paul uses for 'submit'; (4) when it is right not to submit; (5) how the marriage relationship was viewed in first-century culture; and (6) some practical reasons for Paul's instructions to wives and husbands.

We will then be in a better position to consider the three questions in the light of what Paul writes in Colossians and Ephesians. For accurate understanding

---

marriage: *RBMW*, 94, 102 (Ortlund), 122 (Schreiner), 155, 159 (S. Lewis Johnson), 296 (Gregg Johnson), 402 (Elliot). Position A is also energetically advanced in O'Brien 1999, 398–418, 436–437. Note that Eerdmans withdrew O'Brien's commentary on 15 August 2016 for non-compliance with accepted standards regarding acknowledgment of secondary sources.

5. *RBMW*, 162–166.
6. For examples of complementarians accepting mutual submission, see Stott 1979, 207–208, 215, 232–236; Piper 2009, 77–79, 95–96.
7. *M&W*, 271–290. Payne 2015, 6, refers to Eph. 5:2: 'Paul's call to both wives and husbands is to defer to and nurture one another. Christ is the model for all believers, wives as well as husbands.'

it will be important to pay close attention to context, to the flow of Paul's argument and to his exact words.

Preliminary topics

1. Relationship of Colossians and Ephesians

Paul's letters to the Colossians and to the Ephesians, with his letter to Philemon, were written at approximately the same time, during one of his imprisonments.[8] Though Paul had ministered for a substantial period in Ephesus, he may not have visited Colossae (Col. 1:4, 9; 2:1). The church there had been founded by Epaphras, who was in prison with Paul at the time of writing (Col. 1:7; 4:12–13; Phlm. 23). They talked together about the church in Colossae (Col. 1:8). This may have helped Paul decide what would be most useful for him to say in his letter to the Colossians.

The letters which Paul wrote to churches at this time were intended for circulation from church to church (Col. 4:15–16).[9] Tychicus was to carry the letters (Eph. 6:21–22; Col. 4:7–9). As the letter carrier, he would be expected to explain the letters to the recipients.[10] The 'household code' section of Ephesians (5:22 – 6:9) is substantially more detailed than the corresponding section of Colossians (3:18 – 4:1). Perhaps Tychicus raised questions with Paul about household relationships, which Paul decided to cover at more length in the Ephesian letter. Whether Tychicus did this or not, it is appropriate to consider these two letters together.

2. Submission and hierarchies

Being willing to take the lowest place for the good of others is at the heart of Christian love and living. Jesus taught this and also lived it, both in his ministry and supremely at the cross (Mark 10:42–45; John 13:1–17; 15:12–17; Phil. 2:5–8). Because Paul's view of the world is Christ-centred, this theme is often picked up in his teaching:

---

8. Possibly in Rome, but more probably in Caesarea: see Mosse 2007, 210–215.
9. This seems to be confirmed in the case of Ephesians by the absence of remarks and greetings for individuals and by a textual query in 1:1 concerning the destination. Ephesus was a regional centre, being the Roman provincial capital of Asia Minor: Arnold 1993a, 249.
10. For the role of the letter carrier as expositor of the letter, see the discussion of Phoebe in chapter 14, 298.

- 'loving, . . . preferring one another in honour' (Rom. 12:10);
- 'I became a slave to all' (1 Cor. 9:19);
- 'I urge you, brothers and sisters, to be subject to such people and to everyone joining in the work and labouring' (1 Cor. 16:15–16);
- 'ourselves [apostles] as your slaves because of Jesus' (2 Cor. 4:5);
- 'through love, serve one another as slaves' (Gal. 5:13);
- 'walk worthy of the calling by which you were called with all humility, bearing with one another in love' (Eph. 4:1–2; and see 5:1–2);
- 'having the same love, . . . in humility esteeming others as surpassing yourself' (Phil. 2:2–3);
- 'Epaphras, our beloved fellow slave' (Col. 1:7);[11]
- 'clothe yourselves . . . with humility, . . . love' (Col. 3:12–14).

The fellowship of God's church is therefore built not on hierarchies but on humble love.

However, this does not mean that Paul is opposed to all hierarchy. He endorses the existence and exercise of authority where appropriate. For example, believers should submit to civil government, because it is God's provision for the active restraint of evil (Rom. 13:1–7). And he endorses the appropriate exercise of authority by parents over children. We know this because one of the qualifications for eldership is that elders should have their children under proper control (1 Tim. 3:4–5 – 'having children in subjection'). Paul is innocent of today's Western cultural distaste for hierarchies.[12]

3. The ideas associated with 'submitting'

To gain an accurate understanding of what Paul means by 'submitting' we need to be sensitive to linguistic and cultural differences. Most people know what a 'submission' is in professional wrestling. Hearing the English word 'submitting',

---

11. Of course the 'slavery' of which Paul writes in some of these texts is not to be understood woodenly, as if exactly like the evil human institution of slavery. It is a vivid metaphorical usage, which connotes taking the low place of humble service. It does not imply Paul's or God's approval of human slavery.

12. In 1 Tim. 3:4–5 the parent's concern is not the children's personality (submissiveness) but the social stance in which they live (as subordinate to the parent). On hierarchies, compare the remarks of the avowedly liberal, atheist writer Jonathan Haidt: 'When I began graduate school I subscribed to the common liberal belief that hierarchy = power = exploitation = evil. But . . . I discovered that I was wrong.' Haidt 2012, 167.

we think of yielding to the will or authority of another person, with connotations of surrender to a superior force. Lists of synonyms include 'succumbing' and 'acquiescing'. The related adjective 'submissive' brings to mind words like 'docile', 'compliant' or even 'doormat'.

These are not the connotations of the Greek verb *hupotassō*, which Paul uses in Colossians 3:18 and elsewhere. This is derived from *hupo*, meaning 'under', and *tassō*, meaning 'set'/'rank'/'arrange', as in Luke 7:8, where the centurion says, 'I am a man ranked [*tassō*] under [*hupo*] authority.' The primary idea of *hupotassō* is to put in subjection, to rank under.[13]

Because *hupotassō* carries the idea of being ranked below someone else, it is apt both for submission to authorities and for submission in personal relationships between equals. In the former case there is an objective ranking in a hierarchy: for example, believers are under the authority of the civil government, and must therefore behave in submission to that authority. In the latter case, the ranking is subjective: believers are to rank themselves below others *as if* in a hierarchy; that is, they are to treat others as more important than themselves, for this is the essence of Christian humility (Rom. 12:10; Phil. 2:3).

Grudem says that Paul's use of *hupotassō* implies a hierarchy of husband over wife. He claims that *hupotassō* is always used of submission to an authority. He says that no-one has yet produced any examples in ancient Greek literature, either inside or outside the New Testament, where *hupotassō*, applied to a relationship between persons, does not carry this sense of being subject to an authority.[14]

This claim is overstated, as can be seen from Paul's use of the same word in 1 Corinthians. In 16:15–16 Paul issues a call to humility, in which he urges his Corinthian readers to submit to the household of Stephanas and to all co-workers:

> You know that the household of Stephanas were the first converts in Achaia, and they
> have devoted themselves to the service [*diakonia*] of the Lord's people. I urge you,
> brothers and sisters, to submit [*hupotassō*] to such people and to everyone who joins
> in the work [*sunergeō*] and labours at it.   (NIV)

---

13. It does not quite correspond to the English word 'submit', which we do not use
    transitively in the relevant sense – I cannot 'submit' another person to myself; for
    this meaning we have to use other verbs, such as 'subject' or 'subordinate'. In this
    book I follow the more contemporary convention of transliterating the Greek letter
    upsilon with a 'u' (thus, *hupotassō*), not the convention of using a 'y' (*hypotassō*).

14. *EFBT*, 191, 250.

Grudem argues that this example is in fact submission to a hierarchy, because some of the household of Stephanas were elders in the Corinthian church, and what Paul means is that the Corinthians should submit to these elders, who are in authority over them. His source for this is a letter written by Clement of Rome to the Corinthians perhaps some forty years after Paul's letter.

But Paul says nothing here about eldership or hierarchy. He does not say that the Corinthians should submit to those of Stephanas's household who became elders, in distinction from others. He says the Corinthians should submit to the household of Stephanas, who put themselves at the service of the Lord's people, and to everyone who joins in the work (all co-workers). The reference to service is not limited to eldership, and the reference to co-workers does not imply any statement about their particular role in the life of the church. Grudem himself says that to be a co-worker (*sunergos*) does not imply having authority.[15] Paul's point is about the submission of believers to other believers who serve. Unless this was an unusual household, those who are submitted to will include women and slaves.

Moreover, Grudem's citation from Clement does not justify his hierarchical reading of 1 Corinthians 16:15–16. Referring to the ministry of the apostles, Clement writes: '[P]reaching everywhere in country and town, they appointed their firstfruits, when they had proved them by the Spirit, to be bishops and deacons unto them that should believe' (1 Clement 42.4). What this general statement tells us is that, from among the converts in each place, the apostles appointed elders and deacons. This adds nothing to our understanding of 16:15–16 as regards the point at issue.

Another use of *hupotassō* without any hierarchical reference is found in 1 Corinthians 14:32, where Paul says that the spirits of prophets are subject to prophets. This may mean that the act of prophesying is under a prophet's own control. An alternative interpretation is that each prophet's prophesying is subject to control or evaluation by other prophets. Either way, there is no implication of a one-way hierarchy of authority.

These examples show that it is possible for Paul to use *hupotassō* where no actual hierarchy is in view.[16]

Grudem's reasoning skips over an essential interpretive decision which has to be made when we read the texts concerning wives' submission. Does Paul mean that wives should submit because their husbands *are* in authority over

---

15. *EFBT*, 248–251.

16. The same can be said of the related noun *hupotagē*. See Gal. 2:5.

them? Or does Paul mean that wives should behave *as if* their husbands ranked above them, even though in Christ husbands and wives are not in a hierarchy but are on an equal footing as brothers and sisters? On the first view submission is appropriate because the wife should recognize the husband's authoritative position. On the second view submission is appropriate simply as an expression of Christian humility. On either view the idea of ranking is central to Paul's meaning. The question is whether it is an objective ranking, reflecting the existence of an actual hierarchy, or whether it is a subjective ranking, reflecting a deliberate choice to behave with humility towards another person. This makes a real difference to Paul's readers, since the first view affirms a husband's unilateral authority and the second does not.

4. *When not to submit*

Understanding submission in terms of ranking raises another important question. If this is what submission means, does it involve unquestioning obedience to the other person?

Complementarians and egalitarians alike agree that Christian submission is not the same thing as unquestioning obedience. There are circumstances in which it would be wrong to submit. When some were contending that the good news of Christ meant that circumcision was essential, Paul says he 'did not yield in submission even for a moment, so that the truth of the gospel might be preserved' (Gal. 2:5, ESV). When Peter temporarily took up the wrong side on this issue Paul 'opposed him to his face' (Gal. 2:11, ESV).

The submission to one another that Paul instructs in Ephesians 5:21 is 'in the fear [*phobos*] of Christ', meaning 'out of reverence for Christ' (as in ESV, NIV, NRSV). This provides both a reason for the submission and a limit upon it. So, when 5:24 refers to the wife's submission to the husband as being 'in everything', this is not an absolute statement, such that she should be a partner even in wrongdoing; rather, it means that this attitude of submission applies in all areas of their life together.

Submission should not extend to doing anything that is against the Lord's will. The Danvers Statement rightly affirms:

> In all of life Christ is the supreme authority and guide for men and women, so that
> no earthly submission – domestic, religious, or civil – ever implies a mandate to follow
> a human authority into sin (Dan 3:10–18; Acts 4:19–20; 5:27–29; 1 Pet 3:1–2).[17]

---

17. See also Esth. 4:16.

5. How the marriage relationship was viewed in first-century culture

Paul's letters to the Colossians, to the Ephesians and to Titus were written to Christians in Hellenic societies.[18] As we saw in chapter 2, the usual arrangement was that the husband was firmly in charge. The pithy (and to our ears, shocking) summary in the famous Athenian speech 'Against Neaera' conveys the flavour of how formal and unequal the relationship could be in traditional Greek culture, and how some men viewed their wives: 'We keep mistresses for our enjoyment, concubines to serve our person each day, but we have wives for the bearing of legitimate offspring and to be faithful guardians of the household.'[19] In Graeco-Roman culture husbands often had only distant relationships with their wives. In first-century Hellenism, wives were often still treated as their husbands' property.[20] In the home the husband's word was supposed to be law. This imbalance was all the more pronounced because women usually married at a young age, typically around fourteen years old, and their husbands were usually significantly older.[21]

This is not to say that the situation was uniform, either as regards affection or as regards the balance of power of husband and wife. There are plenty of ancient tombstone inscriptions which testify to close affection. As to power, even in the fourth century BC Aristotle had remarked that, if the wife was an heiress, she would rule the husband.[22] In the first century among the Roman elite there was a trend of 'new women', who neglected their household duties, sought the same freedom as men to engage in illicit liaisons, and avoided childbearing.[23] But the general picture remained that the husband was usually in authority over the wife.

---

18. Respectively Colossae, Ephesus and Crete. In Paul's time Ephesus was an important city of the Roman Empire but it preserved its Greek roots in its political and cultural institutions: *WITC*, 60 (Baugh).

19. Demosthenes 59.122. See Peterman 1999, 163. This speech (probably not written by Demosthenes) is from the fourth century BC but in Hellenic society women's status was largely unchanged by Paul's time: see chapter 2, 24. It should warn us not to imagine husband–wife relationships in modern Western terms when reading Paul's letter. The 'mistresses' were *hetairai*, meaning courtesans. The 'concubines' were probably not concubines properly so called but female slaves in the household. See Scheidel 2008.

20. Stark 1996, 122. *M&W*, 33.

21. Many brides were married in their early or mid-teens to men who were some ten years older than they were: Winter 2000, 287. See also *WITC*, 42 (Baugh).

22. Aristotle, *Nicomachean Ethics* 8.10.

23. Winter 2004.

This was also true for Jews. Jewish culture gave a religious reason for wives to obey husbands. As Josephus wrote: 'Let her, therefore, be obedient to him . . . for God hath given authority to the husband.'[24]

However, within the fellowship of the church, personal relations were altered. There is ample evidence in the New Testament that the equality of men and women in the gospel had a powerful impact. The Christian message transformed women's relationships with men. Women became men's sisters in Christ, equal in standing before God and active partners in the gospel (Acts 2:16–18; Rom. 16:1–12; Gal. 3:28). This had an impact on the nature of the marriage relationship (1 Cor. 7).

6. Some practical reasons for Paul's emphases

Both love and humility are part of truly Christian living. However, in Paul's more specific remarks about husbands and wives in Colossians and Ephesians there is a clear contrast of emphasis: he tells wives to submit, husbands to love. In the next chapter we will consider possible theological reasons for this apparent distinction. But first we will consider whether there may be practical reasons for it. Does the historical context of culture and the Christian message shed any light on this contrasting emphasis?

We may take it that, as is usual in his letters, Paul gives instructions which he judges to be relevant and important for his readers.

Human nature being what it is, we may suppose that after men became Christian believers, they would still be tempted to adhere to the cultural stereotype of the autocratic master of the household, demanding unquestioning service from others in the household, including their wives. This supposition is corroborated by the additional instruction to husbands in Colossians 3:19 that they must not act harshly towards their wives. It may be inferred from this instruction that husbands were behaving in this way at Colossae. Perhaps Epaphras expressed concern about this. Paul decided that he needed to make clear that it was not acceptable. It is unsurprising that in the prevailing culture the husbands particularly needed to hear Paul's emphasis on humble, gentle love, especially as regards their wives.

But what about the wives? Given that most women were in subjection to their husbands, why did Paul judge that he should emphasize to them that Christian behaviour involved ranking themselves below their husbands?

The social impact of the gospel provides an answer. This is particularly clear in the parallel case of slaves, who in the eyes of the law were items of property.

---

24. Josephus, *Against Apion* 2.25 (Whiston's translation).

Under the laws of the Roman Empire, subject to certain restrictions, a master was entitled even to kill slaves which he owned.[25] But when both master and slave were converted to Christ, they became equals and brothers (Gal. 3:28). This brotherhood became such a powerful new reality in Christian communities that Paul had to remind slaves who had Christian masters not to be disrespectful to them, as being brothers (1 Tim. 6:1–2). It is likely that the equality of believers in Christ was embraced with similar enthusiasm by previously downtrodden wives.

Human nature being what it is, we may reasonably infer that within the fellowship of the church, where all were Christian brothers and sisters, the new-found equality of women was leading some wives to become disrespectful, thinking that humility towards their husbands was no longer appropriate. This explains Paul's judgment that he should emphasize submission by wives to their husbands.

The later letter to Titus provides a further example of Paul tailoring his reminders in accordance with his judgment about what needs to be said. His earlier contrast of emphasis (wives to submit, husbands to love) is not reproduced in that letter. Instead he writes about wives both submitting to their husbands and loving them (2:4–5), without including any instructions specifically for husbands. And in that letter he adds an important practical reason for wives' submission: they must 'be subject to their husbands, so that no one will malign the word of God' (2:5, NIV). Paul wants to avoid creating unnecessary barriers to the Christian message. This instruction makes obvious sense in a culture where husbands were generally expected to be in charge.

We have set the scene by considering the six preliminary topics. We are now better prepared for looking into Colossians and Ephesians to find answers to the disputed questions.

Colossians and the three disputed questions

We begin with Colossians. In the light of Paul's brief instructions to husbands and wives in the church at Colossae (3:18–19), what can be said about the three questions? Is the husband the authoritative leader of the wife? Is submission one-way or mutual? Are husbands' and wives' responsibilities differentiated?

In this letter Paul does not use a 'head' metaphor in relation to the husband.[26] He instructs wives to submit 'as is fitting in the Lord' (3:18). This could mean

---

25. Buckland 1921, 63–65.
26. In 1:18; 2:10, 19, Christ is the head.

either that submission is itself fitting in the Lord or that submission should be done in a way that is fitting in the Lord. He does not explain further. This instruction to submit is consistent with a one-way submission to a husband's authority. On the other hand, Paul's command to humility applies to all (3:12) and he envisages Christian believers, who include husbands and wives, teaching and admonishing one another (3:16). This outlook does not seem to be consistent with a one-way, hierarchical relationship. And Paul metaphorically describes Epaphras, the evangelist who founded the Colossian church, as a fellow slave (1:7). This may suggest that the kind of submission that is fitting in the Lord is mutual submission.

The fact that different instructions are given to husbands and to wives might indicate differentiated responsibilities. On the other hand, the command to love, which is specific to husbands in 3:19, is applied to all believers in 3:14.[27] So all believers are commanded both to act humbly towards others and to love them. This does not establish differing responsibilities for husband and wife.

We must conclude that none of the three questions can be definitively answered from Colossians.

Does comparing the three pairs show Paul's approval of a hierarchical view of marriage?

Some who take positions A or B on the spectrum of interpretations would challenge the conclusion that none of our three questions can be definitively answered from Colossians. They argue for an implication from the context: the household code[28] in Colossians is laid out in a clear pattern in which Paul addresses first the subordinate person of each pair and then the person in authority: wife then husband (3:18–19), child then father (3:20–21), slave then master (3:22 – 4:1). Precisely the same pattern appears in Ephesians 5:22 – 6:9. This then implies Paul's endorsement of the authority of husbands, fathers and slave masters. Peter O'Brien refers to these three relationships as 'divinely ordered'.[29]

---

27. In 3:19 the verb is *agapaō*; in 3:14 the noun is *agapē*. Both refer to active care, not romantic love.

28. There is a substantial literature comparing Paul's text with other ancient household codes, which it is unnecessary to consider here.

29. O'Brien 1999, 399, 404–409, 412, 447–448. In regard to slavery, can O'Brien really mean this in the sense of 'divinely ordained' or does he only mean that God has regulated it? Startlingly, his meaning seems to be the former, because on 409 he

The fundamental difficulty with this argument is that it presupposes a degree of similarity between the three relationships which we do not find either in these two texts or in what we can discern from elsewhere about how Paul views them. As we shall see, although Paul approves of the parent–child relationship as a hierarchy, he does not approve of the master–slave hierarchy. Accordingly, these comparisons cannot tell us whether he thinks that marriage ought to be a hierarchical relationship or not.

That *children* should honour their parents is divinely ordained (Eph. 6:1–2). The term 'obey' in Colossians 3:20 and Ephesians 6:1 shows Paul's expectation that parents will issue instructions to their children which the children are under obligation to obey. This is not merely a fact of life but is something of which he positively approves, as we have already seen from 1 Timothy 3:4–5.

Paul's view of the *slavery* relationship is quite different. There is a superficial similarity, because he uses the same term 'obey' when addressing slaves. He tells them to obey their masters in everything (Col. 3:22; compare Eph. 6:5). But it does not follow that he is indicating his approval of the authority of slave owners over their slaves. While Paul accepts the institution of slavery as a fact of life in the society in which he lives, when we look more closely at what he writes it is clear that he disapproves of it and outmanoeuvres it.

In the Colossian letter he states that in Christ there is no distinction between slave and free (3:11), a proposition as startling to slave owners as to slaves. He appeals to Philemon, in terms which leave Philemon no real choice, to receive his converted slave, Onesimus, as a beloved brother (Phlm. 8–21); this is inconsistent with Philemon treating Onesimus as his property. Paul also makes plain elsewhere that slavery is an evil (1 Tim. 1:10), which has no place in the kingdom of God (1 Cor. 7:21–23; 12:13; Gal. 3:28). We must understand, therefore, that by instructing slaves to live in obedience to their masters, Paul is not giving his approval to the position of slave owners. Rather, he is instructing Christian slaves in truly Christian conduct (Col. 3:12). They should live obediently because it is the Lord Christ they are serving (3:22–24). Rather than take matters into their own hands, they should trust that God will judge masters for wrongs that they do (3:25).[30]

---

refers to the places of persons in the three relationships as their 'place within the created order'. Compare *RBMW*, 166 (Knight). But see also *RBMW*, 170–171, where Knight recognizes that slavery is not a parallel case.

30. Verse 25 has misbehaving masters in view, not misbehaving slaves. This is clear from the phrase *ouk estin prosōpolēpsia* – 'there is no respect of persons'. God shows no deference to the social and legal position of slave owners.

In Ephesians, similarly, Paul instructs slaves to obey their masters, not because of the masters' position but on the basis that the slaves are really slaves of Christ (6:5–6). This qualifies their duty to obey and is potentially far-reaching in its practical effects. Slaves who are serving Christ will no longer obey instructions that harm others, or that conflict with the Christian standard of sexual behaviour, or that give effect to unkindness, selfishness, arrogance or dishonesty. Then, after telling slaves to *serve with goodwill*, as serving the Lord rather than people, Paul instructs the masters to *do the same to their slaves* (6:7–9)! This reciprocal mutuality of service, as between master and slave, is revolutionary. It is a particular application to slave owners of the Christian duty mandated in Galatians 5:13 ('serve as slaves of one another'). These instructions undermine the hierarchy of slave ownership.[31]

We must conclude that, when Paul instructs slaves to obey their masters, this does not imply his approval of the authority of slave masters. It is correspondingly hazardous to argue that, when Paul instructs wives to submit to their husbands in everything, this implies his positive endorsement of the unilateral authority of husbands over their wives which existed in the prevailing culture. Comparison of the three pairs of relationships does not establish this implication. We need to look more closely at the context.

Having seen that Colossians does not resolve the three questions, we will concentrate in the next chapter on Paul's fuller exposition in Ephesians.

Summary of chapter 3

1. Colossians and Ephesians were written at about the same time and were intended for circulation from church to church, so are appropriately considered together.
2. Paul is not opposed to hierarchies where they are appropriate.
3. The word 'submit' (*hupotassō*) carries the idea of being ranked below someone else. But Paul's instruction to wives to submit does not of itself imply the existence of a hierarchy in marriage. We have to decide whether he means that wives should submit because their husbands *are* in authority over them or whether he means that wives should behave *as if* their husbands ranked above them.

---

31. Again, in Titus 2:9 Paul's instruction to slaves to be subject to their masters is not based on the masters' hierarchical position. The reason he gives is to adorn the teaching of God the Saviour. Compare Titus 2:5.

4. Submission in Christian relationships does not mean giving unquestioning obedience to another person. There is no Christian duty to follow another person into wrongdoing.

5. There was not a uniform view of marriage in first-century culture, but typically the husband had unilateral authority over the wife.

6. Paul's instructions to wives to submit, and to husbands to love, are partly driven by practical considerations.

7. Paul endorses the authority of parents over children but not of slave owners over slaves. Comparing the three household relationships (wife to husband, child to father, slave to master) does not establish that Paul approves of husbands having unilateral authority over their wives.

Questions to consider

1. Are you instinctively for or against hierarchies? Why?

2. Is 'submission' a negative word? Should it be?

3. What is the social impact of the gospel in your culture? What are your personal experiences of this?

4. MARRIAGE PORTRAYS THE SAVIOUR: EPHESIANS 5

> How sweet are your words to my taste,
> sweeter than honey to my mouth!
>
> (Ps. 119:103, NIV)

The big picture of Ephesians 5

In chapter 3 we noted a spectrum of positions on marriage and identified three
disputed questions. We now continue our search for answers by looking more
closely at Ephesians 5.

Paul's theme in Ephesians 5 is stated in verses 1–2. He is giving instruction
on how Christian believers (both men and women) should live as imitators of
God, following the model of the self-giving love of Christ. His remarks about
holy lives in verses 3–16 bring us to verse 17 ('do not be foolish but understand
what the Lord's will is').

We can understand more accurately what Paul writes next if we observe the
structure of his thought. The layout in ESV, NASB and NKJV ends a paragraph at
verse 21, interposes a heading and starts a new paragraph with verse 22. This is
to be regretted because it tends to obscure his train of reasoning. In his Greek
text Paul has written in verses 18–22: 'And do not become drunk with wine . . .
but be filled by the Spirit, . . . speaking . . . , giving thanks always . . . , submitting
to one another . . . , wives to their husbands.'[1] The submission of wives (v. 22)

---

1. Based on a choice between variant manuscripts, it is generally considered that v. 22
   does not have its own verb, so that what wives are to do in relation to their husbands

is a particular example of the Spirit-filled submission of which Paul writes in verse 21. The way that husbands and wives relate to each other (vv. 22–33) is part of the outcome of being filled by the Holy Spirit so as to live this Christlike way of life.

In 1 Corinthians 7 Paul set human marriage in the context that the Messiah had come and the end of all things was in sight. Here in Ephesians 5 he further develops this perspective. He portrays the relationship of husband and wife as reflecting the relationship of the Messiah and his body, the church. In this way he teaches both about marriage and about Christ and the church. The union of husband and wife (v. 31) points forward to the mystery of Christ's union with his church (vv. 29–30, 32).

Paul's comparison of the husband and the Messiah sheds light on his view of the marriage relationship. However, we need to proceed carefully, not jumping to hasty conclusions.

Paul's *kephalē* metaphor

Our first interpretive question is whether Paul is intending to depict the husband as having unilateral authority over his wife. As we saw in chapter 3, the instruction to wives to submit (5:22, 24) does not tell us the answer, because submission could be either because husbands have such authority or because wives are instructed to behave as if their husbands were above them, even though they are not. Nor, as we saw, do we get a clear answer from comparisons with children and slaves (6:1–9).

However, those who adopt positions A or B on the spectrum find an answer in Paul's use of the word 'head' (*kephalē*) in verse 23, where he describes the husband as head of the wife. Grudem argues that this word conveys the idea of a governing authority (in other words, a lord or ruler). Paul is therefore teaching that husbands should exercise unilateral authority over their wives, albeit in a loving manner (v. 25). Payne argues that this is a misunderstanding of Paul's meaning.[2] Which view is correct?

We need to start by recognizing that to describe one person as head of another is to use a metaphor. In English we regularly use the term 'head' to mean the person in charge. We know what is meant by the head coach, the head

---

is implied from the 'submitting' of v. 21: *M&W*, 278–279. For a dissenting minority view, see Gurry 2018.

2. *EFBT*, 43, 201–211; *M&W*, 278–290.

gardener, the head waiter, the head of sales. This is such a standard usage that we do not even think of it as a metaphor. So, when in English we read 'the husband is head of the wife' (v. 23), it seems obvious that Paul means that the husband is in charge of the wife, that is, he is the authority figure who rules over her. But metaphors used in one culture and language are not necessarily the same as metaphors used in other cultures and languages. So the uses of 'head' as a metaphor in English are not a safe guide to the uses of *kephalē* as a metaphor in first-century Greek. We need to look at actual usage.

The use of 'head' to mean the person in charge was unknown in classical Greek. But Paul would have been aware of such a metaphor in Hebrew, from his reading of the Old Testament.

After Paul's time this metaphor gained wider currency in Greek, partly as a result of the way that commentators living in patriarchal cultures interpreted Paul's writings. However, when Paul wrote to the Ephesians, 'head' as chief or ruler was not a standardized or widely used metaphor in the Greek language. As far as studies show, it had only started to creep slowly into Greek usage as a result of a translation choice made in the Septuagint (about second century BC). In the Septuagint there is a very small number of instances where the Hebrew word for 'head', possibly used as a figure of speech for the leading person (or sometimes the most prominent person), was translated literally as *kephalē*.[3]

---

3. There are about 170 instances where the translators used another Greek word to translate the Hebrew word for 'head' when used to mean a leader or ruler (*M&W*, 119). The exact number of exceptional instances where the Septuagint seems to use *kephalē* in some sense of 'leader' or 'ruler' is debated: see chapter 7, 119. We do not know why the translator chose to translate into Greek literally in these exceptional instances; this could have been because he was unsure of the intended meaning of the Hebrew, so left the reader to decide what it meant. In *EFBT*, 544–551, Grudem gives what he says are over fifty examples of the Greek word for 'head' (*kephalē*) meaning 'authority over/ruler' in ancient literature. The meaning of *kephalē* in many of his examples is disputed. Because this usage was unknown in classical Greek the earliest examples Grudem gives are from the Septuagint. Outside the Septuagint the only examples Grudem claims from an author who was writing prior to Paul are from Philo, who was familiar with the Septuagint. But from Philo we have two clear examples of 'head' used as a metaphor not for ruler but for 'source of life'. For details of these two examples, see the discussion of *kephalē* in chapter 7, in relation to Paul's metaphorical usage in 1 Cor. 11. (Paul's usage there is rather different from that in Eph. 5, without any mention of a 'body', so it provides limited help for understanding his usage in Eph. 5.)

Writers are free to create, adapt or reuse a metaphor as they wish, provided they make their meaning clear. In Ephesians 5 Paul uses the term 'head' in conjunction with 'body'. It may therefore help to notice some possibilities of how *kephalē* could potentially be used in a head and body metaphor, given how people thought about the functions of the head in relation to the body at the time when Paul was writing.

Hippocratic medicine ascribed to the head at least three roles: one was that it provided life and nourishment to the body; a second was that it was the origin of sperm, which was believed to be a drop of brain; a third was that the head ruled over the body. The first role was obvious to all, without any medical knowledge: food and water enter via the head, so the head nourishes us and gives us life. The second role had been taught before Hippocrates, by Alcmaeon (early fifth century BC). (It is not until the end of the first century AD that we find a clear statement that sperm originates in the testes.) The third role was controversial, because Aristotle and others taught, in opposition to Hippocrates, that the body was ruled not by the head but by the heart.[4]

Thus if a Greek writer used the term 'head' metaphorically in relation to a 'body', this could readily indicate something like 'source of life' or 'source of life and nourishment'. Less obviously, if the writer thought Hippocrates was right and Aristotle was wrong, it could indicate something like 'ruler'.

Grudem argues for the latter use, while also admitting this is not the only possibility.[5] He places great emphasis on lexical studies in order to argue for the meaning 'person in authority' in Ephesians 5. He looks for metaphorical uses of 'head' (*kephalē*) elsewhere, finds numerous examples where he judges that it is used of a ruler and then reads Ephesians 5 accordingly.[6] Some writers have followed him in placing strong emphasis on how *kephalē* has been used metaphorically in other writings outside the New Testament. We will take a further look at these studies in chapter 7. But their usefulness should not be overstated. Usage by others elsewhere is by its nature inconclusive evidence,

---

4. Arnold 1994, 352–353. Prioreschi 1996, 174, 274–281. Hippocrates died about 375 BC, shortly after Aristotle was born. In *M&W*, 288, Payne cites Hippocrates' view that the veins nourished the body from the head. See also *M&W*, 122–123.

5. *EFBT*, 567: 'it is an elementary fact of life that we receive nourishment through our mouths, and thus in a sense through our heads, and this idea was plain to the ancient world as well; therefore, the idea that a metaphor would occur in which "head" meant "source" is not impossible.'

6. *EFBT*, 201–211, 544–599.

even when it predates Paul's letters. Such studies can show some possibilities, but no more. Paul was not bound to follow what others had done.

In fact, Paul's usage was new. No example has been found, whether in the Septuagint or in other Greek literature, where an earlier writer had used a head and body metaphor in which the head stood for a man or husband and the body stood for a woman or wife.

Given that Paul's usage was new, and that *kephalē* was not a standardized metaphor with a single meaning, usage elsewhere cannot definitively determine Paul's meaning in Ephesians 5. The meaning must be discerned from the context.[7]

The context and Paul's use of *kephalē*

Paul uses *kephalē* metaphorically of Christ in Ephesians 1:22. His exact meaning there is a matter of debate among commentators. However, since it is used in association with a reference to Christ being far above all rule and authority (1:21), he is probably intending to convey the idea of Christ as the person at the top, and therefore the ruler.[8] This is in line with how 'head' had been used metaphorically in Hebrew.

Paul uses a *kephalē* metaphor a second time in 4:15. The context of this verse shows that he is here conveying a different idea (see 4:16). The metaphor here is that the Messiah, as head, is the source of the body's (the church's) nourishment and growth.[9] This usage exploits the consensus view in Greek medicine that the head enabled the body to live and grow. Paul has in mind here that Christ, as the body's source of life and sustenance, provides for the body the full salvation which is described in verses 13 and 16, which is complete maturity in the likeness of Christ and in unity with Christ.

---

7. This is rightly acknowledged by Köstenberger 1994, 264.
8. In this text the Messiah is said to be 'head above all things for the church'. The church, for whom he rules, is perhaps also part of the 'all things' over which he rules. For the Messiah as 'Lord', see further Phil. 3:20; 2 Pet. 1:11.
9. Köstenberger 1994, 265, agrees that Paul's use of *kephalē* in Ephesians is not rigidly uniform. O'Brien 1999, 313, correctly notes that in Eph. 4:16 Christ as head is the source of the body's growth. He contradicts this on 413, where he asserts that in all instances in the letter prior to Eph. 5:23 'head' signifies 'ruler' or 'authority' rather than 'source', and that Eph. 4:15 describes Christ's rule over his people (which is not correct: there is no such description in Eph. 4:15–16).

Paul applies a *kephalē* metaphor to the Messiah a third time in 5:23. But here he applies the metaphor also to the husband. Here Paul makes an explicit connection between the husband's position as head and the wife's submission. After instructing wives' submission in verse 22, he adds: 'For a husband is head of the wife as also the Messiah is head of the church, himself saviour of the body.' What sense does Paul intend here? Is he applying the Ephesians 1 sense (ruler, lord over all things) or the Ephesians 4 sense (source of life and sustenance, and hence of full salvation), or both senses, or some other, third sense? Since a third sense would carry a risk of confusing his readers, it seems reasonable to begin by considering senses he has already used.

Is Paul's application of the head metaphor to the husband intended to indicate that the husband is properly to be regarded as the ruler of the wife? For the reasons explained above, the bare fact that Paul instructs the wives to submit to their husbands does not tell us whether in 5:23 he is using the 'head' metaphor to mean 'lord'. However, those who adopt positions A or B point to Paul's further descriptions of the nature of wives' submission to husbands. In verse 22 wives are to submit to husbands 'as to the Lord' and in verse 24 'as the church submits to Christ' (ESV).

These two phrases, taken on their own, are certainly consistent with interpreting Paul's 'head' metaphor in 5:23 as referring to lordship. For it is uncontroversial that the Lord Jesus Christ is the one who rules over his church. Nevertheless, these phrases are also consistent with interpreting 'head' as not referring to lordship. By using these phrases Paul is pointing to the *motive for* and *extent of* wives' submission. The *motive* is that submission is part and parcel of serving Christ. Paul has already highlighted this motive in verse 21 ('out of reverence for Christ'). In *extent*, the wives' submission is to be as comprehensive as the church's submission to Christ, who is the Lord; Paul spells this out explicitly when he adds 'in everything' in verse 24. Submission with this motive and to this extent is closely comparable to what Paul asks of slaves towards their masters (6:5–8; Col. 3:22–24). It does not carry a necessary implication that Paul is using *kephalē* to indicate that the husband has God-given authority over his wife.

Four features of the immediate context show that he is using the Ephesians 4 sense. These are (1) Paul's use of apposition in verse 23; (2) the theme of saviourhood in verses 25–33; (3) Paul's use of Genesis; and (4) the first word of verse 24.

1. Paul's use of apposition in verse 23
Placing a noun or noun phrase next to another noun or noun phrase, both of them having the same syntactic relation to the other elements of the sentence,

is a standard grammatical construction; the second noun or noun phrase explains the meaning of the first. Because it is a standard construction, it has been given the technical label of apposition.

As a thoughtful writer, Paul must be aware that he has already used the *kephalē* metaphor twice in this letter, on the first occasion to say something about Christ's lordship (see 1:20–22) and on the second occasion to say something about Christ's saviourhood (see 4:13–16). He needs to indicate to his readers in what sense they are to understand the *kephalē* metaphor here, as an analogy for the husband's role. So he explains in what way the husband is head of the wife. It is 'as also the Messiah is head of the church, himself saviour of the body'. He places 'himself saviour of the body' in apposition with 'head of the church'. This explains the comparison that he is making between Christ as head and the husband as head. It is a comparison with Christ's headship as saviour of the body, not with his headship as lord over the church.

The task which Paul designates for the husband is therefore analogous to Christ's saviourhood.[10] As saviour, Christ secures the safety and welfare of the church which is his body: he is the source of its life and sustenance, the one who nourishes it, the one who enables it to live and to grow into unity with him. Christ fulfils this function for the church in the highest sense; the husband is to fulfil it in a lesser sense for his wife.

It is to be regretted that in many English versions Paul's apposition of 'saviour of the body' alongside 'head of the church' is not clearly visible. For example, ESV renders verse 23 as: 'For the husband is the head of the wife even as Christ is the head of the church, his body, *and* is himself its Saviour'; and NIV renders it as: 'For the husband is the head of the wife as Christ is the head of the church, his body, *of which* he is the Saviour' (emphases added). The correspondence of 'head' to 'saviour' is not clear in these translations. The insertion of 'and' by ESV and 'of which' by NIV, which are not in the Greek text, open the door to reading Paul as making two separate points – first, that the husband is head of the wife as Christ is lord of the church, and second, that Christ is also the saviour of the church. These translations do not sufficiently reflect Paul's careful choice of words. But some other versions, such as ASV and NASB, accurately reflect the way that Paul places 'saviour of the body' in apposition to 'head of the church'.[11]

---

10. *M&W*, 283–284.

11. ASV: 'the husband is the head of the wife, as Christ also is the head of the church, being himself the saviour of the body.' NASB: 'the husband is the head of the wife, as Christ also is the head of the church, He Himself being the Savior of the body.'

The interpretation of headship in verse 23 as saviourhood rather than lordship is not driven by egalitarian presuppositions. It is driven by Paul's precise words. Even J. Armitage Robinson, who believed that the wife was beneath the husband's authority, saw that the phrase 'himself saviour of the body' was added 'to interpret the special sense in which Christ is here called "the head of the church"'.[12] Similarly, John Stott, though for other reasons he took a largely complementarian position, reached the same conclusion concerning the meaning of this part of Paul's letter:

> In order to understand the nature of the husband's headship in the new
> society which God has inaugurated, we need to look at Jesus Christ. For Jesus
> Christ is the context in which Paul uses and develops the words 'headship'
> and 'submission'. . . . he defines it in relation to the headship of Christ the
> redeemer: . . . (verse 23). Now Christ's headship of his church has already been
> described in 4:15–16. It is from Christ as head that the body derives its health
> and grows into maturity. His headship expresses care rather than control,
> responsibility rather than rule. This truth is endorsed by the surprising
> addition of the words *and is himself its Saviour.* The head of the body is the
> saviour of the body; the characteristic of his headship is not so much lordship
> as saviourhood.[13]

But what about contrary arguments? How is the appositional phrase 'himself saviour of the body' interpreted by writers who insist that by 'head' Paul here means 'lord'?

Grudem does not offer an interpretation of 'himself saviour of the body'; instead he repeatedly cites verse 23 without including this phrase. The chapter in *RBMW* on Ephesians 5 similarly omits this phrase when it cites verse 23, and it expounds the meaning of this verse as if the phrase were not in the text. Hurley and Sandom similarly ignore it. Lincoln regards the phrase as 'an additional thought which disturbs the flow of the argument'; in other words, it is an irrelevant digression. Arnold says it is not relevant to the husband because the husband fulfils no role for his wife analogous to that of saviour. Smith acknowledges that Paul 'might seem to say that the husband is the saviour of

---

12. Robinson 1909, 124.
13. Stott 1979, 225. The words which I have omitted include the phrase 'Although he
   grounds the husband's headship in creation'; Stott argues this from elsewhere, not
   from Ephesians, because it is not there.

his wife as Christ is the saviour of the church', but then makes a point similar to Arnold's.[14]

The view that Paul's phrase 'himself saviour of the body' is of no relevance to his argument, and does not apply to the husband, discounts the significance of the apposition. It also disregards the immediate context. For Paul goes on to expound the husband's responsibility as head by continuing his analogy with Christ's saving role, as we see next.

2. The theme of saviourhood in verses 25–33

Any doubt about whether Paul's reference to saviourhood in verse 23 is intended to apply to the husband should be set at rest by the contents of verses 25–33. Paul goes on to develop the idea of the husband's headship as saviourhood by repeating it four times in different words. He draws out multiple similarities between what the Messiah does for the church in his role as saviour and what a husband should do for his wife. If any patriarchal reader missed Paul's signal in verse 23 that in this context to be head means to behave like a loving saviour, by these repetitions Paul puts his meaning beyond doubt:

- verse 25: to love her and to give himself up for her;
- verse 28: to love her as his own body;
- verses 29–30: to nourish her and to care for her just as the Messiah does for his body;
- verse 33: to love her as himself.

These instructions are about the husband rendering loving service in imitation of the Messiah's actions as saviour. Not one of them is about the husband ruling over his wife. Every occurrence of the English word 'love' (vv. 25, 28, 33) translates *agapaō*, which denotes active care, as in verse 2. Paul's instructions are all directed to the husband's calling to display the incomparable riches of Christ's gracious love through the way that he lovingly serves and nurtures his wife. Knight correctly states: 'Ephesians says that because a husband loves his wife,

---

14. *EFBT*, 41, 183, 440, 442, 492, 552, 586; *RBMW*, 164–165 (Knight); Hurley 1981, 138–148, 164–165; Sandom 2012, 128–143; Lincoln 1990, 371 (note that Lincoln does not accept Pauline authorship); Arnold 2010, 382; Smith 2012, 199 (she also asserts that the Greek word order shows that only Christ is the focus of the phrase, but gives no reasons for this; I have not been able to discover any). When considering this phrase in v. 23, several commentators also make reference to the first word of v. 24; we will consider this further aspect of the discussion separately below.

he will give his life for her good.'[15] Paul's comparison of the husband's responsibility as head with Christ's role as saviour could not be any clearer.

Smith rightly acknowledges that what Paul says about the saving and cleansing work of Christ is not a literal statement about how husbands are to love their wives but rather that earthly husbands are to model their behaviour towards their wives on Christ's sacrificial love for his church. To maintain, nevertheless, her stance on the meaning of 'head' as 'ruler', she says: 'Paul is basing his instructions to wives on the fact that the husband is the head of the wife, not because he is her saviour.'[16] But this interpretation conflicts with the whole thrust of what Paul writes. Verse 23, which includes the phrase about Christ as saviour, is presented by Paul as a reason for wives' submission. And Paul then depicts the husband as following the model of Christ's saving love, giving himself up for his wife (as Smith acknowledges), not as following the model of Christ's authoritative rule. To adapt a phrase of C. S. Lewis, if Ephesians 5 crowns the husband, it is with a crown of thorns.[17]

3. Paul's use of Genesis

Those who take a hierarchical view of the meaning of a husband's headship find support in Genesis 2. We will look at Genesis 2 in chapter 5. For the present we notice that Paul's sole citation from Genesis is in 5:31, where he quotes Genesis 2:24 ('For this reason a man will leave his father and mother and be united to his wife, and the two will become one flesh', NIV).

This verse is about the unity of husband and wife. Paul links it with the unity of Christ and the church (5:30, 32). This reinforces the headship metaphor in its sense of saviourhood, as introduced in 4:12–16, which depicted Christ's work of salvation as achieving the unity of the church as one mature body in union with him.

Thus Paul's use of Genesis in Ephesians 5 emphasizes the union of husband and wife, as reflecting the union of Christ and the church. This is part of the saviourhood theme. It makes no reference to any idea of headship as authority.[18]

---

15. *RBMW*, 168.

16. Smith 2012, 117–119.

17. Lewis 1960, 149.

18. When Paul says of Gen. 2:24 'I speak of Christ and the church' (v. 32), he may imply a further development of his analogy between husband/wife and Christ/church. Just as a man leaves home (his father and mother) and is joined to his wife, and the two become one flesh, so Christ left his heavenly home to become the saviour of mankind, taking on human flesh in order to become one with us and so to save us (compare Phil. 2:6–8; Heb. 2:14).

4. The first word of verse 24

After stating in verse 23 that a husband is the head of the wife as Christ is head of the church, being its saviour, Paul next writes: 'But [*alla*] as the church submits to the Messiah, so also the wives to the husbands in all things.'

The first word, *alla*, is an adversative conjunction. Its function is to introduce an idea which contrasts with what has gone before. It tells us that in Paul's mind verse 24 contrasts in some way with verse 23. However, if Paul is referring in verse 23 to the husband being head in the sense of ruling over the wife, this creates a puzzle. If in verse 23 the husband is the 'lord', the one holding authority, it directly follows in logical progression that the wife must submit to him, as stated in verse 24. It seems that on the hierarchical interpretation verse 24 is not a *contrast* with verse 23 but a *logical consequence* of it, so Paul has inexplicably used the wrong word to introduce verse 24.

Translators who interpret verse 23 as meaning that the husband is lord of the wife are therefore faced with a serious difficulty, because with their interpretation it makes little sense that Paul starts verse 24 with 'But' (*alla*). Consequently, they often do not translate Paul's word accurately. Various strategies have been adopted:

- Tyndale (1534), and the translators of the Geneva Bible (New Testament, 1557) and the KJV (1611), followed the logic of their hierarchical view of marriage in accordance with the culture of their times. They boldly reversed Paul's meaning, replacing 'but' with 'therefore'. To modern eyes this is brazen. 'Therefore' introduces something that evidently follows. 'But' introduces something that does not evidently follow. This tradition of mistranslation has subsequently been reproduced in at least eight other English versions.
- ESV, NIV and some other versions also reinterpret what Paul writes but are not so audacious as to say the exact opposite. They replace 'but' with 'now'.[19]
- Others, such as RSV and NRSV, are more coy. They similarly believe Paul cannot have meant quite what he wrote, so are unwilling to translate *alla* accurately; but they cannot bring themselves to translate it by a word that does not match its meaning, so they miss it out, leaving it untranslated.

---

19. The Preface of the ESV states that in 'rendering connectives, the ESV follows the path that seems to make the ongoing flow of thought clearest in English'. LSJ does not list 'now' as even a possible meaning of *alla*.

These are translation strategies of last resort. Their use is a warning. It suggests that the flow of Paul's thought may not have been correctly understood by these translators.

Commentators have sought to explain Paul's choice of *alla* to connect verse 24 with verse 23. The first step in their reasoning is a focus on the final phrase of verse 23 – 'himself saviour of the church'. They argue that with this phrase Paul veers off-piste, because it is irrelevant to his argument, which they say is about the husband's lordship over the wife, not saviourhood. Paul's use of *alla* is then explained in two ways. Some say that *alla* merely signals a return, after this digression, to what is relevant and significant, that is, to the point of interest. Others say that the contrast is between what Paul actually means and what readers may mistakenly understand from the last phrase of verse 23: that is, in Paul's mind his comparison of the husband to the Messiah is limited to lordship and does not extend to saviourhood, so by using *alla* he warns his readers not to misunderstand him as meaning that the husband is to serve his wife like a saviour.[20]

These explanations for Paul's use of *alla* are technically feasible, within the available flexibility of how language can work. But they do not fit the context. We cannot justifiably maintain that Paul is going off-piste with the topic of saviourhood in the final phrase of verse 23. The idea of the husband acting like a saviour towards his wife, as Christ is saviour of the church, is of central relevance to Paul's exposition. As we have seen, Paul develops this very point with emphatic repetition in verses 25–33. It is hard for commentators to miss this, so they end up contradicting their own arguments. For example, O'Brien makes clear, as he must, that from verse 25 onwards Paul is instructing husbands to follow the model of Christ's saving love, even to the extent of making the ultimate sacrifice. This is the husband as saviour, the very thing that O'Brien's exposition of verses 23–24 denies.[21]

There is a subsidiary difficulty. If the potential misunderstanding against which Paul is warning his readers is a misunderstanding of the husband's role,

---

20. See Robinson 1909, 124, 205; Barth 1974, 619; Lincoln 1990, 372; *RBMW*, 174 (Knight, relying on F. F. Bruce and J. Armitage Robinson); O'Brien 1999, 415–416; Arnold 2010, 382; Smith 2012, 119. For readers in warm climates: to go off-piste is to deviate from the proper track (a metaphor from skiing).

21. O'Brien 1999, 413–416; 419–424. As we have seen, Smith 2012, 118–119, contradicts her own arguments in similar fashion, treating Paul's reference to Christ as saviour in v. 23 as an irrelevant aside, while also admitting that Paul is presenting Christ's saviourhood as the model for husbands to follow.

verse 24 should contain a contrasting statement about what the husband should do. But it does not. Verse 24 does not say: 'But the husband is to exercise authority over his wife.' Verse 24 is not a statement about what husbands are to do, such as would provide the supposed contrast with the end of verse 23. Instead, verse 24 is directed at wives.

The difficulties in translating the text and in understanding the flow of Paul's thought are eased if we stop trying to maintain the view that 'head' means 'ruler' or 'lord' in verse 23 and instead accept the plain meaning of verse 23. Paul is indicating what the husband's headship is like, namely, like Christ's headship of the church in his role as saviour. The contrast signalled by *alla* is not a contrast with what readers may mistakenly draw from the last phrase of verse 23 alone. It is a contrast with what readers may infer from the whole of verse 23.

We need to attend to the flow of Paul's thought. In verse 21 he has given a reason for the submission of wives which he instructs in verse 22, namely, reverence for Christ. Verse 23 commences with *hoti*, meaning 'because'. So in verses 23–24 he is giving an additional reason for wives' submission. All of verse 23 is relevant to his argument. In the course of stating this additional reason Paul does indeed want to guard against potential misunderstanding. He is anticipating an objection. The misunderstanding he has in view is an erroneous reaction to the husband's headship being modelled on Christ's saviourhood. If the husband's role is merely to be the wife's 'saviour', wives may conclude that they need not submit after all. But (*alla*) they must. *Although* Paul is comparing the husband's headship to only one aspect of the Messiah's headship, namely saviourhood, Paul *nevertheless* wants wives to submit to their husbands as the church submits to the Messiah. They are to submit despite the fact that in a Christian marriage their husbands are not in authority over them. And one of the reasons encouraging such submission is that their husbands are called to be their heads, their sources of life and sustenance, loving them with a love like the practical, saving love of Christ.[22]

We can now return to the disputed questions.

The first question: unilateral authority of the husband?

The general understanding in the ancient world was that husbands should have unilateral authority over their wives. If, rather than merely regulating how a

---

22. The egalitarian exposition in *DBE*, 398 (Webb) is not satisfactory. It misses Paul's reasoning and gives temporary cultural reasons for a wife's submission.

husband's authority is used, Paul intends believers to depart from this understanding, he needs to redefine what it means for a believer to be a husband. This is what he does in Ephesians 5. He designates the husband as 'head', explaining and expounding this term not in the sense of an authoritative leader of the wife but as the one who lovingly sacrifices himself for her good. The meaning which Paul ascribes to 'head' in Ephesians 5 does not establish husbands' unilateral authority over their wives. Rightly understood in context, it contradicts it.

Given Paul's evident approval of the exercise of God-given authority, his omission to tell husbands to exercise authority over their wives is striking. We see a contrast with what Josephus wrote about the husband's authority being God-given (see chapter 3, 40). If Paul had believed that God's design gave husbands unilateral authority over their wives, this would have been the most obvious reason for him to give for wives' submission. He cannot give this reason because it does not accord with his view of the marriage relationship (compare 1 Cor. 7:3–5). Instead, Paul redefines the husband's responsibility in terms of saviourhood; this is his guide to the conduct of husbands. When he tells wives to be subject to their husbands, this is his guide to the conduct of wives; this does not mean, and Paul does not say, that husbands should behave as masters over their wives.

Some may still object that, while Christ is the saviour of the church, he is also her lord; so Paul's emphasis on headship as saviourhood does not prevent the husband's headship extending also to being master over his wife.

However, this does not reflect what Paul says. Paul does not instruct husbands, either here or anywhere else in his writings, to be lord over their wives or to exercise unilateral authority over them. In Ephesians 5 he does not expound 'head' as 'lord'. He does not write in verse 23: 'For a husband is head of the wife as also the Messiah is head of the church, himself lord over the body.' Had he done so, his meaning would have been different. Nor does he say here that a husband's conduct towards his wife should be in *every* respect like Christ's relation to the church; rather, he is focusing on a particular aspect of the Messiah's role. The tasks modelled by the Messiah and allotted to the husband in verses 25–29 are tasks of saving power rather than tasks of authoritative command. These are not the same thing. The surgeon who cuts out your cancer and the helicopter winchman who rescues you from the raging sea have saving power, but not commanding authority; if they give you instructions, you would be wise to follow them, but you are under no obligation to do so.

Some have further argued that the relation of husband to wife should be hierarchical, on the grounds that there are some scriptures which speak figuratively about God being Israel's 'husband'.[23] But Paul makes clear that the point of his analogy is to describe the husband's proper actions towards his wife by comparison with Christ's saviourhood. Accordingly, his exposition gives no support to a hierarchical analysis. There is no scripture which says that a husband should relate to his wife as God relates to Israel.[24]

The second question: one-way or mutual submission?

According to Ephesians 5:21, part of the outcome of being filled by the Holy Spirit, so as to live a Christlike life, is 'submitting to one another out of reverence for Christ' (ESV). In the prior context, from 5:1 to 5:21, Paul's remarks are addressed to all believers who read or hear the letter. There is nothing in verses 1–21 about one believer being ranked more highly than another in some existing hierarchy. Nor is there anything in verses 1–21 about the exercise of authority by one believer over another. Verse 21 is itself part of a single sentence which commences at verse 18 (or possibly at v. 17) and which is of general application to believers. There is no limitation on the application of verse 21 to any particular group within the fellowship of the church.

These contextual features indicate that the submission which Paul instructs in verse 21 is a voluntary, mutual submission of believers to one another. O'Brien rightly accepts that the Greek grammar emphasizes its voluntary character. Even Chrysostom, who held that husbands were placed in commanding authority over their wives, acknowledged that, according to Paul, both partners were to love each other and submit to each other.[25]

---

23. *RBMW*, 243 (Poythress).
24. It is also sometimes said that God's Fatherhood has implications for men's authority over women. But Scripture does not anywhere say this. Jesus resists the idea that God's Fatherhood stands as a model for leadership in Christian relationships. In Matt. 23:1–12 he addresses both crowds and disciples, and therefore both men and women, when he says that they have one Father in heaven, and that they are all 'brothers', and no-one among them should be called 'father'.
25. O'Brien 1999, 411: 'The use of the middle voice of this verb (cf. Col. 3:18) emphasizes the voluntary character of the submission.' We do not have a 'middle voice' in English, but only 'active' and 'passive'. The nearest we can get to expressing the middle voice is to say that we do something to ourselves (here, ranking ourselves below others). Purely as a matter of form, the verb could be alternatively understood as being in the passive voice; the use of the middle voice is determined from the

If a first-century Christian husband is ten years older than his wife, and better educated, and regarded by society as more important than a woman, how can he put verse 21 into practice? How can he rank his wife as more important than himself in a relationship which society has made so unequal? Paul gives the answer in verses 25–31. The husband can express his submission by his humble and loving self-sacrifice. He can step down from the throne which he occupies in fallen human society (compare Gen. 3:16) and give himself up for his wife (5:25; compare Phil. 2:5–8).

In Ephesians 5:24 Paul says that wives must submit *in everything*. If this were one-way-only submission to a higher authority, it would be in conflict with 1 Corinthians 7:3–5, where Paul states that the wife has authority over the husband's body. Once we understand the submission of husband and wife in Ephesians 5 to be mutual, this conflict disappears.

Moreover, when we compare Paul's remarks about wives' submission with what immediately follows, we find a notable difference. Paul gives to children and slaves the more pointed instruction that they should obey (6:1, 5). Why does he not use this word also to the wives? Probably because he is not thinking of Christian marriage as a hierarchical relationship and he does not want to say anything that might encourage husbands to act as lords over their wives.

These considerations all suggest that Paul regards the marriage relationship as a suitable setting for the mutual submission of which he writes in verse 21, rather than a special exception to it. Once it is understood that the husband's headship does not involve unilateral authority over his wife, there is no difficulty in applying to marriage the mutual submission of believers to one another of which Paul writes in verse 21.

But there are some objections to this interpretation which we have not yet considered. The weightiest of these is that Paul cannot have intended mutual submission of husband and wife in Ephesians 5 because he compares the relationship of husband and wife with the relationship between Christ and the church. This is one-way-only submission, for Christ and the church are not in mutual submission to one another.[26]

It is right to say that the church submits to Christ in an asymmetrical relationship. We may also accept that the relationship of husband and wife, as

---

context. In *RBMW*, 162, 164, Knight agrees that the submission here in view is voluntary. In Homily 10 on Colossians 3:18–25 Chrysostom said: 'See how again he has exhorted to reciprocity. . . . From being loved, the wife too becomes loving; and from her being submissive, the husband becomes yielding.'

26. *EFBT*, 190.

envisaged by Paul, is not fully symmetrical. But the objection is nevertheless unpersuasive, because the uniqueness of Christ and the irreversibility of his relationship with the church are not incompatible with a two-way submission of Christ and the church. Jesus Christ himself exemplifies the kind of submission that Paul has in mind. He treats others as more important than himself, even though they are not. He washes his disciples' feet (John 13:1–15). He chooses to take the lowest-ranking place, as the slave of all, and gives up his life as a ransom for many (Mark 10:42–45; Phil. 2:7–8). To apply a complementarian term, this is 'functional subordination'. In other words, Jesus is in no sense inferior to the church but he voluntarily adopts the lowly and submissive position of serving the church as a slave. The church, in turn, submits itself to him, taking up its cross and following him (Mark 8:34). In this way the relationship of Christ and the church involves mutual submission.

Of course, the analogy of Christ and church with husband and wife is not precise. The church's submission largely follows chronologically after Christ's taking of the lowest place, while the mutual submission of husband and wife happens at the same time. But no analogy is ever exact. The husband's responsibility to imitate his saviour by his conduct towards his wife is consistent with the mutual submission required by 1 Corinthians 7:3–5 and Ephesians 5:21.

In appendix 2, I consider further arguments which are advanced against mutual submission. These do not alter the conclusions that Paul envisages believers generally submitting to one another, and that he envisages this as applying also within marriage.

The third question: does Paul differentiate the responsibilities of husbands and wives?

There is an obvious biological difference between women, who can bear and nurse children, and men, who cannot. Beyond this sphere, many egalitarians object to the notion of any definite and fixed differentiation of the responsibilities of husband and wife, even in the very specific and limited sense of the husband taking first responsibility for self-sacrificing service. They point to the words addressed to all believers in 5:2: 'walk in love, just as the Messiah loved us and gave himself up for us as an offering and sacrifice to God.' They rightly point out that the husband's responsibility to love as described in verse 25 is no different in quality from the instruction to love in verse 2, which is addressed to all believers, who include wives. Similarly, the submission expected of wives in verse 22 is expected of all believers in verse 21. Some claim additionally that any definite and fixed differentiation of responsibility is ruled out by Galatians 3:28.

I do not see how this egalitarian objection can realistically be sustained. Verse 23 says that the husband is head of the wife as Christ is head of the church, saviour of the body. The metaphor of 'head' and 'body' is asymmetrical and involves a strong distinction. If Paul had meant to convey that there was to be no difference in the responsibilities of husband and wife set out in this passage, he would scarcely have chosen this metaphor. A metaphor in which one partner is presented as 'head' and the other as 'body' seems entirely unsuitable for such a purpose. The same is true of Paul's analogy of Christ and the church for the relation of husband and wife. This analogy could not convey to his readers an idea that there is no difference between the calling of a husband and of a wife; on the contrary it conveys that there is a difference. To maintain a fully egalitarian position it is necessary to say that Paul's metaphor and comparison are fully reversible, and could be applied to the wife as 'head' and the husband as 'body'. This seems a considerable stretch, given Paul's reliance on the husband's calling as 'head' as part of his reasoning.[27]

All believers are called to imitate Christ, but in the context of marriage Paul places a particular emphasis on the husband's responsibility of self-sacrifice. By comparing the husband to the head and to the Messiah, while comparing the wife to the body and to the church, Paul makes his meaning clear. The husband is called to a first responsibility for self-sacrificial service, as the Messiah took the lead in giving himself for his church (see Eph. 2:1–10; Phil. 2:6–8; Rom. 5:8; 1 John 4:10). Husbands cannot excuse themselves from this responsibility by saying that there is no qualitative difference in the behaviour expected of them and the behaviour expected of their wives.

This may become clearer if we consider leadership in the Christian community. Jesus taught his disciples that they should love others and serve them as if their slaves (John 13:1–17, *doulos* = slave) and that whoever wanted to be a leader among them must be the slave of all: see Mark 10:42–45, where the concept of 'leader' is represented by 'great' (*megas*) and 'first' (*prōtos*). There is no qualitative difference between serving as a slave and serving as slave of all, but we do not draw the conclusion from this that there is no such thing as leadership in the community of believers. Similarly, the lack of a qualitative difference between the ordinary calling of every Christian to love and serve and

---

27. Alternatively, some maintain a fully egalitarian position by arguing that the metaphor and comparison were apt in first-century conditions but Paul would say something different today. Compare *DBE*, 199–204 (Marshall). This is not impossible, but again it seems a considerable stretch, given the nature of the metaphor and of the comparison.

the special calling of the husband to go first in love and service within the marriage does not nullify the husband's calling.

Does Galatians 3:28 rule out any definite and fixed differentiation of responsibility? It does not. Paul's point is that in the new creation in Christ all are equally 'sons' of God (3:26) and all barriers to unity of fellowship are broken down. In Christ this is true here and now, anticipating the age to come. With God, there is no graduated 'respect of persons' (Rom. 2:11; Eph. 6:9). But God can still call people to responsibilities that differ in some way. Equality is not an obstacle to different callings in this present life.

No doubt it is difficult for scholars with a strong commitment to egalitarianism to hear this, and to take on board what Paul says about the husband's special obligation. But I suggest it is clear in Ephesians 5, because of the asymmetrical head–body metaphor and the asymmetrical Christ–church comparison, that Paul is calling the husband to go first in self-sacrifice. This is what the Messiah did for his body, the church. While this is not different in kind from the wife's Christian obligation of unselfish love for her husband, it is an intensification of the husband's responsibility to love.[28]

The beauty of Paul's vision of marriage

In chapter 3 we noted some likely practical reasons for Paul's instructions for wives to submit and for husbands to love. Having considered Ephesians 5 we see, alongside the practical reasons, deeper, theological reasons.

We learned from 1 Corinthians 7 that the coming of the Messiah demands a new perspective. New creation has begun. Human marriage is a temporary institution. While the old creation continues, marriage will still have a proper place as part of that creation, but is it now really anything more than a temporary preventive remedy for sexual immorality?

In his letter to the Ephesians Paul uses his understanding of God's purpose for the church to give a profound answer to this question. He continues to hold together creation in the background and redemption and new creation in the foreground. His view remains Christ-centred. The great mystery which Paul proclaims is God's great plan of salvation, to bring everything and everyone into unity in the Messiah, to the glory of God (Eph. 1:9–10; see also 3:1–11;

---

28. On the human level, it seems only fair that the husband should bear this heightened responsibility, given that the most difficult and dangerous incidents of marriage (pregnancy and childbearing) are borne solely by the wife.

4:12–16; 6:19; Col. 1:25–27; 2:2; 4:3; 1 Tim. 3:16). The church's function is therefore to display, both now and in the age to come, the incomparable riches of God's grace and love expressed in Christ (Eph. 2:7–10; 3:10; 3:21 – 4:1; 5:1–2). The union of husband and wife (5:31) points to the great mystery of the union of Christ with his church (vv. 29–30, 32). For this reason, marriage is not only a relationship of mutual submission (as in 1 Cor. 7:3–5). In addition, in the context of God's great plan of salvation, it makes sense for Paul to place particular emphasis on the responsibility of the husband to care for his wife with a self-sacrificial love which reflects and portrays the love of Christ the saviour for his bride, the church.[29]

This vision of marriage gives no encouragement to husbands to be masters over their wives, whether in the first century or the twenty-first. What about the wives themselves? If in Paul's day the new-found equality of women with men in the fellowship of Christ led some Christian wives to think that submission was no longer appropriate, today there may be a different but parallel issue. The newly established equality of women with men in secular Western society could lead wives to think that the Christian attitude of submission is no longer fitting for them. Paul would say it remains appropriate, in imitation of the humility of Christ.

When husband and wife live in accordance with Ephesians 5, appropriately displaying in their relationship the humility of Jesus Christ and his sacrificial love for his church, this is winsome and compellingly attractive. 'How sweet are your words to my taste, sweeter than honey to my mouth!' (Ps. 119:103, NIV).

Leadership of the household?

We have concentrated in this chapter on the relationship of husband and wife. We have seen a limited form of leadership allotted to the husband, in the

---

29. His instructions for husbands in Eph. 5 are more than three times the length of his instructions for wives. For a range of different interpretations of 5:31–32, see commentaries, such as O'Brien 1999, 429–435. The interpretation in the text above fits with the immediate and broader context in the letter. It understands Paul's use of 'mystery' in a way that is consistent with his other uses of this term both in the same letter and elsewhere. It is consistent with Paul's use of *de* in v. 32, which is a weak 'but' and can properly be translated 'and', as in ESV. It makes sense of Paul's choice of *plen* to commence v. 33: the topic of v. 32 is Christ and the church; in v. 33 he returns to what he wants to emphasize in regard to the behaviour of husband and wife. (Paul's typical use of *plen* is explained in chapter 8, 150.)

sense of a heightened obligation of loving self-sacrifice for the benefit of his wife. What about the leadership of the household more generally?

In both Greek and Roman settings, slaves were legally incapable of marriage.[30] Paul's remarks about the behaviour of wives and husbands in Ephesians 5 are therefore directed primarily to free persons, especially the social stratum who presided over households with slaves.[31] The usual expectation of Roman, Greek and Jewish society was that the husband was the overall ruler of the household. However, Paul does not say anything in Ephesians or Colossians which specifically endorses that arrangement. This raises at least the possibility that he envisages husband and wife having joint leadership of the household. This would be an unsurprising position for him to take, given his belief in equal authority in marriage (1 Cor. 7).

Joint leadership would be consistent with 1 Timothy 5:14, where Paul advises younger widows to marry, bear children and rule over their households.[32] Unless he envisages these widows becoming masters of their households to the exclusion of their new husbands, which seems very unlikely, this suggests joint responsibility for the leadership of the household. But we should recognize that Paul is not prescriptive about the balance of the responsibilities of husband and wife in this respect. We will return to this topic of responsibility for the family in the next chapter.

Summary of chapter 4

1. The only marriage at the completion of the new creation will be the union between Christ and his people. In Ephesians 5 Paul teaches that marriage in the present age is to be seen as a pointer to that reality. The way that husbands and wives relate to each other is to be understood as part of the outcome of being filled by the Holy Spirit so as to live a Christlike way of life.

---

30. Ogden 1996, 129–131; Buckland 1921, 106. However, this did not stop slaves often living in a relation similar to marriage: Buckland 1921, 65.
31. Compare *DBE*, 374–375 (Fee).
32. Translations such as 'take care of their homes' or 'keep house' do not bring out the strength of the term that Paul uses here, which is *oikodespoteō* – 'be master of the household'. ESV translates the related noun *oikodespotēs* as 'master of the/a house' in Matt. 10:25; 13:27, 52; 20:1, 11; 21:33; 24:43; Mark 14:14; Luke 12:39; 13:25; 14:21; 22:11.

2. Paul uses a 'head' metaphor to describe both Christ's relation to the church and the husband's calling in marriage. In Greek this was not a standardized metaphor with a single meaning, so its meaning has to be determined from the context. In Ephesians 1:21–23 the focus is probably on Christ's lordship and in 4:13–16 it is on Christ's saviourhood. Four features show that it is the latter meaning which Paul applies to the husband. These are (a) Paul's apposition of 'head of the church' and 'himself saviour of the body' in 5:23; (b) Paul's theme of saviourhood in 5:25–33; (c) his use of Genesis in 5:31–32; and (d) the first word of 5:24 (*alla*, 'but'), which can only be explained in a way that fits the context if Paul is comparing the husband with Christ as saviour rather than as lord.

3. The meaning of the husband's headship, as shown by the head–body metaphor and the Christ–church comparison, is that he has a particular obligation of loving self-sacrifice for the benefit of his wife. If the husband has any crown, it is a crown of thorns.

4. Wives are to behave as if their husbands were their masters. This does not mean that husbands are masters of their wives. The reasons given by Paul for the wife's submission are the example of and reverence for Christ (vv. 1–2, 21–22) and the husband's responsibility of self-sacrificial service (vv. 22–23). He does not give a reason based on a God-given unilateral authority of the husband.

5. The submission which Paul instructs in verse 21 is a voluntary, mutual submission of believers to one another. Husbands are not exempted from this as regards their wives.

6. In the limited and particular sense explained above, Paul makes a differentiation in the responsibilities of husbands and wives. The egalitarian view which denies any definite differentiation of responsibilities is not consistent with Paul's use of the head–body metaphor and the Christ–church comparison.

7. Marriages lived according to the model of Ephesians 5 are capable of being a wonderful demonstration of the humility of Jesus Christ and his sacrificial love for his church.

8. Paul appears to envisage joint leadership of the household and is not prescriptive about the balance of men's and women's responsibilities for the family.

Questions to consider

1. At present, do you think that in Ephesians 5 Paul is comparing the husband's role in marriage with Christ's saviourhood rather than Christ's lordship? Why or why not?

2. Are there some ideas in chapter 4 which are new to you, or which have challenged your views on the relationship between husband and wife? In what ways?

3. Does Paul's teaching in Ephesians 5 have some practical implications that you consider you should think about and work on? What are they?

5. CREATION AND LIFE: GENESIS 1 – 3 AND BEYOND

> For the word of God is alive and active. Sharper than any double-edged sword, it penetrates even to dividing soul and spirit, joints and marrow; it judges the thoughts and attitudes of the heart.
>
> (Heb. 4:12, NIV)

Man and woman in Genesis

Interpretation of the early chapters of Genesis plays a pivotal role in Grudem's exposition of a complementarian viewpoint in his major work, *EFBT*. He presents ten arguments said to show male headship (in his sense) before the fall, six of which rely on Genesis. Similarly, *RBMW* devotes a whole chapter to deriving male headship from Genesis 1 – 3. Because this forms such a foundational element of the complementarian outlook, I devote the major part of the present chapter to assessing these interpretations,[1] before moving on to marriage and women's leadership in the Old Testament more generally.

---

1. *EFBT*, 25–41; *RBMW*, 86–104 (Ortlund). Ray Ortlund's chapter includes many criticisms of egalitarian interpretations of Gen. 1 – 3 put forward by G. Bilezikian, *Beyond Sex Roles: What the Bible Says about a Woman's Place in Church and Family* (Grand Rapids: Baker, 1985); and A. B. Spencer, *Beyond the Curse: Women Called to Ministry* (Nashville: Thomas Nelson, 1985). It is unnecessary to review the details of these criticisms here because our focus will be on whether Grudem's and Ortlund's complementarian interpretations are justified from the text. The early chapters of Genesis give rise to some more general controversies over interpretation; I explain my approach to these chapters in the Preface.

Complementarians and egalitarians differ in their understanding of man and woman before the fall, and therefore differ also in their understanding of the impact of the fall.

Grudem acknowledges an innate equality of man and woman before the fall, while also identifying a unique male leadership role, which involves a unilateral authority of husband over wife. After the fall, male rule continues, but in a corrupted form. He reads Genesis 3:16 ('he will rule over you') as referring to a harsh distortion of what was originally benevolent male leadership authority.

Payne sees God's original design in creation as making men and women fully equal, without any male leadership role. So how does he read Genesis 3:16? In his view it describes an entirely new situation, which is contrary to God's original design. In other words, male rule over women, or men's rule over their wives, only began as an adverse consequence of the fall.[2]

Before proceeding further, we may note what the New Testament derives from Genesis regarding marriage:

- Jesus refers to God's institution of marriage in Genesis 2 to teach that divorce falls short of God's purpose (Matt. 19:2–9; Mark 10:2–12); but he says nothing about a husband's authority or leadership. The Genesis verses which he cites show only the equality of men and women in God's image (Gen. 1:27) and the unity of husband and wife (Gen. 2:24).
- Paul teaches on marriage in 1 Corinthians 7, Ephesians 5 and Colossians 3; in this teaching the only Genesis passage he cites is Genesis 2:24 (in Eph. 5:31; see also 1 Cor. 6:16). Paul does not derive from Genesis any express proposition about a husband's unilateral authority over his wife.[3]
- Peter teaches about marriage in 1 Peter 3, but in doing so he makes no reference to Genesis 1 – 3.

Since, as far as we know, Jesus, Paul and Peter did not derive anything from Genesis 1 – 3 concerning a husband's unilateral authority in Christian marriage, we should proceed with caution.

---

2. *M&W*, 41–54.

3. Paul makes further references to Gen. 2 or 3 in passages which are not about marriage. We consider 1 Cor. 11:2–16 in chapters 7 and 8, and 1 Tim. 2 in chapters 11 to 13. Schreiner agrees that neither of these New Testament passages is specifically about husband and wife: *WITC*, 177–179. See also *EFBT*, 296–299; *RBMW*, 183 (Moo).

Narrative structure

It is well known that Genesis 1:1 to 2:3 presents a narrative scheme of seven
days. We should also notice how the Hebrew narrative structure continues in
Genesis 2 – 3, because some of our questions will be answered by recognizing
the writer's emphases and connections.

The seven days are followed in 2:4 – 3:24 by seven scenes, arranged in a
concentric symmetry (inverted parallelism). The seven scenes may be summarized as follows:

A   (2:4–17) creation of the man;
  B   (2:18–25) creation of woman and animals, relationships among
      creatures;
    C   (3:1–5) dialogue about eating the fruit;
      D   (3:6–7) narrative of eating the fruit;[4]
    C'   (3:8–13) dialogue about eating the fruit;
  B'   (3:14–21) punishment of creatures, hostile relationships among
      them;
A'   (3:22–24) expulsion of the man.

The second of these scenes (2:18–25) itself consists of seven steps, arranged
in a forward symmetry. The seven steps in the second scene are as follows:

A   (v. 18) problem: the man is alone;
  B   (v. 19) God acts;
    C   (v. 20a) the man acts;
A'   (v. 20b) problem: still no helper for the man;
  B'   (vv. 21–22) God acts;
    C'   (v. 23) the man acts;
A"   (vv. 24–25) problem solved.[5]

---

4. Italic type indicates the climactic point of the structure.

5. See Walsh 2001, 21–23, 39–41. Some commentators divide scene D from scene C'
   at 3:9 rather than 3:8. See Wenham 1987, 50. There is also a debate about whether
   the first half of 2:4 properly belongs with what precedes it or with what follows it.
   These details make no difference for our present purposes. The different analysis
   of narrative structure in *Me&W*, 48, is less persuasive; it is said to be confirmed
   by the questions but there is no question to the serpent. See also footnote 19 below.

Male rule in Genesis 1 – 3

If we look for what the early chapters of Genesis say *expressly* about anything connected with ideas of human rule, authority or leadership, we find only two points:

- In 1:26–28 God makes mankind, male and female, to fill the earth, subdue it and rule over the other creatures. This is joint rule by man and woman.
- In 3:16, after the fall, God pronounces to the woman that the man will rule over her.

These scriptures present a contrasting picture: before the fall, mankind's rule over creation was joint, by man and woman together; after the fall, man will rule over woman, at least in the marriage relationship. This is God's decree, in the sense that it is the outworking of judgment, but it is not presented as God's original design for human beings. Grudem agrees that the man's rule as described in 3:16 is a result of the fall, and in that form it is not something to be deliberately perpetuated or increased.[6]

However, Ortlund and Grudem put forward a concept which they call male 'headship', which they find in Genesis 1 – 3. By God's design, the man is given authority and responsibility to lead and teach the woman. Ortlund's definition of male headship is: 'In the partnership of two spiritually equal human beings, man and woman, the man bears the primary responsibility to lead the partnership in a God-glorifying direction.'[7]

The difficulty that complementarians must address is plain. In the text Adam is not given any instructions before the fall about leading the partnership in a God-glorifying direction or about acting in any way as 'head' of his wife. Nor do we see him leading Eve or teaching her. So how do Ortlund and Grudem derive this idea of headship from the text?

On examination, we find that they rely entirely on implication.[8] Some of the implications are more in the realm of possibility than others, but the critical point is that none of them is a necessary implication, as we shall see.

---

6. *EFBT*, 40.

7. *RBMW*, 86. See also *EFBT*, 30–40.

8. See also complementarian Craig Blomberg: 'The upshot of our survey of Genesis 1 – 3 is that there are hints of a divinely intended male headship in God's original scheme': Blomberg 2005, 132.

Genesis 1 – 2 and authoritative headship?

The Hebrew word *'ādām*, which is translated 'mankind' in NIV in Genesis 1:26 and 5:2, or 'man' in some versions, refers in those texts to both male and female human beings. Grudem relies on God's naming of the human race as 'man' in Genesis 5:1–2 as giving a 'hint' of male leadership. Similarly, Ortlund says that God's naming of the human race as 'man' in 1:26 'whispers male headship'. Their careful choices of the words 'hint' and 'whispers' speak eloquently of the weakness of this argument for establishing a doctrine. This is a case of implication being in the eye of the beholder.[9]

Complementarian writers sometimes assert that Eve did not receive God's command first-hand, but was taught it by Adam. But the text does not show this. It does not say whether Eve was instructed about God's command concerning the forbidden fruit by Adam, by God, or by both.[10]

Grudem further relies on the order of creation: the man first, then the woman. He says to be born first was to have a leadership role, and that the first readers of Genesis would have understood Adam's leadership because of the system of primogeniture in the ancient world.[11] This is another proposal about an implication from the text. Again, the problem is that it is not clear enough for establishing a firm doctrine. Nothing is said about it in the text. Nor does the narrative allude to ideas of primogeniture, for Adam and Eve are not born, they are created or formed. Nor is such an idea picked up elsewhere in the Bible, despite multiple opportunities for doing so. The description 'firstborn' is applied

---

9. See further *DBE*, 79–80 (Hess). Such implications are a recurring feature of the wider debate. For examples from the egalitarian side see *DBE*, 111 (Belleville, reading Num. 12:15 as implying that the congregation of Israel viewed Miriam's role as essential to its mission, refusing to move ahead until she was restored to leadership); Tidball 2012, 175 (reading Luke 21:1–4 as praising a woman over a man).

10. *EFBT*, 36: 'Adam told her of the command.' Some commentators have tried to work out who instructed Eve by close examination of the differences between God's command to the man in 2:16–17 and the woman's recitation of God's command in 3:2–3. In the command to Adam in 2:16–17, 'you shall not eat' is singular. In Eve's recitation in 3:2–3, 'you shall not eat' is plural. But these differences do not provide a definitive answer to the question. Mowczko 2015a advances an egalitarian reading by arguing that God must have given the command to both Adam and Eve together on an occasion between 2:17 and 3:2. Maybe. But Eve's use of the plural could also be read as no more than her acknowledgment that the command applies both to her and to Adam.

11. *EFBT*, 67. Contrast *DBE*, 84 (Hess).

to Christ (Rom. 8:29; Col. 1:15, 18; Heb. 1:6; Rev. 1:5), and Christ is sometimes compared with Adam, yet there is no scripture that refers to Adam as the firstborn. As regards order, in Genesis 1 the humans who are to rule over creation are created last, not first, so the writer does not appear to regard priority of order of creation as showing priority of authority. This element of Grudem's argument does not really depend on Genesis 2, since Genesis 2 does not itself say anything expressly about headship for Adam. Instead it depends on Grudem's interpretation of 1 Timothy 2:12–13, which we shall come to in chapters 11 to 13.

Ortlund's interpretation of Genesis 2:18–25 is that God makes the woman the 'helper' and man the 'head'. Within this, he makes a number of points that will command wide assent:

- Verse 23, where the man's partner is revealed to him, is to be understood as the man's cry of joy and recognition.
- The woman was created as man's equal partner to help him, a helper 'corresponding to him'. This means that the woman is 'suitable for the man, on his level, in contrast to the animals'.
- The woman is made to help the man, and not vice versa, and this shows that men and women are different and 'non-reversible'.

The depiction of woman as created to be man's helper is evidently a significant feature of the narrative. (Paul picks it up in 1 Cor. 11:8–9, which we will consider in chapters 7 and 8.) It firmly suggests difference, and leaves open the possibility that the difference has something to do with leadership, but the text leaves the difference undeveloped. So how does Ortlund arrive at his view of headship?

He says, 'A man, just by virtue of his manhood, is called to lead for God', and he gives three reasons:

1. In verse 23 the man names his partner 'woman'. Grudem also relies on this. Ortlund says it is a 'sovereign act' which 'not only arose out of his own sense of headship, it also made his headship clear to Eve'. This is by far their strongest argument for an implication of male authority from the text.

When God calls the light 'day' and the darkness 'night', this is an exercise of authority (1:5, and see 1:8, 10). In a similar way, Adam's naming of the animals in 2:19–20 is an exercise of the authority given to humans in 1:26–28, as God's image-bearers, to rule over the creatures. And after the fall the man can be understood as exercising rule over his wife by giving her the personal name 'Eve' (3:20, in the context of 3:16).

However, while the giving of a name can be an exercise of authority, it is not necessarily so. In Genesis 16:13, when Hagar gives a name to the Lord, this is not an exercise of authority by her and does not imply her headship over God.

The question is whether Adam's cry of joy and recognition in 2:23 should be understood as carrying an implication that Adam is at that moment exercising authority over the woman. We can see from the contrast between 1:5 (God naming creation) and 16:13 (Hagar naming God) that whether there is such an implication depends on the relationship between the namer and the named. If we assume Adam's authoritative headship, it would follow that the naming could properly be understood as an exercise of authority. If we do not assume such headship, the naming is not an exercise of authority. Either way, the arguments are circular. Genesis 2:23 on its own cannot tell us whether there is an implication of authority or not.

If we attend to the text, we find that it offers its own interpretation of the significance of the man's joyous recognition of the woman. It is not the point made by Ortlund and Grudem. What the writer wants readers to understand from verse 23 is plainly stated in verse 24, which begins with 'For this reason', and which is about the union of husband and wife in marriage. The differentiation and similarity of man and woman enable this union to be achieved.

This message is reinforced by the narrative structure. The union of 2:24 is the last of the seven steps in the second scene. The scene starts with the problem that the man is alone, without a helper (v. 18). This problem, which is 'not good', stands out by contrast with the 'good' and 'very good' of chapters 1–2 up to this point (1:4, 10, 12, 18, 21, 25, 31; 2:9, 12), and it is emphasized by repetition (2:20). In the final step the problem is solved: man is no longer alone, and instead he is united with an intimate companion who corresponds to him; man and woman are joined in the close alliance which we call marriage. This is the writer's own emphasis. The writer states nothing about headship in Ortlund's or Grudem's sense.

Moreover, there is no appeal or allusion to verse 23 anywhere in the Bible for the purpose of indicating male headship.

The strongest of the complementarian arguments therefore fails to establish authoritative male headship.

2. Ortlund's second reason refers to verse 24. According to this verse a man leaves his father and mother in order to join his wife in marriage. Ortlund says: 'His wife does not leave her family to initiate the new household; this is the responsibility of the head.' Certainly this text indicates a positive action on the part of the man in leaving his father and mother. But the text is silent about

whether or not the woman likewise leaves her family. And in verse 24 the man's action of leaving is the means by which his need, not to be alone, is met. There is nothing here about responsibility as 'head' in Ortlund's or Grudem's sense. Verse 24 fails to confirm male headship; instead, it celebrates the unity of man and woman in marriage.[12]

3. The word 'helper' in 2:18 is said by Ortlund to denote 'subordination', which is 'entailed in the very nature of a helping role'. Grudem similarly relies on Eve's role as helper of Adam.[13] They both acknowledge that in Scripture God is often stated to be the helper of his people, but both insist that someone who helps is adopting a subordinate role.

The problem with this reasoning is that it depends upon a connotation of the English word 'helper'. In English we commonly think of a helper as a subordinate or junior assistant. This connotation is lacking from the Hebrew word '*ēzer*, which carries the idea of 'strength' and is here translated 'helper'. It refers to a military protector in Isaiah 30:5 (where Pharaoh's help will not avail) and in Daniel 11:34 (with 'little' added, diluting the usual force of meaning). It refers to God as 'strength' or 'help' in numerous texts.[14] For example, Deuteronomy 33:26 speaks of God riding across the heavens to help, and on the clouds in his majesty; in Deuteronomy 33:29 God is Israel's shield and help and glorious sword; in Psalms 121 and 124 Israel's help comes from the Maker of heaven and earth. In these scriptures God is depicted as a powerful ally for needy Israel; in none of them is there any sense of God adopting a subordinate role, such that Israel is God's leader.

The natural reading of Genesis 2 in Hebrew is therefore that woman is made to be man's powerful ally. There is no implication that she is his junior assistant.

---

12. In addition, by describing the man as leaving his family, v. 24 notably fails to endorse the ancient patriarchal and patrilocal pattern. According to that pattern, when a patriarch's son marries, the son does not leave his family but instead the wife leaves her family.

13. Grudem also refers to 1 Cor. 11:9, but this does not add anything to the argument. It is common ground between complementarians and evangelical egalitarians that the Genesis account presents the woman as made to be the man's helper.

14. Exod. 18:4; Deut. 33:7, 26, 29; Pss 20:2; 33:20; 70:5; 89:19; 115:9–11; 121:1–2; 124:8; 146:5; Hos. 13:9. See further *M&W*, 44–45; *DBE*, 86 (Hess); Wenham 1987, 68; Atkinson 1990, 68–69. *M&W*, 44, states that '*ēzer* always refers to a superior or equal. But this may go too far. In Ezek. 12:14 the identity of the helpers is uncertain, but they appear to be subordinates.

This is consistent with woman being made from man's side, which does not indicate a hierarchy.

Moreover, Grudem acknowledges from Genesis 2:18 that the woman is not to help the man as one who is inferior to him; rather she is to be a help 'corresponding to him' (Hebrew, *kĕnegdô*), that is, 'equal and adequate to himself'. The creation mandate of 1:26–28 is given by God to man and woman together. Obviously man is utterly unable to fulfil this on his own. He needs a helper different from and complementary to himself. Their alliance will enable them to fulfil the mandate. Genesis 2:18 and 20 contain no implication of man's authority over woman. Staunch complementarian James Hurley agrees that the term 'helper' does not here contain an implication of subordination or of a junior assistant. Even Luther considered that before the fall the woman was fully Adam's equal.[15]

Genesis 3 and authoritative headship?

Ortlund reads Genesis 3 as supporting his concept of male headship. Is his reasoning satisfactory?

- He argues that the serpent addressed Eve first in order to strike at Adam's headship. But this is mere assertion, with no basis in the text. It would be as easy to say that the serpent addressed Eve first because she was the more dominant character and, if she could be led astray, Adam was likely to follow her; this would be equally without any basis in the text. Moreover it was not Adam's authority that the serpent challenged, but God's (v. 4).[16]
- According to Ortlund, Eve usurped Adam's headship, and Adam sinned by listening to his wife and thereby abandoning his headship. But the text

---

15. *EFBT*, 119. Hurley 1981, 209. Luther, in Pelikan 1958, 115 (Gen. 2:18): 'If the woman had not been deceived by the serpent and had not sinned, she would have been the equal of Adam in all respects. . . . Therefore Eve was not like the woman of today; her state was far better and more excellent, and she was in no respect inferior to Adam, whether you count the qualities of the body or those of the mind.' See also Chrysostom, *1 Corinthians*, Homily 26: 'she was not subjected as soon as she was made; nor, when He brought her to the man, did either she hear any such thing from God, nor did the man say any such word to her: he said indeed that she was "bone of his bone, and flesh of his flesh" (Gen. ii. 23): but *of rule or subjection he no where made mention unto her*' (emphasis added).

16. For this last point see *DBE*, 89 (Hess).

does not say this. The text depicts the serpent deceiving Eve into taking
and eating the forbidden fruit (vv. 1–6, 13), and Adam receiving the fruit
from her and eating (vv. 6, 17). Nothing is said about Eve usurping
Adam's headship or about Adam abandoning his headship; the story is
not presented in those terms. The reason given in the text for it being
wrong for Adam to listen to his wife is that he listened to her instead
of obeying God's command not to eat the forbidden fruit (v. 17). Even
Grudem rebuts this element of Ortlund's interpretation as not justified
by the text.[17]

- Ortlund says that God calls out to Adam first (v. 9) because Adam is the
  head. Grudem says the same. But it is unclear how they know this. The
  text does not say that this is the reason. It could equally be suggested
  that the reason was that Adam had received the command first. Or there
  could be some other reason. The text does not state a reason. One could
  say, with as little justification, that Eve is the head because in verses
  16–17 God addresses Eve before Adam.

- The sentence on the woman in verse 16 includes that her desire will be
  for her husband, and that he will rule over her. Ortlund draws attention
  to the similar expression in 4:7 and suggests that the woman will desire
  mastery over her husband. This is a persuasive reading, which Grudem
  also notes, but it says nothing about male headship before the fall.
  Ortlund then proposes that 'he will rule over you' in verse 16 should
  be read as referring to man's rightful rule over woman, as if the text said
  'you will desire mastery over him but he must rule over you'. This is a
  minority reading which not even Grudem supports. The text presents
  the man's rule over the woman as a negative consequence of the fall.

- Perhaps conscious that his first interpretation may not command
  acceptance, Ortlund offers an alternative, in which the word 'rule'
  in verse 16 connotes 'the exercise of ungodly domination'. Grudem
  follows a similar line, proposing that it connotes rule that is forceful
  and sometimes harsh, and hence a distortion of man's rule before the
  fall. But this again lacks a basis in the text. The text uses an ordinary
  word for rule, which does not have a connotation of ungodly domination
  or harshness. The same word is used of God's rule in Judges 8:23. It is
  often used of political rulers. In Isaiah 19:4 it is used of rule by a cruel
  king, but the connotation of cruelty in that context does not come from
  the word 'rule'; it is provided by words that describe the king as cruel

---

17. *EFBT*, 69–70.

and fierce. The interpretation of verse 16 to refer to a distortion of a previous ruling role is without any textual warrant. It is directly contrary to the plain meaning of the text, which is explicit that the rule of the husband is a result of the fall.[18] The narrative structure confirms this. The statement of male rule is in the sixth scene (B' in the symmetrical structure). It corresponds to the second scene (B), where the writer's emphasis was on the unity of man and woman which brought that scene to its conclusion (2:24–25).[19] The writer's own contrast is therefore not between benevolent rule and harsh rule but between the united alliance of 2:24–25 and the competitive disharmony of 3:16, where the man is now on top. The conclusion that ought to be drawn from this text is that, if or in so far as there was a God-given distinctiveness of the husband's role in marriage before the fall, it certainly did *not* consist of ruling over the wife.

- Ortlund's next point is that God addresses Adam in verse 17 with an introductory statement or indictment; this is different from the way that God addresses Eve in verse 16; and that God told Adam alone that he would die (v. 19). These factors are said to demonstrate Adam's headship. How this is so, Ortlund does not explain; there is no mention of headship in the text. It can perhaps be seen as an implication if one starts out from a belief in male headship, but the text does not demand to be understood in this sense.

Referring to 3:17, Ortlund goes on to say that Adam's disobedience was 'the pivotal factor' in the fall, not Eve's. Grudem develops this observation. He contends that 'male headship in marriage before the fall' is shown by the fact that Adam, not Eve, had a special role in representing the entire human race: although Eve sinned first, the New Testament does not say 'as in Eve all die' but 'as in Adam all die, so also in Christ shall all be made alive' (1 Cor. 15:22).

---

18. In *EFBT*, 39–40, Grudem expands the idea of the fall as involving a distortion of previous roles by saying that the curse of pain in raising food from the ground in 3:17–19 was on Adam's particular area of responsibility and the curse of pain in bearing children in 3:16 was on Eve's particular area of responsibility. He does not explain why he thinks that a farmer is necessarily head over a mother. Moreover, his conception of fully separated roles does not arise from the text: see below under 'Who should protect and provide?', 86–89.

19. The second half of the sevenfold structure of 2:4 to 3:24 is divided a little differently by Waltke 2001, 81, following Dorsey, but the literary correspondence of harmonious unity in B and disharmonious male rule in B' (3:16) remains the same.

He also refers to the parallels between Adam and Christ in 1 Corinthians 15:45–49 and Romans 5:12–21.[20]

This argument about the fall confuses two separate ideas. Representation is not the same thing as authoritative headship. If I say that an ambassador represents the Government of the United States of America, so that, for good or ill, the ambassador's words and actions are the words and actions of the US Government, and so that an attack on the ambassador is an attack on the USA, I am not implying that the ambassador leads the US Government or rules the USA.

In these scriptures Adam is indeed seen as representing all of humanity. Paul's interpretation reflects the shape and wording of the Genesis narrative, where the account of the exclusion from the garden mentions only 'the man' (3:22–24; contrasting in the narrative structure with 2:4–17, or more precisely with 2:15–17, where the man is placed in the garden).[21] We can express the basic idea by saying: Adam was created first and all have their source from him; he sinned; his fall is seen as representing the fall of all humanity. This basic idea has led to much discussion and debate over how this is to be fully understood, including whether and in what sense Adam's fall is the cause of subsequent sinfulness. But we do not need to enter into that debate; we can see that this basic idea is about representation, not about rule. In 1 Corinthians 15 and Romans 5 Paul is speaking of Adam's representation of humanity, not of ruling over humanity. Nor is he saying anything about Adam as ruler of his wife.[22]

In a concluding appeal Ortlund observes, without conscious irony: 'all of us know the stripping experience of discovering, to our dismay, that we have been making the Bible say things it does not really say.' The distinctive feature of complementarian interpretations of Genesis 1 – 3 is that they are based on implication rather than on the express words. In this way they make the Bible say things that it does not actually say. From the express words, the only definite point made about unique male rule, leadership or authority is that the rule of the man over the woman is to be understood as one of the negative consequences of the fall (3:16).[23]

---

20. *EFBT*, 30–31.
21. This chimes with the use of the word *'ādām* as meaning 'man' in the sense of 'mankind', as in Gen. 1:26 and 5:2.
22. Some say the Adam typology also carries an idea about mankind's rule over creation, but this possible further element does not support men's rule over women.
23. There is a wide range of views among Christians concerning theories of evolution and to what extent these are in conflict with Genesis. According to evolutionary

GENESIS 1 – 3 AND BEYOND

The Danvers Statement argues that gender role distinctions, and hence male headship, should find an echo in every human heart. This is said with good intentions. But listening to one's heart can be risky. Hebrews 4:12 says (NIV): 'For the word of God is alive and active. Sharper than any double-edged sword, it penetrates even to dividing soul and spirit, joints and marrow; it judges the thoughts and attitudes of the heart.' Genesis 3:16 has this effect. It reveals that the desire to rule over others comes from fallen hearts.

What does it mean to be male or female?

In a video discussion in which Don Carson, John Piper and Tim Keller discuss The Gospel Coalition's commitment to complementarianism, Piper poses the question, 'What does it mean to grow up to be a man and not a woman?' or vice versa. He says that egalitarians are unable to answer this question.[24]

This may or may not be so, but we should note that it is not a question that the Bible directly addresses. In the course of the present book we look at many Bible passages about men and women. We see differentiated instructions for men and for women about honourable conduct in gathered worship (1 Cor. 11:2–16). We see instructions specifically to husbands and wives on living in imitation of Christ (Eph. 5; 1 Pet. 3). But nowhere will we see any instructions in the Bible saying what a man should do in order to be a real man or what a woman should do in order to be a real woman. There are none. 'Manhood' and 'womanhood' are not terms or concepts that are used in the Bible. (1 Cor. 16:13 calls both sexes to mature behaviour; it is not a prescription for masculinity.)

---

understandings, male dominance has been hard-wired into many creatures for millions of years: see, for example, Peterson 2018, 1–11, referring to lobsters and numerous scientific papers. Suppose this theory should be broadly accepted: would it contradict the idea that the rule of man over woman is to be understood as resulting from the fall, because male dominance is older than mankind? It would not. The Genesis story distinguishes Eden from the rest of creation (2:5–9). When God forms mankind from what already exists (2:7), he is doing something special. He is making a unique creature in his own image (1:26–27) to copy and follow through his work of ordering the world (2:15; 1:28), a creature in which male and female are equal (1:27; 2:18), and which has the potential of living for ever in his presence (2:9, 16). These differences from the animals (1:25–26; 2:20) are marred by the fall (3:16, 22).

24. Carson [no date].

This lack of instructions should not be a surprise. In Genesis 1:27, being male and female are matters of God-given nature; they are not themselves roles which humans are commanded to fulfil.[25]

Differentiation of man and woman

While being male or female is not a role, and the headship concepts put forward by Ortlund and Grudem do not find explicit support in the Genesis text, the fact still remains that the Genesis narrative presents the woman as created separately from the man, and she is made to be the man's powerful ally. What conclusions follow from this?

An initial conclusion is that there is a clear differentiation between man and woman. While the main explicit emphasis is the essential similarity and unity of man and woman (2:23–24), nevertheless differentiation is conveyed by the clear narrative presentation of woman as being made for man and by the use of the word 'helper'.

God, who is Israel's helper, can do things which Israel cannot do. Similarly, we may say, women can do things which men cannot do. If any egalitarians claim that according to 2:18–24 there are ultimately no differences of nature or aptitudes between men and women, such a claim cannot be sustained. Men and women are *different*.

The egalitarian side is sometimes shy of acknowledging innate differences between men and women. Such a perspective was aptly challenged by a female journalist with a droll comment on reactions to a TV quiz show in the UK:

> Some people [were] upset that the final of *University Challenge* was between two all-male teams, on the grounds that this was 'sexist'. Really? I live with a man who not only answers more questions on *UC* every week than I do, he often answers more than most of the contestants combined. Does this make me feel like a dumb blonde?

---

25. Giles 2000, 200–201, objects to the term 'role'. 'In our very being we *are* differentiated, we are not simply acting out sex roles. . . . To suggest that God has differentiated the sexes simply by allocating differing roles is a novel idea which cannot be supported from the Scriptures. The Bible insists that our maleness and femaleness is grounded in our God-given nature.' It is right to acknowledge that we live in an imperfect world (Gen. 3; Rom. 8:20–22) and that there are people born with intersex conditions or who experience gender dysphoria, but this does not alter the point concerning God's original design of human beings as male and female.

On the contrary, I find the systemising male brain a rich source of comedy. For what does it profit a man to recall the Treaty of Westphalia, yet lose the worming tablets for the cat? He also arranges his books in alphabetic order within chronological. And his proudest boast is that while on holiday in North Wales in 1974, he won a hubcap identification competition. Who could compete with that? Who would want to?[26]

I am not suggesting that all men are or should be like the journalist's husband. But God has made men and women to be different, and they should be allowed to be different. Both similarity and difference are God's good gift. For man and woman to be fully united in marriage, similarity and difference are both necessary. It is through these gifts of similarity and sexual difference that God creates communities.

But how is the God-ordained differentiation of man and woman intended to work out in practice? The man was formed first, and the woman was made for the sake of the man. Does this mean that the man is to be the leader and the woman the follower? This would fit with such a view, but it does not establish it.

To see this limitation of the Genesis text more clearly, let us suppose someone were wanting to establish that *women* are ordained by God to be the *leaders of men*. They could easily use the same kinds of arguments from implication that complementarians use, proceeding as follows:

- In Genesis 2 the woman is described as man's *'ēzer*.
- Even some complementarian scholars accept that to be an *'ēzer* (strength, or helper) does not imply subordination. God is Israel's *'ēzer*. The usual implication is that the *'ēzer* is more powerful than the needy one who receives the help.

---

26. Pearson 2017. There is a substantial scientific literature debating the extent of empirical differences between men and women. For example, Baron-Cohen 2003 presents an evidence-based argument that in general the female brain is predominantly hard-wired for empathy, and that the male brain is predominantly hard-wired for understanding and building systems, and that these traits, while partly determined by culture and socialization, are also partly determined by biology. (He does not claim that this is an invariable pattern or that every individual fits clearly into it.) For a spirited defence of a contrasting view, see Fine 2010. The debate over the conclusions to be drawn from empirical research might be constructively advanced by explicitly recognizing some innate characteristics as 'pre-wired', and subject to the possibility of changes, rather than 'hard-wired': see Haidt 2012, 152–153.

- We see in the narrative that the woman is made for the man because of his inadequacy and need, that is, he is alone and he needs help.
- Genesis 2 is adding further detail to the order of creation presented in Genesis 1 in which mankind is created last; it presents the woman as formed last of all, the pinnacle of God's beautiful creation.
- Therefore it is implied that the woman was originally intended to be the strong leader of the man.
- This understanding also sheds light on Genesis 3:16; in the fall, woman misuses her leadership; therefore it is taken away from her and given to the man instead.

But no-one would be convinced. The argument would not persuade anyone who did not have a prior commitment to women's leadership of men. Setting on one side our cultural resistance to excluding all men from leadership, the decisive reasons for not being convinced *from the text* are that (1) the argument depends entirely on supposed implications; and (2) the Genesis writer does not draw a conclusion about leadership. The Genesis writer's own conclusion focuses on the unity of man and woman (2:24). For the same reasons, the complementarian arguments from Genesis 2 cannot convince anyone who does not have a prior commitment to the idea of male leadership. Issues concerning male leadership must depend upon other scriptures.[27]

Church history teaches us the need for great caution in using implications from Scripture to establish Christian doctrine. It can be hazardous to go beyond what is written.

One doctrinal example will suffice to press home this point. The New Testament describes Jesus' death on the cross as a ransom (Mark 10:45; 1 Tim. 2:6). It is implicit in the concept of a ransom that it is costly and that it results in liberation from bondage. The costliness of Christ's death and its liberating effects are both mentioned expressly elsewhere in the New Testament (for example, 1 Cor. 6:20; Heb. 2:15). We therefore accept these implications of the ransom concept. But it is also implicit in the idea of a ransom that a payment is made to someone. The 'whole world lies in the power of the evil one' (1 John 5:19, ESV). So Scripture could reasonably be said to imply that the ransom was paid to the evil one.

---

27. In chapter 4, we have seen a limited form of leadership by the husband based on Eph. 5. Paul further refers to this part of Genesis in 1 Cor. 11 (which we will consider in chapters 7 and 8) and in 1 Tim. 2 (which we will consider in chapters 11 to 13).

In the early centuries of church history patristic writers such as Origen and Gregory the Great taught that the ransom was paid to the devil. But Scripture never actually says this. Over time it began to be appreciated that this doctrine of payment led to various errors. It gave the evil one an exaggerated status. It suggested that the devil had legitimate rights over human beings, which had to be satisfied. The doctrine was ultimately, and rightly, discarded. Debatable implications are not a sufficient basis for a doctrine.

In the same way, it is not appropriate to build a doctrine of male headship on debatable implications from Genesis 1 – 3. Genesis does not establish that before the fall there was a male leadership role which involved a unilateral authority of husband over wife.

Pursuing the principle of canonical interpretation, we should next check whether this conclusion is confirmed or called into question by the remainder of the Old Testament.

Marriage in the Old Testament

Ortlund suggests a creation principle that male headship is expressed by taking the initiative to form a marriage.[28] But we do not see in the Old Testament an invariable pattern of male initiative in this respect. If it had been understood that this was a God-ordained male prerogative, Boaz would have been affronted or shocked by Ruth's proposal of marriage. Instead, he commended Ruth for taking the initiative in asking him to marry her (Ruth 3:7–14).

In practice, in Old Testament marriages, husbands are usually in charge. Sarah calls her husband, Abraham, her 'lord' (Gen. 18:12).[29] This is exactly what we might expect from Genesis 3:16 ('he will rule over you'). But this does not tell us whether God's original design for men and women was that husbands ought to be in charge of their wives.

There is no Old Testament law which says that a wife must obey her husband. Nor does the Old Testament establish such a law through its narratives. In the story related in 1 Samuel 25 Nabal refuses David's request for provisions. Nabal's wife, Abigail, flouts the foolish and dangerous position adopted by her husband and provides abundant supplies. The

---

28. *RBMW*, 92.

29. We will look at this text in more detail in chapter 6.

text presents this as a positive action, and she is warmly commended for it.[30]

We can search the whole of the Old Testament for a text which says that men ought to exercise authority over their wives, but we will not find it, because it is not there.[31] The absence of any such text is consistent with our understanding that Genesis does not teach a creation principle of unilateral male authority in marriage.

Who should protect and provide?

We saw in chapter 4 that Paul was not prescriptive about the balance of the roles of husband and wife as leaders of the household. But complementarians say that the husband has primary responsibility to provide for and protect his wife and family, whereas the wife has primary responsibility to care for the home and nurture the children. Grudem bases this on numerous scripture references and on 'the internal testimony from both men's and women's hearts'.[32]

Grudem draws a stronger distinction than is justified. His reasoning is faulty, for he relies mainly on scriptures which are descriptive rather than prescriptive. Even where the scriptures give instructions, there is no instance where they explicitly allocate contrasting general responsibilities as between husbands and

---

30. In *EFBT*, 154–155, Grudem makes the point that Abigail does not disobey a direct command stated to her by her husband. This is correct, but makes no material difference. She is plainly flouting the authority which the prevailing culture gave to her husband. Grudem rightly acknowledges that she acts contrary to her husband's intent. In other words, she disobeys him.

31. The nearest thing in the Bible to an explicit unilateral authority of husband over wife is in legal regulations under the old covenant which permitted a Jewish husband to nullify formal pledges made by his wife provided he acted promptly (Num. 30). This authority only extended to releasing her from a vow. This regulation may be viewed in the same way that Jesus viewed the law's provision for divorce, as an accommodation to fallen human nature (Matt. 19:8). This regulation does not contain any command to a husband to exercise authority over his wife. See also *EFBT*, 434 ('The Bible never tells husbands to attempt to force submission on their wives').

32. *EFBT*, 44–45.

wives in the way that he proposes.[33] The Old Testament depicts both parents, not mothers alone, as responsible for teaching children how they should live.[34] And the subjective testimony of men's and women's hearts is not a valid doctrinal argument.

To protect and provide is good. A husband who is fulfilling the responsibility defined by Paul in Ephesians 5:25–30 should protect and provide, so far as lies in his power. Otherwise, he is not fulfilling that responsibility. Moreover, it is of course women who bear children. In the agricultural society depicted in the early chapters of Genesis, as in many other cultures, we may suppose that their ability to work in the fields is reduced while pregnant or while nursing small children. They need to be provided for.

But does Scripture prescribe firm and invariable social roles? In Genesis 1:28 it is both man and woman who are commanded to fill and subdue the earth. In Genesis 2:15–18 the woman is to be the man's powerful ally in the care of the garden. These scriptures do not prescribe firmly separated spheres of responsibility for men and women.[35]

---

33. His New Testament references are Matt. 2:13–14; Eph. 5:25; 1 Tim. 5:3–16, especially 8, 10; Titus 2:5; 1 Pet. 3:7. These fall short of establishing the view that he puts forward. Moreover, he makes an unwarranted assumption when he says of 1 Tim. 5:8 that, because of the historical context, the gender-neutral term *tis* (anyone) refers to men as having a duty to provide for others. His assumption is in conflict with 5:16, where Paul says that, if any believing woman has widows (meaning, 'has relatives or household members who are widows' – see 5:8), she should assist them (that is, provide for their needs).

34. Prov. 1:8 states, 'Listen, my son, to your father's instruction and do not forsake your mother's teaching' (NIV). Prov. 6:20 says, 'keep your father's command and do not forsake your mother's teaching' (NIV). In Deut. 6:4–9 the command to teach children is addressed to 'Israel', and therefore to both fathers and mothers.

35. Both Augustine and Aquinas, holding a low view of women's intelligence and abilities, mistakenly taught that the bearing of children was the only way in which woman was man's helper: Augustine, *Literal Commentary on Genesis* 9.5 ('If it were not the case that the woman was created to be man's helper specifically for the production of children, then why would she have been created as a "helper"? Was it so that she might work the land with him? No . . . a male would have made a better assistant. One can also posit that the reason for her creation as a helper had to do with the companionship she could provide for the man. . . . Yet for company and conversation, how much more agreeable it is for two male friends to dwell together than for a man and a woman! . . . I cannot think of any reason

The fullest biblical description of an ideal wife is in Proverbs 31:10–31. While her husband is seated with the elders at the city gate (v. 23), the 'wife of noble character' or 'wife of strength' is a businesswoman who works both within and outside the home, earning money and providing for her husband and for the whole household (vv. 12–19, 21–22, 24), helping the poor from her means (v. 20), watching over the household (v. 27), and receiving honour both in the family and in the public sphere (vv. 28–31).

Grudem's remarks about this text seem to view it through mid-twentieth-century American spectacles. He protests against seeing the woman as providing for the family. Verse 15 'just means she puts out the food for the day'. He does not acknowledge that the wife is portrayed as a manufacturer (vv. 13, 24), entrepreneurial farmer (v. 16) and commercial trader (v. 18).[36] Other complementarians acknowledge more fully what this text shows. 'She will not let us say there is anything intrinsically wrong with a wife and mother owning property or running a business and having and supervising employees.' 'The different roles she takes on outside of the home show there are any number of jobs a woman can have. Many of them would have involved working with men and in some instances having authority over them.'[37] Scripture explicitly calls women, not just men, to be providers (1 Tim. 5:16).

The Proverbs text is a ringing affirmation of the dignity and abilities of women. But this wifely role is not presented as a command. It is portrayed as an ideal,[38] described in terms of the social conditions prevailing among the wealthy at the time of writing. Social conditions, people and family circumstances vary. Hopefully no-one is so foolish as to insist, on the basis of this scripture, that every wife must be the breadwinner, through manufacturing, farming and trading, and also take responsibility for running the home (v. 27) and caring for the children and domestic staff (v. 15), while her husband sits at the contemporary equivalent of the city gate. Similarly, other descriptive passages should not be read as prescriptive.

(note 35 *cont.*) for a woman's being made as a man's helper, if we dismiss the reason of procreation'); Aquinas, *Summa Theologica*, Part 1, Question 92, Article 1, Answer 1 ('It was necessary for woman to be made, as the Scripture says, as a "helper" to man; not, indeed, as a helpmate in other works, as some say, since man can be more efficiently helped by another man in other works; but as a helper in the work of generation').

36. *EFBT*, 155–157.

37. Smith 2012, 210; Sandom 2012, 187.

38. Each line begins with a successive letter of the complete Hebrew alphabet.

As for provision, so also for protection. The fact that in the Old Testament it is men who go to war does not give us God's prescription for the family. In the Old Testament men are protectors; so also, as occasion arises, are women. They protect their families and they protect others. Abigail protects her husband and the men in her household from a violent death (1 Sam. 25). Rahab protects the male spies (Josh. 2). An unnamed woman protects the people of Thebez from being burned to death (Judg. 9:50–55). The unnamed 'wise woman' of Abel Beth Maakah protects the men and women of her city from an invading army (2 Sam. 20). Esther protects her people, the Jews, from being massacred (Esth. 2:19 – 9:19).

Where Scripture is not prescriptive, we have no justification for insisting on a single preferred blueprint. There are many pressures on the family and on the nurture of children. The Industrial Revolution had the consequence of separating work from home. Economic and cultural changes have dislocated the extended family. With the rise of the cult of the individual, 'me first' is falsely seen as a virtue. It is right for Christians to be concerned about how best to respond to all these changes, but this is not best done by treating patterns of life that reflect particular moments in human culture as if they were biblical instructions.

Insisting on an unduly prescriptive vision has been a characteristic failing of some complementarian literature, commending a culturally preferred pattern into which the entrepreneurial wife of Proverbs 31 would certainly not fit. Some recent complementarian writings have partly corrected this tendency.[39]

What if Genesis 2 – 3 teaches authoritative male headship?

We have seen that there are reasons for not accepting Grudem's and Ortlund's interpretations of Genesis 2 – 3. But what if Genesis 2 – 3 ought to be

---

39. Complementarian Aimee Byrd, writing from a cessationist perspective, has challenged some of the stereotypes and has promoted McKinley's analysis that Scripture shows women as necessary allies to men in multiple ways: (1) by warning them to turn away from evil; (2) as cobelligerents against evil enemies; (3) by mediating the word of the Lord; (4) by giving wise instruction and counsel; (5) by collaboration in service to others; (6) by responding to God as examples of faithfulness; and (7) by influencing men from a gift of empathy and relatedness: Byrd 2016, 139–140, 152, 178–188.

understood as teaching that there was authoritative male headship before the fall? What consequences would follow?

It would not follow that now, in Christ, the husband should rule the wife. Although Christ came to undo sin and its consequences, this does not mean that redemption in Christ takes us back to before the fall. There is no road back to Eden. The purpose of redemption in Christ goes forwards, not backwards. As Isaac Watts puts it, 'In Him the tribes of Adam boast more blessings than their father lost.'[40]

God's great purpose is a new heaven and earth, a new creation in which God reigns and where all rebellion is ended, which has been inaugurated in Christ and will be finally brought to fulfilment in him.[41] In the light of God's great purpose of new creation, we should not be surprised that Paul's teaching on marriage in 1 Corinthians 7 makes no clear backward reference to Genesis 1 – 2 (despite 1 Cor. 6:16). Nor should we be surprised that when Paul writes about the relations of husband and wife in Ephesians 5 his only reference to the institution of marriage in Genesis 2:24 is a revelation of its spiritual signifi-cance, as pointing forward to the union of Christ and his church (5:31). 'For this world in its present form is passing away' (1 Cor. 7:31).

Grudem's stated purpose at the start of his book is to present a clear positive statement of his complementarian view. The title of his first chapter is 'A Biblical Vision of Manhood and Womanhood as Created by God'. As presented, his viewpoint is founded on his interpretation of the creation story.[42] But if our objective is to understand accurately what Scripture teaches concerning Christian behaviour in marriage, this approach is not sufficiently based on God's redemptive purposes in Christ. It gives disproportionate prominence to creation. The truths of creation must be seen in the light of the truths of redemption. Grudem's reasoning does not sufficiently acknowledge the perspective which Paul emphasizes in 1 Corinthians 7:29–31 (see chapter 2 above). Teaching about creation cannot provide a definitive answer concerning Christian marriage, because we must go beyond the question 'How did God order the original cre-ation before the fall?' and ask also 'What is God's purpose for human beings redeemed in Christ?' and 'In the light of that purpose, how are we to live now?'

We are not living in Genesis 2 or in Genesis 3, but after the resurrection of Jesus Christ from the dead, and after the gift of the Holy Spirit, and in

40. From the hymn 'Jesus Shall Reign Where'er the Sun'.
41. See Matt. 19:28; John 1:1; 3:3; 19:30; 20:1, 19, 22; Rom. 8:1–23; 1 Cor. 11:11; 15:1–26; 2 Cor. 5:17–19; Gal. 6:14–15; Eph. 2:10; 4:24; Titus 3:5; Rev. 21.
42. *EFBT*, 25, 29–42.

anticipation of Christ's return and of the general resurrection. Human marriage will not have a place in the new creation (Matt. 22:30). In marriage Christian believers are called to live a kingdom life of self-sacrificial love in this present world, in anticipation of the fullness of the new creation where 'male and female' will not have the same significance as at present.

If it were demonstrated that Genesis 2 presented authoritative male headship before the fall, it would still need to be separately established that this model is intended to be adhered to in a Christian marriage lived in anticipation of the new creation. But once we fully appreciate what Paul says about equality and mutual submission in 1 Corinthians 7 and Ephesians 5, we see that it is a mistake to insist on a hierarchical model for Christian marriage. This is so, irrespective of how we interpret Genesis 2 – 3.

Women's leadership and authority in the Old Testament

Enlarging the focus beyond the relationship of husband and wife, some commentators find in the Old Testament a wider principle of male leadership. 'Leadership and teaching were reserved for men; priests, prophets and kings were men. There were exceptions with regard to prophecy, but these are few and far between.'[43] The phrase 'reserved for men' is used to indicate that this was not merely how things were but was also how God ordained them to be. Underlying this analysis is a notion that God has established a normative principle of authoritative male leadership.[44]

We must therefore ask whether the Old Testament substantiates a principle that women ought never to lead men or exercise authority over them. Such a principle cannot be established merely by the observation that nearly all leadership of, and authority over, the people of God in the Old Testament was exercised by men. The question is not whether women often became leaders. Nor is the question whether equal numbers of men and women are gifted for leadership. The question is whether women's leadership and exercise of authority, on the rare occasions where we see it, had God's approval or disapproval.

It had God's approval. Miriam was a prophet and a leader of the people of Israel (Exod. 15:20–21; Mic. 6:4). Deborah led the people of Israel, decided

---

43. FIEC 'Women in Ministry Statement'.

44. There is also a more specific argument based on a claim that the ministry of teaching in the Old Testament was reserved to male priests. This is considered in chapter 14.

their disputes, instructed them to go into battle and prophesied (Judg. 4 – 5). Huldah prophesied and thereby instructed the king and influenced the nation (2 Kgs 22:14 – 23:3). These activities are presented in the texts as God-given. Isaiah's wife was herself a prophet (Isa. 8:3).[45]

The significance of Miriam is disputed. We only have brief glimpses of her. In Exodus 15 she leads the women in celebration. In Numbers 12 she and Aaron step out of line and criticize Moses, and she is struck with a skin disease for doing so. Because of her prominence she is listed in the genealogy in 1 Chronicles 6:1–3 along with men. Later, Micah prophesies to Israel in God's name: 'I brought you up out of Egypt and redeemed you from the land of slavery' (Mic. 6:4, NIV), and continues (as literally translated from the Hebrew by Grudem): 'I sent before you Moses, Aaron, and Miriam.' The natural understanding of this is that these three were leaders provided by God when bringing the people up out of Egypt. This is the meaning given in many English translations, including CJB, CEB, GW, GNT, NET, NIV, NOG, NLV, and VOICE. Grudem reads 'I sent before you' as meaning only that Moses, Aaron and Miriam were literally at the front of the people, when Moses was leading them.[46] This seems an unduly wooden reading of the text and also rather unlikely. Even if the phrase should be read literally, it would be strange to mention Moses, Aaron and Miriam as being at the front of the people of Israel if that position had no significance. Aaron certainly had a leading role (Exod. 7:1–2).

Nevertheless, it is fair to say that the information we have about Miriam's leadership is brief, and falls short of being completely definitive about her role. If she were the only example of women's leadership in the Old Testament, we might be uncertain what conclusion we should reach.

We know relatively little about Huldah, but enough to reach a conclusion. In the time of King Josiah a scroll of the law is found during repair works at the temple. The king is alarmed at the contents. To inquire what should be done he sends a delegation of important officials, including the high priest, not to Jeremiah or to Zephaniah[47] but to Huldah. The fact that she is not summoned or brought to the king, but instead receives a delegation, shows the high esteem in which she is held. She instructs them to tell the king that the judgment

---

45. This should not be a surprise. Despite the system of Levitical priests, all men and women were expected to fear God and relate to him themselves (Exod. 19:6; Deut. 31:12). See further Berman 2008, 169.

46. *EFBT*, 143–145.

47. Jeremiah had begun his ministry five years earlier and Zephaniah was in his prime: Tidball 2012, 119.

foretold in the scroll will happen, but not in his lifetime, because he has repented (2 Kgs 22:3–20). This triggers a revival in Israel (23:1–25). Grudem's answer to the example of Huldah is that her prophecy is delivered privately to the delegation.[48] But this answer does not meet the point that as God's spokesman she gives authoritative instructions to both the high priest and the king. This is not consistent with a principle that women may never provide authoritative leadership to men.

Neither would such a principle be consistent with the role of Deborah, the prophet and the wife of Lappidoth (Judg. 4:4), about whom we have fuller information. First we should note the context in which her story is set. She exemplifies a theme in Judges that God calls and uses people without being bound by how people are ranked by human culture. The story immediately preceding that of Deborah is the story of Ehud, the left-handed deliverer (Judg. 3:12–30). In ancient Near East culture, the right hand was associated with strength, authority and wisdom; the left with weakness, foolishness and waywardness.[49] The story immediately following Deborah's is that of Gideon, described as the youngest member of the weakest clan (Judg. 6:15). The three stories demonstrate that, contrary to the prevailing human culture, God's call to leadership is not excluded by left-handedness (Ehud), by gender (Deborah), by the laws of primogeniture (Gideon) or by human weakness (Gideon again).

English translations of Judges 4:4 do not agree on whether Deborah was 'judging' Israel or 'leading' Israel. The Hebrew word used means to judge or govern. But if we approach the text without a preconception that women's leadership is impossible, there is no difficulty in understanding it. In the book of Judges the functions of governing and judging are not divided. That the word is used to refer to governing, and not only to judging, is unmistakably clear both from Judges 2:16–19 and from the book as a whole. The successive leaders whom God raises up for Israel do more than decide disputes: they lead the people. Deborah is such a leader, as the account of her leadership in Judges 4 – 5 shows. In the course of that leadership she exercises authority over men and gives instructions to men. Her God-given leadership is inconsistent with a supposed principle that women may never lead men and never exercise authority over them.

Grudem raises four points about Deborah with a view to reducing her significance.[50] The first is that she 'affirmed male leadership over God's people'

---

48. *EFBT*, 138.

49. See Gen. 48:12–20; Exod. 15:6, 12; Isa. 48:13; Ps. 110:1; Eccl. 10:2; Matt. 25:33, 41.

50. *EFBT*, 132–136.

when she 'encouraged' Barak to take Israel into battle (Judg. 4:6–7, 14). On reading the text, we see that the nature of the 'encouragement' was that she summoned Barak and instructed him to take Israel into battle. This does not diminish her authority but highlights it. She affirms Barak's leadership of the army by exercising her authority over him.

Grudem's next point is that the text does not say that Deborah ruled over God's people or taught them publicly or led them militarily. He also argues that when she judged disputes (4:5) she did so privately. But these points cannot be supported from the text. That she is the overall ruler and exercises authority over men is plain from any fair reading of Judges 4 – 5. (And we may note in passing that there is no basis in the text for excluding her husband from those under her authority.) There is no basis for the argument that she did not give instruction in public. Justice was normally delivered in public in ancient Israel, no less than in Western democracies today.[51] The palm tree where she sat was a public place (Judg. 4:5). And even if her judicial decisions had been given privately, by making them she still exercised authority over men. And to say that she did not lead Israel militarily is like saying that the President of the USA does not lead the armed forces because as commander-in-chief he only issues instructions to his generals and does not normally go onto the battlefield.

Grudem next argues that the Bible views Deborah's 'judgeship' as a rebuke against the absence of male leadership. It is implicit in this argument that she was indeed exercising leadership over men. Whether it was a rebuke or not,[52] it does not change the fact that God called her to lead Israel, and this is inconsistent with a principle that women may never lead men or exercise authority over them. The text presents her leadership in a positive light.

Grudem's final point is that we must use caution in drawing examples to imitate from the book of Judges. Indeed we must. But this has no impact on the significance of Deborah as showing that God may call women to lead men.[53]

---

51. See Deut. 17:5; Josh. 20:6, 9; Isa. 29:21; Amos 5:10, 12, 15.

52. Hurley 1981, 47, observes that there is no evidence in the text for the view that Deborah's calling constituted a shaming of Israel.

53. It is instructive to compare Calvin's reasoning. He relies on what he calls 'the ordinary rules of government'. He writes in his commentary on 1 Timothy: 'If any one bring forward, by way of objection, Deborah (Judges 4:4) and others of the same class, of whom we read that they were at one time appointed by the command of God to govern the people, the answer is easy. Extraordinary acts done by God do not overturn the ordinary rules of government, by which he intended that we

A less well-known example of a woman exercising leadership is the wise woman of 2 Samuel 20. Her actions are presented positively. The city of Abel Beth Maakah is under military attack because a traitor has taken refuge there. She takes the initiative to resolve the situation. She shouts instructions to the attackers to bring their commander so she can speak to him. She negotiates an agreement with him, to spare the city if the traitor is killed. She informs her people what they need to do. They comply. The siege is lifted.

Scripture does not teach a principle that women may never lead men.[54]

Summary of chapter 5

1. The complementarian interpretation of Genesis 1 – 3, which argues for male leadership authority, lacks explicit support in the biblical text. It depends on implications which are at best uncertain. None of them is a necessary implication from the text.
2. To be male or female is a created fact of life. The presentation of woman as made to be man's powerful ally indicates a definite differentiation of men and women.
3. The Genesis text does not define or develop this differentiation. It leaves open the possibility that other scriptures could indicate responsibilities of leadership. But it does not establish male rule. The rule of a man over his wife, as described in Genesis 3:16, is presented as a negative consequence of the fall. This is not something to be deliberately perpetuated or increased.

---

should be bound.' He explains that government by women 'has always been regarded by all wise persons as a monstrous thing'. Thus Calvin admits that God commanded Deborah to govern, but regards this as 'monstrous' and implies that God is not 'wise'. This is not brother Calvin at his best. He does not perceive how outrageous his reasoning is. It provides a graphic illustration of the distorting impact of culture upon interpretation.

54. Some writers refer to Isa. 3:12, where rule by 'women' is regarded negatively. If this translation is correct (contrast CEB, GNT, NET, TPT), there are two viable ways of reading v. 12a in the context of 3:1 – 4:1. Probably it should be read as part of the situation that provokes God's judgment. In that event, it is a reference to the haughty women seen in v. 16. Alternatively, if it should be understood as part of the situation that results from God's judgment, it is a feature of a disaster in which most of the mature men have been killed (see 3:25; 4:1). Either way, it cannot properly be read as a prohibition of any rule by a woman.

4. There is no Old Testament text which says that husbands ought to exercise authority over their wives.

5. Scripture is not prescriptive about the balance of roles of husband and wife in caring for the family. The description of the noble wife in Proverbs 31, who is both breadwinner and runs the home, sets out an idealized picture in a particular historical and cultural setting. People's circumstances, abilities and giftings vary. To regard Proverbs 31 as a mandatory prescription would be to misunderstand it.

6. Teaching about creation cannot provide a definitive answer concerning Christian marriage, because we must go beyond the question 'How did God order the original creation before the fall?' and ask also 'What is God's purpose for redeemed human beings?' and 'In the light of that purpose, how are we to live now?'

7. The institution of marriage in Genesis 2:24 has spiritual significance as pointing forward to the union of Christ and his church (Eph. 5:31). Even if the complementarian interpretation of Genesis 1 – 3 were correct, it would not follow that in Christ the husband should rule the wife. Redemption in Christ is taking believers forward into the new creation, not backwards to before the fall.

8. Old Testament examples of women's leadership with God's approval are inconsistent with there being a principle that women may never lead men or exercise authority over them.

Questions to consider

1. When is it acceptable to base Christian doctrines on implications from Scripture rather than express statements?

2. What is your own understanding of Genesis 3:16 and its significance?

3. Does Deborah or the noble wife of Proverbs 31 have any relevance today for society, for the church or for your own life? If so, in what ways?

6. SUBMISSION AND HONOUR: 1 PETER

These are the ones I look on with favour:
   those who are humble and contrite in spirit,
   and who tremble at my word.

(Isa. 66:2, NIV)

Peter's focus

Peter's first letter was written perhaps some ten years after Paul's first letter to the Corinthians and seven years after Paul's letter to the Ephesians.[1] Peter writes:

> Wives, in the same way [*homoiōs*] submit [*hupotassō*] yourselves to your own husbands. . . . Sarah . . . obeyed Abraham and called him her lord. You are her daughters if you do what is right and do not give way to fear. (1 Pet. 3:1, 6, NIV)

Based on this passage, it is often stated that Peter puts forward a hierarchical view of marriage. But is this right? If it is, it clashes with the equality and mutuality that we found in Paul's letters.[2]

In Ephesians 5:15 – 6:9 Paul was writing about behaviour within the fellowship of the church and in Christian households. What Peter writes about marriage is set in a different context. Peter's focus is on Christian behaviour among pagans. Believers are God's people (2:9) living as exiles and foreigners in an unbelieving, pagan culture (1:1, 17; 2:11). His instructions to household slaves (2:18–25) and

---

1. For discussion of dates, see Mosse 2007, 304, 310, 316.
2. See chapters 2 to 4 above.

to wives (3:1–6) do not assume that the slaves' masters or the wives' husbands are believers. Peter's overall message is summarized at 2:12 (NIV): 'Live such good lives among the pagans that, though they accuse you of doing wrong, they may see your good deeds and glorify God on the day he visits us.' He is particularly concerned to encourage believers who are suffering, persecuted or otherwise mistreated (for example, 1:6; 2:20; 3:9, 14, 16; 4:1, 12–16, 19; 5:9–10).

Close attention to what Peter writes will reveal that his view is very much in line with Paul's.

Peter's theme

How should believers live in this hostile context? Peter's theme is that they should follow the example of Christ, in humble love and submission, and without retaliation.

Jesus taught that God's kingdom would be inherited by the meek (Matt. 5:5, understood in the light of 4:17, 23; 5:3, 10; 6:10, 33) and that his followers, when mistreated, were not to retaliate but to humbly bless those who mistreated them (Matt. 5:38–44). He was the Messiah, God's chosen king. He told Pilate that his kingdom was not from this world; if it had been, his servants would have fought to prevent his arrest (John 18:36). Instead of exercising the coercive power available to him (Matt. 26:53), he won the decisive victory for God's kingdom by his self-giving love at the cross. Thus, as we saw in chapters 3 and 4, to be imitators of the Messiah (Eph. 5:1–2), believers are called not to rule over other people but to be the 'slave' of others, as Jesus both taught and lived.

Peter's view of the world, like Paul's, is Christ-centred. Those who follow Jesus are the people of God's new kingdom (1 Pet. 2:9). They must behave with Christlike meekness and humble love to each other, to outsiders, and particularly to anyone who mistreats them (for example, 1:22; 2:18–19; 3:8–9, 16; 4:8). Peter's call to submission is expressly based on Christ's example (2:13, 18–21). At the cross, Jesus endured unjust suffering meekly and without retaliating (for example, 2:21–24; 3:17–18; 4:1–2). Believers' lives are a continuation of the Messiah's sufferings (4:13–14; see also Phil. 3:10; Col. 1:24).

Submission and honour in wider society

In regard to relationships with those outside the Christian community, Peter instructs submission in 2:13. This verse is difficult to render into natural English. It says: 'be subject [*hupotassō*] to every human creation [*ktisis*].'

Some English versions use here the word 'authority', but this word is not in the text and it risks causing misunderstanding by reminding readers of what Paul writes in Romans 13:1–7, where he calls for submission to 'authorities' which are 'instituted by God'. Here, the reference is not to God-ordained authorities but to human institutions, as is clearly brought out in the ESV ('Be subject for the Lord's sake to every human institution').

The contrast between the two passages is instructive. In Romans 13:1–7, having referred to authorities as God-ordained, Paul does not include slave masters in his examples. Peter has only referred to human institutions, so is able to give slave masters as an example at 2:18. He is appealing to his readers, for the sake of the good name of Christ, to live with meekness in every arrangement of human society, without reference to whether the arrangement has God's approval. Believers should think of themselves as 'God's slaves'; from this lowly position they should give honour to all among whom they live (2:16–17).

Submission: hierarchical or mutual?

We saw in chapter 3 that 'submission' does not have to do with docility but with ranking oneself beneath other people, treating them as more important. In his letter Peter highlights some specific contexts for meek and submissive behaviour, which include household slaves to their masters (2:18), wives to their husbands (3:1) and younger people to elders (5:5).

Is Peter here thinking of submission as voluntary and mutual or as compulsory in a one-way hierarchy? The general answer is not hard to find. Peter makes clear that all his readers should be humble-minded (*tapeinophrosunē*) (3:8). He makes clear that 'all' includes the elders, who are called to be examples to the flock, and who are expressly forbidden to be lords over those in their care (5:3, loudly echoing Mark 10:42–45). In 5:5 the younger people are to be subject to the elders *by following the example which the elders have set*: 'In the same way [*homoiōs*; that is, in the way exemplified in the behaviour of the elders], younger ones, be subject to the elders; all of you [that is, both the younger ones and the elders] clothing yourselves with humility [*tapeinophrosunē*] towards one another.' This can only work if the elders are in fact setting an example of humility. Peter's letter cannot reasonably be read as meaning that Christian masters, Christian husbands or church elders are not called to exhibit humble behaviour.[3]

---

3. Knight agrees that mutual submission is seen in 1 Pet. 5:5 (*RBMW*, 163).

But does this mutually submissive behaviour apply between husband and wife?

First Peter 3:1–7 has often been read as if it were Peter's endorsement of a hierarchical view of marriage, in which men's role is to be 'lord' over their wives, whose role is to be subordinate. We need to examine whether this is what Peter means. We begin by looking at his instructions to wives in verses 1–6.

Instructions to wives in 3:1–6

Peter was writing within Hellenic culture (1:1). As we saw above in chapters 2 and 3, it was taken for granted as a general rule that wives were under the commanding authority of their husbands. There would ordinarily be no question about whether wives should submit; they would have no choice but to do so. We therefore need to ask why Peter judged that he should instruct Christian wives to submit to their husbands.

An obvious answer is that Christian teaching mandated that women be treated differently from the way they were generally treated in wider society. In line with the example of Jesus, women were treated as of equal worth with men, and as equal recipients of God's grace and promises and of spiritual gifts. We see this directly or indirectly over and over again in the pages of the New Testament.[4] Over time this was a major factor in the growth of the gospel across the Greek and Roman world.[5] Because of this new perspective, Christian wives might conclude that submission to husbands was no longer appropriate. Peter agrees with the starting point (women's equality in Christ), as he makes clear in 3:7, but he disagrees with the conclusion. Despite the equality of women with men, he still urges submission of wives to husbands.

In order to understand Peter's viewpoint accurately, we need to note the three reasons which he gives for wives' submission, and two reasons that he does not give.

Peter's first reason for wives' submission is evangelistic. He recognizes in 3:1 that he is addressing some wives whose husbands are not believers. Society's

---

4. Examples include Acts 2:17–18; 16:13–15; Rom. 16:1–16; 1 Cor. 7:3–5; 11:11–12; 12:1–11; Gal. 3:26–29.

5. Stark 1996, 95–128. Note that this applied across all sectors of society, whether the people involved were rich or poor. This change in women's status is to be distinguished from the 'new women' trend in Roman society, which applied only to some of the elite; see chapter 3, 39.

expectation at this time is that a wife should follow her husband's religion.[6] Thus the gospel has already subverted the authority of these husbands. Peter gives wise counsel to avoid further inflaming the situation and to commend the gospel to husbands by means of their wives' pure, reverent and otherwise submissive conduct (vv. 1–2). This is a particular example of his concern in this letter for witness to outsiders (see also 2:12; 3:15–16).[7] Paul has a similar concern in mind in Titus 2:5, where he says that wives should be subject to their husbands so that no-one will speak evil of God's word.

Peter's second reason is that a gentle (*praüs*) and quiet (*hēsuchios*) spirit is pleasing to God (3:4). This has often been misinterpreted as a statement about women being allocated a distinctively subservient role, in contrast to men. But that is not what Peter is saying. It is a statement about a proper Christian attitude, which should be equally true of men, and was true of Jesus himself. In the same letter, see 1:17; 2:13, 18–19, 23; 3:7–9, 15–16 (*praütēs*); 5:5.[8]

Peter's third reason is the example of holy women of the past, in particular Sarah, who was obedient to Abraham (3:5–6). He commends this as a good example for Christian wives to follow. We will examine this further after we have looked at Peter's instructions to husbands.

There are two further reasons which Peter could have given, if he had thought they were good reasons. First, he does not rely directly on a cultural reason. He does not say that wives should submit because in Hellenic society husbands have authority over their wives, so that wives must live accordingly. He could hardly do so, given that the wives have already challenged their husbands' culturally derived authority by rejecting their husbands' religion and becoming obedient to the gospel.

Second, he does not give a reason based on a concept of God's creation order for men and women. He does not say that God's design is for husbands to be in a position of authority over their wives. This would have been an obvious reason to give for wives' submission if Peter believed it to be true. Those who interpret this part of Peter's letter as endorsing a God-given

---

6. *DBE*, 226 (Davids); Plutarch, *Moralia*, 'Advice to Bride and Groom', 19.

7. For a corresponding contemporary example, we could consider the task of commending Christian faith in traditional Muslim cultures. Newly converted women (if allowed to remain in a Muslim household) could cause great offence by demanding that their traditional Muslim husbands treat them as equals. This could tend to repel their husbands from Christian faith rather than commend it to them.

8. See also Matt. 5:5 (*praüs*); 11:29 (*praüs*); 21:5 (*praüs*); Gal. 5:23 (*praütēs*); 1 Thess. 4:11 (*hēsuchazō*); 2 Thess. 3:12 (*hēsuchia*); 1 Tim. 2:2–3 (*hēsuchios*); Titus 3:2 (*praütēs*).

unilateral authority of husband over wife are adding a reason which Peter does not give.[9]

However, we need to consider whether, although Peter did not state explicitly that God's design placed husbands in authority over their wives, he nevertheless believed it to be the case.

Is Peter supporting a hierarchical view of marriage?

Some complementarian commentators agree with egalitarians that Scripture does not teach that husbands have unilateral authority to rule over their wives.[10] Others disagree. Although Peter presents submission, meekness and paying honour to others as part of following Christ's example, and although he does not say that God has placed husbands in a position of authority over their wives, they argue that he is nonetheless teaching a hierarchical understanding of marriage. Two main reasons are given for this.

The first is that Peter's instruction to wives to submit is introduced in 3:1 by 'in the same way' (*homoiōs*). This is said to refer back to the submission of household slaves to their masters (2:18). Grudem's argument is that, as slaves submit to the authority of their masters, so also wives submit to the authority of their husbands.[11]

Grudem is correct to say that *homoiōs* refers back to what Peter has earlier written, but the argument is mistaken. Peter does not say that slaves should submit to their masters because God has put masters in authority over them. Where authority exists, an instruction to submit does not necessarily imply that the authority is endorsed by the writer of the instruction. The hierarchy involved in slavery is a fact of life for Peter's readers, but Peter expresses no approval of it and does not suggest that God has instituted this human arrangement. Peter does not endorse the authority of slave masters. But he does give reasons for slaves to submit to their masters. They are to submit in reverent fear of God (2:18) and mindful of the example of Christ (2:19–25). Submission is therefore part of following Christ.

---

9. *M&W*, 276.

10. For example, Storms [no date] states: 'Husbands are never commanded to rule their wives'; 'Headship is not the power of a superior over an inferior'; 'Headship is never to be identified with the issuing of commands'; and 'Headship means honoring one's wife. See 1 Peter 3:7.'

11. *RBMW*, 198–199.

'In the same way' in 3:1 refers back to three things that Peter has just written: the call to all believers to be submissive (2:15–17), the instruction to slaves to be submissive even to unjust masters (2:18–21) and the example of Christ's submission to those who unjustly caused his suffering (2:21–24). These are the analogies for wives' submission to their husbands. In sum, Peter's point is not that God has put husbands in authority over wives but that to submit is truly Christlike conduct.

The second argument for hierarchy springs from verse 6, where Peter relates that Sarah obeyed Abraham and called him 'lord'. Some say this shows that husbands are to be lords over their wives. In other words, Peter is not only commending Sarah's behaviour as a model for wives to follow but also making an implied statement about a husband's authority over his wife.

However, as Claire Smith correctly observes, 'neither Peter nor Paul holds the husbands accountable for their wives' submission or tells husbands to make their wives submit'.[12] How can this be, if husbands are in truth called by God to be masters over their wives? The conclusion to be drawn is that God does not call husbands to be masters over their wives, and that Peter understood this.

We may ask, why did Peter, despite the cultural context in which he lived, not believe that husbands were called by God to exercise authority over their wives?

The short answer is because this is not God's perspective as revealed to humanity. There is no scripture, whether in 1 Peter, in Genesis, in Ephesians or anywhere else in the whole of the Bible, which instructs husbands to exercise unilateral rule over their wives.[13] This is a stubborn fact which hierarchical understandings of marriage have yet to come to terms with.

In addition, the argument which sees an implied statement about a husband's authority in verse 6 cannot stand with the nature of the instructions that Peter gives to Christian husbands in verse 7, to which we must turn next.

Peter's instructions to husbands

In verse 7 Peter addresses husbands. He does not say that husbands are in the position of lords over their wives. On the contrary, he indicates that husbands

---

12. Smith 2012, 134.
13. Against *DBE*, 387 (Webb). The prophecies cited by Webb, which use punishment of women as a metaphor for God's judgment (Jer. 13:20–27; Ezek. 16:32–42; 23:22–30; Hos. 2:1–3, 10), do not give a husband 'implied authority to physically discipline his wife'.

must follow the same kind of behaviour that he has been setting out from 2:13 onwards. Just as his instructions for wives start with 'in the same way' (*homoiōs*), so as to refer back to what he has written earlier in the letter, so also his instructions for husbands start with *homoiōs*, again referring back to the instructions that he has already given.

The structure of Peter's extended discussion is as follows:

1. As slaves of God, all Christians are to submit in every arrangement of human society, giving honour to everyone (2:13–17).
2. Household slaves are to submit to masters (2:18–20).
3. Christ's suffering stands as an example to follow (2:21–25).
4. In the same way (*homoiōs*), wives are to submit to husbands, with a gentle and quiet spirit (3:1–6).
5. Husbands are to behave in the same way (*homoiōs*), with gentleness and giving honour to their wives (3:7).
6. All are to act humbly (3:8).

Wayne Grudem argues that Peter's discussion should not be understood in this way. He says that in 3:7 *homoiōs* is not used in its primary sense of 'in the same way'. Instead, it should be understood in a weak sense of 'also' or 'continuing in the same area of discussion'. Grudem reasons that the idea of similarity to the submission of wives does not apply in verse 7. He says it is excluded by the fact that here, unlike in 2:18 and 3:1, 'Peter does not command submission to any authority but rather the considerate use of that authority'.[14]

But Peter does not instruct husbands to exercise any authority at all, and he does instruct them to adopt an attitude of submission and to pay honour to their wives, as we will see more fully below.

Grudem's argument misses Peter's main point and rejects the primary meaning of *homoiōs* without justification. In Peter's thinking the relevant authority is God, because Christians are 'slaves of God' (2:16). This is the lowly position from which Christians must act, giving honour to others. Both leading up to and following this section, there is a clear, repeated theme of submission as truly Christian conduct (2:13, 18, 21–23; 3:1, 5, 7–9; 5:3, 5–6), which is reinforced by Peter's uses of *homoiōs* in 3:1, 3:7 and 5:5. The whole thrust of Peter's extended discussion depends upon the similarity of the points that he makes in succession, concerning first, all Christians (2:13–17), then household

---

14. *RBMW*, 203.

slaves (2:18–20), then Christ's example (2:21–25), then wives (3:1–6), then husbands (3:7), and at 3:8–9 all Christians again.

Grudem himself says elsewhere, '*homoiōs* never seems to mean merely "also" when a suitable referent for actual similarity is near at hand . . . , for then the idea of comparison can hardly be kept from the reader's mind'.[15] Precisely so. Here Peter's whole train of thought emphasizes the similarities. There is no sufficient ground for sharply distinguishing the behaviour expected of husbands from the behaviour of the other kinds of people mentioned.

However, the particular nature of the similar conduct expected of the husband in 3:7 is rather unclear in most English versions. This is because they follow a tradition of translation which does not provide an accurate rendering of Peter's text. To this we must turn next.

Translation issues and Peter's three points for husbands

Grudem notes that the NIV's use of the word 'respect' in 3:7, instead of 'honour', is too weak.[16] But the translation issues go beyond this.

In the Greek text the language used tells us that 3:1–7 is part of a larger whole which includes (at least) everything from 2:13 to 3:9.[17] This is not apparent in most English versions, because clear English style generally requires short sentences, each with a main verb. At 2:13 Peter commands submission. At 2:17 he issues crisp imperatives: 'Honour [*timaō*] everyone, love the brotherhood [the family of believers], fear God, honour [*timaō*] the emperor.' These imperatives are then followed by a series of participles describing how this honouring works out in some further practical situations:

household slaves, *being subject* in all fear to their masters (2:18)

in the same way [*homoiōs*], wives *being subject* to their husbands (3:1)

the men [husbands] in the same way [*homoiōs*], . . . *paying honour* [*timē*] (3:7)

---

15. *RBMW*, 198.

16. *RBMW*, 203–205.

17. Smith recognizes this. Thus her contrary argument, that *homoiōs* in 3:1 means merely 'also', does not reflect the flow of Peter's reasoning as shown in the features of the text. See Smith 2012, 135–136.

This continues into 3:8–9:

> but the end [*telos*]: all of one mind, sympathetic, brotherly-loving, tender-hearted, humble-minded, *not rendering* evil for evil

In addition to the separation of Peter's discussion into short sentences, two further features of English versions are particularly liable to result in misunderstanding of what Peter writes:

1. They start a new sentence and a new paragraph at 3:8 with the word 'Finally'. This can give the impression that Peter is moving on to a different point at verse 8. This is not so. Verse 8 is his summary of what he has been saying from 2:13 onwards. The 'end' (*telos*) of the various descriptions of how to live is that all believers (including wives and husbands) should live in the submissive way instructed in 2:13–17, and so in the humble and loving way depicted in 3:8–9. This is the 'end' in the sense of the objective, so it is also the 'end' in the sense of a summary conclusion.

2. Many versions follow a tradition of translation of 3:7 which contains a mistake.[18] For example, the NIV says: 'Husbands, in the same way be considerate as you live with your wives, and treat them with respect as the weaker partner and as heirs with you of the gracious gift of life.' This translation appears to make two points: the first point is that husbands should be considerate; in the second point the idea of 'respect' is somehow linked, paradoxically, to the wife being 'the weaker partner'. Compared with the Greek, this is a muddle. In the Greek we can usefully distinguish three elements in what Peter writes in this part of verse 7, which can be translated as follows (with numbers added for clarity):

> [1] the men [that is, husbands] in the same way
> [2] dwelling with [them] according to knowledge as with a weaker vessel the female,
> [3] showing [them] honour as also co-heirs of the grace of life.

Unlike most English versions, NASB translates verse 7 correctly: 'You husbands in the same way, live with your wives in an understanding way, as with someone weaker, since she is a woman; and show her honor as a fellow heir of the grace of life, so that your prayers will not be hindered.'

---

18. In appendix 1 I flag a warning about the tendency of English versions to follow a tradition of how translation has been done before, even when there is a mistake.

So Peter's three points here, leading up to what he says about prayer, are as follows:

[1] Husbands should behave in the same way as previously stated for household slaves (2:18–25) and wives (3:1–6), that is, in a humbly submissive way.

[2] Husbands should live with their wives in a way that is considerate of their wives' being less strong than they are.

[3] Husbands should honour their wives, who are not in a subordinate position but who are equal with their husbands in having the high standing of being heirs of God's gift of life.

Peter's first point is similar to Paul's concept of humble, mutual submission between husband and wife.[19] Points [2] and [3] further explain point [1].

In Peter's second point, he has in mind that husbands generally have greater muscle strength than their wives. The word 'vessel' translates *skeuos*, which means a container, and which can therefore be used to refer to the human body (1 Thess. 4:4, ESV, NIV, NRSV), particularly as a container of eternal treasure (2 Cor. 4:7). He has just described the very precious and lasting treasure of wives' gentle spirit in verse 4. The phrase 'weaker vessel' therefore refers to the weaker female body which contains that treasure and not, as some have argued, to the relative weakness of women's social position in marriage or society. Peter has told wives to behave with a gentle spirit. 'In the same way' husbands should also be gentle, using their physical strength to serve their wives with kindness, not to coerce or mistreat them.[20]

Peter's third point assumes that the wives are believers. He combines his emphasis on paying honour to all and his belief in the equality of men and women in Christ. This last aspect is similar to what Paul writes in Galatians

---

19. This is more or less the opposite of Grudem's argument in *EFBT*, 191, that husbands are never told to submit to their wives.

20. In some qualities other than muscle strength, women tend to be stronger than men (for example, in stamina, endurance of pain and endurance of cold temperatures) but such matters are not relevant to Peter's point. For the argument that Peter is referring to wives being in a subordinate position in the marriage, see Hurley 1981, 156; Smith 2012, 147. But this is not justified by the text. The description 'weaker vessel' is not apt to convey such an idea. This can be illustrated by substituting 'slave' for 'wife'. To convey that a slave was in a subordinate position, a writer would not say that the slave was 'a weaker vessel' than their master.

3:26–29, where there is no distinction in Christ between men and women because all inherit the promise as 'sons' of God. The paying of honour to the wife in 3:7 is not a concession to her relative physical weakness but a recognition of her high status.

We may note that the honouring of another person may take place either in a situation where the person honoured is in authority over the person who pays honour (as in 2:17 – honour the emperor) or where there is no such authority (again as in 2:17 – honour everyone). An instruction to pay honour does not necessarily imply that such authority exists.

Honour was a concept of central social importance in the Mediterranean societies in which Peter lived and ministered. This is not the case in Western societies today, so it is easy for us to miss the force of what Peter writes about it. A person could gain great honour by being adopted into a high-status family. For example, Octavian's honour status rose enormously when it became known that Julius Caesar had adopted him as his son and named him as his heir. Octavian subsequently became the Emperor Augustus, and as Caesar's son styled himself 'son of god'. There was no higher honour status than this in Gentile society. To be born into or adopted into the true God's family, and named as an heir of the true God, was even greater than this: it was the highest honour status imaginable. This is the Christian believer's position (see 1:4 'inheritance'; 1:23 'born anew'; 2:9 'a people belonging to God').[21]

In most English versions the connection of 3:7 with 2:17 is not apparent: one would not appreciate from those versions that Peter says 'honour [*timaō*] everyone, honour [*timaō*] the emperor' and then 'men, render honour [*timē*] to your wives'. But this would have been clear to Peter's first readers, who should not have misunderstood 3:1–7 as affirming that men have a God-given status of being lords over their wives. He has told wives to submit to their husbands. 'In the same way' husbands are to pay honour to their wives.

Thus in 3:7 Peter is instructing husbands to show their submissive conduct, like that of wives (3:1), of Christ (2:21), of household slaves (2:18) and of all believers (2:13). They are to do this by honouring their wives in view of their shared highest possible status as God's heirs in God's family. This speaks of equality between husband and wife as fellow Christians, and a voluntary giving

---

21. See deSilva 2000, 23–29. The Bible does not replace honour–shame with other valid categories such as innocence–guilt or power–fear. It uses all of these. It recalibrates honour–shame. See Georges 2017. Strictly speaking the Latin word which Octavian used for 'god' (*divus*) meant 'deified', the idea being that Caesar became a god when he died.

of honour by husband to wife. Beyond doubt, Peter is not here saying that God has designed a hierarchy in which a husband is in authority over his wife.

In Peter's thought as in Paul's, husbands are not viewed as being in authority over their wives. They are called to adopt a position of humility towards them. In relation to their wives, husbands are not exempt from Christian submission.

Complementarian John Piper rightly summarizes from 1 Peter 2 – 3 in this way: 'So, as we saw in Ephesians 5, submission is a wider Christian virtue for all of us to pursue, and it has its unique and fitting expressions in various relationships.'[22]

The example of Sarah and Abraham

Having identified Peter's reasoning, it is instructive to look further at the example of Sarah and Abraham (3:6). This illuminates his instructions both to wives and to husbands.

Peter says that Sarah called Abraham her lord. There is only one place in the Old Testament where Sarah refers to Abraham as her 'lord' (*kurios*), and that is in Genesis 18:12. This tells us that Peter has in mind the story told in Genesis 18.

Commentators have made heavy weather of Peter's illustration, because Sarah only calls Abraham 'lord' in a muttered laugh of disbelief (18:12).

> Unfortunately the single example of Sarah calling Abraham 'lord' occurs when she expresses amused scepticism to herself about God's promise of a child, which hardly seems an ideal example to choose. Peter's comments do not fit comfortably with Genesis . . . perhaps we should not expect to find profound theology and contextually accurate quotations in Peter's simple instructions.[23]

Such negativity is misplaced. Peter is a gifted preacher (as we see in Acts 2). The illustration is a brilliant choice: wry, provocative and deeply appropriate. Its superficial unsuitability tickles readers' interest and forces them to think (compare 1:18; gold was one of the most imperishable things known). We may readily imagine Peter's eyes twinkling as he tells Silvanus what he wants to say (5:12).

Peter has been emphasizing that reverent fear of God may require submission even in unfavourable circumstances (2:18, 23; 3:1). Just so, upon the visitors' arrival, Abraham instructs Sarah to do heavy labour at the most unsuitable time

---

22. Piper 2009, 96. (It does not follow that Piper would agree with the present chapter.)
23. Tidball 2012, 246. See further *DBE*, 231–234 (Davids).

of the day, when it is too hot to do anything but sit (Gen. 18:1, 6). And the larger picture is that God is calling her to submit to Abraham in marital intercourse (18:10–12), in a situation where they are both too old to have a child (18:11–12) and where the husband to whom she is called to submit is someone who repeatedly makes bad decisions in their marriage, especially in sexual matters (Gen. 12:11–13; 16:1–6; and afterwards 20:1–13). From Abraham's track record she has grounds for fear (compare 1 Pet. 3:6). But despite her initially negative reaction, and despite all the reasons for distrusting and resisting Abraham, she submits to God's will, and the child of promise is born (18:10; 21:1–2). This is a wonderfully encouraging illustration of submission to God, and therefore also to husband, in adverse circumstances. Wives can be Sarah's righteous daughters by following her example (Isa. 51:1–2; 1 Pet. 3:6).[24]

Following on immediately from 3:6, Peter says that husbands should in the same way (*homoiōs*) render honour (*timē*) to their wives (v. 7). He is therefore telling husbands to behave towards their wives not only as household slaves to masters (2:18–25) and as wives to husbands (3:1–6), but also more specifically as Sarah behaved submissively to Abraham, because of her submission to God. As we have noted, this exhibits essentially the same revolutionary outlook as Paul's teaching on mutual submission in marriage.

For readers who take the trouble to consider the details of the story, there is a yet further impact for husbands in the same direction, although whether Peter had this in mind we cannot be sure. In verse 6 Peter's foreground focus is on Sarah. In the background is her husband, who in the immediate story is also a model of submissive behaviour – but to others, not to his wife. He pays honour to his important visitors by following the conventions of ancient Near Eastern hospitality to the utmost degree. Although he is resting in the heat of the day, he hurries to meet them, and bows low to them (Gen. 18:1–2). He calls himself their servant, and speaks and acts towards them in a way that shows that serving them is a privilege (18:3–5). In ancient Near Eastern culture a high-status person like Abraham, who was the ninety-nine-year-old head of a large group of people, would demean himself by running, but Abraham chooses the low place of dishonour by running to the herd to select a calf (18:7). And he adopts the role of a household slave, bringing the visitors refreshments and

---

24. I am indebted to John Stevens for his perceptive comments which set me on the path to this understanding. Note that Peter's allusion is to this particular episode in Abraham's and Sarah's life together. The natural reading of it is not affected by Sarah's forcefulness on a later occasion, when it was God's will for Abraham to follow the instruction which she gave to him: Gen. 21:8–14.

then standing back while they eat (18:8). By serving the visitors Abraham acts as a slave of the Lord God (18:1, 13, 22). This links both to 1 Peter 2:16 (believers must live as God's slaves) and to 2:18 (household slaves must live submissively). These details supply an additional resonance to what Peter says next (3:7). If Peter is instructing the husbands to act submissively, 'in the same way' that Sarah did, in practice this means also following the example of Abraham himself, who honoured the visitors by taking the lowest place and energetically serving them as a slave, with the twist that the husbands must now give to their own wives the honour that Abraham gave to his important visitors.[25]

'These are the ones I look on with favour: those who are humble and contrite in spirit, and who tremble at my word' (Isa. 66:2, NIV). This is what both Sarah and Abraham did. This biblical teaching applies to husbands, just as much as to wives.

Dangers of coercive power

First Peter 3:1–7 has a sad story of misuse in church history.

Over time, under the influence of traditional patriarchal culture, the church lost sight of the meaning of the New Testament teaching. The church took Peter's remarks as authorizing the use of coercive power by husbands as lords over their wives. While doubtless many who held a hierarchical view of marriage nevertheless acted with kindness and gentleness towards their wives, others did not. The church's misunderstanding of Peter's teaching led to abuse and cruelty which was said to be justified by Scripture. This is typified by the notes referring to 1 Peter 3:7 in Becke's Bible (1549), which state:

> He dwelleth wyth his wyfe according to knowledge, that taketh her as a necessarye healper . . . And if she be not obedient and healpfull unto hym, endevoureth to beate the feare of God into her heade, that therby she maye be compelled to learne her dutie and do it.

This interpretation was culture-driven. The commentator's cultural spectacles blinded him from seeing what Peter actually wrote.[26] He somehow missed the

---

25. That the husband should serve the wife is the same outlook as Paul's (Eph. 5:25, exemplifying 5:1–2 and Gal. 5:13).

26. Such views are not confined to the past. Grudem expresses his shock at a present-day example of the same view in *EFBT*, 491, n. 5.

theological theme running through Peter's letter (and through the whole New Testament), that God's kingdom is based on meek, self-giving love, not on the exercise of coercive power. This is shown supremely in the cross. It is the cross that wins the decisive victory of the kingdom and opens the door to the life of the resurrection. God's people are called to implement and live out that victory in the same way, that is, by humble self-giving love, not by exercising coercive power over other people, whether their spouses or anyone else. It is the meek who are to inherit the earth (Matt. 5:5).

Some egalitarian writers claim that teaching on a wife's unilateral submission can encourage the continuation of domestic abuse, because it leads some pastors, to whom abused wives go for support, to advise them to submit to the abuse without taking any steps to bring it to an end. Regrettably, such advice has sometimes been given. Grudem usefully observes:

> This is a terrible misuse of Scripture. Yes, the Bible tells us there will be times when we must 'suffer for righteousness' sake' (1 Peter 3:14), but several biblical examples show people escaping danger when they are able to do so.

After referring to 1 Samuel 19:10; 2 Corinthians 11:32–33; Luke 4:29–30; John 8:59; 10:39; 1 Corinthians 6:19–20; Proverbs 22:3; 27:12, he continues:

> Therefore when we become aware of a situation where a wife is being abused by her husband, we should take whatever steps we can . . . in order to protect the abused and bring an end to the violence. 'Rescue the weak and the needy; deliver them from the hand of the wicked' (Psalm 82:4).[27]

One only has to read the book of Acts to be reminded that in the face of mistreatment of any kind there is always a wise judgment to be made: when to submit, when to resist, when to flee (see also Matt. 5:39; 12:9–14; 10:23).

As a footnote to this section we may notice that in church history the misuse of coercive power has gone far beyond the domestic sphere, with dreadful results. God has allocated coercive power not to the church but to civil authorities responsible for maintaining civil order (Rom. 13:1–7), but this has not stopped the church from being keen to acquire it. Whenever the church has acquired worldly power, it has been intoxicated by it. Intrusive coercions such as the imposition of legal penalties for not attending public worship are merely

---

27. *EFBT*, 492–493. Claire Smith has a useful chapter on dealing with domestic abuse: Smith 2012, 181–194.

the tip of the iceberg. The church stands shamed by the brutality of the Crusades, the tortures of the Inquisition, the burning of heretics and its justification of slavery. The humility of 1 Peter 3:1, 7–8 and 5:2–6 is an altogether better way.

Submission and leadership

As we noted above, Peter sees the Christian obligation of mutual submission as extending to the elders, who are called to be examples to the flock and who are expressly forbidden to behave as lords over those in their care (5:3). Expositions of Ephesians and 1 Peter as showing mutual submission in Christian relationships have given rise to an anxiety about Christian leadership. Some complementarians worry that an emphasis on mutual submission results in the erosion of any meaningful notion of authority in the church, whether exercised by men or even by women.[28]

This is a needless anxiety. Most good leadership takes place by inspiration and example, as Jesus, Paul and Peter demonstrated. The apostles' letters are also examples of positive leadership: they combine a servant spirit with the issuing of instructions and advice which they expect believers to follow. Mutual submission does not remove leaders' ability to decide what is right, adhere to it, exemplify it, urge it and, where appropriate, command it. Paul was very firm when the situation required (see 1 and 2 Corinthians and Galatians).

There is still a place for authoritative church discipline. If people claim to follow Christ but persistently refuse to live in a way that honours him, something has to be done to preserve the integrity of the church. But what should be done is nothing like the coercion and cruelty applied by church authorities all too often in history. Kingdom values are reflected in the relative mildness of the New Testament's instructions for this situation: the strongest sanction which is authorized is to rebuke such people and to forbid them from participating in the fellowship of the church, in the hope that they may change their minds.[29] In Christian relationships among men and women mutual submission is the norm, exclusion is an exceptional last resort, and forcible coercion is never authorized.

---

28. *WITC*, 252 (Yarbrough), citing Margaret Elizabeth Köstenberger.
29. See Matt. 18:8–17; 1 Cor. 5:1–5, 9–13; 2 Cor. 2:6–11; 1 Tim. 1:19–20; 2 Tim. 2:24–26; 3:1–5; 2 John 7–11.

Summary of chapter 6

1. Peter's view of life is Christ-centred. The example of our Lord's humble love and submission is prominent in Peter's first letter.

2. Peter discusses how this applies to a variety of situations in which Christian believers should give honour to others, including marriage.

3. Peter's reasons for submission of wives to husbands include: (a) to win them over; (b) a gentle spirit is pleasing to God; and (c) the example of holy women of the past, such as Sarah. She is a wonderfully encouraging illustration of submission to God, and therefore also to her husband, in adverse circumstances (3:1–6). Peter's analogies for wives' submission are the call to all believers to be submissive (2:15–17), the instruction to slaves to be submissive even to unjust masters (2:18–21) and the example of Christ's submission to those who unjustly caused his suffering (2:21–24). His reasons do not include that God's design has placed husbands in a position of unilateral authority over their wives. This would have been a highly relevant reason for him to give if he had believed it to be true. There is no scripture anywhere in the Bible which instructs husbands to exercise unilateral authority over their wives.

4. Husbands are to behave 'in the same way', with gentleness, and paying honour to their wives (3:7). This points to mutual submission.

5. To be named as an heir of the true God is the highest possible honour status. Husband and wife are equally 'heirs of the grace of life'. Accurately translated, carefully read and rightly understood, 1 Peter 3:1–7 does not endorse a unilateral authority of husband over wife.

6. Patriarchal culture has misused 1 Peter 3:1–7. Husbands should not coerce their wives. Where there is domestic abuse, steps should be taken to bring it to an end.

7. Mutual submission in Christian relationships is consistent with appropriate leadership. Christian leadership in the church does not involve the exercise of forcible coercive power over other people. Where church discipline is required, the strongest proper sanction is exclusion and nothing more.

Questions to consider

1. What do you find interesting or surprising in chapter 6? Are there any take-home lessons?

2. How important is the concept of 'honour' in the culture in which you live? How does Christian faith affect the way you see it?

3. At present, how relevant are 1 Peter 2:18–23 and 3:1 to your own life and to the lives of your friends?

The unfolding of your words gives light.
(Ps. 119:130, ESV)

The thickets surrounding 1 Corinthians 11:2–16

From our study so far, we may say that marriage is a relationship of equality and mutual submission. It also involves a differentiation of responsibility which goes beyond the obvious biological differences, namely, the Christian husband is called to a particular responsibility to take the initiative in self-sacrificial love for his wife. But some commentators derive rather different views of male–female relations from 1 Corinthians 11:2–16.

Among the details of Paul's instructions are some points which make uncomfortable reading for those with an egalitarian view. In verse 3 he says that the man is head of woman. And in verses 9–10 (ESV) we read: 'Neither was man created for woman, but woman for man. That is why a wife ought to have a symbol of authority on her head.' Paul seems to be saying that a wife ought to wear something on her head to show that she is under her husband's authority. For those complementarians who hold a hierarchical view of male–female relations, this is a key passage. The ESV's interpretation is music to their ears, and anathema to committed egalitarians.

How should this passage be understood? In most English versions, verses 2–16 seem to be a jumble of thoughts about head coverings and hair, with obscure and impenetrable reasoning. Historically, there have been differences of view among commentators over the extent to which Paul is writing about covering the head with a garment, or about hairstyles, or both.[1] Commentators regularly throw up their hands in despair. Some declare that the practical situation which Paul was addressing can no longer be positively identified and that it is impossible to follow his train of thought.

In chapter 1 I warned of the need to hack our way through thickets to find the path. Paul's train of thought in 1 Corinthians 11:2–16 lies hidden under a tangle of misconception, misunderstanding and mistranslation. A great deal of hacking away has to be undertaken. The effort will be worthwhile. After six thickets have been cut away, the reward will be an internally consistent interpretation, which takes account of every detail of Paul's text, in which everything has its place in a connected train of reasoning and which sits comfortably with what he writes elsewhere. When we do Paul the honour of assuming that he is presenting a coherent, logical and consistent argument, his meaning becomes clear.[2]

The first thicket: the doctrine of the Trinity

Discussion of 1 Corinthians 11:3 has generated a substantial literature re-examining the doctrine of the Trinity.

Grudem draws a parallel between (1) the relationship of God the Father and God the Son and (2) the headship–submission relationship of male to female. His principal purpose is to answer a claim by some egalitarians that authority and submission cannot coexist among equals. His argument relies on Paul's statement in verse 3 that God is head of the Messiah. He uses this to advance a concept called 'the eternal subordination of the Son'. He claims that the very nature of God is at stake, because (he says) egalitarians are modifying the doctrine of the Trinity in order to maintain their view of marriage.[3]

His particular understanding of the doctrine of the Trinity has generated considerable controversy among conservative theologians. Some agree with

---

1. *M&W*, 146, 150–151.
2. Stackhouse 2015 writes of a 'pattern of doubleness', because he sees two themes in tension – privileging of the male and affirmation of male–female equality. He appears to have reservations about Paul's accuracy as an interpreter of the Old Testament (see 82). In the present book I find consistency rather than tension.
3. *EFBT*, 42, 45–48.

him; many others (both complementarian and egalitarian) view him as re-introducing the ancient heresy of subordinationism in a new guise, and as denying the equality of Father and Son. Complementarians who are persuaded by 'eternal subordination' add it to their arsenal and deploy it in the debate. Complementarians who think it is a distortion of the doctrine of the Trinity regard it as an unwelcome distraction which harms their cause. Egalitarians regard it as further proof of the dangers of complementarianism.

Fortunately, for present purposes this thicket can be quickly cleared. This controversy over the doctrine of the Trinity is a potentially important matter in its own right. But it is not necessary or even appropriate to enter into it in order to understand what Paul writes in 1 Corinthians 11. Paul does not use the terms 'Father', 'Son' or 'Holy Spirit'. The doctrine of the Trinity is not the topic which he is addressing. He is writing about the appropriate conduct of men and women while praying and prophesying. His meaning should be determined by examining the flow of his argument in its context. It is not reasonable to think that what he means can be safely or convincingly settled by appeal to nuances of the doctrine of the Trinity.[4]

The second thicket: unjustified conclusions from word studies

Verse 3 says: 'But I want you to realize that the Messiah is the head [*kephalē*] of every man, and the man is head [*kephalē*] of woman, and God is head [*kephalē*] of the Messiah.'

The two main views on the metaphorical meaning of *kephalē* in verse 3 are that it means 'authority over' or 'source'.[5]

Grudem writes:

> In this verse, 'head' refers to one who is in a position of authority over the other, as this Greek word (*kephalē*) uniformly does whenever it is used in ancient literature to say that one person is 'head' of another person or group.

---

4. The converse is also true. The contours of the doctrine of the Trinity are not dependent on a resolution of the egalitarian–complementarian debate. For a recent discussion which charts declining acceptance of Grudem's view of the Trinity, see Giles 2017.
5. A third view is that it indicates prominence. This is advanced by Perriman 1998, 13–40, 59, 197–199. See also Tidball 2012, 213, and the citation in *EFBT*, 592, of Thiselton's tentative endorsement.

[T]he authors and editors of all the English lexicons for ancient Greek now agree (1) that the meaning 'leader, chief, person in authority' clearly exists for [*kephalē*] and (2) the meaning 'source' simply does not exist.[6]

There are two problems with these statements. The first is a problem of analysis. Grudem's assessment of the available evidence is erroneous, with the result that his conclusion concerning the usage of *kephalē* is incorrect. The second is a problem of method. Even if his conclusion about metaphorical usage elsewhere were correct, this would not determine Paul's meaning in verse 3.

Grudem's word studies

Grudem has put much labour into studying how *kephalē* is used metaphorically elsewhere. He denies that it is ever used in the sense of 'source'. He accepts it is sometimes used to mean 'beginning', but says: 'Even in those cases where the sense "beginning" is appropriate, there is no idea of "beginning" without authority; rather, the person who is the "head" is always the one in authority.'[7]

Payne says that study of lexicons and examples leads to an almost opposite conclusion, namely, both metaphorical senses occur, but the sense 'authority over' is unusual, while the sense 'source' is amply attested in lexicons of secular Greek usage.[8]

On close examination, it appears that Grudem's analysis has been influenced by confirmation bias, with the result that he has overstated his case and reached an incorrect conclusion concerning usage.

Was *kephalē* used as a metaphor for 'source'? The answer is yes. Payne demonstrates that there are well-attested examples of the use of *kephalē* to mean 'source' prior to or roughly contemporary with Paul's time. For example, there are two clear examples in Philo (died about 45–50) where *kephalē* is used as a metaphor for 'source'.[9] Moreover, Grudem's focus on whether a person

---

6. *EFBT*, 45–46, 590.

7. *EFBT*, 582.

8. *M&W*, 117–128, 136–137.

9. Philo, in *On Rewards and Punishments* 125, states: '[T]he virtuous one, whether single man or people, will be the head [*kephalē*] of the human race and all the others like the limbs of a body which draw their life from the forces in the head.' Here the person described as 'head' is said to be the source of life for the people described as limbs. But Grudem lists this as an example of 'head' meaning 'authority over': *EFBT*, 546. Again, Philo in *On the Preliminary Studies* 61 (*Congr.* 61) states: '[O]f all the members of the clan here described Esau is the progenitor [*genarches*], the head

described as head in the sense of 'beginning' happens to be also in a position of authority rather misses the point, which is to discover what the metaphor was intended to convey.[10]

Was *kephalē* used as a metaphor for 'authority over'? The answer is again yes, though with some qualifications as regards date of use. Many of Grudem's examples of *kephalē* being used to mean 'ruler/chief/authority' are after Paul's time, so are of limited assistance. The more relevant examples are those which are before or contemporary with Paul. Grudem particularly refers to the use of *kephalē* in the Septuagint translation of the Old Testament from Hebrew into Greek. In the Hebrew the word for 'head' is frequently used metaphorically, as in English, to refer to a ruler, chief or leader. Depending on one's understanding of the meaning of the original Hebrew, there are a few instances (from about one to about six) where the Hebrew word for 'head' means 'ruler' and the translator chose to render this into Greek as *kephalē*. This could have influenced Paul's usage, since he was familiar both with the Septuagint and with the Hebrew scriptures.

But it is important to appreciate that, even though some Septuagint translators showed a strong tendency to prefer literal renderings and to stretch Greek words beyond their usual meanings in order to stay close to the Hebrew text, this literal translation of the Hebrew 'head' metaphor as *kephalē* was only adopted in a tiny minority of instances. This is inexplicable if *kephalē* was a well-known metaphor in Greek for a person in authority at the time the Septuagint was produced. Uses of it in that sense in Greek, prior to Paul, are very rare.

Accordingly, while in the first century there was nothing to prevent a Greek writer using *kephalē* metaphorically to mean 'chief/ruler/authority', he would need to take deliberate steps to make his meaning clear for his readers, as it was not widely used as a metaphor in that sense.

[*kephalē*] as it were of the whole creature.' This translation again plainly shows 'head' in the sense of 'source'. The figurative use of 'head' as meaning 'progenitor' echoes the ancient belief that sperm originated in the brain (see chapter 4, 49). Grudem accepts this translation as correct but argues unconvincingly that there is ambiguity here, and that the meaning of *genarches* as used here might possibly be 'ruler of created beings': *EFBT*, 579. The latter meaning indicates a god. Grudem does not offer an explanation either of how Philo regards Esau as a god or of how Esau rules the clan from his grave. The clan is here allegorical, representing certain vices, but an allegory needs to make sense. See further *Mc&W*, 123–128, where Payne also provides further examples of 'head' as 'source' in Greek literature.

10. See *EFBT*, 202–204, 544, 582, 589, 591, 595.

We noted in chapter 4 that in this respect first-century Greek stands in contrast to English, where we regularly use 'head' to mean the person in charge. This feature of English is shared by Latin and German (as well as Hebrew). Between them, Latin, German and English account for a substantial proportion of the Bible commentaries that have been written. This feature has been liable to lead to an over-hasty assumption about Paul's meaning. He was writing in Greek to Greek speakers, for whom *kephalē* was not a metaphor with a single standardized meaning.

Paul's own usage of *kephalē* as a metaphor varies. In Ephesians 1:22 he uses it to refer to the person in the top position: all things are under Christ's feet and he is the head above all things for the church. This is easy for English speakers to take in a sense which conveys an idea of authority. Elsewhere he uses 'head' metaphorically as meaning source of life and nourishment. Clear examples of this latter kind of metaphorical usage by Paul include Ephesians 4:15–16 (Christ is the head from whom the whole body grows) and Colossians 2:19 (Christ is the head from whom the whole body grows and is nourished).[11] It is true, of course, that the Messiah is also lord of his church, but that is not the point that Paul is making by using the metaphor of Christ as 'head' in these latter examples.

In short, usage elsewhere than in 1 Corinthians 11:3 shows more than one metaphorical use. Both 'authority' and 'source' are possibilities to consider.

Metaphorical meaning is not determined by usage elsewhere but by context

Grudem and Payne adopt contrasting approaches to interpretation.

Based on his word studies of *kephalē*, Grudem reads verse 3 as meaning that Christ is the authority over every man, man is the authority over woman and God is the authority over Christ. He does not offer a connected interpretation of verses 2–16 as a whole. He pays relatively limited attention to the context of Paul's words.

Payne's approach is to examine verses 2–16 in full, paying attention to context, including the cultural situation in first-century Corinth and Paul's related teaching elsewhere, in order to propose an interpretation which seeks to understand Paul's argument as a whole, and each of its subsidiary steps.

---

11. Similarly, in Col. 1:15–16 Christ is the source of creation ('in him all things were created') and in v. 18 he is 'the head of the body, the church, who is its beginning', that is, he is the source of the church. Eph. 5:23 (where Christ is the head who saves the body) was discussed above in chapter 4.

Payne presents this in over 100 pages, amounting to eight chapters of his book.[12]

In the context of my experience of junior school, the head was the teacher who was in charge of the school. In the context of geography lessons at senior school, the head of the river was its source. In the context of college rowing at Oxford, the head of the river was the team which was in the winning position in the competition. Meaning depends on context.

Payne's approach is therefore the sounder method. The surveys of usage of *kephalē* are of considerable interest, but seeing how words are used elsewhere can only show us a range of possibilities. The meaning and intent of Paul's metaphor in 1 Corinthians 11 must be sought primarily from the internal logic of what he writes in the particular context.[13] This vital step is missing from Grudem's approach.

Even if prior to Paul's time *kephalē* had been used metaphorically only to indicate 'authority', Paul remained free to use this existing metaphor, or adapt it, or make up a new one in which he used *kephalē* in some other sense. If there was more than one possible usage, or if he was coining a new metaphor, it was up to him to make his meaning clear for his readers. Context is king.

The third thicket: authority structures

According to complementarian interpretations, verse 3 is about a hierarchy of authority relationships (God » Christ » man » woman) and the overall point which Paul is making in verses 2–16 is: 'if women pray and prophesy in church, they should do so under the authority of male headship.'[14]

A commonly held complementarian view is that Paul instructs women to veil their heads during worship because a veil symbolized that married women were under their husbands' authority; the veil therefore functioned as a symbol of the authority and order of gender relationships.[15] A minority of complementarian commentators believe that Paul is not writing about veils but only

---

12. *M&W*, 110, 109–215. Most of what he writes is well reasoned and, where it refers to historical information, appropriately evidenced. I have benefited greatly from his exposition.
13. This is rightly accepted in Köstenberger 1994, 264.
14. *RBMW*, 129 (Schreiner).
15. Smith 2012, 70. So also Schreiner in *RBMW*, 117–132.

about hairstyles. Nevertheless, they still consider that his overall point is about maintaining authoritative male headship.[16]

Let us therefore review the possibility that Paul is using *kephalē* to mean 'authority over'. How well does this hierarchical interpretation fit what he writes?

Eight red lights for the hierarchical interpretation

When we set the hierarchical interpretation next to Paul's text, eight points stand out as red lights, warning us not to proceed. All but the eighth are internal to verses 2–16.

1. The role of verse 3 in Paul's reasoning and the non-use of the third couplet

Verse 3 presents three pairs of 'head' relationships: Christ–man, man–woman, God–Christ. I will call these 'couplets'. It is clear, and not controversial, that this verse functions as a keynote statement undergirding the argument which Paul then presents. Schreiner says verse 3 is 'fundamental to the whole passage'. Smith says it 'lays the foundation for what follows'; it is a 'summary statement of principle, functioning a bit like a heading . . . that informs the rest of the passage', and it 'provides the framework for Paul's instructions'.[17]

But on the hierarchical interpretation Paul fails to make full use of that framework. He does not pick up and use the third couplet (God–Christ) anywhere in his argument. We should expect to find Paul relying on God's authority over Christ in order to explain or support his instructions. But he does not.

The question for anyone who thinks Paul is talking about authority relationships in this passage is: please tell us how the third couplet of verse 3 functions in Paul's argument. Where in verses 4–16 does Paul write about the authority of God over Christ?[18]

---

16. For example, Hurley 1981, 162–181.
17. *RBMW*, 122 (Schreiner); Smith 2012, 58, 64, 65.
18. The reason Schreiner gives for Paul's inclusion of the third couplet in 11:3 is the possibility that some might think that the authority of man over woman makes woman unequal and inferior; he says that this is impliedly rebutted by Paul's reference in v. 3 to God's headship over Christ (*RBMW*, 122). But this theory does not identify for the third couplet any direct role in the connected argument that Paul advances from v. 4 onwards. Similarly, on Smith's interpretation the third couplet plays no actual part in Paul's reasoning and instructions. It is left hanging and unused. For Paul, who is a thoughtful writer, this is an improbable rhetorical

2. The mistranslation of verse 10

Verse 10 says: 'Because of this a woman ought to have authority [*exousia*] over [*epi*] her head.'

The basic structure of Paul's argument in verses 5–10 is plain from the way it is put together and is agreed by commentators of all persuasions. In this structure, verse 10 is a conclusion about the proper behaviour of women. In Paul's mind this conclusion *is consistent with* what he says about women's behaviour in verses 5–6. It *stands in contrast with* what he says about the proper behaviour for men in verse 7. And it *follows from* his reasoning in verses 7–9. Given this structure, on the hierarchical interpretation verse 10 must be about a woman's behaviour showing that she is under a man's authority.

In order to maintain the hierarchical interpretation and make the meaning of verse 10 fit into this structure, translators offer a bold paraphrase of this verse as stating that a woman ought to have a 'sign' or 'symbol' of authority on her head (for example, ASV, EHV, ESV, MOUNCE, NASB, NKJV, NRSV, NIV 1984, RV). The translators' idea is that Paul is here referring to a veil on the woman's head, and that this is a symbol of her husband's authority over her. But this paraphrase is entirely lacking in linguistic or textual support:

- The added words 'sign of' or 'symbol of' are a creative invention. They do not reflect any words in the Greek text.
- The paraphrase reverses the meaning of the expression 'have authority'. The translators' paraphrase is not intended to convey anything about the woman's authority. It is intended to convey the opposite, namely, that she is in subjection to someone else's authority. But when a person has authority over something or someone, it means they are in charge of them or in control of them. The word *exousia* is very commonly used.

---

strategy. Cottrell 1997 puts forward a rather different proposal for v. 3. He says the main point is the middle couplet (because woman is subordinate to man); the function of the first couplet is an illustration or analogy for the man's role (because Christ is the head over every man) and the function of the third couplet is to provide an illustration or analogy for the woman's role (because Christ is subordinate to the Father). But Paul says nothing to show that this is the purpose of the first and third couplets – how is the reader supposed to know this? Moreover, on this view the first and third couplets play no role in Paul's extended argument from v. 4 onwards. This is not a plausible interpretation. Note also that when Paul does write on the topic of the Son submitting to the Father (1 Cor. 15:24, 28), he does not use a 'head' metaphor.

It occurs over 100 times in the New Testament alone. No-one has found any other example, whether in the Bible or in the whole of ancient Greek literature, in which a phrase about a person having authority (*exousia*) is used in a reversed sense of being in subjection to an authority rather than being the possessor of the authority. The Greek text speaks not of an authority to which a woman is subject but of authority that she ought herself to have.[19]

• Exactly the same Greek expression for authority over (*exousian . . . epi*) is used in Luke 10:19, where Jesus says to the seventy-two: 'I have given you authority . . . over [*exousian . . . epi*] all the power of the enemy.' This means what it says. The seventy-two were not put in subjection under the power of the enemy, nor were they given a sign of their subjection to the enemy. There is no warrant for understanding this same Greek expression any differently in 1 Corinthians 11:10. The translation is straightforward: the woman ought to have authority over her head.

Some translators may have felt that their paraphrase was a valid rendering either because their own culture taught them that women could not exercise authority, or because they thought that Paul endorsed patriarchal culture; hence Paul must have meant that a woman was under a man's authority. But that is not what Paul writes.

The stated 'Rationale' for the Danvers Statement deplores 'the increasing prevalence and acceptance of hermeneutical oddities devised to reinterpret apparently plain meanings of Biblical texts'. But the complementarian paraphrase of verse 10 (as in the ESV) is a prime example of such an oddity, which reverses the plain meaning of Paul's words.

This flawed paraphrase of verse 10 should be discarded as having no proper basis in the text and as being diametrically contrary to what the text actually says. NIV 2011 has corrected it to 'a woman ought to have authority over her own head'. The meaning of this in context is explained in chapter 8 below.

---

19. Hurley 1981, 175–177, interpreting Paul's instructions as concerning hair rather than veils, sees the difficulty that the Greek text speaks of the woman's authority. To maintain nonetheless a hierarchical interpretation, his proposal is that the woman's hair is both a sign of her authority with respect to the rest of creation and a sign of the man's authority over her. This remarkable proposal would make the expression 'have authority' mean two opposite things at the same time, neither of which corresponds to Paul's actual words.

3. The relationship of verse 11 to verse 10

Any interpretation has to take into account the relationship between verse 11 and verse 10. Verse 11 starts with *plen*, which is most often translated into English as 'nevertheless', 'however' or 'yet'. A typical translation of verse 11 reads: 'Nevertheless, in the Lord *woman is not independent of man*, nor is man independent of woman' (NIV, emphasis added).

According to the hierarchical interpretation, Paul has just made a statement in verse 10 about a woman being under man's authority. He now qualifies what he has said. The qualification in verse 11 balances up what he has said about women's subjection in verse 10 by pointing to the mutual interdependence of men and women. The purpose of this qualification is to make plain that women are not inferior beings, of less value than men.[20]

The first problem here is that this explanation treats verse 10 as saying something different from what it actually says. But even if the paraphrase of verse 10 were correct, the explanation is in conflict with the text of verse 11. If Paul is wanting to balance a statement about a woman being under man's authority, he should start verse 11 with 'Nevertheless, in the Lord *man is not independent of woman*.' As written by Paul, verse 11 is the wrong way round for this explanation. Instead of pointing to man's status as interdependent, to make clear that man is not superior, he starts with woman's dependence upon man, thereby apparently re-emphasizing her inferiority. This would be a reinforcement, not a contrast. The explanation does not work.

4. The absence of the necessary clues to Paul's metaphor, if he means 'authority'

Paul says he wants his readers to 'know' or 'understand' his framework statement (v. 3). We expect him to employ it to justify his instructions. Since 'head' as a metaphor could be used in more than one way, Paul needs to signal clearly what he means by it. In particular, if he means 'head' as a metaphor for authority, he needs to give this signal promptly and clearly, since at the time of writing *kephalē* was not widely used as a metaphor in that sense among Greek speakers.

If he means 'authority', he fails to give the needed signals. If verse 3 is supposed to introduce a passage about the authority of God, of Christ and of man, how is it that Paul's only clear reference to authority anywhere in verses 4–16 is to the authority of a woman (v. 10)?

---

20. *RBMW*, 127 (Schreiner).

5. The order of the couplets in verse 3

If Paul were thinking in hierarchical terms, involving a structure of authority relationships, it would be natural for him to state the couplets in verse 3 in a hierarchical order: God » Christ; Christ » man; man » woman. But he does not. His order is: Christ » man; man » woman; God » Christ. This suggests to the reader that in verse 3 he is not thinking in terms of a hierarchy of authorities. It is an early signal that he has something else in mind.

6. The equal balance of instructions to men and women

According to the hierarchical interpretation, the practical situation which Paul is addressing is women's failure to show their submission to men, and his concern is the maintenance of proper order in worship, being an order in which women are under men's authority.[21] If this is a correct understanding of Paul's concern, we should expect the main burden of Paul's instructions to be directed at the behaviour required of women.

But this is not what we find in Paul's text. His first instruction is to men, and this is followed by an instruction to women (vv. 4–6). Next, Paul gives another instruction to men, coupled with an instruction to women (vv. 7–10). Verses 11–12 treat men and women as equals, as complementarian interpreters accept. Paul then gives a final instruction to women, coupled with a final instruction to men (vv. 13–15). It is simply not the case that Paul's instructions are mainly directed at the proper behaviour of women. They are directed equally to men and women.

7. The nature of the instructions to men

If the burden of Paul's concern is that women should be in subjection to men, we should expect this to be reflected in the nature of the instructions which Paul gives to men. There are instructions to men in verses 4, 7 and 14. But in those instructions there is not a word telling men to behave on the basis that women are in subjection to them.

8. Inconsistency with chapter 7

Just four chapters earlier, in strong and revolutionary terms, Paul has affirmed the equality of men and women in personal relations (as we saw in chapter 2). If he is now saying that by reason of the creation order men in fact have unilateral authority over women, he is contradicting himself. This is not an acceptable analysis. Paul's writings sometimes fill out, develop or qualify things

---

21. *RBMW*, 118 (Schreiner).

he has written previously, but they do not flatly contradict what he has written previously.

The significance of the red lights

To arrive at the hierarchical destination, it is necessary to drive through all eight of the red lights. Taken in combination they justify a secure conclusion that it is not correct to understand Paul's concern as being about women's subjection or to understand 'head' as metaphorically denoting 'authority' in this passage.

Red lights 1–3 are of special importance, since they are compelling considerations which depend directly on the structure and words of Paul's text. To hold to a hierarchical interpretation, it is necessary to disregard the rhetorical function of Paul's framework statement, to reverse the meaning of the plain words of verse 10 and to accept that Paul somehow wrote verse 11 the wrong way round. We can have confidence that this interpretation cannot be correct.

Having rejected the hierarchical interpretation, we can move on to the next major disputed question, which is whether Paul's concerns are about the veiling or unveiling of women and men or only about hairstyles.

The fourth thicket: veils

Many interpreters, not only complementarian but also egalitarian,[22] believe that in 11:2–16 Paul is teaching about the appropriate use of veils or other garments for covering the head during corporate worship: women's heads should be covered, men's should not. The alternative possibility is that Paul is writing only about hairstyles.

In order to consider the veils interpretation, we need to look first at the context in Corinth, and then at whether this interpretation is consistent with Paul's text.

Cultural context

Culturally, the people to whom Paul was writing at Corinth were a mixture of Roman, Greek and Jewish.[23] What do we know about the significance of head coverings and hair for these people?

---

22. Fee 1987, 496–497.

23. The names of people mentioned in 1 Corinthians are a mixture of Latin names and Greek names; some were Jews (Acts 18:5–8; 1 Cor. 7:18; 12:13). Paul wrote to them in Greek. While important public inscriptions in Corinth were often in Latin, Greek graffiti are found on pottery at Corinth: Gill 1990, 259.

First, hair.

There are contemporary and near-contemporary descriptions by Seneca, Juvenal, Pseudo-Phocylides and Dio Chrysostom of men behaving as women, with homosexual connotations, either by wearing long hair hanging down loose or by fastening it up in a woman's style. In the pagan cult of Dionysus, which was practised at Corinth, men wore effeminate long hair to be like women and indicate their sexual availability to other men for homosexual liaisons.[24]

The same cult also provided opportunities for women to throw off sexual restraint.[25] 'Women's hair was a prime object of male lust in the ancient Mediterranean world.'[26] A woman of looser morals might let her hair down to take part in pagan revels, or to indicate that she was a prostitute for hire. In either event, she was indicating a willingness to be an object of male lust. A faithful married woman did not normally let her hair down in public.[27]

Many Corinthian believers came from a background of idol worship (12:2) and some continued to frequent pagan temples (8:10; 10:14–22). In the church in Corinth there were issues of inappropriate sexual behaviour, both heterosexual and homosexual (5:1–2, 9–13; 6:9–11, 12–20; 7:2; 10:8). In this context of idolatry and sexual licence in Corinth, men's long hair and women's loose hair seen in a public or semi-public setting each had shameful implications of sexual impropriety.[28]

What about head coverings?

Bruce Winter has argued that respectable married Roman women were required always to wear a veil in public as a sign of their marriage, and that this applied in Corinth, which was a Roman colony.[29] But this goes beyond the

---

24. For references, see *M&W*, 176.

25. Information about the cult of Dionysus at Corinth is given in Payne 2006. See further *M&W*, 142–144, 162–166. *WITC*, 54 (Baugh), also confirms that loose hair was associated with lascivious worship of Dionysus. See also Gill 1990, 255, referring to Livy.

26. Keener 1993, 585, citing Apuleius, *Metamorphoses* 2.8–9; *Sifre* Num. 11.2.3. Keener 1996 cites additionally Chariton, *Chaereas* 1.13.11; 1.14.1; ARN 14, §35B; *Sifre* Num. 11.2.1; p. Sanh. 6:4, §1. The sexual attraction of hair flowing down is also acknowledged in Song 4:1.

27. Hair might be let down in the special case of mourning: Hurley 1981, 261.

28. Paul's perspective is very different from that of twenty-first-century liberal society. His reliance on Gen. 2:24 in 1 Cor. 6:16 implies that in his view there is no such thing as sexual intercourse that is merely recreational and without personal meaning.

29. Winter 2003, 77–82.

evidence. For example, veiled wives depicted on tombstones, and statues of an
empress with veiled head, do not prove that married women were always veiled
when out and about from day to day. And if a head covering, as worn at a
wedding, was capable of indicating a woman's married status, it does not follow
that she was required to wear such a covering whenever she went out. Gill has
pointed out that public marble portraits of women at Corinth, presumably of
members of wealthy and prestigious families, most frequently show them bare-
headed. This suggests that it was socially acceptable for women to be seen
bare-headed in public in Corinth.[30] Hurley's detailed study reaches the same
conclusion. He states:

> Graeco-Roman practice of the day, as evidenced by art and literature, did not include
> mandatory veiling of any sort. Facial veiling was unknown and whether or not women
> pulled their shawls (*palla*, Latin; *himation* or *peribolaion*, Greek) over their heads was a
> matter of indifference.

---

30. Gill 1990, 251. *EFBT*, 334–335, relying on information from Winter, is insufficiently
    cautious in this respect. Winter also refers to an account, written in the first century,
    of a prominent Roman who, about two hundred years previously, had divorced his
    wife for going out without a veil: Valerius Maximus, *Memorable Doings and Sayings*
    6.3.10 ('*Horridum C. quoque Sulpicii Galli maritale supercilium: nam uxorem dimisit, quod
    eam capite aperto foris versatam cognoverat.*' My translation: 'There was also the grim
    marital arrogance of Gaius Sulpicius Gallus; for he divorced his wife because he
    had recognized her around outdoors with her head bare'). But Valerius reports this
    as something notable and harsh; it does not establish what was common practice in
    Corinth two hundred years later. (Confusingly, Plutarch appears to have understood
    the same historical incident in the opposite sense that women were formerly not
    allowed to cover their heads at all, and that Gallus divorced his wife because she
    pulled her cloak over her head: see *M&W*, 158.) In this area of study there is a
    general issue of inferring more uniformity from historical evidence than is really
    justified. Some commentators confuse expressions of personal preference with
    societal expectations. Some mistakenly project onto Paul's time the more restrictive
    veiling customs applied to women in other times and cultures. Some refer to
    aspirational prescriptions by pagan or Jewish moralists for the dress habits of
    the elite woman, overlooking the question to what extent such prescriptions
    were actually followed, and by whom. The Corinthian church was a socially mixed
    community, containing only a few elite persons (1:26). Payne sounds a prudent
    note of caution about the variations of customs from place to place: *M&W*, 31–35.
    See also Perriman 1998, 113.

Payne's study, which includes consideration of Winter's analysis, comes to the same conclusion as Hurley's. From the available evidence we can be confident that, at the time when Paul was writing, it was not generally regarded as shameful in Roman, Greek or Jewish contexts for a woman to be seen unveiled, with her hair visible, in a public or semi-public situation, provided that it was fastened up.[31]

This is corroborated by the New Testament itself. Both Paul and Peter felt the need to issue warnings against the conspicuous display of elaborate hairstyles (1 Tim. 2:9; 1 Pet. 3:3).[32] Such a warning would not have been needed if women habitually concealed their hair under a garment when outside their own living quarters. Women's hair must have been regularly on display. Significantly, the apostles' remedial advice in each case was not that women should veil their heads or otherwise cover their hair but that their styles should not be extravagant. What the apostles rebuked was the elaborate braiding with gold ornaments, not the fact that the women's hair was unveiled and visible.[33]

Conversely, it was culturally acceptable for a man to cover his head with a garment during religious worship. Roman men covered their heads when

---

31. Hurley 1981, 269; see further 66–68, 254–271. *M&W*, 150–162. The coincidence of Hurley's and Payne's views is striking, since they are both well researched, and Hurley writes from a complementarian and Payne from an egalitarian perspective. Moreover, even if there had been some social pressure towards veiling in public settings, this pressure would have been less strong in Christian assemblies in the early days. Christian meetings for worship took place in homes: see 1 Cor. 16:19. While unbelievers might come in (1 Cor. 14:24), fellow believers were regarded as family (1 Cor. 4:15; 11:33; 14:26; 1 Thess. 4:9–10; 1 Tim. 3:15). Corporate worship was therefore only a semi-public occasion.

32. 1 Timothy was written to Ephesus (1 Tim. 1:3). Like Corinth, Ephesus was a Roman colony. Because Corinth had been re-founded as a Roman colony after the earlier destruction of the Greek city, there was probably a higher proportion of Roman cultural influence in Corinth than in Ephesus, but the difference was only a matter of degree. 1 Peter was written to Pontus, Galatia, Cappadocia, Asia and Bithynia (1 Pet. 1:1).

33. During the first century the display of the elite woman's braided hair became ever more elaborate, such that the high beehive of closely woven curls took her attendants hours to achieve: Freisenbruch 2010, 149–150. We can be confident that this fashion would not have developed if women's hair had been hidden from public view.

making a pagan offering (as did Roman women).[34] Covering of the head was not compulsory for Jewish men generally, but God's law required the Jewish high priest to wear a turban on his head to carry out his priestly duties, and required the other priests to wear caps (Exod. 28:4, 37–41; 29:6–9; 39:28). Head coverings for men were not regarded as disgraceful among Jews.[35]

Thus, the cultural background did not render it disgraceful for women to be unveiled, or for men to cover their heads, while praying or prophesying.

Does the veils interpretation fit what Paul writes?

With this background in mind, we may consider whether Paul is writing about covering women's heads with a veiling garment and uncovering men's heads. There are at least six difficulties in interpreting this passage as being concerned with veils:

1. If Paul is writing about veiling, we might expect him to mention veils, or some other garment used for covering the head. Some English versions do indeed mention veils. But in the Greek text there is no mention of any actual garment on a person's head, whether a veil or any other kind of garment. The only use of a term denoting a garment is in verse 15 (*peribolaion* – something thrown around). This means a wrap, mantle or cloak (as in Heb. 1:12). But the use of this word in verse 15 is figurative, referring to the function of a woman's hair.

2. The veils interpretation has Paul prohibiting *men* from praying or prophesying with their heads covered with a garment in verses 4 and 7, on the basis that this would cause disgrace to them and to Christ. But there was no cultural reason which made it disgraceful. And it is unlikely that Paul, as a Jew, and knowing that God's law required the high priest to cover his head during worship, regarded it as disgraceful for religious reasons for a man to pray or prophesy with a garment on his head.

Two theories have been advanced to try to explain how, despite the Jewish law, Paul might have regarded a man's head covering, during prayer or prophecy, as disgraceful. But neither theory is persuasive:

- Some have speculated that Paul disapproves of head coverings for men in Corinth both because in Roman society head coverings were employed

---

34. *M&W*, 155.

35. Customs for Jewish men's head coverings varied from place to place. I have not found evidence of a firm custom applicable to Jewish men in Corinth.

as signs of high status and more particularly because Roman men covered their heads when making a pagan offering.[36] But Paul does not say anything that points to these explanations. Moreover, a Roman woman making a pagan offering in a public setting would likewise pull her garment up over her head while doing so,[37] so if Paul were concerned about this Roman custom he should tell women to uncover their heads also. This is not what he says.

- Others have drawn a comparison with what Paul writes in 2 Corinthians 3:12–18 and have suggested that a man must pray or prophesy with his head uncovered as a visible demonstration that God has now set believers free in Christ to worship him 'with unveiled face'.[38] Unlike in 1 Corinthians 11, in 2 Corinthians 3 Paul does indeed use the word for a veil worn on the head (*kalumma*). He uses it literally in 3:13 to refer to Moses' use of a veil, and figuratively in 3:14–16. But in 3:16–18, when Paul writes figuratively of the 'unveiled' experience of the Christian beholding the glory of the Lord, he says nothing that would confine this to Christian men. If Paul's concern in 1 Corinthians 11 were that the mode of dress during worship should reflect the freedom of the new covenant, he should be saying that neither men nor women should veil their heads while praying or prophesying. This is not what he says.

3. The veils interpretation has Paul prohibiting *women* from praying or prophesying with unveiled heads in verses 5–6 and 13, on the basis that this would cause disgrace. But the passage itself does not reveal any intelligible reason for regarding this as disgraceful. Nor does Corinthian culture provide a convincing reason. As we have seen, in the prevailing culture it was not disgraceful for a woman's hair to be on view, provided it was fastened up and not let down loose. And the apostles had no objection to a woman's hair being visible.

4. The veils interpretation is unable to make sense of verse 10, which says that a woman ought to have authority over her head. The hierarchical version of the veils interpretation adopts the extreme measure of reversing the meaning of Paul's words and adding to them, so as to make them refer to a veil worn as a

---

36. Tidball 2012, 214, citing Winter.
37. Finney 2010, 38.
38. Prior 1993, 181.

sign of subjection. The non-hierarchical version says that what Paul means in verse 10 remains a mystery or cannot be confidently stated.[39]

5. In the structure of Paul's argument, the function of verses 13–15 is to provide additional reasons for his instructions. But on the veils interpretation the reasons do not make sense; on the contrary, verse 15 undermines his supposed instruction about how women should dress.

In the ESV verses 13–15 state:

> [13]Judge for yourselves: is it proper for a wife to pray to God with her head uncovered? [14]Does not nature itself teach you that if a man wears long hair it is a disgrace for him, [15]but if a woman has long hair, it is her glory? For her hair is given to her for [*anti*] a covering [*peribolaion*].

If the instruction in verse 13 means that it is improper for a woman to pray without wearing a veil, verses 14–15 do not provide an intelligible reason for that instruction. On the contrary, these verses contradict the need to wear a veil. If a woman should be covered when praying, and her hair is given to her by God 'for a covering', she has no need of a veil.

Schreiner points out that *anti* does not always indicate substitution; it may instead indicate equivalence. But this does not help.[40] Whether the woman's hair is given to her 'instead of' a covering (NTE, YLT), 'as' a covering (NIV) or 'for' a covering (ESV), the logic is that no further covering, such as a veil, is needed. Reading the passage as concerned with veils has the result that Paul contradicts himself by giving a reason which leads to the opposite position from the one which he has supposedly been arguing for.

Some suggest that, in using the term *peribolaion*, Paul has in mind not merely a wrap or cloak but more specifically a prayer shawl.[41] Again, this proposal does not help. If Paul is saying in verse 15 that a woman's hair is given to her for (or as, or instead of) a prayer shawl, it follows that her hair is the only prayer shawl that she needs.

---

39. *RBMW*, 125–127 (Schreiner); *EFBT*, 338–339. Fee 1987, 521; *DBE*, 155–157 (Fee); Tidball 2012, 218–219.

40. *RBMW*, 119. In support of the translation of Greek *anti* as 'as' or 'for', see Rom. 12:17; 1 Thess. 5:15. But if the meaning is 'instead', the point remains substantially the same.

41. See Tidball 2012, 214–215.

To try to resolve the contradiction, some have suggested Paul's thinking is: because a woman has long hair, it is natural that she should use a long garment to cover her head. This suggestion has Paul relying on a flimsy argument. Moreover, he has not mentioned any long garment in verses 4–13. And men also wore long garments, so the suggestion sits ill with the distinction that he is making between women and men in verses 14–15.

6. The veils interpretation runs into a further obstacle at verse 16. The passage ends with 'If anyone thinks to be contentious, we do not have such [*toioutos*] a custom, nor do the churches of God.' The Greek word *toioutos* means 'such' or 'of this kind'. This verse indicates that Paul has in mind a single custom which he wants the Corinthians to discontinue.

On the veils interpretation verse 16 creates multiple difficulties when translated in accordance with what it actually says. The phrase 'we do not have such a custom' cannot refer specifically and solely to what immediately precedes it in verse 15, since that verse states Paul's own view. To say of it 'we do not have such a custom' would be a direct contradiction of what he has just written. The phrase must therefore have a wider reference back into Paul's discussion. But on the veils interpretation Paul has not been discussing a single custom. On that interpretation he has been identifying and banning three customs, namely, men praying or prophesying with veiled heads (vv. 4, 7), women praying or prophesying with unveiled heads (vv. 5–6, 10, 13), and men having long hair (v. 14).

The translators of some English versions (including NIV, NASB, RSV), appreciating that Paul's conclusion in verse 16 does not fit their veils interpretation, change 'we do not have *such* a custom' to 'we have no *other* custom'. This is presumably intended to prevent verse 16 conflicting (as they see it) with verse 15 and to mean that Paul and his co-workers do not have any practice that is different from the variety of instructions that Paul has given in the preceding verses.

But this is not a plausible or justifiable translation. There is no known example of *toioutos* as meaning 'other'. This is the opposite of its ordinary meaning.[42] The veils interpretation does not fit what Paul actually writes in verse 16.

For the above six reasons, the view that Paul's concern in verses 2–16 is the veiling of women's heads and uncovering of men's heads cannot be

---

42. Fee 1987, 530; *M&W*, 208.

sustained. If that interpretation falls away, the only available alternative is that he is writing about hairstyles throughout. But can this alternative be correct? From most English versions, such an understanding could not even be guessed at.

The fifth thicket: translating for veils or only for hairstyles?

The structure
The first step towards clarity of translation is to notice the structure of this part of Paul's letter. It is plain that 10:31 – 11:1 concludes the previous topic (food offered to idols) and that 11:17 introduces a new topic (the Lord's Supper). There is no language between verse 2 and verse 16 which signals a change of topic. This structure therefore suggests that verses 2–16 are dealing with a single topic. On any view, verses 14–15 are unquestionably about hair. It is therefore reasonable to try out a working hypothesis that the whole passage must somehow be about hair.

The culture
How would such a hypothesis fit into the historical and cultural context which we sketched above? How hair was worn during worship would have implications for sexual propriety. It would make sense for Paul to be concerned about this. It was not appropriate, when the church assembled for worship, for men who took part by praying or prophesying to wear their hair like that of women, since this could be seen as a hint of availability for homosexual liaisons. Nor was it appropriate for women who took part by praying or prophesying to let their hair down, which could similarly be thought to suggest a willingness to engage in sexual misconduct. Paul did not need to spell out these implications for his Corinthian readers, who knew perfectly well what went on in Corinth. He contents himself with giving the necessary instructions and (as we shall see) providing reasons for them.

The words
The critical move which enables us to clear the thicket is to understand the adjective *akatakaluptos*, which appears as a description of a woman's head in verse 5 and is used again in verse 13. This is an unusual word, which occurs nowhere else in the New Testament. It can refer to having hair hanging down loose, as opposed to its being fastened up on top of or behind the head. This meaning can be seen from its use in the Septuagint in Leviticus 13:45, where it refers to a person's hair. English translations of Leviticus 13:45 use the terms

'unkempt' (NIV), 'go loose' (ASV), 'hang loose' (RSV and ESV) and 'dishevelled' (NRSV).[43]

Thus verse 5 may be translated: 'And every woman praying or prophesying with her hair let down loose on [*akatakaluptos*] her head dishonours her head . . .' And verse 13: 'Judge among yourselves: Is it fitting for a woman to pray to God with her hair let down [*akatakaluptos*]?'

Comparing verse 5 with verse 13 we see that in using this adjective it is not necessary to refer expressly to the head: to say that a woman is *akatakaluptos* has the same meaning as saying that her head is *akatakaluptos*. In Greek the '*a*' at the beginning of the word has the meaning 'not'. So, when this word is used, we can say that the woman's hair is not *katakaluptos*, that is, it is not fastened up. Paul wants the women to pray or prophesy with their hair fastened up, not hanging down loose.

In verses 6 and 7 Paul uses the related verb *katakaluptō*. Again, this is an uncommon word, not used anywhere else in the New Testament. It is made up of the preposition *kata*, which has a wide range of meanings, and *kaluptō*, the primary meaning of which is 'cover'. So English versions conventionally render *katakaluptō* as 'cover'.[44] But comparison with verse 5 enables us to be more precise. Both from the make-up of the word itself (its lack of the initial '*a*'), and from Paul's flow of thought in verses 5–6, we can see that the verb *katakaluptō* here denotes having a particular kind of covering, one which is the opposite of the adjective *akatakaluptos*. In other words, this verb refers to having one's hair fastened up.

So verse 6 is saying: 'For if a woman does not have her hair fastened up [*katakaluptō*], she should be shorn, and since it is a disgrace for a woman to have her hair shorn or shaved, she should fasten it up [*katakaluptō*].'

Now that we have seen what Paul is saying in verses 5–6 about women's hair, we can look at how to translate verse 4, which is about men. What is this verse saying about a man's hairstyle?

Many English versions refer here to a man's head being 'covered'. But there is no Greek word for 'covered' in the text. Literally, verse 4 says: 'Every man

---

43. Philo may also use the same word to refer to hair let down loose: Philo, *The Special Laws* 3.60, referring to Num. 5:18. NIV translates Num. 5:18 as referring to the priest loosening a woman's hair. Hurley 1981, 262, concurs in this interpretation of Num. 5:18. However, this piece of evidence is unclear, because Philo also mentions removing a woman's 'kerchief', though the biblical text does not. See *RBMW*, 118 (Schreiner); Fee 1987, 509.

44. See also the Septuagint of Gen. 38:15 and Isa. 6:2.

praying or prophesying having down from head dishonours his head.' Here, the phrase 'having down from head' is '*kata* [down from[45]] *kephalēs* [head] *echōn* [having]'. On the basis that Paul is dealing with a single topic in this passage, it is natural to read this consistently with verse 5, where Paul criticizes the Corinthian practice of having women's hair hanging down loose while praying or prophesying, and with verse 14, which refers to long hair on a man as dishonouring. On this basis verse 4 is also about hair. Thus verse 4 may be translated: 'Every man praying or prophesying with long hair hanging down dishonours his head.'

The idiom 'having down from head' is admittedly not a very clear way of referring to having long hair hanging down. This is why translators have struggled to know how best to render verse 4. But there is biblical precedent for it.[46] And Paul has a good reason for using this particular expression. Verse 4 contains a word-play on what he has written in verse 2. The last two words of verse 2 are *paradoseis katechete*, meaning 'you are holding fast the traditions'. The verb *katechō* ('have down', in the sense 'hold fast') is a compound derived from *kata* (here meaning 'down') and *echō*, meaning 'have'. So in verse 2 Paul is commending the Corinthians by way of general introduction because they *kata-echō* the traditions (= hold them fast); then in verse 4 he is censuring the men because they *kata echō* the head (= have long hair hanging down). This word-play explains Paul's choice of words. It emphasizes the contrast between

---

45. Greek *kata* plus a genitive of place means 'down from' (as Matt. 8:32; Acts 27:14).
46. The same expression *kata kephalēs* ('down from head') is used in the Septuagint of Esth. 6:12 to describe Haman when he goes home in grief and frustration after being humiliated before Mordecai. The setting is the Persian Empire in the fifth century BC. Artefacts from the Persian Empire show some elaborate hairstyles for high-status men, including hair arranged to project behind the head. When Alcibiades, the fifth-century BC Athenian statesman, adopted a Persian lifestyle, this involved 'tying his hair up in a bun': Stuttard 2018, 195. If the Septuagint translator of Esth. 6:12 had understood the relevant expression in the original Hebrew (literally, 'covered') in its ordinary literal sense, *kata kephalēs* would have been a strange translation to adopt. But the translation is explicable if the translator was using *kata kephalēs* in the same sense as is used by Paul. Whether rightly or wrongly, it seems the translator understood that Haman went home with his hair untied and hanging down loose. This would express grief and shame. (Some commentators also discuss a quotation from Plutarch, where he uses the expression *kata . . . kephalēs*, but this is not directly relevant, since in that instance Plutarch expressly says that it is the person's toga that is down over his head.)

verse 2, which is a general commendation of the Corinthians for holding to the traditions delivered to them, and what follows in verses 3–16, where Paul is critical of the Corinthians for adopting a custom that they did not receive from him or his colleagues.[47]

This understanding reveals how verses 4 and 5 relate to each other. Paul writes first about men's disgraceful long hair hanging down in verse 4, then women's disgraceful long hair hanging down in verse 5.[48]

Returning now to verse 7, this says, as regards a man's hair: 'For indeed a man ought not to fasten up his hair on [*katakaluptō*] his head . . .' The reason for this additional instruction will be explained below.

Verse 16 can now be translated and understood without difficulty and in faithful accordance with the Greek text. It says that neither Paul nor the churches have 'such a custom' – that is, they do not have the Corinthian custom of men and women praying and prophesying with long hair hanging down.

The sixth thicket: translating for husband and wife or only for man and woman?

There is another translation issue which needs to be resolved.

In verses 2–16 Paul makes frequent use of the words *anēr* and *gunē*. In Greek writing *anēr* is used generally for a man and more specifically for a husband, and *gunē* is used generally for a woman and more specifically for a wife. When a writer intends the more specific meaning this is usually made obvious by a clear verbal clue. For example, a phrase such as 'his woman' would mean 'his wife'.[49]

---

47. Note that Paul continues his rhetorical flourish in v. 4 by shifting the word-play from *kata* and *echō* to *kata* and *kephalē*: 'Every man praying or prophesying *kata kephalēs echōn* [having down from head] *kataischunei* [dishonours] *ten kephalēn autou* [his head].' The word-play includes a deliberate ambiguity in the phrase 'dishonours his head'. Literally, it refers to dishonouring the man's own head; metaphorically, in view of v. 3, it refers to dishonouring the Messiah.

48. This sequence of thought is made clearer in English if we translate the first word of v. 5 (*de*) as 'and'. This is a common translation of *de*. It may also be translated as 'but'. The choice depends on context.

49. Examples of how verbal clues are given to show when husband or wife are in mind, not merely man or woman, may be seen in Rom. 7:2; 1 Cor. 7:2, 12, 39; Eph. 5:22. See *EFBT*, 297–298.

The ESV seeks to bring out an interpretation of 1 Corinthians 11 as being based on authority structures in marriage by sometimes translating *anēr* as 'husband' and *gunē* as 'wife'. This approach is driven by a belief that Paul is writing about veiling, coupled with a further belief that a veil was a sign that a woman was married (see ESV's footnote to v. 5).

This is not a helpful or correct approach to translating the text, for several reasons:

1. As we have seen, Paul is not writing about authority.
2. As we have seen, Paul is not writing about veils.
3. While (as we shall see below) the concept of marriage between one man and one woman plays an important part in Paul's reasoning, his thought also ranges more widely. For example, verse 11 refers to the spiritual unity of man and woman in the Lord; this is not limited to husband and wife but applies to all believers. His instructions about behaviour do not apply only to married people but to all men and women who lead in prayer or who prophesy.
4. The ESV's approach results in confusing oscillations and anomalies. In the ESV of verse 3 *anēr* is translated as 'man' in the first couplet and as 'husband' in the second couplet. But 'husband' is not mentioned again anywhere in the passage. Verses 4–5 become asymmetrical, with verse 4 seeming to apply to all men and verse 5 applying only to wives. Having referred to wives in verses 3–6, ESV makes Paul switch over to 'woman' in verses 7–9, back to 'wife' in verse 10, then to 'woman' in verses 11–12, back to 'wife' in verse 13, and then finally to 'woman' in verse 15. These multiple switches of meaning are not justified by any verbal features of the text. Nor do they illuminate the flow of Paul's reasoning.
5. The appropriate verbal clues for the meanings 'husband' and 'wife' rather than 'man' and 'woman' are not present anywhere in the text. Thus the NIV translates *anēr* and *gunē* as respectively 'man' and 'woman' throughout the passage. This retains the open texture of Paul's wording and allows his argument to be heard.[50]

To clear the path, we have had to work hard, cutting away misconceptions that Paul's meaning can be discerned by considering the doctrine of the

---

50. Schreiner agrees that, because of the lack of verbal clues to show that husband and wife are meant, this passage must refer to men and women in general: *WTTC*, 178. Smith 2012, 62–63, also agrees.

Trinity, or directly from word studies, or that he is writing about a hierarchical structure of men's authority over women, or about the wearing of veils, or giving instructions specifically to husbands and wives. 'The unfolding of your words gives light' (Ps. 119:130, ESV). At last, we are ready to unfold the words of verses 2–16 and gain some light. This will be the subject of our next chapter.

Summary of chapter 7

1. First Corinthians 11:3 is a framework statement which acts as a heading to Paul's remarks about praying and prophesying. It undergirds his reasoning.
2. Paul's meaning cannot be safely or convincingly settled by appeal to fine nuances of the doctrine of the Trinity.
3. Word studies show that 'authority over' and 'source' are possible metaphorical uses of *kephalē* (head) in verse 3. Usage elsewhere cannot determine Paul's intended meaning in this verse. This must be sought by examining the context.
4. The hierarchical interpretation which sees Paul's concern as being about men's authority over women cannot be right, because it conflicts with the text in eight respects. Of particular importance, the hierarchical interpretation makes it necessary to disregard the function of Paul's framework statement, to mistranslate verse 10 and to accept that Paul wrote verse 11 the wrong way around.
5. In the relevant cultural context, women's hair was regularly on display rather than hidden by a veil (compare 1 Tim. 2:9; 1 Pet. 3:3). But pagan practices in Corinth encouraged dishonourable sexual behaviour, both heterosexual and homosexual, and this was an issue for the Corinthian church. Men's long hair, and women's long hair let down loose instead of fastened up on top of the head, both suggested a willingness to engage in such conduct.
6. There are multiple difficulties in reading the passage as concerned with veils. Paul is writing about how hair is worn, not about the veiling of women. Properly translated, verses 2–16 are about hairstyles throughout, not about veils.
7. The NIV is correct to translate *anēr* and *gunē* as respectively 'man' and 'woman' throughout the passage, and not as 'husband' and 'wife'.

Questions to consider

1. At this stage, what are your reactions to the discussion of how verse 10 should be translated?

2. Does chapter 7 persuade you that 1 Corinthians 11:2–16 is about hair, not veils? If so, why? If not, why not?

3. Do you currently think that Paul is writing about a hierarchy of authorities in verses 2–16, or not? Does your view have any practical consequences for you? What are they?

> They were all filled with the Holy Spirit and spoke the word of God
> boldly.   (Acts 4:31, NIV)

Paul's outline

Having cleared away some misconceptions about 1 Corinthians 11:2–16, we can turn to the more positive task of identifying the steps in Paul's reasoning and gaining a coherent understanding of what he writes.

Paul is here giving instructions about assembled worship in a semi-public setting. This is part of a longer discussion of worship which occupies 1 Corinthians 11 – 14. During worship, unbelievers or enquirers may come in (14:24). He does not want the Corinthians to cause anyone to stumble (10:32). After discussing several aspects of assembled worship, he concludes with the crisp summary: 'All things should be done decently and with order' (14:40).[1]

Orderliness is a particular focus in chapter 14, decency and honour in 11:2–16. Here Paul is concerned with sexual propriety, against a Corinthian background of immorality, both heterosexual and homosexual.

We have seen that a hierarchical interpretation of head as authority does not fit with what Paul writes. The most widely held alternative is to understand head

---

1. Some have argued from the phrase 'when you come together' in 11:17–18 that in 11:2–16 Paul is not concerned with assembled worship. This is unpersuasive: see chapter 9, 167.

as source. The next step is to try this out, combined with our understanding that Paul is writing about hairstyles throughout. If we accept that Paul's theological motif in verse 3 is sources, and that his subject matter is hairstyles worn during assembled worship, we will find that he is making a continuous, logical and connected argument.[2]

On that basis, his progression of thought in verses 2–16 is as follows:

- Verse 2 is an introductory remark.
- Verse 3 is a brief theological statement concerning sources of creation and redemption of men and women, which undergirds Paul's subsequent reasoning in verses 4–12.
- Verse 4 is Paul's instruction to men, and verses 5–6 his instruction to women, concerning long hair hanging down.
- Verses 7–12 contain his theological reasoning, unpacking his keynote statement, and including a further instruction about hair to men in verse 7 and to women in verse 10. The first two couplets from verse 3 are employed in verses 7–10. The third couplet is employed in verses 11–12.
- Verses 13–15 give additional supporting reasons – verse 13 from the Corinthians' own sense of propriety, and verses 14–15 from nature.
- Verse 16 is Paul's concluding remark.

A sources and hairstyles interpretation, verse by verse

[2] And I praise you that in all things you have remembered me and you are holding fast the traditions just as I handed them on to you.
Paul commends the Corinthians for holding fast the traditions that he had delivered to them. These traditions evidently did not include wearing long hair hanging down while praying or prophesying, so he now needs to instruct them.

---

2. It is therefore unnecessary to discuss in detail the third proposal, that *kephalē* indicates prominence. Certainly, *kephalē* is sometimes used metaphorically in that sense. But Paul gives no signal that this is the meaning of his metaphor. Compared with the sources proposal, this meaning is a poor fit with what Paul writes and does not illuminate the flow of his argument.

*³ But I want you to realize that the Messiah is the head of every man [anēr], and the man is head of woman, and God is head of the Messiah.*³
His argument is Christ-centred. He starts from the facts of creation and redemption, viewed in the light of the Messiah's work. If 'head' connotes 'source', the three couplets in verse 3 are in an order that is both logical and chronological:

- *The Messiah is the source of every man.* The first couplet refers to the creation of man in Genesis 1 – 2. Paul has already reminded his readers at 1 Corinthians 8:6 that the Messiah is the agent of creation, including the creation of Paul and his readers ('Jesus Christ, through whom are all things and we through him'; see also John 1:3; Col. 1:16; Heb. 1:2). With this insight, therefore, the Messiah was understood as the source of all men in creation (and in particular of Adam, the representative everyman). In the Genesis account, 'man' sometimes means mankind (human beings) and sometimes specifically a male (see chapter 5 above). Paul exploits a similar ambiguity here (*anēr* can include women, as in Acts 17:34). This is the first step and the first couplet.
- *The man is source of woman.* In the account in Genesis 2, man was the source of woman (Gen. 2:21–24). This is the second step and the second couplet.
- *God is source of the Messiah.* Mankind fell under the lure of the serpent (Gen. 3) and a deliverer was promised (Gen. 3:15). Logically and chronologically the coming of the deliverer from God is a subsequent step. Earlier in the letter Paul has already referred to the Messiah as having come from God to bring redemption (1 Cor. 1:30 NIV: 'Christ Jesus, who has become for us wisdom from God – that is, our righteousness, holiness and redemption'; see also John 3:16–17; Gal. 4:4–5). The third couplet therefore refers primarily to the Messiah having come from God as the promised redeemer.

Before moving on we need to note that the third couplet also has a secondary reference. It completes a circle, because it ends with the Messiah, where the first couplet began. Therefore, the third couplet implies that all these facts of

---

3. My translation tries to reflect the Greek accurately by using the same English word order as NASB and NRSV, not ESV or NIV. However, the differing order seems to make little difference to how an English reader understands the meaning of the couplets.

creation and redemption (the Messiah being the source of every man, the man being source of woman and God being source of the Messiah) come from God.

Paul's framework statement in verse 3 undergirds the instructions which he gives and provides the theological basis of his reasoning through to verse 12. This reasoning involves an ordered application of the ideas contained in the three couplets, each being reflected in turn in his exposition.[4] The first couplet (the Messiah as creative source of man) underlies verses 4 and 7a. The second couplet (man as source of woman in creation) underlies verses 5–6 and 7b–10. The third couplet (primarily, God as source of Messiah and, secondarily, both creation and redemption being from God) underlies verses 11–12. These applications are further explained below. Paul's underlying idea is that these statements about sources point to God's creative and redemptive purposes for men and women, and hence to what is or is not honourable behaviour.

[4] Every man praying or prophesying with long hair hanging down dishonours his head. [5] And every woman praying or prophesying with her hair let down loose on her head dishonours her head – it is just the same as the shaved woman.

Remarks about dishonour can be somewhat opaque to people in modern Western cultures, but Paul's characterization of the issues in these terms would have been readily understandable in the honour–shame culture within which he was writing.

The statement that the Messiah is the head/source of every man carries with it an allusion to the purpose for which man was created. Every man who prays or prophesies with long hair hanging down like the hair of a woman (hinting at his availability for homosexual liaisons) is dishonouring the Messiah, his source, because his behaviour looks like a rejection of the purpose assigned to him at creation.

Similarly, the statement that the man is head/source of woman carries with it an allusion to the purpose for which woman was created. Every woman who prays or prophesies with her hair down, hinting at availability for illicit sexual relations, is dishonouring man, her source in creation, because she appears to be rejecting her creation calling to be one man's exclusive partner in a monogamous marriage.

This understanding of Paul's meaning in verses 4–5 follows by implication from what he has said in verse 3 and is subsequently confirmed by verses 7–9. The 'shaved woman' is explained next.

---

4. *DBE*, 146, 152 (Fee) misses this.

⁶ For if a woman does not have her hair fastened up, she should be shorn, and since it is a disgrace for a woman to have her hair shorn or shaved, she should fasten it up.

Paul's argument is: If a woman insists on having her hair hanging loose, this insistence shows that she is determined to be sexually promiscuous. In that case she deserves to receive the punishment and disgrace of an adulteress, which is to have her hair cut off.[5] She should avoid this by fastening up her long hair (*katakaluptō*).

⁷ For indeed a man ought not to fasten up his hair on his head, since he is the image and glory of God; but the woman is the glory of man.

Here Paul provides further explanation and justification. He has just indicated that a woman should *katakaluptō*, that is, fasten up her long hair. He now makes clear that a man should not *katakaluptō*. To do this would be to adopt a woman's hairstyle. The point of the instruction in verse 7 is that Paul does not want his ban on men's long hair hanging down (v. 4) to be taken as suggesting that long hair on a man is acceptable provided that it is fastened up (compare v. 14). The man should not behave effeminately (by having long hair) at all, because of his calling to be the image and glory of God.[6] This echoes the first couplet, which referred to the creation of every man. If every man is made to be the image of God, God's representative, he should be creative, procreating and filling the earth. If a man behaved as a woman, this would be a rejection of this creation calling.

Verse 7 twice uses the term 'glory': man is the image and glory of God, and woman is the glory of man.[7] The word 'glory' has multiple shades of meaning. The meaning which fits the context here is the rich sense of something that one glories in or takes delight in, and which also reflects honour back onto oneself, as in 1 Thessalonians 2:20 ('you are our glory and our joy').[8]

---

5. *M&W*, 172; Hurley 1981, 169.
6. The image of God is 'the royal function or office of human beings as God's representatives and agents in the world, given authorized power to share in God's rule over the earth's resources and creatures': Middleton 1994, 11–12.
7. In referring to the woman, Paul is careful not to repeat 'image and', as if woman were man's image, because he knows from Gen. 1:27 that woman is God's image, not man's image.
8. Compare the honour and dishonour in Prov. 12:4: 'A good wife is the crown of her husband, but she who brings shame is like rottenness in his bones' (NRSV).

Paul's remark is derived directly from the creation story, where God takes delight in mankind, who is the image set up in God's honour (Gen. 1:27, 31). Consistently with being the image and glory of God, man should not dishonour God by rejecting his creation calling. In turn, woman is man's 'glory'. He rightly takes delight in her (Gen. 2:23), not (sexually) in another man.

⁸ For man is not from woman, but woman from man; ⁹ for also neither was man created because of the woman, but woman because of the man.

We earlier noted the need for the reader to receive confirmation of the meaning of the head metaphor which Paul uses in verse 3. The meaning 'source' has been suggested by his allusion to the creation story in verse 7. The points that Paul picks up next from the creation story (verses 8–9) are transparently about sources. These points therefore provide definite confirmation of this meaning.

The contents of verses 8 and 9 are a double explanatory reason for what he has just said in verse 7, in the format: 'for . . . ; for also . . .' They are based on Genesis 2:18, 23–24.⁹ The first part of the explanation is 'for man is not from woman, but woman from man'. The second part of the explanation is 'for also neither was man created because of the woman, but woman because of the man'. This explanation picks up the second couplet of verse 3, where Paul referred to man being the source of woman. In this double explanation Paul goes beyond mere allusion and implication. He explicitly joins together *source* in creation (v. 8) with *purpose* of creation (v. 9).

Many English versions translate verse 9 in a similar way to NIV: 'neither was man created for [*dia*] woman, but woman for [*dia*] man.' Some have read this as if Paul were making a point about subordination, namely, that woman was created for the use of the man, as his junior assistant, whereas man, as the person in charge, was not created for the woman to use. But the Greek preposition *dia*, when followed (as here) by a noun in the accusative case, is regularly translated into English as 'because of' or 'for the sake of', and this meaning fits the context. Paul's point is not about hierarchy but about purpose. Paul's reasoning is still concerned with God's purposes for men and women, as derived from Genesis 1 – 2. He is following through on the basic ideas in the first two couplets of verse 3: through Christ, who is the agent of creation, every

---

9. On Paul's reliance on the details of the Genesis creation accounts, see my remarks in the Preface.

man is made to be God's steward of the earth; then woman is made from man in order to be his helper (Gen. 1:27–28; 2:18–24).

We saw in chapter 5 that this means woman is made to be man's powerful ally. Part of her purpose is to help the man in the care of God's creation (1:28; 2:15). And, since it is not good for the man to be alone, she will answer his need by being his intimate companion (Gen. 2:18, 24). One aspect of God's purpose for the woman is of particular relevance in the present context: she is to be man's sexual partner in monogamous heterosexual marriage (Gen. 2:18, 20, 24). By joining together in this way they will be able to fulfil the command to multiply and to subdue the earth (Gen. 1:27–28). Sexual relations outside such a marriage are not consistent with these purposes, so it is dishonourable for these activities to be hinted at by the way men and women wear their hair during public worship, whether by a man's long hair hanging down (1 Cor. 11:4), by a woman's long hair hanging loose (v. 5) or (probably only hypothetically in the Corinthian assembly) by a man's long hair being fastened up (v. 7).

The negative elements in verses 8–9 ('man is not from woman'; 'neither was man created because of the woman') serve to emphasize Paul's point about purpose because they emphasize the order of creation and the differentiation of man and woman. Paul may have in mind not only that human sexuality depends upon differentiation but also that it has an irreversible order, for procreation is accomplished by the man giving and the woman receiving.[10]

[10] Because of this a woman ought to have authority over her head, because of the messengers.

On the basis that the whole passage is about hair, and is not about men's authority over women, the meaning of 'Because of this a woman ought to have authority over her head' becomes clear.

We noted above that in Paul's structure:

- verse 10 is a conclusion about the proper behaviour of women;
- this conclusion *is consistent with* what he says about women's behaviour in verses 5–6;

---

10. We noted in chapter 5 that this differentiation of man and woman could permit a distinctive responsibility of leadership for the man, but that the Genesis text did not go as far as affirming such a responsibility. So also here. Although Paul emphasizes differentiation between man and woman, he makes no statement here about any male leadership.

- it *stands in contrast with* what he says about the proper behaviour for men in verse 7;
- and it *follows from* his reasoning in verses 7–9.

Paul says in verse 10 that a woman ought to have authority over her head. In context, this means that she ought to exercise her authority over it by fastening up her hair. This *is consistent with* what Paul says about women's behaviour in verses 5–6 (they should not have their hair hanging down loose when praying or prophesying but should fasten it up). It *stands in contrast with* what he says about the proper behaviour for men in verse 7 (a man should not fasten up his hair). And we may readily see how verse 10 *follows from* his reasoning in verses 7–9. Verse 10 starts with 'Because of this', which refers back to those verses. In other words, because of God's creation purposes for man and woman, in which woman is to be man's faithful partner, she should fasten up her hair, for unfastened hair at Corinth would imply willingness to be an unfaithful partner.[11]

At the end of the verse Paul gives an additional reason for a woman to exercise control over her hair: literally, 'because of the messengers'. The word he uses for messenger is *angelos*. When the context shows that a messenger is from the spiritual realm, it is customary to translate this word into English as 'angel' (see Heb. 1:13–14).

Paul may have in mind here that angels rejoiced at creation ('when I laid the earth's foundation . . . all the angels shouted for joy' – Job 38:4–7, NIV) and they now observe how the church, the pilot project of God's new creation, lives and worships (see 1 Cor. 4:9; 1 Tim. 5:21; Luke 15:10). If the women are not ashamed to let their hair down in the presence of fellow believers, they should at least be ashamed to do so in the presence of angels. Conceivably, there might also be a glance back to 1 Corinthians 6:3, where Paul indicates that in the age to come Christian believers will judge angels, for the woman's exercise of authority over her own head, and her praying and prophesying, show the angels her status in Christ. Or perhaps, if she is going to judge angels, she should show her ability to make right judgments now, by fastening up her hair.

However, there is nothing in the context which indicates that heavenly messengers are meant. It seems more likely that Paul has human messengers in mind. He is concerned about appearances. In the words concluding the previous

---

11. Padgett 2011, 112, places a different interpretation on v. 10. He takes it to mean that women ought to have freedom to wear their hair however they want. But this interpretation runs contrary to the whole thrust of Paul's reasoning.

section of the letter and leading into this section Paul has stated his concern
that the Corinthians should do everything for the glory of God, not giving unnecessary offence to anyone, so that others may be saved (10:31–33; see also
9:19–22). A similar concern surfaces again later in this section on worship
(14:23). Paul's point may be that honourable behaviour will avoid outsiders or
spies concluding, and reporting back to others, especially civic authorities
or synagogue leaders, that Christians have loose sexual morals.[12]

The recipients of his letter in Corinth, where he had previously ministered
in person, would have been in a good position to know whether Paul meant
'angels' or 'human messengers'. If not, they could ask the bearer of the letter
what Paul had in mind.[13] We are not in that position, and cannot ask, so must
leave the question open. This uncertainty does not affect the overall understanding of what Paul is saying in verses 2–16.[14]

[11]*Nevertheless, in the Lord woman is not separate from man, nor is man separate from woman.*

We noted earlier that the first word of verse 11 is *plen*, which is often translated
as 'nevertheless'. Paul typically uses *plen* to introduce a contrast, in the sense of
highlighting for his readers something that he particularly wants to emphasize
as important, and which differs from what he has just said in the preceding
sentence.[15] In the context of the 'sources' interpretation, Paul is using *plen* in
verse 11 in his usual way.

He has been focusing on God's creation purposes for men and women. But
in chapter 7 Paul was teaching that those purposes, though they remain valid in
this present life, have been relativized and reduced in importance by the coming
of Christ to redeem the world, so that the new creation has begun and the end
is in sight.[16] He has the same double perspective here (creation and, more
importantly, redemption). He maintains a consistency of perspective by means
of the qualification which he introduces with *plen*.

---

12. Compare Paul's parallel but different concern about spies in Gal. 2:4. Winter 2003,
88–91, in the context of his 'veils' interpretation of 1 Cor. 11, favours the view that
Paul is referring to human messengers.
13. The bearer was probably Titus. See 2 Cor. 7:2–16 and Mosse 2007, 304–307.
14. Use of the English term 'messengers' reflects the open connotations of Paul's
choice of word, provided it is understood that the messengers could be earthly
or heavenly.
15. See his other four uses of this word in Eph. 5:33; Phil. 1:18; 3:16; 4:14.
16. See chapter 2 above.

Verses 7–9 were about creation, with implicit reference to the union of man and woman in marriage in order to fulfil God's creation purpose, and verse 10 was a statement about something that a woman should do on her own, that is, to control her hair. But what is the position 'in the Lord', that is, in the Messiah, who came from God, as signalled in the third couplet of verse 3? This is more important than what he has just said about creation.[17] The position is: 'in the Lord woman is not separate from [*chōris*] man, nor is man separate from woman.' This refers to the unity of man and woman redeemed in Christ.[18] This unity in the Lord goes beyond the created unity available to husband and wife (Gen. 2:24); it is a deeper and broader unity of men and women, who are now redeemed together, being united in the Messiah. This is a similar line of thought to Galatians 3:28: 'there is not "male and female" [Gen. 1:27], for you are all one in Christ Jesus.'

Note also that verse 11 begins the right way around. Because verse 10 is a statement about what a woman should do on her own, verse 11, in order to be a contrast, needs to begin with a statement about woman not being separate from man. It does.

So Paul is saying that the most important thing here is that God has redeemed men and women so as to be united in Christ. Throughout verses 4–10 Paul has been *differentiating* between men and women as created beings, whose differing hairstyles should be consistent with the complementarity of their sexuality. But now he is taking up the primary meaning of the third couplet of verse 3 and emphasizing that in Christ they are *not separated* from each other. This spiritual unity is expressed in the fact that men and women are together leading in worship by praying and prophesying.

[12] For just as the woman is from the man, so also is the man through the woman. And all these things are from God.
Next, Paul adds further support for his qualification to the separation of men and women.

---

17. Contrasted with the Genesis creation, this redemption in the Lord brings into existence a new creation, as Paul says in 2 Cor. 5:17 ('if anyone is in Christ: a new creation!'). See further Titus 3:5 (*palingenesia*) with Matt. 19:28.

18. 'Separate from' is an ordinary meaning of *chōris*: compare 2 Cor. 12:3; Eph. 2:12; Heb. 11:40. Payne says in *M&W*, 191, following Thiselton, that the translation 'independent of', which is used in many English versions (including ESV, NIV, NRSV), adds a nuance which is absent from the Greek word.

In verse 12 Paul makes two statements. First, he says 'for just as the woman is from the man, so also is the man through the woman'. Here he is deriving support from creation. Even in creation men and women are not fully separated but derive life from one another. Second, he adds 'and all these things are from God'.[19]

Here he exploits the secondary meaning of the third couplet. We saw above that it completes a circle, ending with the Messiah, where the first couplet began, implying that both creation and redemption come from God. All these things that Paul has been writing about come from God, namely, the Messiah being the source of every man in creation, man being the source of woman in creation, God being the source of the Messiah who unites men and women in redemption, and the interdependence of man and woman in creation.

The implications of these two statements are that (1) creation affirms that men and women need each other's contribution; and (2) because everything is from God, he should be honoured in how Christian believers, both men and women, make their vocal contributions to worship.

Here Paul reaches the end of his deployment of the ideas from the three couplets. Next, he adds some different lines of reasoning in support of what he has said about hairstyles worn by men and women during assembled worship.

[13] Judge among yourselves: Is it fitting for a woman to pray to God with her hair let down?
To reinforce his point about women's appropriate behaviour, Paul now adds a cultural argument. He invites the Corinthians to judge for themselves whether it is proper for a woman to pray in the assembly with her hair let down. They were able to make this judgment because in Corinth they well knew that hair let down, other than in a fully private setting or the special case of a bereavement, suggested illicit sexual availability.

[14] Does not even nature herself teach you that indeed if a man wears long hair, it is a dishonour to him, [15] but if a woman has long hair, it is her glory? For long hair is given to her for a wrap.
Paul now moves on to an argument from nature. He reinforces the point made in verse 7, where he made clear that the solution to the men's long hair hanging

---

19. Greek: *ta de panta ek tou theou*. The word *panta* with the definite article *ta* commonly refers back to what has just been mentioned – as in 1 Cor. 12:6, 17; 2 Cor. 4:15; 5:18. Hence the translation 'all these things' brings out the meaning more fully than 'all things'.

down was not that it should be fastened up. He is now indicating that the men's hair should be short.

Verse 14 only makes sense when interpreted in its historical and cultural context. Paul is not stupid. He knows perfectly well that, left to nature, a man's hair will grow long, so he cannot mean that long hair in itself is unnatural for a man. And he cannot mean that having long hair is inherently dishonourable for a man, for a Jew (like Paul himself) who took a vow was under obligation not to cut his hair during the period of the vow (Num. 6:1–21; Judg. 16:17; see also Acts 18:18; 21:20–26).

Paul is not concerned with men's long hair in general. His concern arises in the cultural context, where it implies dishonourable availability for homosexual liaisons. Paul's reasoning is implied, because it is not necessary for him to spell it out: for men to wear long hair in Corinth is dishonourable because homosexual liaisons are against nature (in modern terms, human biology) as created by God. When he mentions 'nature' and 'dishonour' he is using the same terminology as in his critique of homosexual activities in Romans 1:26–27.[20]

Paul did not use an argument from biology in verse 13, to restrict women's loose hair, because it is not against human nature for a woman to be sexually available to a man. But he now makes a different argument from nature as regards women.

A woman's long hair is her natural, created glory – it is given to her as (or 'for' or 'instead of') a wrap; in other words, it is a beautiful, natural covering. When wrapped around (fastened up), it crowns her head.

The lesson from nature in verses 14–15 is that a woman's long hair is a glorious wrap for her, but it is not fitting for a man to adopt, or appear to adopt, the sexual role of a woman by making his hair look like a woman's hair. Therefore, in the cultural context at Corinth, to be aligned with what is in accordance with nature, men should wear their hair short.

---

20. *M&W*, 201–204, suggests that Paul here uses 'nature' in the Stoic sense of the origin and guarantor of culture, so that the appeal is to what appears natural, as regards the length of men's hair, in the particular cultural setting (compare Fee 1987, 526–527). The word for 'nature' here is *phusis*. The context in 1 Cor. 11 does not require this unusual meaning. Paul is not giving Stoic instruction to Stoics. No other use of *phusis* in the New Testament is a reference to culture. Consider Rom. 1:26; 2:14, 27; 11:21, 24; Gal. 2:15; 4:8; Eph. 2:3; Jas 3:7; 2 Pet. 1:4.

[16] And if anyone thinks to be contentious about this, we do not have such a custom, nor do the churches of God.

Paul now concludes his topic of hairstyles and sexual propriety during worship with his final reason. The Corinthians should accept what he writes because the custom of men and women praying and prophesying with long hair let down was the Corinthians' own; it was not something Paul had taught them (compare v. 2); nor was it a custom that was adopted in other assemblies of God's people.

Ten pointers

From the above commentary, we can pick out the following pointers to the substantial correctness of a sources and hairstyles interpretation:

1. The order in which the three couplets are stated in verse 3, which is logical and chronological, not hierarchical.
2. Paul's ordered use of each of the three couplets in verses 4–12, in the same order in which they were set out in verse 3.
3. Paul's confirmations of the meaning 'source' for 'head'.
4. Paul's linkage of sources to purposes to justify his instructions.
5. The plain meaning of verse 10, regarding the authority that a woman ought to have.
6. The nature of the contrast between verse 11 and verse 10.
7. The absence of any mention in verses 4–16 of Christ's authority over man, of man's authority over woman or of God's authority over Christ.
8. The consistency of Paul's reasoning throughout.
9. The lack of any pressure to mistranslate, whether in verse 10, verse 16 or anywhere else.
10. Full consistency with 1 Corinthians 7, where Paul treats men and women as equals in personal relations, and where his perspective holds creation and new creation together, with the latter being more important.

In sum, this sources and hairstyles interpretation is based on the precise words of what Paul writes. It takes into account the historical and cultural context. It is internally consistent. It shows how Paul's argument proceeds from the keynote statement of verse 3 in a smoothly logical and coherent way. And it is in harmony with what Paul writes elsewhere in the same letter.

Objections to a sources interpretation

Complementarian writings sometimes depict a 'sources' interpretation as a modern idea, newly invented by egalitarians to support their position.[21] But this is a mistake. Such an interpretation is attested in commentators whose native language was Greek and who were much closer to Paul's time than to the modern era. For example, Cyril of Alexandria (died 444) understood 'head' in verse 3 to mean 'source'.[22] Cyril was certainly not influenced by modern egalitarianism. He understood this metaphor in accordance with its context, just as Paul's first readers, who were Greek speakers, would have been able to do. Ambrosiaster, although writing in Latin, also understood 'head' as 'source' in verse 3.[23]

Schreiner rightly acknowledges that in verse 8, where Paul says that woman came from man, this obviously suggests the idea of 'source'. He nonetheless denies that verse 8 assists with understanding the meaning of 'head' in verse 3. The reason he gives is that 'Paul uses this argument from source to prove that woman is the glory of man'.[24] But this is no reason at all; it is an acknowledgment that Paul is using an argument from source.

---

21. For example, Smith 2012, 59, advises her readers that interpreting *kephalē* in 1 Cor. 11:3 as 'authority over' is the historic understanding while interpreting it as 'source' has been argued 'in recent years'.

22. *De Recte Fide ad Arcadiam* 1.1.5.5(2).63. The full quotation is cited by Grudem in *EFBT*, 569. Grudem's own translation of Cyril's text reads: 'Christ is the head of every man: for man was made through him. . . . "the head of a woman is the man", for she was taken out of his flesh. . . . And similarly, "the head of Christ is God", for he is from him according to nature.' Grudem prefers to say that Cyril understands the metaphor of 'head' as meaning 'beginning' rather than 'source', but in the context of the quotation there is no material difference, as it is clear that Cyril is referring to man being made through Christ, to woman being derived from man in creation, and to Christ as coming from God. Some further citations from other ancient authors are given in *M&W*, 131, 136–137. Grudem disputes their significance, but it is not necessary to discuss them. The clear example from Cyril is sufficient to demonstrate that understanding 'head' as connoting 'source' in 1 Cor. 11:3 is not a modern idea, and was apparent to an educated Greek-speaking reader many centuries ago.

23. Ambrosiaster was writing no later than 384. For references, see *M&W*, 137.

24. *RBMW*, 122. In Schreiner 2018, 232, he links this expressly to Gen. 2:21–23.

Based on Grudem's analysis, Schreiner states that the metaphorical meaning 'source' for *kephalē* is 'never certainly attested'.[25] This is mistaken, as we saw when we considered Grudem's word studies. There are clear examples both in secular works and in Paul's letters. Schreiner fairly acknowledges that the meaning 'source' is possible in both Colossians 2:19 and Ephesians 4:15. But in any event it is context that finally determines the meaning of a metaphor.

Schreiner says that *kephalē* never bears the meaning 'source' in the Septuagint.[26] It is not necessary to examine whether this is correct, for Paul was under no obligation to limit himself to metaphors found in the Septuagint. It is Paul's own usage in context that determines the meaning of his metaphor. His usage was intelligible to Greek-speaking readers, as we see from Cyril and from the fact that there are examples of a similar usage by Philo. Moreover, the Jewish element in the Corinthian church should not have had any difficulty in understanding this metaphor, since biblical Hebrew, like secular Greek, linked 'head' with the concept of 'beginning' or 'source' (see, for example, Ps. 111:10, where 'the fear of the LORD is the beginning of wisdom', and the Hebrew word for 'beginning' is closely related to the Hebrew word for 'head').

It is sometimes said that a sources interpretation ascribes an unsatisfactory meaning to the first couplet, to the effect that Christ is the creative source of every man, for Christ is also the creative source of every woman. This is not a strong objection. Paul is free to choose the points which will support his argument, and hence to draw out that in God's creation Christ is the source of every man (which, as in Genesis, need not mean only every male) and, from the account in Genesis 2, that man is the source of woman. If the objection were sound, it would apply with equal force to the meaning ascribed to the first couplet by the hierarchical interpretation, since Christ is the authority over every woman just as much as over every man. Yet complementarian commentators do not see this as a valid objection to their interpretation.

It is also sometimes objected that 'head' as 'source' in verse 3 is unlikely, because the source relationships differ widely in their nature. Christ is not the source of man in the same way as man is the source of woman, and God is not the source of Christ in either of those two ways.[27] It is true that the source relationships differ widely. But this is not a valid objection. There is no justification for reading Paul's metaphor so woodenly as to require three identical relationships. The differences are obvious, and they do not impact on the points

---

25. *RBMW*, 119.
26. *RBMW*, 119.
27. Smith 2012, 60.

that Paul is making. If the objection were valid, it would apply just as much to an interpretation in terms of authority structures. On such an interpretation the authority of Christ over man, the authority of man over woman and the authority of God over Christ all differ greatly from each other. But complementarians do not view this as a valid objection to their interpretation.

The objections to a sources interpretation are unpersuasive.

Significance of Paul's teaching

'They were all filled with the Holy Spirit and spoke the word of God boldly' (Acts 4:31, NIV). Unholiness and speaking by the power of the Holy Spirit do not belong together.

Paul teaches that there should be a holy propriety in vocal contributions to assembled worship. His concern arises from the motives in 10:31 – 11:1: a concern for God's honour, and not giving unnecessary offence, so that Christian faith may be effectively commended to outsiders.

He has strong words to say about hairstyles for men and women in Corinth when they undertake the prominent task of praying or prophesying in the assembly. His concern is not about hair itself, but about the licentious message given by their hairstyles. Their conduct should honour God's purposes for men and women in creation. Those purposes include faithful, monogamous, heterosexual marriage (which Jesus expressly endorsed: see Matt. 19:3–9). But, more than that, though differentiated by their sexuality in creation, in redemption man and woman are united in the Lord. Men and women are interdependent and need each other's contributions. Prayer and prophecy should be undertaken by men and women in a way that honours God, the source both of creation and of redemption.

In cultures where loose long hair on men or women does not convey connotations of sexual impropriety, the specifics of Paul's instructions will not apply. But the principles remain the same. Men and women are not differentiated in their experience of redemption in Christ, but in this present life men and women are created to be different and complementary. God has revealed his purposes for human sexuality. Those who lead worship in prayer or by prophecy should not appear to condone forms and circumstances of sexual conduct which are contrary to those purposes.

The Danvers Statement cites verses 2–16 in support of the proposition: 'some governing and teaching roles within the church are restricted to men.' But this view depends upon importing into the passage words which are not there. Even if verses 2–16 were interpreted as being about veils rather than hair, and even if 'head' connoted 'authority' rather than 'source', Paul still says nothing explicit in this passage about restricting women's participation in governing and teaching roles within the church. A requirement to have a decorous hairstyle or to cover the head is not a restriction on participation in governing and teaching roles.[28]

The FIEC Women in Ministry Statement says: 'Paul roots the prohibition . . . of 1 Corinthians 11 both in creation (vv. 8–9) and the nature of the Godhead (v. 3).' This misreads what Paul draws from Genesis and relies on the misguided attempt to enlist the doctrine of the Trinity into the contest. It is not clear what relevant 'prohibition' is in view, since in 1 Corinthians 11 Paul places no restriction on the worship activities which women may lead.

We have seen that in 1 Corinthians 11 Paul is not writing for the purpose of defending an authority structure of man over woman. His remarks are directed to men as much as to women. If notions of male authority over women and restrictions on women's ministry are to be supported, this needs to be done by reference to other passages of Scripture.

Summary of chapter 8

1. Once we accept that Paul's theological motif in 1 Corinthians 11:3 is sources, and that his subject matter is hairstyles worn by those who prophesy or pray aloud during assembled worship, we find that he is making a continuous, logical and connected argument. There are at least ten pointers to the substantial correctness of a sources and hairstyles interpretation of what Paul writes. The objections to a sources interpretation are unpersuasive.

2. Paul's concern is not about hair itself, but about the dishonourable message given by the Corinthians' hairstyles. Their conduct should honour God's purposes for men and women as taught in Genesis and should not appear dishonouring and contrary to those purposes. Relevantly, those purposes involve faithful, monogamous, heterosexual marriage. Paul also emphasizes redemption in Christ: though differentiated by their sexuality in creation, in redemption man and woman are united in the Lord. Men and women are

---

28. Curiously, the CBE Statement refers to 1 Cor. 11:2–16 as a text which appears to 'restrict the full redemptive freedom of women' and must therefore be interpreted in relation to 'the broader teaching of Scripture'. Contrary to this assessment, Paul's text contains no apparent restriction on women's ministry or redemptive freedom as compared with men's.

interdependent and need each other's contributions. Prayer and prophecy should be undertaken by men and women in a way that honours God, the source both of creation and of redemption.

3. Paul says nothing in this passage about male authority over women. Nor does he say anything about reserving some governing and teaching roles within the church to men. If notions of male authority over women and restrictions on women's ministry are to be supported, this needs to be done by reference to other passages of Scripture.

Questions to consider

1. What ideas in chapter 8 are new to you? What do you think of them?
2. The Danvers Statement cites 1 Corinthians 11:2–16 in support of restricting some governing and teaching roles within the church to men. What do you think are the reasons for this citation?
3. Does Paul's teaching in 1 Corinthians 11:2–16 have practical implications in your own church context? What are they?

9. SILENT WOMEN? 1 CORINTHIANS 14

> Your word is a lamp for my feet,
>   a light on my path.
>   (Ps. 119:105, NIV)

Shameful speech?

First Corinthians 14:34–35 (ESV) says:

> [34] [T]he women should keep silent in the churches. For they are not permitted
> to speak, but should be in submission [*hupotassō*], as the Law also says. [35] If there is
> anything they desire to learn, let them ask their husbands at home. For it is shameful
> for a woman to speak in church.

Interpreting these verses is problematic. When read in the context of what Paul
writes elsewhere about women's vocal participation in worship, not least in the
same letter, they do not seem to fit in.

This apparent requirement for women, unlike men, to be silent in the
churches raises a head-on challenge to the egalitarian position on women's
ministries.

But complementarians also face a challenge here, because of the difficulty
of finding an interpretation which satisfactorily resolves the seeming contradiction. David Pawson speaks for many when he says:

> It would be foolish to deny that this is a 'difficult' passage (even to
> understand, never mind integrate!). The writer confesses to having found

no fully satisfying exposition, but is comforted by the fact that no one else
has either![1]

Discussions of verses 34–35 have focused on three main questions: (1) How
do they relate to verse 33? (2) What exactly does Paul mean in verses 34–35?
(3) Are these verses authentic?

In this chapter we consider the first two of these questions. The debate over
whether these verses are authentic is considered in the next chapter.

Relationship of verses 34–35 to verse 33

Paul's original Greek text would have had very little punctuation, not even
spaces between words, and quite likely no punctuation at all. English versions
are therefore free to decide how to present the relationship between verse 33
and verses 34–35.

The presentation in the ESV is typical of a number of modern versions. It
makes a paragraph division which splits verse 33 into two and attaches the
second half of it to verse 34:

> [29]Let two or three prophets speak, and let the others weigh what is said. [30]If a
> revelation is made to another sitting there, let the first be silent. [31]For you can all
> prophesy one by one, so that all may learn and all be encouraged, [32]and the spirits of
> prophets are subject to prophets. [33]For God is not a God of confusion but of peace.
> As in all the churches of the saints, [34]the women should keep silent in the churches.

In contrast, the traditional layout keeps verse 33 intact and puts a paragraph
break between the end of verse 33 and the beginning of verse 34, as currently
seen in the NIV:

> [29]Two or three prophets should speak, and the others should weigh carefully what
> is said. [30]And if a revelation comes to someone who is sitting down, the first speaker
> should stop. [31]For you can all prophesy in turn so that everyone may be instructed
> and encouraged. [32]The spirits of prophets are subject to the control of prophets.
> [33]For God is not a God of disorder but of peace – as in all the congregations of
> the Lord's people.
> [34]Women should remain silent in the churches.

---

1. Pawson 1988, 66, referring to 1 Cor. 14:33–38.

This traditional presentation was used for many centuries. It can be seen in very ancient surviving manuscript copies.[2]

Those who depart from the ancient layout argue that there is a lack of clear meaning in the statement 'for God is not a God of confusion but of peace, as in all the churches of the saints'. The reasoning is: (1) if taken word for word, it does not make much sense, as the Corinthians did not need to be told that God was the same in every congregation; and (2) to make sense of it, some additional words are needed to make Paul's point clear, for example, 'as *I teach* in all the churches of the saints'.[3]

This is a weak argument.

First, those who argue for the new layout see a problem where none exists. Paul's phrase 'for [*gar*] God is not a God of confusion but of peace' reads naturally as an additional point expressed parenthetically. Inserting a parenthetical comment introduced by *gar* is a standard Pauline usage.[4]

Once we understand that the *gar* phrase is parenthetical, we see that the concluding phrase of verse 33, 'as in all the churches of the saints', refers back to verses 31–32. This makes perfectly good sense. Paul's meaning is the same as if he had written: 'and the spirits of prophets are subject to prophets, as in all the churches of the saints, for God is not a God of confusion but of peace.' Paul's point is that orderly prophecy, as practised in churches everywhere other than Corinth, faithfully reflects God's peace.

Second, the new layout imposes an improbably clumsy construction which uses the phrase 'in the churches' (*en tais ekklēsiais*) twice in close proximity in the same sentence. Instead of solving a problem, it introduces one.

---

2. For example, in Codex Sinaiticus (fourth century). This can be seen online at <http://www.codexsinaiticus.org>. Ancient manuscripts generally show vv. 34–35 as a separate paragraph: Lavrinoviča 2017. Grudem appears to suggest, incorrectly, that the division between v. 33 and v. 34 was introduced in 1551 (*EFBT*, 234–235).

3. For (1), see *EFBT*, 234. The extra words as per (2) are added in Chrysostom, *1 Corinthians*, Homily 36 (in Greek) and in Codex Fuldensis (in Latin), presumably by analogy with 1 Cor. 4:17. In *RBMW*, 133, Carson wants a longer addition: 'The sentence can be salvaged only by understanding an additional phrase, such as: "and this principle must be operative in your church, as in all the congregations of the saints".'

4. For example, in Eph. 5:8–10 the phrase starting with *gar* in v. 9 is additional and parenthetical: 'walk as children of light – for [*gar*] the fruit of the light is in all goodness and righteousness and truth – proving what is pleasing to the Lord.' Other examples include Rom. 5:12–14; 7:1; 2 Cor. 5:6–8; 6:1–3. See Clarke 2001.

In addition, we will see in the next chapter that verses 34–35 are a unit which appears in different places in different manuscripts. In its alternative position, no part of verse 33 is attached to those verses.

In sum, there is no sufficient reason for departing from the traditional layout so as to split verse 33 into two. To do so is unwarranted and problematic.[5]

The context of verses 34–35

Having looked at the structural relationship between verses 34–35 and verse 33, we turn to the second question: what exactly does Paul mean? This is a difficult question because of the apparent inconsistency of these verses with other scriptures, especially other parts of the same letter and the overall thrust of his argument. To appreciate the extent of the inconsistency within 1 Corinthians, we first need to examine the context.

Earlier in the letter Paul has given instructions for when women, as well as men, are praying aloud and prophesying (11:2–16; see also Acts 2:16–18; 21:9).

Following on from 11:2–16, and continuing to address both men and women, he writes about the Lord's Supper, about spiritual gifts and about the primacy of unselfish love (11:17 – 14:1). In doing so he teaches in chapter 12 the giftedness of every person in 'the body of Christ', and so of both men and women.

It is uncontroversial that when he addresses his readers as 'brothers' (plural of *adelphos*), this is used as a generic term which includes women (11:33; 12:1; 14:6, 20, 26, 39).[6] In chapter 14 he says to the Corinthian believers, both men and women, that they should eagerly desire spiritual gifts, especially prophecy (v. 1). He says that he would like *all of them* to speak in tongues and even more to prophesy (v. 5). He gives detailed instructions for the exercise of these gifts in 14:1–25. Much like teaching (14:26), prophesying involves speaking to the assembled church for edification, encouragement and consolation (14:3–4).

---

5. We will see in chapter 10, 187, that Paul has a particular reason for pulling forward the *gar* phrase into a parenthetical position.
6. This is like the English word 'brother', with the plural 'brethren', which carried the same generic meaning until the twentieth century, but in contemporary English this meaning is not reliably understood unless spelled out as 'brothers and sisters'. See the entry for 'Brother', as meaning 'fellow-christian', with the plural 'brethren', in *The Shorter Oxford English Dictionary*, 3rd ed. (1944).

The problems that Paul is addressing towards the end of chapter 14 are plain from what he writes in verses 26–33 and 36–38. In their corporate worship the Corinthians were speaking in tongues and prophesying more than one at a time. And too many people were speaking in tongues. This was disorderly and unedifying. It was also disproportionate, since there should be space also for psalms (v. 26 – see also Eph. 5:19; Col. 3:16) and for teaching (v. 26). In verse 26 his word for teaching is *didachē*. This is the same word he uses for the kind of teaching he would himself deliver in the assembly (14:6). It appears here that both men and women may teach the assembly.[7]

So both speakers in tongues and prophets must exercise self-control. Two or three speakers in tongues are to contribute, each in turn, and be interpreted, and if there is no interpreter they are to exercise their gift silently (vv. 27–28). Similarly, two or three prophets are to contribute one by one, and the others are to weigh what is said (vv. 29–32). God is a God of peace, not of disorder (v. 33).

The Corinthians' disorderly worship is in contrast to what other churches do, and draws strong rebuke (vv. 33, 36–38). Verses 39–40 provide a summary which concludes Paul's discussion of worship before he moves on to the subject of the resurrection in chapter 15.

The nature of the inconsistency

In chapter 11 of his letter Paul gave instructions about the hairstyles of both men and women when they prayed or prophesied in the Corinthian church, as we saw above in chapters 7 and 8. But he placed no restriction on the *scope* of women's participation, compared with that of men.

Some scholarly discussions treat the issue of inconsistency as if the clash were solely with 11:2–16. But that considerably underplays the problem. While the inconsistent context starts at 11:2, it continues through to 14:33 (see especially 12:4–12; 14:1, 12, 24, 26, 29, 31). In chapters 12 and 14 Paul says 'all' over and over again (12:6, 11, 12, 13, 19, 26; 14:5, 18, 23, 24, 31). The immediate context at 14:26–33 is about orderliness and restraint, not about any general bans on types of speaking or on who may do it. The whole thrust up to verse 33 is that he positively wants all believers to exercise their spiritual gifts, but in a proper manner. Before verse 34 there is no trace of any restriction on who may contribute in accordance with their gifts.

---

7. This is consistent with what Paul writes about teaching in Col. 3:16. We consider teaching, and the significance of 1 Tim. 2:12, in chapters 11 to 13 below.

But if women must keep silent in the churches, they cannot engage in any of the speaking activities which Paul has discussed: praying aloud, prophecy, speaking in tongues, interpretation, bringing a psalm or teaching. Thus the inconsistency of verses 34–35 with what has gone before is sudden, stark and startling.

Verses 34–35 are likewise discordant with what follows after:

- In verse 39 Paul tells the *adelphoi* (brothers and sisters) to be eager to prophesy. A woman cannot both prophesy and remain silent.
- In 16:15–16 he tells the *adelphoi* to submit (*hupotassō* – the same verb as in 14:34) to the household of Stephanas and to everyone working together and labouring. Unless, very unusually, Stephanas had an exclusively male household, that would mean men among the believers submitting to both men and women. This is in line with what Paul writes elsewhere (see the topic of mutual submission discussed in chapters 3 and 4 above); but it is a different picture from the unilateral submission of all women as a group, which is demanded in verse 34 ('they should be put in subjection').[8]

Unsatisfactory attempts at harmonization

Many attempts have been made to resolve the inconsistency of verses 34–35 with their context. As Don Carson graphically puts it, 'The solutions that have been advanced are, like devils in certain instances of demon possession, legion.'[9]

This search for a solution has mostly been a modern activity. In traditional cultures women's silence was generally expected, so verses 34–35 excited relatively little concern. Public speaking by women, such as in Rome by the female orator Hortensia in the first century BC, occurred only as remarkable exceptions to the general rule. Tertullian (about 200) considered that women had the right to prophesy but should otherwise be silent. Chrysostom (about 390) was unconcerned about the exception for prophesying, because he considered that women's prophesying had ceased in the distant past, leaving complete silence

---

8. Grudem in *EFBT*, 193, 248–251, says that in 16:15–16 Paul is referring only to submission to male elders. This is mistaken (see the discussion in chapter 3, 36–37 above).
9. *RBMW*, 133.

as the order of the day. He saw no difficulty in explaining verses 34–35: 'And what may be the cause of setting them under so great subjection? Because the woman is in some sort a weaker being and easily carried away and light minded.'[10]

Many solutions propose that the ban on women's speaking in the assembly, although on the face of it unqualified, is only intended to be partial. So it is said, for example, the ban is only on asking questions, or on noisy or disruptive chatter, or on speaking in tongues, or on speaking to any less purpose than prophesying, or on failing to conform to the proper order of worship, or on teaching falsely, or on making an uneducated contribution.[11]

The primary obstacle to all solutions of this kind is that silence is enjoined in unqualified terms and this unqualified ban is stated three times ('women should be silent', 'they are not permitted to speak', 'it is disgraceful for a woman to speak in an assembly'). Each such phrase, even on its own, indicates a complete ban on women's speaking in the assembly. And the forcefulness of the complete ban is intensified by the rhetorical use of repetition. To make the same point three times in different ways was a common device in both Jewish and Graeco-Roman discourse for expressing maximal emphasis.[12] This combination of unqualified words and threefold repetition is therefore an extreme difficulty for all proposals that only a particular kind of speaking is being prohibited. Moreover, the contrast between the negative ban on speaking in the assembly and the positive suggestion of asking husbands at home (v. 35)

---

10. Tertullian, *Against Marcion* 5.8; Chrysostom, *1 Corinthians*, Homily 26 (cessation of prophesying); Homily 36 (the quotation in the text). Where Chrysostom perceives a difficulty requiring a solution, he says so: see, for example, what he says about 14:21–25, in the same homily. Since he regarded the women of his own times as incompetent, he was untroubled by vv. 34–35.

11. For details of a range of such proposals, and some others considered below, see *RBMW*, 138–139, 145–146 (Carson); *EFBT*, 238–247; *DBE*, 164–171 (Keener); *M&W*, 220–224; Fee 1987, 702–705; Bailey 2011, 410–417; Tidball 2012, 225–229; Schreiner 2018, 297–298.

12. For an Old Testament example, see Eccl. 8:17. For Greek, see Hermogenes, *Peri Ideōn (On Types of Style)* 287. For repetition in Roman oratory, see Quintilian, *Institutio Oratoria* 6.1.1–2, and the opening words of Cicero's *First Oration against Catiline*: '*quo usque tandem abutere, Catilina, patientia nostra? quam diu etiam furor iste tuus nos eludet? quem ad finem sese effrenata jactabit audacia?*' My translation: 'Until when, Catiline, will you keep on abusing our patience? How much longer will you mock us with your madness? When will you stop flailing around with your effrontery?'

reflects the widespread cultural distinction between the silence which was expected of women in the public sphere and their freedom to speak in private at home.[13]

Recognizing the absolute terms of the ban, some have sought a solution in limiting 11:2–16 instead. They suggest that this earlier section of the letter (1) was only concerned with private home or small-group gatherings rather than with the public assembly; or (2) made a temporary concession which Paul changed his mind about; or (3) regulated a practice which Paul allowed to pass for the sake of argument. All of these suggestions fail.

As to (1), Paul's concerns about honour and shame make a private context unlikely for 11:2–16. Another problem for this theory of private prophesying is that in 14:1–31 Paul wants prophecy to be for the benefit of the assembly, not something done in a corner. And in any event, a hard and fast distinction between small groups and public assemblies is unlikely in circumstances where the churches met in homes (Acts 18:7; Rom. 16:5; 1 Cor. 16:19; Col. 4:15; Phlm. 2), perhaps typically in the semi-public areas of dining room or courtyard.[14] The discussion in 11:2–16 is visibly part of a longer section about worship. The continuity from 11:2–16 to what follows is shown by 11:17 ('I do not give praise') picking up the language of 11:2 ('I praise you'). Verses 17–18 ('when you come together') cannot properly bear the weight of implying that verses 2–16 are about something done when people are not together. Most decisively, even if verses 2–16 were somehow limited to small, fully private meetings, this would still not provide a solution, because it would not remove the inconsistency of 14:34–35 with 12:1 – 14:33, which advocates of this theory agree are primarily about public worship.

As to (2), a temporary concession would jar both with Acts 2:16–18 and with 1 Corinthians 12:1 – 14:33, and Paul's change of mind would have had to occur after 14:31. This is not credible.

---

13. Some of these suggestions are additionally problematic because the behaviour in question would be no more desirable if done by men. Some commentators have pointed out that questions from uneducated people were not culturally acceptable. But this is of little help in explaining what Paul writes, because some women were educated and some men were not.

14. The most convenient places for meeting were in the homes of the wealthy. The dining room was a large room constructed for entertaining guests. The partly covered courtyard space could accommodate a meeting of perhaps from one to two hundred. On early Christian meeting places, see Capper 2005, 121–127. Other possible meeting places are discussed in Osiek 1997, 33–34; Brookins 2014, 148–150; Adams 2015.

As to (3), if Paul intended to ban women from all speaking in the assembly, he would scarcely have written what he did in chapter 11 for the sake of argument. Why would he waste valuable time and writing materials and issue instructions concerning prophecy by women in the presence of men if he intended to ban women from opening their mouths? Furthermore, the theory does not provide an answer to the problem, because it does not explain the inconsistency between verses 34–35 and what he writes about every member participation in chapter 12 and in chapter 14 up to verse 33.

Some have proposed that the ban on women's speaking in 14:34–35 applies only to wives, and that the women praying and prophesying in 11:2–16 are unmarried. But it is not reasonably possible to read 11:2–16 as being limited in that way, because there is nothing in the text to justify it. Such a limited application could not be guessed at before readers arrived at 14:34. Furthermore, even if 11:2–16 could be read in that limited way, the inconsistency of verses 34–35 with 12:1 – 14:33 would remain unresolved.

It is not unfair to say: 'Unsuccessful solutions abound, characterised by avoidance of the plain meaning of the text.'[15]

Armin Baum has proposed a different approach.[16] He relies on considerations of cultural background. He says that women's speaking is permitted in 11:2–16 because it there takes place on the conditions that it is (1) with men's permission and (2) in a way that is consistent with the preservation of women's chastity, whereas women's speaking is prohibited in 14:34–35 because in the latter context those two conditions are not fulfilled. He considers that verses 34–35 are an answer to the question: 'What do female church members have to do if their husbands and/or male church leaders do not permit them to speak in public church gatherings?' But there is no indication of this question in what Paul writes. Verses 34–35 state a general rule. He says nothing about male permission in 11:2–16 or about its absence in 14:34–35. There is no indication at verse 34 that Paul is turning his attention from speaking that has husbands' or male church leaders' permission to speaking that lacks that permission. In verse 34 the lack of permission is general and is supported by the law, not by a man withholding permission. And the proposal leaves unresolved the contradiction between verses 34–35 and 12:1 – 14:33, where Paul instructs the believers, both men and women, to use their speaking gifts in the assembly.

Recognizing that verses 34–35 on their face are inconsistent with Paul's teaching, and acknowledging the failure of proposals for harmonizing them

---

15. Capper 2005, 301.
16. Baum 2014.

with Paul's position, some have suggested that verses 34–35 state the position adopted by the Corinthians, which Paul then rebukes in verses 36–38. In support of this theory, it is widely agreed that Paul briefly cites wrong positions adopted by the Corinthians in various parts of this letter, in order to discuss and correct them (for example, in 6:12; 7:1; 8:1). However, the suggestion does not work here. Verses 36–38 are not framed as a protest against what he has just written in verses 34–35, but as a protest against *anyone who does not accept* what he has just written.[17] In addition, because verses 34–35 contain argumentation (two clauses starting with 'for') they are quite unlike the other instances where Paul quotes the Corinthians.

One proposal remains for consideration. The current front runner among interpretations proposed by those on the complementarian side of the discussion is that verses 34–35 are a prohibition on women taking part vocally in the evaluation of prophecies.[18] This is said to be implied from the context. We must consider whether this front runner can get as far as the finishing line.

Women not to evaluate prophecies?

Evaluating prophecies is an activity mentioned in verse 29. It is not spelled out explicitly in that verse that the results of the evaluation are spoken audibly in the assembly, but this seems to be implied from the context, and Paul's words are generally understood in this sense. The evaluation is one of the means for ensuring that what is said is edifying (v. 26).

Verse 29 as a whole covers two points: two or three prophets should speak (29a) and the others should evaluate what is said (29b). The front-running theory is that the first point is expanded in verses 30–33 (or 30–33a), which deal with orderly prophesying, and that the second point is expanded in verses 34–35 (or 33b–35), which state who may take part in the evaluation, namely, not women, who must remain silent.

This theory has a number of points in its favour. First, it proposes a unified context for verses 29–36, which is prophecies and their evaluation. Second, the logic of the suggested structure is appealing. Third, the words for being silent (*sigaō*) and for submitting (*hupotassō*), both of which are used in verse 34, also appear respectively in verses 28 and 30 (*sigaō*) and in verse 32 (*hupotassō*), where

---

17. Carson explains this with thoroughness in *RBMW*, 139–142.
18. Hurley 1981, 188–191; *RBMW*, 142–144 (Carson); *EFBT*, 233–235; Hensley 2012. This interpretation was first suggested in 1962 (see *M&W*, 222).

they are qualified by their immediate context. So it is appropriate to look for applicable contextual qualifications when the same words are used again in verse 34.

However, despite its evident attractions, this theory suffers from the fatal defect that it bears no proper relation to the words in the text. This can be seen from the following ten considerations:

1. Although verses 29–33 are about prophets, there is not actually anything in the lead-in to verses 34–35 which indicates that they are to be understood as an expansion or qualification of what Paul has said about prophets.

2. Verses 34–35 themselves do not contain any express mention either of prophecies or of evaluation.

3. Like other theories which limit verses 34–35 to a particular kind of speaking, this theory runs up against the problem of the threefold absolute ban on all speaking. These verses do not contain even so much as an implied pointer that, despite this forceful and unqualified ban, their real purpose is much narrower, namely, only to stop women from stating their evaluations of prophecies. As Schreiner pithily puts it: 'Paul forbids speaking in general and gives no clue that judging prophecies is specifically in view.'[19]

4. Despite the negative assessment from points 1–3, let us see whether the context can somehow imply the proposed limitation on verses 34–35. We can see that the subject of prophesying and of evaluating prophecies is mentioned before (in vv. 29–32) and that prophets and prophesying are mentioned again after (in vv. 37, 39). So verses 34–35 might have something to do with those topics. But how can we get to the proposed limitation that the ban on women's speaking relates *specifically and only to evaluation*? There is no verbal signal in verses 34–35 to point to that conclusion, and there is nothing in Paul's earlier or subsequent reasoning which points to it. Are readers supposed to deduce that the ban is on evaluation by women because it is clear from 11:2 – 14:33 that Paul permits women to prophesy? This does not follow, because it is equally clear from 11:2 – 14:33 that women are given spiritual gifts, including gifts of discernment, and in 14:26–31 Paul is permitting men and women to evaluate prophecies (see further point 8 below).

5. Even if we regard verses 34–35 as having something to do with the evaluation of prophecy, this does not resolve the inconsistency with the remainder of the letter. In fact, it highlights it even further. Paul's goal for prophecy and interpretation (vv. 29–30) is that all may learn (*manthanō*) together in the assembly (v. 31). But verses 34–35 are clearly indicating that women

19. Schreiner 2018, 297.

cannot even ask a question in the assembly for the purpose of learning. If they 'wish to learn [*manthanō*] anything' they must ask their husbands at home.[20]

6. Grudem seeks to explain the instruction to ask husbands at home as an anti-avoidance measure: women might otherwise artfully evade the restriction on evaluating prophecies by dressing up their evaluations in the form of questions posed in the assembly.[21] But this proposal does not advance the argument, since it first has to be shown from the text that verses 34–35 are aimed specifically at restricting the evaluation of prophecies. The indication that women should ask their questions at home instead of in the assembly is the only stated example of the practical effect of the ban. Asking questions is not on the face of it the same activity as giving an evaluation of whether a prophecy is from the Lord. If Paul intended to ban women only from evaluating prophecy in the assembly, he was clumsily misleading his readers by including, as his only example, a different activity.

7. Associated with this theory is an idea that evaluation must be by male teaching elders who have authority over the assembly. But this is not what 14:29 says about who exercises the gift of discernment. Evaluation is by the other prophets, not by male teaching elders. Paul nowhere presents this gift as exercised by a separate male group of teachers or elders who stand over the prophets in order to evaluate what they say. Moreover, Paul does not regard prophets (or those among them who have the gift of discernment) as less authoritative than teachers. He lists prophets after only apostles, and before teachers (12:28; compare Eph. 2:20). If we say that Paul's concern in verses 34–35 is to do with maintaining a proper authority structure, we are missing the main force of what Paul is writing. From chapter 12 onwards he is concerned to secure the proper exercise of spiritual gifts. He does not say anything about the proper exercise of gifts being secured through appropriate authority structures. Paul's key to the proper exercise of gifts is the primacy of unselfish love (chapter 13). Love uses gifts not selfishly or thoughtlessly but in order to build others up. This is given practical expression in chapter 14.

8. Let us consider 14:29 more closely. It says: 'the others should discern.' Who are 'the others'? There are three possibilities of who 'the others' could refer to.

---

20. Reflecting a variation in manuscripts, UBS 4th edition here shows *manthanein* shortened to *mathein*. Codex Sinaiticus has *manthanein*. But there is no difference in meaning. Here ESV translates accurately as 'If there is anything they desire to learn'. NIV softens this to 'If they want to inquire about something'.

21. *EFBT*, 234.

(1) The natural reading is that it refers to the other prophets. On the basis of 11:2 – 14:29 this group includes both men and women. (2) The first possibility may be refined by suggesting that those who discern are all those members of the group of prophets who have the gift of discernment mentioned in 12:10. There is nothing from 12:1 to 14:29 which indicates that the gift of discernment, unlike other gifts, is allotted to men only. (3) Just conceivably, the phrase 'the others' could refer to the whole assembly. If so, women are again included. So, whichever of these three possibilities is correct, 'the others' in verse 29, who evaluate prophecy in the assembly, include women. Thus the theory that in verses 34–35 Paul is excluding women from evaluating prophecy stands in direct conflict with verse 29.

9. When Grudem discusses the rival theory that Paul's concern was only to get rid of noisy or disruptive chatter, he rightly says that this view does not fit Paul's solution, for if this had been the problem, Paul would have expressly forbidden women's disorderly speech, not all speech by women.[22] But precisely the same objection applies to the 'weighing of prophecies' theory. If the problem that Paul perceived had been the weighing of prophecies by women in the assembly, he would have expressly forbidden women to weigh prophecies; instead verses 34–35 forbid them to speak at all.

10. The concluding reason given for the ban in verse 35 is that it is disgraceful for a woman to speak in the assembly. This reason is inconsistent with banning evaluation of prophecies by women while permitting prophecy by women. If 'speak' is understood with its ordinary width, it rules out both prophesying and evaluation. If 'speak' is read in some specially limited sense (for example, 'chatter'), it rules out neither prophesying nor evaluation.

After making all possible allowances for the flexibility of language, the distance between Paul's actual words and the proposed interpretation remains too great. It requires that, when Paul stated with emphatic threefold repetition that women *must be silent* in the assemblies, that they are *not permitted to speak* and that it is *disgraceful for them to speak* in the assembly, what he really meant was something quite different. He intended to convey that, with appropriate decorum and orderliness, women may pray aloud in the assembly (11:5, 13), may speak in tongues in the assembly (14:5, 27), may interpret tongues in the assembly (14:13, 27), may teach in the assembly (14:26), may offer a psalm in the assembly (14:26) and may prophesy in the assembly (11:5; 14:5), but may not evaluate prophecies in the assembly. This interpretation of his intent is not credible, and readers could not realistically be expected to glean this

---

22. *EFBT*, 245.

meaning.[23] It is all the more implausible after he has written in 14:29: 'Let two or three prophets [who include women] speak and the others [who also include women] discern.'

Assessed objectively, the 'evaluation of prophecies' theory cannot be accepted, because in the respects enumerated it does not match the text.

The consequence is that no theory has yet been put forward which satisfactorily resolves the contradictions between verses 34–35 and the surrounding context.

This unresolved lack of harmony between verses 34–35 and their context is not the only problem with these verses. The puzzle is made even more perplexing by the two reasons given in these verses for women's silence. To these we now turn.

The first reason for women's silence: the law

The first reason is in verse 34, which states: 'for it is not permitted to them to speak but they should be put in subjection as also the law says.'

Paul's intimate knowledge of and reliance upon the Hebrew scriptures is apparent throughout his writings. When he uses the expression 'the law says', he refers to something specific in the Old Testament, as we see in Romans 3:10–20 and 1 Corinthians 9:8–9.[24] But in the case of verse 34 the Old Testament passage to which he refers has not been positively identified. There is no other place in Paul's writings where his explicitly intended Old Testament reference is uncertain.

However, the problem with verse 34 goes beyond a question merely of uncertainty. The problem is not just about selecting the correct Old Testament passage. The problem is that there is no passage in the Old Testament which is suitable for selection.

---

23. In fact, as far as we know, for about 1,900 years this interpretation never occurred to anyone: *M&W*, 222–223. However, not too much importance should be attached to the length of time, since for most of this period it was believed, for cultural reasons, that women should generally be silent in a public assembly, so, as we have seen, the intended meaning of vv. 34–35 excited relatively little concern.

24. Paul most often uses 'the law' to refer to the law of Moses (Rom. 7:7; 1 Cor. 9:8–9; Gal. 3:10, 12). He also uses it once to refer to Genesis (Gal. 4:21–23), once to one or more psalms (Rom. 3:10–20) and once to Isaiah (1 Cor. 14:21).

The phrase 'as also the law says' could be taken to refer (1) to the whole of 'it is not permitted to them to speak but they should be put in subjection' or (2) only to 'they should be put in subjection'. Either way, the problem is the same. Nowhere in the Old Testament is there any explicit statement that women are not permitted to speak in an assembly of God's people or any explicit command that they should be put in subjection. The same is true if 'women' is read as 'wives'.

Could Paul be referring to an Old Testament requirement that is implied rather than explicit? This is unlikely, because Paul is not merely alluding to something that can be inferred from the Old Testament: his phrase is 'as also the law *says*'. To satisfy this phrase, we would expect to find a reasonably explicit statement. But, even if an implied requirement would do, no text can be identified that carries such an implication. In addition, such a requirement would not be consistent with the Old Testament taken as a whole.

As regards speaking in the Christian worship assembly, there is no exact analogy for this in the Old Testament. There is no mention in the Old Testament of local gatherings in synagogues. The system of centralized worship at the temple, with its ritual sacrifices and Levitical male priesthood, is not carried over into the life of the New Testament church. In chapter 5 we looked at what roles were open to women in answer to God's call in Old Testament times. An implied requirement that women must not even speak in any gathering of God's people does not fit with what we know about the roles of Miriam (a co-leader of the whole people), Deborah (prophet, ruler and judge of the whole people) and Huldah (the prophet who directed the nation by speaking to the delegation sent by the king). In particular, how could Deborah carry out her God-given role as ruler or judge if she was not allowed to speak when people were assembled in her presence?

As regards subjection, the nearest scripture is God's pronouncement to the woman in Genesis 3:16: 'he will rule over you.' Various commentators, starting in the early centuries after Paul, have suggested that Genesis 3:16 was his intended reference. But this statement in Genesis 3:16 is not a command to men to put their wives, or women more generally, in subjection. It is presented as a negative consequence of the fall, not as an instruction for men to follow, as Grudem agrees.[25]

Paul teaches in 1 Corinthians, as elsewhere, that Christ came to rescue from judgment and to undo the consequences of human sin (see 1 Cor. 1:30; 6:11, 19–20; 10:24; 12:7). It would therefore make no sense for Paul to transform

---

25. *EFBT*, 40.

Genesis 3:16 from a consequence into a command and apply it to the believing community. This would not advance the work of Christ but fight against it.

The idea that Genesis 3:16 commanded men to rule over women appeared plausible in cultures where it was taken for granted that women were inferior to men and should be in subjection to them. But once these cultural spectacles are removed the radical difference between consequence and command is plainly seen.

Carson accepts that Paul is not referring to Genesis 3:16. He makes a proposal which seems to be driven by his interpretation of Paul's reasoning in 1 Corinthians 11:8–9 and 1 Timothy 2:13, rather than arising from the text of verse 34 itself. He says Paul has in mind 'the creation order in Genesis 2:20b–24', which in his view suggests 'that because man was made first and woman was made for man, some kind of pattern has been laid down regarding the roles the two play'.[26]

The insufficiency of Carson's proposal is evident from his careful choice of words. As we saw in chapter 5, the making of man and woman separately as depicted in Genesis 2, so that woman was made to be man's ally, makes a positive differentiation between men and women. But Genesis 2 does not say anything, either directly or indirectly, about men putting women in subjection. Even the doughty champion of male rule in churches, John Chrysostom, recognized this.[27] As we further saw in chapter 5, the Genesis writer draws his own explicit conclusion about what we are to get from the passage which Carson identifies, namely, 'That is why a man leaves his father and mother and is united to his wife, and they become one flesh' (2:24, NIV). It would be perverse for Paul to draw, from a passage of Scripture emphasizing the unity of man and woman in marriage, a tangential and even discordant message about putting women in subjection, and to do so on the basis of an unclear implication that is contrary to the equal view of the marriage relationship which he has expressed a few pages earlier (see 1 Corinthians 7, discussed in chapter 2). While Carson is right to see an indication of 'some kind of pattern' for men and women, in the sense that there is a differentiation between them, this is a far cry from saying that women should be put in subjection or prohibited from speaking.

Grudem seemingly recognizes that neither Genesis 3:16 nor Carson's proposal will do, because he does not endorse either. His own suggestion is that

---

26. *RBMW*, 143.

27. Chrysostom, *1 Corinthians*, Homily 26: 'she was not subjected as soon as she was made; nor, when He brought her to the man, did either she hear any such thing from God, nor did the man say any such word to her: . . . of rule or subjection he no where made mention unto her.'

verse 34 refers to 'teaching of the Old Testament in general on men and women'.[28] This fails to answer the difficulty. It simply leaves us with the problem we started with, which is the absence of any identified teaching to the effect of verse 34 in the Old Testament. No satisfactory proposal has been made.

The whole issue becomes even more uncomfortable when we recognize the historical context. There is evidence of a misconception among Greek-speaking Jews in the first century that there was indeed a scripture about a woman's subjection, as cited in verse 34. Such a belief can be seen in the Jewish historian Josephus, writing about 95–100: 'for, says the scripture, "A woman is inferior to her husband in all things." Let her therefore, be obedient to him.'[29] Verse 34 seems to reflect this misconception.

Anyone familiar with the quality of Paul's writing, and more especially anyone who regards the New Testament as God's word, must view with surprise and discomfort a text where Paul apparently refers to an Old Testament scripture which does not exist, but which some Jews of his day mistakenly believed to exist. This instance is unique in Paul's letters.[30]

The second reason for women's silence: cultural disgrace

The second reason given for women's silence is in verse 35: 'for it is disgraceful [aischros] for a woman to speak in an assembly [ekklēsia].' This is a cultural reason.

---

28. *EFBT*, 246.

29. *Against Apion* 2.25, in Whiston's translation. The Greek word translated as 'says the scripture' is *phēsin*, which means 'it says'. Thackeray's translation renders it as 'says the Law'.

30. It is quite unlike the more usual difficulties arising from the way Paul uses identifiable Old Testament texts. Paul is often accused of misquotation or of selecting an out-of-context proof text. The apparent difficulty is usually generated by a failure to understand the nature of his argument, a failure to appreciate the relevance of the whole of the Old Testament passage referred to and a false assumption that an allusion is intended as an exact quotation. A typical example is Eph. 4:8, where in English versions Paul appears to misquote Ps. 68:18 by changing 'received gifts' to 'gave gifts'. But the words 'gave gifts' are not a quotation from v. 18; they are an allusion to 68:9–13 and 35, which are about God giving gifts to his people and strengthening them; and this is exactly what Paul is writing about. English versions have a tendency to inappropriate over-use of quotation marks, which anachronistically imply a modern convention of verbatim quotation.

It is not asserting that speaking is inherently wrong, like child sacrifice or idolatry, but that it generates disgrace. The disgrace arises from community perception that speaking in that particular setting is not fitting behaviour for a woman.

This reason directly reflects the prevailing culture. In a Greek *ekklēsia* (assembly) women were not allowed to speak.[31] Plutarch wrote of the virtuous woman:

> her speech . . . ought to be not for the public, and she ought to be modest and guarded about saying anything in the hearing of outsiders, . . . keeping silence. For a woman ought to do her talking either to her husband or through her husband.[32]

Similarly, in Roman culture women were expected to be silent in a public assembly.[33] The instruction in verse 35 to ask husbands at home echoes a phrase in Livy's *History of Rome*.[34]

Paul has already written in this letter about what is or is not disgraceful (*aischros*) when praying and prophesying in 11:2–16 (see v. 6 and the related verb *kataischunō* in vv. 4–5). In that part of his letter he did not regard it as disgraceful for a woman to speak in the presence of others in Corinth unless she loosed her hair. Is Paul now enforcing a stricter Graeco-Roman cultural perception of the proper conduct of women in an assembly, in direct contradiction of what he wrote previously?

This jarring note compounds the problem of these verses.

The Lord's command

In 14:37 Paul states: 'If anyone regards themselves as a prophet, or spiritual, they should recognize that the things I am writing are a command of the Lord.'

---

31. *RBMW*, 144 (Carson), citing N. G. L. Hammond and H. H. Scullard (eds), *Oxford Classical Dictionary* (Oxford: OUP, 1970), 376.
32. *Moralia*, 'Advice to Bride and Groom', 31–32.
33. Valerius Maximus, *Memorable Doings and Sayings* 3.8.6: '*quid feminae cum contione? si patrius mos servetur, nihil.*' My translation: 'What have women to do with an assembly? If Rome's customs are to be observed, nothing.'
34. In his account of Cato's unsuccessful speech against the repeal of the Oppian law, Livy has Cato castigating women for speaking in public to other women's husbands, when they could have asked their own husbands at home: *History of Rome* (*Ab Urbe Condita Libri*) 34 (written in Latin shortly before the turn of the era from BC to AD).

Some have seen this as a claim that, because he is an apostle, his own words are the Lord's commands.[35] But this is not the way of thinking that Paul displays in this letter. He makes clear when he is claiming to pass on a command given by the Lord and when he is giving an instruction of his own (7:8–12, 19, 25, 39–40; 9:14; 11:23). Accordingly, 14:37 should probably be understood as referring to a command given by the Lord Jesus. Which command is Paul referring to?

The instruction that immediately precedes this statement is verses 34–35. But there is no known command given by Jesus that women must be silent in an assembly.

It makes sense to understand 'the things I am writing' as chapters 13–14.[36] In these chapters Paul first expounds the meaning of the Lord's command to love (John 13:34–35; 15:12–17) and then shows how to put it into practical effect in the use of spiritual gifts, culminating in the instructions to prophets in 14:29–33, which reflect his exposition in 13:4–5.

It is conceivable that someone could understand verses 34–35 as an application of the Lord's command to love, driven by concern to avoid alienating outsiders, somewhat like that in 14:23–25. However, this particular application is hard to imagine of Paul here, given his encouragements in chapter 14 for all believers to exercise their spiritual gifts in the assembly.

Consequences of the lack of harmonization

'Your word is a lamp for my feet, a light on my path' (Ps. 119:105, NIV). This is how it should be. But in this instance the path currently remains unclear.

In view of the lack of a satisfactory solution for the interpretive issues, it is not reasonably possible to base any firm church policies on 1 Corinthians 14:34–35. Since we are at a loss to know exactly what restriction is intended, and at a loss to understand the reasoning, we cannot be confident of how to apply these verses to churches in different times and cultures.[37] The difficulty is particularly acute because the restriction is based on cultural grounds (v. 35) and on a supposed Old Testament scripture which has not been successfully identified (v. 34).

---

35. So Schreiner 2018, 299–300.

36. So Bailey 2011, 418.

37. This is also true of 1 Cor. 15:29. We are unsure what baptism 'for the dead' was.
    Therefore, we do not do it.

Judging from the other contents of 1 Corinthians, neither of the reasons given for women's silence appears Pauline in character. Nor are they derived from Jesus Christ. In the next chapter we will look at the scholarly discussion about whether verses 34–35 are authentic to Paul.

Summary of chapter 9

1. Verses 34–35 form a unit, separate from verse 33. Verse 33 should not be split into two and partly joined onto verse 34 as in some modern versions.
2. The content of these two verses is in severe conflict with the surrounding context. This conflict raises interpretive issues for which no satisfactory solution has been found.
3. Paul seems to say that women's silence is required by a command of the Lord Jesus. This is a further puzzle.
4. In the absence of a satisfactory solution to the interpretive puzzles, we cannot tell what to make of these verses. In particular, we cannot judge whether a restriction on women's speaking which is based on an Old Testament scripture which cannot be identified (v. 34) and on cultural grounds (v. 35) should or should not apply to churches in different times and cultures.

Questions to consider

1. Is there any consensus in your church, or in your discussion group, on how to interpret 1 Corinthians 14:34–35? What views are you aware are held? What is your own view?
2. In your culture, is it disgraceful for a woman to speak to the assembled church? Is your church practice influenced by these verses? How?
3. What do you usually think or do when you read instructions in Paul's letters which puzzle you? Should you do anything else?

The law of the LORD is perfect,
refreshing the soul.
(Ps. 19:7, NIV)

Removing added words

If the Bible as originally given is the church's primary authority for faith and
life, it is important that we have accurate copies of it.

Anyone with access to a reasonably recent English version of the Bible, such
as the NIV, ESV or NRSV, will see that in John 5 the verse numbers jump from
verse 3 to verse 5. Some words from verse 3, together with all of verse 4, have
been removed and put into a footnote.

These words are found in some ancient manuscript copies but not in others.
A decision has therefore had to be taken: are they original or not? The disputed
words were known to Tertullian (about 200), so were certainly of early date,
and they fit smoothly into the text. But scholars have had to work out why they
are in some ancient copies and not in others.

Were they original to John's Gospel, and did they somehow get omitted from
some early copies? Or were they added to it when some early copies were being
made? After study of the available evidence, the majority view is that the
disputed words are not original to John's Gospel. They are words of additional
explanation, which someone wrote into the margin as a comment, and which
were afterwards promoted into the text of some copies on the mistaken assumption that they originally belonged there.

A similar example of the addition of words may be seen at Acts 24:6–7.

Why did the assessment of authenticity change, so that these words, familiar in the KJV, were removed from John 5 and from Acts 24? The answer is that the available evidence changed. The KJV 'was based on half a dozen Greek MSS [manuscript copies], no earlier than the tenth century AD. Today, we know of *5,600* Greek MSS – and some of them are as early as the *second century* AD.'[1]

We must now examine the theory that the words printed in our Bibles as verses 34–35 of 1 Corinthians 14 were not original but a later addition like that in John 5 or in Acts 24.

The question mark over verses 34–35

We saw in chapter 9 that verses 34–35 raise problems of interpretation to which no satisfactory solution has been found. The two reasons for women's silence given in verses 34–35 appear to be more reflective of prevailing Graeco-Roman culture than of Paul's own writings. Could these verses have been added to Paul's letter by someone else?

As churches continued to grow in the decades after Paul's death, they inevitably increased in public visibility. It would not be difficult to imagine that someone who received an early copy of Paul's first letter to the Corinthians, or who was about to circulate a collection of his letters, might have felt concerned about whether what he read in chapters 11 to 14 remained culturally acceptable. He might have thought that 11:2 – 14:40 did not make clear the proper restrictions on women, which he considered were now necessary in order to avoid giving unnecessary offence. If he wrote his view of the proper restrictions in the margin, he could have written what we see in 14:34–35. Is it possible that a marginal comment of this kind got incorporated into the text of the letter when it was copied?

It would be a serious error to start cutting difficult verses out of the Bible on the basis of speculations. But where there is a real question mark over authenticity, it needs to be thoroughly considered. Only someone with a low view of Scripture can be unconcerned about the possibility that inauthentic words have crept in. We need to examine the hard evidence bearing on whether these verses were original to Paul. When I first looked at this question I was very sceptical of the theory that they were not authentic. But when I looked at the totality of the evidence I found that there was a serious issue to be decided.

This brings us to the art and science of text criticism.

---

1. Wallace 2001b (emphases original).

Text criticism

Introduction

The question whether verses 34–35 are authentic involves text criticism (or 'textual criticism'). In any investigation or process of reasoning, the results obtained are influenced by the methods used. I therefore owe the reader an explanation of my viewpoint on text criticism and of how I seek to apply the relevant principles.[2]

Because the Bible has come down to us via handwritten copies of earlier handwritten copies, text criticism could be described in the present context as the archaeology of handwritten copies. Without the benefit of modern pens and papers, writing was hard work. It was difficult to ensure complete accuracy when copying. Scribes got tired and made mistakes. One scribe wrote:

> Because one who does not know how to write thinks it no labour, I will describe it
> for you, if you want to know how great is the burden of writing: it mists the eyes,
> it curves the back, it breaks the belly and the ribs, it fills the kidneys with pain, and
> the body with all kinds of suffering. Therefore . . . as the last port is sweet to the sailor,
> so the last line to the scribe.[3]

Changes could also be introduced deliberately, if the scribe was convinced that a correction was needed to the manuscript that was being copied.

The orthodox Christian belief that the Bible is God's revelation strictly applies only to the texts as originally written. It is therefore important for Christian scholars to be as sure as possible that the church is using accurate copies and not treating spurious alterations as Scripture. Scholars therefore have to examine and evaluate the differences between manuscript copies in order to reach a conclusion about the most accurate representation of an author's finished text.[4] Copies in the original language have a primary role, but significant help can also be gained

---

2. Readers seeking additional detail on the general principles of text criticism may usefully consult chapter 1 of Bird 2010.

3. Florentius of Valeranica (tenth century). Translation by Biggs, 2014.

4. This description assumes there was a single finished version, written by the original author or authors; this assumption does not always apply straightforwardly (for example, in the Psalms, where material from one psalm may be reused in another). There is an academic debate about whether it makes sense to speak of trying to recover the original text of the Bible. This is a sterile debate. We want to get as close as we possibly can.

from early translations and sometimes from lectionaries or from quotations or allusions in other writings.

Because there are so many manuscripts, the number of variant readings is very large. The vast majority are not significant. Either the difficulty can be easily resolved, because the evidence permits identification of the likely original text, or any remaining uncertainty consists of a trivial variation which makes no material difference to the overall meaning. But in a very small proportion of instances the remaining differences have more significance and the solution is less clear.

Principles to apply

It is sometimes said that the art of text criticism was invented in the eighteenth century by the Lutheran scholar Johann Bengel. He certainly began a process of systematization. But the need for careful assessment of copies and selection of variant readings was well known in the ancient world. Origen and Jerome wrote about it, and from surviving evidence Bishop Victor of Capua (died 554) appears to have been an accomplished text critic as well as a considerable scholar.[5] Careful scribes added marks which gave information about variants (textual differences). Sometimes there is evidence of sharp disagreements between scribes in their judgments concerning the correct text. In the Codex Vaticanus (fourth century) there is a later marginal note, written in Greek, referring to a change made in two letters of a word in Hebrews 1:3: 'Fool and knave, leave the old reading, do not change it.'[6]

A distinction is made between external and internal evidence. External evidence is evidence of or about the manuscripts themselves, such as their date, provenance, relationship to other manuscripts, and so on. So, for example, if a particular variant only appears in one late manuscript, it can safely be rejected. Internal evidence consists of matters such as stylistic features, inconsistencies and grammatical or spelling errors visible in the words of the text itself.

Internal evidence is of two kinds – intrinsic and transcriptional. Intrinsic evidence is concerned with discerning the author's probable intention from context, style, vocabulary, and the like (we began to look at this in chapter 9). Transcriptional evidence is concerned with how changes to the text could have come about, for example, by a scribe mishearing a dictated word, or the eye

---

5. *M&W*, 246; Bischoff 1994, 107–108.
6. This can be seen online from the Vatican Library at <http://digi.vatlib.it/view/ MSS_Vat.gr.1209/1516>. For alternative translations of the comment, see Snapp 2017.

jumping over from one word to a similar one; the text critic looks for 'transcriptional probability', which is what a copyist is most likely to have done.

Regarding the use of evidence, we should note in particular:

1. Schools of text criticism differ over the relative importance of external and internal evidence. For present purposes it is not necessary to enter into that debate. My approach here is that all relevant evidence, of whatever kind, should be fully taken into account, being given whatever weight appears appropriate in the particular circumstances.
2. There is a strong reluctance on the part of evangelical scholars to accept any proposed emendation of the text which is not supported by manuscript evidence. This is a wise reluctance, because without it there would be a nearly irresistible temptation to propose that words which someone does not like are not original. This is of obvious relevance to discussions about restrictions on women's ministry. (Temptations to remove things too readily are not confined to the Bible. One editor of works by Euripides is said to have worked 'on a principle somewhat like that of the provincial English dentist – "if you won't miss it, why not have it out?"'[7])
3. Other things being equal, earlier copies are valued more highly than later copies.[8]
4. Scribes tend to smooth out difficulties. So where there is a conflict between a difficult reading and an easier one, the difficult one is generally preferred.
5. Considerations such as 3 and 4 above should not be elevated into hard and fast rules, but applied with discretion.
6. Generally, the form of the text that best allows an explanation of the origin of all known variants is most likely the original. This is often referred to as Bengel's first principle.

Points 3–6 can be simply illustrated. In English texts I have seen examples of 'exasperate' being used in mistake for the less common word 'exacerbate'. Suppose an English manuscript, for which we are dependent on copies,

7. Bird 2010, n. 110, citing R. J. Tarrant, 'The Reader as Author: Collaborative Interpolation in Latin Poetry', in John N. Grant (ed.), *Editing Greek and Latin Texts* (New York: AMS Press, 1989).
8. Dating is carried out largely from examination of the style of writing, including abbreviations and punctuation. Occasionally manuscripts are also carbon dated by scientific tests which destroy a small piece.

originally said: 'If you speak harshly, you will only exacerbate the problem.' Scribes vary in quality from five stars to one star. A one-star scribe making copy 1 mishears dictation and writes: 'If you speak harshly, you will only exasperate the problem.' A later scribe of five-star quality, making copy 2 from copy 1, makes the obvious correction: 'If you speak harshly, you will only exacerbate the problem.' A text critic who examines copy 1 and copy 2 and prefers the earlier and more difficult reading, in accordance with points 3 and 4, would be in error. In accordance with point 5, it is the internal evidence which should be decisive here, because the earlier and more difficult reading does not make sense, while (1) the later reading makes sense and (2) it is easy to see how an earlier error could have occurred. This also illustrates point 6. An educated author would be very unlikely to misuse language in his original text by writing 'you will only exasperate the problem', whereas a less well-educated scribe could mistakenly write 'exasperate' when he should have written 'exacerbate', this mistake being corrected by a later scribe.

Text criticism is a matter of expert judgment, based on knowledge, experience and inference. In evaluating the experts' arguments, my approach is to weigh the expert evidence for and against, assessing the quality of the reasoning and seeking the explanation which best accounts for all the available evidential data, both external and internal. Such an explanation should not conflict with any credible evidence and ideally should resolve every problem.

Marginal glosses and additions

If a scribe missed out a phrase and the mistake was later picked up, the missing words might be written into the margin of the manuscript, with an indication of where they should fit in. In the course of time such indications could wear off or otherwise become invisible or smudged. People might also write an occasional comment in the margin. This meant that a scribe making a later copy of a text with something written in the margin would sometimes have to make a decision whether the marginal words were someone's comment or belonged in the text and, if the latter, where to place them. 'Fool and knave, leave the old reading, do not change it' is obviously a comment, not part of the text of Hebrews 1, but sometimes (as in the case of John 5:3–4) the correct decision was not obvious. If in doubt, scribes would tend to include the words into the main text, rather than miss anything out.[9]

---

9. Schmid 2011, 58 ('The inclination of scribes, at least in the view of the ancients, seems to have been toward the inclusion of marginal material into the main text'). See also Payne 2017a, 616.

Families of manuscripts

Manuscripts are assessed as belonging to different families, according to their characteristic similarities. This provides convenient labels for groups of manuscripts. However, this concept should not be understood rigidly, since cross-fertilization took place when scribes or early text critics cross-checked against manuscripts other than the one being copied.

Were verses 34–35 added to what Paul himself wrote?

There has been considerable debate among scholars concerning whether verses 34–35 of 1 Corinthians 14 are added text, particularly since the respected evangelical scholar Gordon Fee concluded in his 1987 commentary that they were not authentic.[10]

The disputed text consists of thirty-six words. It is therefore very similar in length to the addition at John 5:3–4 (thirty-two words). The special feature of the external evidence about these two verses is that there is no extant manuscript from which the two verses are entirely absent. Instead, there are (1) manuscripts which have them in a different place and (2) manuscripts which some experts interpret as indicating the prior existence of earlier manuscripts from which they were absent.

The intrinsic evidence

Is it intrinsically probable that Paul wrote the words which we see in verses 34–35? In chapter 9 we surveyed three relevant features of the intrinsic evidence: (1) no satisfactory solution has been found to the inconsistencies between verses 34–35 and what Paul writes in 11:2 – 14:33; 14:39; and 16:15–16;[11] and

---

10. Fee 1987. Fee clarified his arguments in Fee 1994, 272–281. A revised edition of Fee's commentary was published in 2014.

11. In *M&W*, 261–262, Payne has pointed out a possible further inconsistency, which arises from Paul's attitude, throughout this letter, of tender concern for those who are in a weaker position: those with weak consciences (8:4–13), the poor (11:20–22, 33; 16:1–3) and those who are weaker or less honoured or less presentable (12:21–26). This is a reminder of the church's role as a new household which gives an honoured place to those whom society sees as weaker or of less value. Among these expressions of concern, what is said about women in 14:34–35 strikes a somewhat discordant note. But this is perhaps not a weighty point, for the argument is a matter of impression only.

(2) no satisfactory solution has been found to the apparently mistaken reliance on a non-existent scripture supposedly from the Old Testament, which is hard to believe of Paul; while (3) the words of the two verses are such as could have been written a little later, by someone who wanted to indicate what was acceptable in the prevailing culture as churches grew in public visibility.

In addition, chapter 14 makes good sense and reads better with the two verses omitted. Without those verses the last part of the chapter would read as follows:

> [29] And two or three prophets should speak, and the others discern. [30] And if a revelation comes to another sitting by, the first should be silent. [31] For you can all prophesy one by one so that all may learn and all be encouraged, [32] and the spirits of prophets are subject to prophets, [33] for [gar] God is not of disorder but of peace, as in all the congregations of the holy people. [36] Or did the word of God go out from you? Or are you the only people it has come to? [37] If anyone thinks they are a prophet or spiritual, they should acknowledge that what I am writing to you is the Lord's command. [38] But if anyone does not recognize this, they will not be recognized.
>
> [39] So then, my brothers and sisters [adelphos], be eager to prophesy, and do not forbid speaking in tongues. [40] But all things should be done decently and with order.

In the absence of verses 34–35 all problems of inconsistency disappear. There is no longer a problem concerning what command of the Lord Paul has in mind at verse 37 (love; see discussion in chapter 9). Verses 36–40 now follow smoothly from verses 29–33. The reference to other churches in verse 33 leads naturally into verse 36, and this explains the order of the phrases in verse 33. Paul pulls forward the *gar* phrase into a parenthetical position so that he can put 'as in all the congregations of the holy people' at the end of his sentence, and so emphasize the contrast between all other congregations and the Corinthians.[12]

---

12. It has also been argued that vv. 36–40 follow smoothly from vv. 26–33 because in the absence of the disputed verses the passage from v. 26 to v. 40 has a chiastic (symmetrically patterned) literary structure. See *M&W*, 254. Paul frequently uses this kind of literary structure in 1 Corinthians: see Bailey 2011, 33–53. But it seems unwise to place overmuch reliance on literary analysis of this kind in Paul's letters, since there is often more than one way of analysing any given passage. Bailey's own analysis is on the basis that vv. 34–35 are necessary to complete a different pattern.

Assessing the external evidence

Philip Payne relies on seven items of external evidence in support of the view that verses 34–35 are a later addition.[13] For present purposes four of these can be dealt with briefly:

1. He relies on editing marks in a manuscript called MS 88 as indicating the existence of a manuscript wholly lacking verses 34–35. His interpretation is logical but is contested, on grounds that others consider substantial.[14]
2. He argues that writings by Clement of Alexandria (died about 215) reflect a text of 1 Corinthians which lacked verses 34–35. In particular, alluding to 1 Corinthians 11:4–5, Clement writes that 'Woman and man are to go to church decently attired, with natural step, embracing silence . . . fit to pray to God'. Payne's point is that this is an odd thing for Clement to write if he knew a text of 1 Corinthians which enjoined silence for women in contrast to men. However, the cited passage could have been written as it was even if Clement was aware of verses 34–35.
3. He says that the apostolic fathers show no sign of awareness of verses 34–35, and gives a long list of authors prior to 200 who do not mention these verses. This is remarkable, since 1 Corinthians was the letter most quoted by Christian writers in the second century. However, this is an argument from silence, so carries little weight.
4. He says there is a high incidence of textual variants in verses 34–35. This is true, but the same can be said of some other scriptures which are accepted as genuine.

We now turn to the three weightier items of external evidence: the variation in the position of verses 34–35 in different manuscripts, the evidence from Codex Fuldensis and the editing marks in Codex Vaticanus.

Variation in the position of verses 34–35: four explanations to consider

In extant manuscripts verses 34–35 appear in two different positions – most often after verse 33, but sometimes after verse 40. This feature is the primary

---

13. *M&W*, 225–253.
14. Kloha 2006, 503–509. Kloha's analysis is based on comparison with Minuscule 915.

reason for Fee's conclusion against authenticity.[15] In theory there are four possible explanations of this variation of position:

1. *Moved down*: Paul dictated[16] verses 34–35 *after verse 33* as part of his main text but someone later moved those two verses down, to after verse 40; most manuscripts are copied from exemplars which retained the original position but some are copied from exemplars showing the lower position.
2. *Moved up*: Paul dictated verses 34–35 *after verse 40* as part of his main text but someone later moved them up, to before verse 36; some manuscripts are copied from exemplars which retained the original position but most are copied from exemplars showing the higher position.
3. *Afterthought*: Paul dictated or perhaps himself wrote verses 34–35 *as an afterthought*, so that it had to be placed in the margin. It was unclear to subsequent copyists where the afterthought was intended to fit; some scribes placed it in the main text after verse 33 and others after verse 40.
4. *Addition*: Someone else (not Paul) wrote verses 34–35 in the margin as a comment; later copyists mistook this as part of the original letter and *added it* into the main text, some in one position and some in the other.

Which manuscripts have one position and which have the other? In the Eastern families of manuscripts, and also in Western manuscripts which were influenced by the Vulgate (the Latin translation produced mainly by Jerome around 400), the disputed verses appear after verse 33. Broadly speaking, the manuscripts which have the disputed verses after verse 40 are those within the Western tradition which were not influenced by the Vulgate. The earliest

---

15. Fee 1987, 701; Fee 1994, 279. *M&W*, 226–227, cites fifty-five studies which conclude that the two verses are a later addition. Smith 2012, 86, summarily dismisses the addition theory on the ground that it 'lacks any evidence'. This is a mistake. She offers no explanation for the differing positions of these verses in different manuscripts. Nor does she consider the evidence which Payne discusses in *M&W* over some twenty-nine pages. Grudem in *EFBT*, 236–237, misunderstands Fee's argument as resting most decisively on the intrinsic evidence and does not fully engage with it. On the egalitarian side Derek and Dianne Tidball similarly dismiss the issue of authenticity on the mistaken basis that the main evidence is intrinsic rather than external: Tidball 2012, 224.
16. That Paul dictated nearly all of the letter is apparent from 1 Cor. 16:21.

currently available is Claromontanus (fifth or sixth century, in both Greek and Latin).[17]

We do not have direct evidence of how or when the divergence first occurred. All we can do is assess the relative likelihood of the possible scenarios.

Examining explanations 1 and 2: *moved down* or *moved up*?

The scenarios for explanations 1 and 2 are that the verses are original to Paul's main text and at some time a copyist moved them either down to a position lower in the letter or up to a position higher in the letter. In principle, such a move could be either accidental or deliberate.

Let us consider first the scenario of an accidental error. A mistake simply of omission when copying would leave the verses out entirely, which is not what we see, so this cannot be the explanation. It is difficult to imagine how an accidental move could be made at all. And, if an accidental move was made, it is difficult to imagine that it remained unnoticed both by the scribe who first made it and by those who made subsequent copies. This appears very unlikely. And a scribe who initially left the two verses out by mistake and then noticed their error while still writing the manuscript would not simply include them in a different place, since this would not correct the error. Carson states that no-one, to his knowledge, argues for an accidental move.[18]

---

17. The original can be viewed at <http://gallica.bnf.fr/ark:/12148/btv1b84683111/
    f328.image> in Greek and on the next page in Latin. Fee 1994, 273–275, says it has
    been demonstrated beyond reasonable doubt that this manuscript (with two others)
    represents a form of text nearly identical to that known to Hippolytus of Rome,
    and therefore must go back at least as far as the late second century. If so, in terms
    of evidential weight for the purposes of text criticism, this puts it on a par with the
    Eastern text. Others say that this conclusion goes beyond the available evidence,
    leaving the history of this form of text a matter of uncertainty. Fee's view on this
    point should at least be taken as a reminder not to overlook explanation (2) when
    considering the possibilities.

18. *RBMW*, 133–137, 145, n. 5. A feasible accidental transposition from the one location
    to the other would require a complex series of events: (1) a mistake of omission is
    made; (2) the mistake is later noticed; (3) the missing text is written in the margin;
    (4) the indication where it truly belongs becomes unclear; (5) as a result, a later
    copyist is faced with a decision on where to put it; (6) this later copyist is unfamiliar
    with Paul's letter and has no access to other copies which would show where it

The other scenario to consider for explanations 1 and 2 is a deliberate transposition. If we are to infer a deliberate move from one position to the other, the need to consider transcriptional probability requires that we identify a likely motive for this deliberate change. The scribe must be convinced both that the verses *cannot belong* where they are found in the manuscript being copied and that moving them to the new location *solves the problem*. If we are to opt for explanation 1 or 2, we need to explain how a scribe could come to that view. During many of the centuries after Paul wrote, when most people believed that women should be silent in public, as far as we can tell from commentaries the relationship between these verses and their context did not cause serious discomfort. A sufficient and credible motive for moving them is therefore lacking.

Moreover, even if we imagine an historically exceptional scribe who was seriously concerned about the seeming contradiction between these verses and their context, this still does not make explanation 1 or 2 probable. Transposition from one position to the other does not resolve or even materially reduce the contradiction and is therefore not explained by the imagined motive. So, even if a scribe was concerned about the contradiction, we are still left without a probable motive for a deliberate move from one position to the other.

Carson opts for explanation 1. He suggests as a motive that in the Eastern position (after v. 33) the verses superficially break up the flow of the argument, and that this is ameliorated if the verses are moved to the Western position (after v. 40). This sits rather uncomfortably with his own analysis that the disputed verses in their Eastern position do not break up the flow and would be understood by readers as part of a logical structure dealing with evaluation of prophecy (see chapter 9, 169–170).

More importantly he acknowledges, as fairly he must, that 'to put verses 34–35 after verse 40 is still to leave some awkwardness'. This is an understatement. Verses 37–40 wrap up a long discussion of assembled worship several chapters long; the scribe would see the verbal similarity of verse 39 with the way Paul indicates that he is bringing other long discussions to their conclusion in 11:33 and 15:58. It is

---

belongs; (7) the later scribe makes the wrong choice concerning where to put it; and (8) those who later reproduce this manuscript are similarly unfamiliar with Paul's letter and similarly have no access to other copies which would act as a corrective. The complexity of this hypothesis counts strongly against it. Moreover, the original mistake is by its nature transcriptionally improbable, since there is no ready explanation for it in this instance (such as jumping from a particular word or phrase to a similar word or phrase on a subsequent line).

hard to see how a scribe would think it even a slight improvement to move verses which are expressly about behaviour in assembled worship to beyond the end of the relevant section. Still less could a scribe have regarded it as an obvious correction which ought to be made. And there is no truly comparable example of such substantial scribal interference anywhere in Paul's letters.[19] Carson relies on John 7:53 – 8:11 as providing a comparable example of displacement. But this undermines his case, since this passage is judged to be an addition, not part of John's Gospel (see NIV 2011). This is Carson's own view of it.[20]

Accordingly, explanations 1 and 2 are not satisfactory because an accidental move is not plausible and because a *probable* motive for a deliberate move has not been identified.

Examining explanations 3 and 4: *afterthought* or *addition*?

Moving on to explanations 3 and 4, the major objection generally advanced against theories involving the incorporation of a marginal gloss or comment arises from the lack of any surviving manuscript from which verses 34–35 are entirely absent. Let us say Paul wrote the letter in about 55. At some point in the next few decades steps were taken to collect and copy this and other Pauline letters. If the marginal text became incorporated a significant time after this process had got under way, one would expect to find some families of

---

19. Payne 2015, 8. Schreiner 2018, 296, suggests that a few scribes thought the discussion on women in vv. 34–35 interrupted Paul's words on prophecy in vv. 29–33 and vv. 37–40, so they moved vv. 34–35 to after v. 40. But this suggestion runs up against the same severe difficulties as Carson's. In addition, if the objective was to keep vv. 29–33 and 37–40 together, why was v. 36 left in its original position? Kloha 2006, 554, suggests that the motive for moving the text from the Eastern to the Western position was to protect women in general, and perhaps Priscilla in particular, from contradicting Paul's teaching on the universal practice of the church (v. 33), by separating the injunction to silence from the practice of all the churches and connecting it instead with the command to do all things decently and in order (v. 40). But it is unclear how, especially in the light of v. 37, this move would provide such 'protection' or what material difference it would make to the extent of contradiction. Verses 34–35 remain discordant with the remainder of chapters 11–14 whether in the Western or in the Eastern position.

20. *RBMW*, 135–136. The incident of the woman taken in adultery is probably historically sound, but that is a different point.

manuscripts wholly lacking the disputed words, because they derived from a copy into which the marginal text had not been incorporated. We do not possess any such family of manuscripts.

But is this a strong objection? All it actually tells us is that, if explanation 3 or 4 is correct, whatever happened, which resulted in the divergence that we see in the manuscripts, must have happened at an early date, before there was extensive copying of the exemplar which lacked verses 34–35. It is right to observe that there is no evidence against the textual divergence having happened at an early date.

The strength of explanation 3 (Paul's own afterthought) is that it fully accounts for the lack of even one extant manuscript from which the disputed words are wholly absent. It also fully accounts for their presence in two different positions. Its transcriptional hypothesis is simple: (1) the words were written in the margin by Paul or his secretary; (2) the indication where they belonged was unclear or later became so; and (3) different copyists took two different decisions about where to insert them. One possible drawback here is that the additional text is thirty-six words long, which is a lot to fit into the margin of an original letter written on papyrus, especially if written in Paul's 'large hand' (Gal. 6:11; 2 Thess. 3:17). Subject to that possible caveat, explanation 3 passes the test of transcriptional probability.

The strength of explanation 4 (addition) is similar or better, provided that the marginal gloss or comment was in existence at or close to the beginning of the process of copying Paul's letters for circulation. The mechanical aspect of the transcriptional hypothesis is identical to that for explanation 3 except that the words were added into the margin without Paul's involvement and the constraint of possibly having too small a margin is eased (because, if we are considering the stage at which Paul's letters are just being copied for wide circulation, there could be more flexibility on margin size).

Relevance of intrinsic evidence to explanations 3 and 4

Leaving aside the probability of a larger margin being available in which to write, the principal difference between explanations 3 and 4 lies in whether it is more likely that Paul or someone else was the author of the additional words.

The intrinsic evidence which we have surveyed makes it hard to believe that Paul wrote them. If he did, we have to accept that he referred to a non-existent Old Testament text, that on the face of it he severely contradicted himself, and that he expressed himself in such an opaque fashion that no subsequent com-mentator has been able to come up with a contextually satisfactory solution to what he really meant. Moreover, if he had intended to indicate second thoughts about women's vocal participation, one might have expected him to have placed the marginal comment adjacent to chapter 11, where he mentions praying and prophesying specifically by women.

Conversely, a motive for someone else to write a marginal comment at the critical time is not hard to find, given the strong views in prevailing culture that women ought not to speak in public. As time passed, church assemblies were gradually becoming more public in character. At 10:31 – 11:1 Paul had laid down a general principle of willingly accepting restrictions on one's own freedom in order to avoid giving unnecessary offence and so to help others to find salvation. He had expressed a particular concern at 14:23 about the impact that behaviour in the assembly could have on outsiders. Outsiders who came into the assembly would be unlikely to receive the good news of Christ if they were shocked by a lack of decorum. In a more public setting, women's silence could therefore be seen as a necessary restriction, with an evangelistic motive. Someone may have considered that it was important to give guidance on this and that a good way of doing it would be to add a comment in the margin. Where would be a good position for such a comment to be written? It is easy to envisage such a person reading chapters 11 to 14 and deciding to add a comment near to where Paul's extended discussion of worship is brought to a close.[21]

The vocabulary of the two disputed verses ('it is not permitted to them to speak') contains a striking echo of the unusual vocabulary which Paul uses in 1 Timothy 2:12 ('I do not permit a woman to teach') and which he wrote about nine years after he had first written to the Corinthians.[22] The same word for permit is used (*epitrepō*), and this is a word which Paul uses nowhere else in any of his letters to indicate a restriction on believers' behaviour. And within this similarity there is a telling contrast. In 1 Timothy it is the author, Paul, who says 'I do not permit'. In verses 34–35 the comment is written elliptically, in the third person ('it is not permitted'), as if referring to a general idea or a rule emanating from elsewhere than the author. This fits with what was popularly believed to be contained in the Jewish law, as evident in verse 34, and with the view of what was proper in the prevailing culture expressed in verse 35.

If someone had the objective of extending Paul's restriction in 1 Timothy 2:11–12, this would also explain the oddity of verse 35a. When imposing a blanket ban on speaking in the assembly, why bother to make this particular point, that women can ask their husbands at home if they wish to learn anything?

---

21. See further Capper 2005, especially 310.

22. Mosse 2007, 304, 311, dates 1 Corinthians in 55 and 1 Timothy in 63–64.

Because, if the person writing the marginal comment is extrapolating from
1 Timothy 2:11–12, he needs to indicate how to implement Paul's instruction
in 1 Timothy 2:11 that women should learn, if the women have questions about
what is taught.

When we take into account the intrinsic evidence in order to make a choice
between explanations 3 and 4, the probability that the author was Paul shrinks
to a low level, so that explanation 4 stands out as the better candidate for
explaining the available evidence.

Carson protests that in explanation 4 'we are asked to believe in a glossator
who is Biblically informed enough to worry about harmonization with
1 Timothy 2 but who is so thick he cannot see that he is introducing a clash
between 1 Corinthians 14 and 1 Corinthians 11'.[23] But this is a caricature of
the step taken by the person who added a comment and it fails to consider the
practical distinction between this step and the further step taken by scribes who
promoted it into the main text:

- If Carson is right, Paul must have been even thicker, because he failed
  to see the apparent contradiction in what he wrote. But in truth, thickness
  does not come into it. A *marginal comment* stating what we have in verses
  34–35 would show thoughtfulness, not dim-wittedness, by someone
  influenced by patriarchal culture. Paul had imposed a restriction on women
  at Ephesus when circumstances required (1 Tim. 2:11–12). With this as a
  precedent, someone might have felt justified in expressing the view that the
  Ephesian restriction should be extended so as to ban speaking by women
  'in the assemblies', in order to avoid giving unnecessary offence in the
  prevailing culture as growing churches increased in public visibility. Was
  this not a principled application of the apostolic guidance in 10:31 – 11:1
  to changed circumstances – a wise strategy for diminishing friction and
  making the Christian gospel more attractive to outsiders (compare Titus
  2:5, 9–10)? An influential place to say it would be in the margin of Paul's
  letter, when it was copied for further circulation.
- Early scribes who *copied it into the main text* may not have been troubled by
  any appearance of inconsistency. Within their cultural context, they may
  readily have assumed that the words they saw in the margin were Paul's
  words, motivated by a concern for not alienating outsiders, and therefore
  being an application of the Lord's command to love, similar to that in
  1 Corinthians 14:23–25.

---

23. *RBMW*, 134.

On the available evidence, which explanation is the most probable?

We do not have direct evidence of any of the four explanations, so it is necessary to make a judgment based on probability. We come back to Bengel's first
principle, which Carson expressly endorses: the form of the text that best allows
an explanation of the origin of all variants is most likely the original.

Judged by this principle, explanations 1 and 2 are found wanting, because
they struggle to account for the two forms in which we find the text. They lack
reasonable probability. An accidental move depends upon such a complex and
improbable hypothesis that no-one argues for it. And the theory of a deliberate
move depends upon a motive which is in itself historically improbable and
which also does not make good sense as a justification for the move. No-one
has come up with a satisfactory explanation of how a scribe could be convinced
both that these verses *cannot belong* in one position and that moving them to the
other position *solves the problem*.

This leaves us to choose between explanations 3 and 4. The choice between
them is not difficult, because, as we have seen, the intrinsic evidence strongly
favours 4 over 3.

We are left with explanation 4, provided that the addition occurred early
enough. There is no evidence against the divergence having occurred at
a suitably early date, and motives are easily found, both for the comment
itself and for its insertion into the text. The requirement of transcriptional
probability is easily satisfied. A marginal comment would not contain any
marks indicating an insertion point. The fact that the words have been inserted
in two different places would reflect the absence of such marks, and also the
absence of any obviously correct place to put them. But in the prevailing
cultural milieu, given the common wisdom that women should be silent in
public gatherings, scribes who saw the comment in the margin may readily
have assumed that the words were Paul's, without being unduly troubled by
concerns about internal contradictions.

Carson takes Fee to task for not referring to the principle that where there
is a conflict between a difficult reading and an easier one, the difficult one is
generally preferred, because scribes tend to smooth out difficulties. He asserts:
'Clearly, on intrinsic grounds inclusion of verses 34–35 after verse 33 is the *lectio
difficilior*, the "harder reading".' He maintains that on the 'harder reading' principle verses 34–35 should be accepted as genuine.

We may agree that treating them as genuine is the harder reading, since they
are inconsistent with so much that Paul writes in the same letter. But explanation 4 has nothing to do with whether a difficulty in the text was smoothed
out, so the 'harder reading' principle is not relevant. Even if it were relevant,

it should be applied with discretion. Carson's mechanistic approach would mean that words which are obviously alien should automatically be regarded as genuine. This cannot be a right approach. The intrinsic difficulties here are such that the 'harder reading' principle cannot sensibly be used as indicating that the verses are authentic, especially when the external textual evidence is best explained by an early marginal comment becoming inserted in two different positions.

Accordingly, there are solid reasons for concluding that verses 34–35 were not written or dictated by Paul the apostle. This is the most probable conclusion.

But what about the absence of extant manuscripts which wholly lack verses 34–35?

If concerns remain about the lack of any extant manuscript from which verses 34 and 35 are entirely absent, there are several points to be considered.

First, if explanation 4 is correct on the basis that the alteration occurred very early in the history of the textual tradition, a shortage of such manuscripts is to be expected.

Second, although we possess many manuscripts of Paul's letters, the evidence is inevitably patchy, both in time and in geography, rather than evenly spread, so we cannot make absolute demands for particular kinds of textual evidence. Copying mistakes occur, and manuscripts are not indestructible. With the passage of time, the earliest copies are no longer available. We cannot insist that, if the verses are an addition, there must necessarily still be extant a manuscript from which verses 34 and 35 are entirely absent.[24]

Third, Payne believes that he has found evidence which shows that many centuries ago such manuscripts were seen by others, even though now no longer extant. To this we now turn.

Codex Fuldensis
Codex Fuldensis is a Latin manuscript containing parts of the New Testament, including 1 Corinthians. It was commissioned by Bishop Victor of Capua, who

---

24. Bird 2010, citing A. E. Housman (ed.), *M. Manilii Astronomicon: Liber Primus* (London: Grant Richards, 1903), refers to an example from a poem by Ovid where 'it took the discovery of the correct text in an inscription to compel editors to print a reading that had not survived in any manuscript'.

read it twice, making corrections both times and noting that he completed these on
May 2, AD 546, and April 12, AD 547. . . . His astute judgments, combined with his
keen interest in ancient manuscripts and his privileged access to them as a bishop,
gives special credibility to his corrections in Codex Fuldensis.[25]

The manuscript is held at Fulda in Germany and it is possible to view it online
to see for oneself the annotations which Victor ordered to be made.[26] Viewing
it makes the issues much easier to understand.

In order to explain what Fuldensis shows I shall describe the text using
chapter and verse numbers, but it should be remembered that these are not in
the manuscript. (Our present system of chapters dates from the thirteenth
century, and verses from the sixteenth century.) In Fuldensis the text is presented
in sections, each starting with a Roman numeral and with the first line of text
written in red ink. Section LXIIII (64) comprises what we call verses 34–40 and
section LXV (65) starts at the first verse of what we call chapter 15. The scribe
who wrote out 1 Corinthians initially included verses 34–35 in the Eastern
position in the main text, where we currently see them in our English versions.
Using English words from the NIV, Figure 1 shows the layout of the two relevant
pages of Codex Fuldensis.

Victor's amendment is signalled by the Latin abbreviation *hd*, written into
the text after the last word of section 63 (that is, after v. 33). This abbreviation
indicates that something is missing from this point (*hic deest* means 'it is missing
here').

What is missing from the main text is set out in the bottom margin. The text
in the margin omits verses 34–35 and consists of the whole of what we call
verses 36–40. The wording in the margin is the same as the main text of verses
36–40, except that a grammatical and spelling correction is made in one word.
(In v. 40, *ordinem* in the margin text corrects *ordine* in the main text; to reflect
this in Figure 1 I have introduced a similar difference in the English, where
'order' in the main text is corrected to 'orderly' in the margin.) The marginal
text is followed by the Latin abbreviation *hs* (*hoc supple* means 'supply this'),
which indicates that this is the text to be supplied at the position shown by *hd*.

Victor is therefore telling the reader: 'There is an alternative text; after reading
verse 33, go straight on to verses 36–40 in the form shown at the foot of the

---

25. *M&W*, 246.
26. The Codex is held by the Hochschul- und Landesbibliothek, shelf-marked 100
    Bonifatianus 1. The most relevant page is hosted at <http://fuldig.hs-fulda.de/
    viewer/resolver?urn=urn%3Anbn%3Ade%3Ahebis%3A66%3Afuldig-2629884>.

If anyone speaks in a tongue, two – or at the
most three – should speak, one at a time,
and someone must interpret.

If there is no interpreter, the speaker should
keep quiet in the church and speak to
himself and to God.

63 Two or three prophets should speak, and
the others should weigh carefully what is
said. And if a revelation comes to someone
who is sitting down, the first speaker
should stop. For you can all prophesy in
turn so that everyone may be instructed
and encouraged.

The spirits of prophets are subject to the
control of prophets. For God is not a God
of disorder but of peace – as in all the
congregations of the Lord's people.   *hd*

64 Women should remain silent in the
churches. They are not allowed to speak,
but must be in submission, as the law says.

If they want to enquire about something, they
should ask their own husbands at home;
for it is disgraceful for a woman to speak
in the church.

Or did the word of God originate with
you? Or are you the only people it has
reached? If anyone thinks they are a
prophet or otherwise gifted by the
Spirit, let them acknowledge that what
I am writing to you is the Lord's com

Or did the word of God originate with you? Or are
you the only people it has reached? If anyone
thinks they are a prophet or otherwise gifted by
the Spirit, let them acknowledge that what I am
writing to you is the Lord's command. But if
anyone ignores this, they will themselves be
ignored. Therefore, my brothers and sisters, be
eager to prophesy, and do not forbid speaking in
tongues. But everything should be done in a fitting
and orderly way.   *hß*

mand. But if anyone ignores this, they
will themselves be ignored.

Therefore, my brothers and sisters, be eager
to prophesy, and do not forbid speaking
in tongues. But everything should be done
in a fitting and order way.

65 Now, brothers and sisters, I want to remind
you of the gospel I preached to you,
which you received and on which you
have taken your stand. By this gospel
you are saved,

If you hold firmly to the word I preached to
you. Otherwise, you have believed in vain.
For what I received I passed on to you as
of first importance: that Christ died for
our sins according to the Scriptures, that
he was buried, that he was raised on the
third day according to the Scriptures,
and that he appeared to Cephas, and then
to the Twelve.

After that, he appeared to more than five
hundred of the brothers and sisters at
the same time, most of whom are
still living, though some have fallen
asleep.

Then he appeared to James, then to all
the apostles,

And last of all he appeared to me
also, as to one abnormally born.
For I am the least of the apostles

Figure 1

page.' In order to make this proposal, Victor must have seen at least one variant
manuscript (let us call it 'pre-Fuldensis') in which verses 36–40 immediately
followed verse 33.

The key question is, what should we infer about pre-Fuldensis? Did it omit
verses 34–35 entirely, or did it include them after verse 40? If it included them
after verse 40 (the Western position), that would not be a surprise, since this is
what we see in manuscripts such as Claromontanus. A similar Western type of
manuscript could have been among those used by Victor. In that event, Codex
Fuldensis would add nothing of weight to the arguments considered above. But
if pre-Fuldensis omitted verses 34–35 entirely, that would provide additional

support for regarding verses 34–35 as a spurious addition deriving from a marginal comment.

Kloha argues that, because the meaning of the hḋ and hŝ symbols is to indicate respectively what is absent and what is to be supplied, they can never indicate a replacement.[27] The problem with this assertion is, as Kloha himself says, 'This, of course, creates an otherwise unattested form of the text' – namely, a very strange text in which the whole of verses 36–40 appears twice. It is not reasonable to suppose that this was how Victor intended the amendment to be read. He cannot have thought that Paul's original contained verses 36–40 twice in close proximity. The text in the bottom margin must therefore be intended as a replacement for some of the main text.

The crucial question is: when the reader has read the text in the bottom margin, what comes next? Where should one rejoin the main text? Scholars have argued for two ways of reading how Victor intends the replacement to operate: (1) use the marginal text to replace section 64, that is, to replace verses 34–40 of the main text; or (2) use the marginal text to replace only what we call verses 36–40.[28]

The first of these has the strong merit of simplicity. The sign which shows where to begin the replacement is at the end of section 63, just before section 64. All the reader has to understand is that the marginal text replaces section 64. After reading the version of section 64 in the margin, one goes next to section 65. In the English shown in Figure 1, it appears reasonably clear that when one reaches the end of the margin text ('everything should be done in a fitting and orderly way'), the eye should continue from where the main text says 'everything should be done in a fitting and order way'. Likewise, in the Latin original this appears reasonably clear, as readers who view Codex Fuldensis online will be able to see for themselves.

The second view is much more complex. On this view the reader has to read the marginal text, then go back into the main text to the beginning of section 64 (at v. 34) and read a limited portion of section 64 (vv. 34 and 35), and then infer that the remainder of section 64 (vv. 36–40), which is not separately delineated in any way, should be skipped. The reader at this point must jump from mid-section (the end of what we call v. 35) to part way down the next page, where section 65 begins.

The difference in complexity supports the former analysis. It is hard to believe that Victor intended to set the reader the difficult task involved in the second view. The much simpler interpretation of what Victor is telling us is:

27. Kloha 2006, 502–503.

28. Of these, (1) is advocated by Payne in M&W, 246–248; (2) is advocated by Shack 2014.

'one reading of section 64 is as shown in the main text [= vv. 34–40] and the other reading of section 64 is as shown in the margin [= vv. 36–40].'[29]

In sum, the issue depends on drawing an inference about Victor's intention. The wholesale replacement of section 64 by the version in the margin (which lacks vv. 34–35) is easy to understand and to follow. The alternative theory about what Victor intended involves a tortuous process.

It is probable, therefore, that Payne's interpretation of Victor's annotations is correct. This was Bruce Metzger's conclusion.[30] If so, then the pre-Fuldensis which Victor saw in Capua in the sixth century was a manuscript which wholly lacked verses 34–35. This constitutes a further item of external evidence supporting explanation 4.

An interesting further question is whether there is any positive indication that Victor preferred one reading to the other. In my view, there is. The main text contains an apparent error, where *ordine* should read *ordinem* (as in the Vulgate).[31] Victor could have indicated a correction to this in the main text, but did not. The better reading is found only in the version in the margin, which replaces section 64. This suggests that Victor preferred the marginal reading, which lacks verses 34–35. In other words, his assessment was probably that verses 34–35 were a spurious addition.[32]

Codex Vaticanus

As further evidence that verses 34–35 were originally a marginal gloss, Payne relies also on interpretation of editing marks visible at verse 33 in Codex

---

29. In addition, note that the correction of a single letter in v. 40 would not be a reason for duplicating the whole of vv. 36–40, since this tiny correction could easily be shown separately. And if Victor intended to show only that vv. 34–35 had two possible positions, could this not have been shown by some method which involved writing out vv. 34–35 a second time, rather than vv. 36–40? This would have been less laborious, since vv. 34–35 are much shorter (thirty-two words in Latin, as compared with forty-seven words).

30. Payne 1995, 245, n. 28.

31. Latin was changing. Word endings were being dropped or shortened. Unlike Victor, the scribe may have regarded *ordine* as acceptable.

32. Payne says that this is further confirmed by comparison with other amendments which Victor made: his tendency was to edit in favour of standard Vulgate readings; thus his edits should be understood as preferences: *M&W*, 248. See also Metzger's point that a scribe would require authorization to re-write such a large amount of text: this implies that Victor regarded the amendment as a correction: *M&W*, 247.

Vaticanus. He concludes that the scribe who wrote this part of Codex Vaticanus in the fourth century indicated, by his marks, that there was a known manuscript from which verses 34–35 were absent. Payne's interpretation of the marks appears cogent and convincing, though it has been disputed by other scholars. Payne has recently answered his critics with a fuller explanation, which has been described by New Testament scholar Larry Hurtado as cogent and impressively thorough, and has been endorsed by a number of other well-known specialists.[33]

It is fair to observe that the editing marks in Codex Vaticanus are only just beginning to be better understood, as a result of Payne's ground-breaking work. This will likely prove to be important work which will impact also on other textual questions, but it is still early days, and it seems wise to see how his analysis of the editing marks in Vaticanus survives scrutiny by other scholars over the next few years.

It is not necessary to reach a firm view regarding the additional evidence from Codex Vaticanus, because the external evidence of the conflicting positions of verses 34–35 in different manuscripts, the external evidence from Codex Fuldensis and the internal evidence are sufficient to result in the conclusion that verses 34–35 were probably an early addition to Paul's text.

Concluding assessment

Some readers may be left with a feeling that cutting out verses 34–35 is just too convenient. This is understandable. We are rightly taught to be highly sceptical of proposals to remove difficult texts from the Bible.

---

33. *M&W*, 232–246. Payne 2017a; Hurtado 2017. Positive assessments have also been expressed by Eldon Jay Epp, Bruce Prior and Fred Schroeder, among others: Payne 2017b. In personal correspondence (2018) Payne has informed me of his new research finding of another nine of the relevant editing marks (distigme-obelos symbols) in the Vaticanus NT, bringing the total to seventeen. All but one of the seventeen have a gap in the text at the exact location of the start of a variant or variants that cumulatively add at least four words not in the original text. The probability that this combination of features is mere chance is close to nil. Only the original 'scribe B' of Vaticanus could introduce those gaps. Since the NA[28] text and the vast majority of text critics agree with scribe B's judgment of the manuscript data in every other case, and since scribe B had access to far more early NT manuscript text than we do today, Payne considers that we have good reason to trust scribe B's judgment that 1 Cor. 14:34–35 is a later addition that was not originally in Paul's letter to Corinth.

It is right to emphasize that we are not here dealing with a case of arguments for inauthenticity based on internal evidence alone. If the problem with these verses were limited to the facts that they are inconsistent with their context, that they contain an apparent error concerning the contents of the Old Testament and that no interpretive solution has been found which satisfactorily makes sense of them, we would leave them standing in the text, acknowledge our limitations and hope for fresh light in the future.

Here, the external evidence also needs to be explained. How has it come about that these words are found in different places in different manuscripts? Something has gone wrong, but what? As we have seen, the most probable solution for this feature of the external evidence is that verses 34–35 are not original to Paul but derive from an early marginal comment which became incorporated into the main text. This is additionally corroborated by Bishop Victor's annotations in Codex Fuldensis, which indicate the existence of a text wholly lacking those two verses. And if Payne's view of the evidence from Codex Vaticanus is correct, that is yet further corroboration.

When we add together the external evidence and the internal evidence, the case for rejecting these two verses is robust. Removing them is not an ideological move; it is going where the evidence leads. In principle this is no different from the rejection of other additions (such as those in John 5 and in Acts 24) which have appeared in the text, have been accepted into our Bibles for a time, and have subsequently been removed when consideration of the available evidence led to the conclusion that they were probably not authentic after all.

At the least, our Bibles should have a footnote, along the lines of: 'Manuscript evidence indicates that verses 34 and 35 may be a later addition, not original to Paul, and should be omitted.' Better, verses 34–35 should be placed in italics or in a footnote, together with an explanation that the nature of the discrepancies in the manuscripts suggests that they are of doubtful authenticity.

'The law of the LORD is perfect, refreshing the soul' (Ps. 19:7, NIV). I am not proposing this here as a criterion of authenticity. But if any readers have felt guilty that their souls have failed to obtain much refreshment from 1 Corinthians 14:34–35, perhaps they may now acquit themselves on the footing that these verses may not after all belong in the Bible.

Summary of chapter 10

1. Belief that Scripture as originally given is God's revelation requires Christian scholars to try to ensure, so far as possible, that the church is using accurate copies and not treating copying errors or spurious alterations as authoritative.

2. The text which is printed as 1 Corinthians 14:34–35 in our current Bibles is probably not authentic. The best explanation of the totality of the evidence currently available is that someone other than Paul wrote verses 34–35 in the margin as an early gloss or comment. Copyists mistook this as part of the original letter and promoted it into the main text, but were unsure where to position it. They inserted it in two different positions (some after v. 33, others after v. 40).

3. This explanation accounts for all the available evidential data, both external and internal. It does not conflict with any credible evidence. It resolves every historical and interpretive problem associated with these verses, including all the relevant features of the evidence from the manuscripts. No other explanation fulfils these criteria.

Questions to consider

1. What do you find interesting or surprising in chapter 10?
2. What is your own view on the authenticity of 1 Corinthians 14:34–35? Why?
3. It is widely agreed that difficult verses should not be removed from the Bible based on internal evidence alone. What good reasons are there for this view? Do any of the reasons strike a chord with your experience of seeking to live as a faithful Christian? In what way?

Do your best to present yourself to God as one approved, a worker
who does not need to be ashamed and who correctly handles the
word of truth.   (2 Tim. 2:15, NIV)

The centre of the storm

The true meaning and intent of Paul's restriction on the activities of women in
1 Timothy 2:12 is a storm centre in the egalitarian–complementarian debate.

According to the NIV, Paul writes: 'I do not permit a woman to teach or to
assume authority over a man; she must be quiet.' But even the translation of
Paul's words is in dispute. What exactly does he mean? How should we set about
interpreting it?

I am not concerned here with the wider controversies among scholars who
do not accept the authority of Scripture, or who do not accept that Paul wrote
this letter. Nor am I directly concerned with later church traditions regarding
church leadership and men's and women's roles. My aim here is to find clarity
on what Paul originally meant.

In the present chapter we consider the general contents of Paul's letter and
the particular contents of chapter 2. This will highlight some severe difficulties
in both egalitarian and complementarian interpretations, because of a lack of
fit with the context. Chapters 12 and 13 will be more positive, looking at further
details of the context in order to find a solution in which all the jigsaw pieces
fit together.

Before proceeding, it will be helpful to clarify the real nature of the
disagreement between the two sides in the debate.

The nature of the disagreement

The debate is often characterized as a choice between an 'absolute' or 'universal' interpretation put forward by complementarians and a 'contingent', 'limited' or 'temporary' interpretation put forward by egalitarians.[1] But this is an over-simplification. In reality both sides propose limitations on the application of Paul's words, in order to avoid inconsistency with what he writes elsewhere.

While a naïve interpreter might assume Paul's words in 1 Timothy 2:12 are intended to apply in an absolute or universal way,[2] no serious complementarian scholar supports such a reading. Complementarians agree with egalitarians that Paul cannot mean in an absolute sense either that women should never teach at all, or that they should never teach men, since both of those propositions are in direct contradiction of what we know about his view of teaching, which includes that in at least some circumstances women may teach, and may teach men.

Complementarians accept that women may properly exercise gifts of teaching in some circumstances: 'no legitimate question exists with reference to either the adequacy or the acceptability of a woman serving in some teaching roles.'[3] The following points are largely common ground among many complementarian and egalitarian scholars:

- Paul refers in approving terms to the fact that his male colleague Timothy had been taught the faith by his grandmother and mother, in contrast to being deceived by false teachers (2 Tim. 1:5; 3:13–15).
- Paul tells Titus to instruct older women to teach what is good (Titus 2:3). He goes on to say that the older women can teach the younger. He evidently envisages that women may be effective and reliable teachers.
- In Romans 12:7 he encourages those who have a gift of teaching to use it. The context is not restricted to men. On the contrary, Paul is emphatic that he is addressing 'everyone' (v. 3). In Romans 15:14 he goes on to affirm that the brothers (including sisters – Greek *adelphos*) are able to 'instruct' one another (NIV). Here 'instruct' is *noutheteō*, which refers to teaching. It is the same word as is used for Paul's admonition in Acts 20:31, and for what leaders do in 1 Thessalonians 5:12, and it is used

---

1. For an example of an egalitarian presentation in terms of 'absolutist' versus 'conditional', see Padgett 1997.
2. As recounted by Smith 2012, 24 (new convert), 30–31 (non-Christian journalist).
3. *RBMW*, 258 (Paige Patterson).

in the same sense. (The related noun *nouthesia* ['instruction'] describes the purpose of the Old Testament in 1 Cor. 10:11.)

- Paul gives instructions about Christian teaching in a context of worship in Colossians 3:16 ('Let the word of the Messiah dwell in you richly, in all wisdom teaching and admonishing one another'). These instructions are addressed to a congregation of both men and women. In that text he places no restriction either on women teaching or on women teaching men. The close juxtaposition of 3:16 with 3:18–19 also suggests that Paul envisages that husband and wife may teach and admonish one another.

- That women may in at least some circumstances teach in a worship context should also be apparent from Paul's words to a mixed congregation in 1 Corinthians 14:26 ('When you assemble, each one has . . . a teaching', NASB).

- With her husband, Priscilla corrected Apollos, a prominent male preacher, and taught him the way of God more accurately, as narrated by Paul's companion, Luke (Acts 18:26). Paul commends Priscilla as one of his co-workers (Rom. 16:3–4). Luke considered Priscilla's correction of Apollos sufficiently important to include it in his short history.[4] Teaching Apollos was no minor task. He was a forceful public exponent of the gospel, with an expansive ministry (Acts 18:24–28). When he moved on to Corinth, his ministry there was more influential with some believers even than Paul's (1 Cor. 1:12). Calvin admits: 'we see that one of the chief teachers of the Church was instructed by a woman.'[5]

- When Paul tells Timothy to entrust his message to reliable 'people' or 'men' who will be able to teach others (2 Tim. 2:2), Paul is not saying that Timothy must choose only males for this task. The Greek word is *anthrōpos*, which usually means 'man' in the sense of a human person, as in 1 Timothy 2:4–5, rather than specifically a male. (It can be used to refer to women only, as in 1 Pet. 3:4.) There is nothing in the context of 2 Timothy 2:2 to show that Paul is instructing Timothy that only men, and not women, may teach.

We should add that complementarians see Colossians 3:16 and 1 Corinthians 14:26 as referring to informal teaching rather than some more formal kind. But Paul's word for 'teach' in Colossians 3:16 is *didaskō*, which is the same as he uses

---

4. Luke also recounts words spoken by women which have come to be accepted as inspired Scripture: Luke 1:42–45, 46–55.

5. Calvin's *Commentary on Acts*, Acts 18:26.

for his own teaching in Colossians 1:28, and the context does not require a difference in meaning. Similarly, his word for 'teaching' in 1 Corinthians 14:26 is *didachē*, which is Paul's word in the same chapter for the kind of teaching he would himself deliver in the assembly (v. 6), and in 1 Corinthians 14 the context shows that the meaning is the same in verse 26 as in verse 6. Elsewhere he uses the same word for the teaching that he wants Timothy to carry out at Ephesus (2 Tim. 4:2), as well as for the teaching which elders must hold on to (Titus 1:9).

Irrespective of the precise interpretation of Colossians 3:16 and 1 Corinthians 14:26, it is clear that both complementarians and egalitarians are faced with the same question, which is to discern what limits Paul intends for 1 Timothy 2:12, so that it is consistent with what he writes and approves elsewhere. To make it consistent, both complementarians and egalitarians therefore propose limitations on the scope of application of what Paul says. But they make different proposals about what the proper limitations are.

The rival limitations

Complementarians believe that there is a God-ordained order in the relations of men and women which finds expression in church life, where the role of authoritative leadership is allocated to men. It is therefore men who must provide authoritative teaching in the church. They argue that in verse 12 the word 'teach' and the word translated in NIV as 'assume authority' are positive words. Paul is not expressing disapproval of the activities mentioned in verse 12. His concern is only that they should not be done by women.

But how is the disapproval of teaching by women in verse 12 harmonized with other passages where Paul evidently approves of teaching by women? Complementarian answers vary on matters of detail but all use the same central idea: Paul's intent is to prohibit women from delivering *authoritative* Christian teaching to men.[6] This is at the heart of his intended limitation upon verse 12.

Egalitarians take a different approach. They reject, as unbiblical, the idea of unique male authority. They believe that men and women are equal in all respects, without distinctions of role in the church. On that basis, Paul's intention cannot have been as complementarians say. Instead, egalitarians say

---

6. Blomberg adds the nuance that the ban is on women fulfilling the senior leadership position in a congregation; on this view women are permitted to teach in less authoritative capacities: Blomberg 2014.

that Paul is placing on women a temporary restriction to deal with a particular problem at Ephesus (the destination of the letter). They argue that in verse 12 the word 'teach' and the word translated in the NIV as 'assume authority' are used negatively, referring to conduct that was inappropriate. There are different theories about what the misconduct was, but the basic point is that Paul's prohibition relates to some particular temporary circumstances. This is the limitation which makes verse 12 consistent with other passages where Paul evidently approves of teaching by women.

My approach will not be to start from any general proposition either about authority or about equality, but instead to start from the context and see what understanding this leads us to.

We will therefore look first at the contents of 1 Timothy. This will help us to see some of the difficulties that complementarians and egalitarians encounter in establishing the rival limitations which they propose. Then in chapters 12 and 13 we will examine the context in more detail. This will lead us to a perhaps unexpected understanding of Paul's words.

Paul's main concern

After the greetings at the beginning of the letter (1:1–2), Paul immediately states his principal topic of concern and makes plain his objective, which is to combat false teaching and promote lives of love, purity and faith:

> As I urged you when I went into Macedonia, stay there in Ephesus so that you may command certain people [*tis*] not to teach false doctrines [*heterodidaskaleō*] any longer or to devote themselves to myths and endless genealogies. Such things promote controversial speculations rather than advancing God's work – which is by faith. The goal of this command is love, which comes from a pure heart and a good conscience and a sincere faith.   (1:3–5, NIV)

In order to advance his purpose of promoting right teaching and godliness (a saved life in Christ, of love, goodness and faith) and combating false teaching and ungodliness, Paul gives Timothy instructions, warnings and advice for him to implement (1:2–5, 18; 3:14–15; 4:6, 11, 15–16; 5:21; 6:2, 13–14), pending Paul's expected further visit (3:14–15; 4:13). Since Paul's instructions had already been given to Timothy face to face, we should understand the purpose of the letter as being to stiffen his resolve, to either remind him of what Paul had said or add to it, and to strengthen his hand in dealing with the issues (see, for example, 1:3, 18; 3:14–16; 4:6–16; 5:21; 6:2, 11–14, 20).

Paul's concept of teaching

Before continuing to identify the context, we must notice that in Paul's thinking combating false teaching and promoting godliness are not two separate tasks; they are part and parcel of a single task.

Western Protestant interpreters too often think of teaching mainly in terms of imparting concepts in something akin to a classroom setting, such as a congregational meeting. But in the New Testament teaching is done by word and deed together, and its objective is to produce lives that are pleasing to God. When Paul writes to the Corinthians to teach them how to live, he does not only give them verbal instructions but points to his own life; he says: 'Follow my example, as I follow the example of Christ' (1 Cor. 11:1, NIV). And he sends Timothy to them, saying, 'He will remind you of my way of life in Christ Jesus, which agrees with what I teach everywhere in every church' (1 Cor. 4:17, NIV). To 'learn the Messiah' is to turn from sinful conduct and live a saved and renewed life of true holiness (Eph. 4:17–24; see also Col. 2:6–7). Holding fast to the apostolic tradition (2 Thess. 2:15) includes living it out, for the outcome of the pattern of apostolic teaching is obedience from the heart (Rom. 6:17).

Thus, the truth that must be passed on by a Christian teacher is not only the truth of who God is, and of the gospel announcement, but also the way of life that God calls for in response; and this truth is taught not only by the teacher's words but also by the teacher's own way of life. (See further Phil. 2:12–15, where Paul's readers are to obey him and thus live for God's pleasure; 4:9, where they must do what they have learned and received and heard and seen in Paul; and 1 Pet. 5:1–4, where elders are to be examples to the flock.) Teaching equips people to do good works (2 Tim. 3:16–17). Similarly, Paul's concern in his letter to Titus is not abstract truth, but truth that is in accordance with godliness (Titus 1:1), which means teaching that produces right living. In Titus 2:1–15 Paul emphasizes strongly and at some length the role of the teacher as an example and the outcome of teaching as godly living (see also Rom. 16:17). Similarly, in 1 Timothy 6:3 teaching is sound or false, depending on whether it accords with godliness.

Grudem agrees that teachers are people who, in the whole of their character and personhood, teach and model for the church, by both life and word.[7]

When English versions translate 1 Timothy 1:3 as referring to the teaching of false 'doctrines', this produces an unduly restricted impression of what Paul is concerned about (*heterodidaskaleō* – 'teach differently'). Bad teaching does not

---

7. *EFBT*, 274–275.

necessarily have anything to do with what we would call 'doctrine'. If Christian teaching is by word and deed, taking place across the whole of life, and producing good behaviour, so also false teaching may be by word and deed, taking place across the whole of life, and producing bad behaviour. False teachers are known by their manner of life (Matt. 7:15–24), and uncaring conduct is a denial of the faith (1 Tim. 5:8).

General contents of the letter

Nearly everything in the letter relates in one way or another to Paul's objective of promoting godliness, purity and love, in Christ, and of combating false teaching, as laid out at the beginning of the letter in 1:3–5.[8] This is true even of Paul's advice to Timothy not to drink water but to take a little wine for the sake of his stomach and his frequent illnesses (5:23), for ill health would hamper Timothy's fulfilment of his instructions for promoting godliness and combating false teaching.

We will look briefly at the general contents of the letter chapter by chapter, noticing some words and ideas which will later play a part in pulling together our contextual understanding of Paul's thinking.

Chapter 1 introduces the topic of combating the ungodliness associated with false teaching (1:4, 6–10; see 1:9 – *asebēs*, 'ungodly'). False teachings oppose (*antikeimai*) the godliness that conforms to sound teaching (1:5, 10–11). False teachers at Ephesus both taught wrong ideas and lived sinfully, rejecting conscience (1:4–6, 19–20). Immoral behaviour is contrary to sound gospel teaching (1:10–11), because Christ Jesus came into the world to save sinners, that is, to deliver them from their sinfulness and renew them as people who give honour to God, as happened in Paul's own case: the violent blasphemer became an example of God's gracious patience (1:12–17). In order to fight the good fight Timothy, by contrast with the false teachers, must have both faith and a good conscience (1:18–19).

Chapter 2 starts with 'therefore' (*oun*), which indicates that the instructions which follow relate to the primary task identified in chapter 1, of combating

---

8. See *M&W*, 296. In v. 4 note Paul's contrast of false teachings with the unusual expression 'stewardship [*oikonomia*] of God in faith'. The meaning of this phrase would be clear to someone (like Timothy) already familiar with Paul's thinking. Paul sees himself and his co-workers as stewards (*oikonomos*) of God's mysteries (1 Cor. 4:1; see also 1 Tim. 3:15–16).

false teaching and promoting a saved life of love and goodness.[9] Through the
true Saviour (1:15; 2:3–4), the aim in chapter 2 is godliness (*eusebia*, 2:2; *theosebeia*,
2:10).

Chapter 3 emphasizes again the link between right belief and right behaviour in 3:2, where being an apt teacher as an elder goes along with a good
character; in 3:9, where deacons must keep the mystery of the faith with a clear
conscience; and in 3:14–16, where Paul writes so that Timothy[10] will know how
to behave in God's household. Paul sees the church as the 'pillar and foundation
of the truth' (3:15); this truth is the mystery of godliness (*eusebia*, 3:16) embodied
by Christ. The appointment of well-qualified elders (3:1–7) and deacons (3:8–
13) will strengthen the church to hold on to the truth and not be swayed by false
teaching.

Chapter 4 contains further reference to false teachings (4:1–5). Paul exhorts
Timothy to teach the truth of godliness (*eusebia*) by both word and example (see
especially 4:6–8, 11–16).

Chapters 5 and 6 continue the same theme. Children and grandchildren of
widows are instructed to show godliness (*eusebeō*) by giving them financial help
(5:4), and widows are told how to live so as to please God (5:5, 10, 14). Elders
who govern and teach well should be rewarded, but elders must be rebuked if
they persist in sin (5:17–20). Good deeds are conspicuous (5:25). Slaves must
behave in a way that does not result in the teaching being blasphemed (6:1–2).
Teaching and life must match. True godliness (*eusebia*) is repeatedly emphasized
(6:3, 5, 6, 11).[11] At 6:3 Paul still has in mind certain persons (*tis*) teaching differently (*heterodidaskaleō*), exactly as in 1:3. The letter concludes with warnings
about love of riches leading people away from faith (6:9–10, 17–19) and with
reminders to Timothy to avoid the false teaching and live blamelessly (6:11–14,
20–21).

In 1 Timothy Paul's aim, therefore, is full salvation, namely, that people in
Ephesus should both come to a knowledge (*epignōsis*) of the truth of salvation
in Christ (see 2:4–5) and live godly lives (see 2:2–3). This stands in contrast to

---

9. As Schreiner notes in *WTTC*, 167. Yarbrough 2018, 280, states that *oun* 'serves to
   introduce a solemn inference from what precedes in order to lay out a vital course
   of action'. Because of the conventions of word order in Greek, *oun* is the second
   word rather than the first.
10. 'You' in 3:14 and 3:15 is singular.
11. The apostle Peter was fond of the word *eusebia* (2 Pet. 1:3, 6, 7; 3:11; see also Acts
    3:12). Paul's letters do not use it until this late period of his life. Tradition suggests
    that he had more contact with Peter in this period.

false teachings, to the character and behaviour of false teachers, and to the results of false teachings.

Introducing the false teachings and false teachers

From what Paul writes we can pick up some features of the false teachings and their practical results, and also some initial information about the false teachers themselves.

The teachings include godless myths and old wives' tales (1:4; 4:7), endless genealogies and useless speculations (1:4), meaningless talk and empty utterances (1:6; 6:20; see also 2 Tim. 2:16–18 – such things advance ungodliness, *asebeia*), misuse of the Jewish law (1:7–8) and rejection of conscience (1:19–20; 4:2; see also 2 Tim. 2:17–19). Rejecting conscience appears to mean insisting on liberty to do ungodly and immoral things that the law and the gospel prohibit (1:8–11). The proper use of the Jewish law is to rule out immoral behaviour, not to regulate what food to eat, but false teachers demand abstinence from certain foods (4:3–5). They also forbid marriage (4:3).

Their teaching is described as 'what is falsely called knowledge [*gnōsis*]' (6:20). Hymenaeus (mentioned in 1:20) and Philetus (only mentioned in the second letter) taught that the general resurrection had already taken place (2 Tim. 2:18).

False teachers are paying attention to deceitful spirits and teachings of demons (4:1) and have been snared by the devil (2 Tim. 2:25–26). The teachers are conceited and lacking in understanding; they have an unhealthy craving for controversy, contradictions and disputes about words, and are depraved in mind, bereft of the truth and ungodly (6:3–5, 20; see also 2 Tim. 2:14, 23). They have a form of godliness (*eusebia*) but not its reality (2 Tim. 3:5; 1 Tim. 4:7; 6:3). They see *eusebia* as a means of increasing their wealth (6:5; compare 6:17–19).

The qualifications for elders and deacons major on character and behaviour. They are designed to ensure that no false teachers may be appointed, not only by reference to their beliefs but by ruling out those who are immoral, quarrelsome, intemperate, conceited, lacking in self-control or lovers of money.

To avoid making an unwarranted assumption, we should note that the letter does not say explicitly whether there is a single brand of false teaching with all the elements mentioned or whether there are variations. In the next two chapters we will look at the wider historical context and also examine parts of the letter in more detail, in order to complete the picture.

Having introduced Paul's letter, we may go on to consider some of the difficulties which egalitarians and complementarians encounter in trying to establish the rival limitations which they propose for 1 Timothy 2:12.

Difficulties for all

Three difficulties are shared by all interpreters. The first is our relative ignorance of the circumstances in Ephesus which were concerning Paul. We have some knowledge of the Ephesian church and its situation from careful study of the New Testament, and some general information about Ephesian society from wider historical sources. We will look at this in more detail in chapter 12. But our information is fragmentary, and is only a small proportion of what Paul himself and Timothy, the first reader of the letter, knew about life in Ephesus and in the Ephesian church.

The second difficulty is to determine the intended meaning of the verb *authenteō* which Paul uses in verse 12, in its form as an infinitive (*authentein*). The difficulty arises because the word is rare, and has a range of possible meanings. English translations of it include the following:

- 'instigate conflict toward' (ISV),
- 'control' (CEB),
- 'lord it over' (TLB),
- 'dictate to' (TLV),
- 'try to dictate to' (NTE),
- 'usurp authority over' (KJV, BRG, GNV),
- 'assume authority over' (NIV),
- 'have dominion over' (ASV),
- 'rule over' (WE),
- 'exercise authority over' (NASB, ESV),
- 'use authority over' (DRA),
- 'have authority over' (RSV, NRSV).

Most evangelical egalitarians select a negative meaning, taking Paul to be concerned about the nature of the activity which he restricts, while most complementarians select a positive meaning, taking Paul to be concerned only about the fact that the activity is done by women. By adopting the ambiguous expression 'assume authority over' the NIV has provided a translation which leaves the reader to decide whether the meaning is positive (take up proper authority) or negative (seize authority illegitimately). I am therefore using the NIV translation for the present, pending closer consideration in chapters 12 and 13.

The third difficulty arises from the highly compressed nature of Paul's writing in this passage, which makes it relatively difficult to interpret and gives rise to many questions. The most extreme example is the shift in 2:15 from '*she* will be saved' to 'if *they* remain . . .', where there is a jump from singular to plural without an intervening identification of the plural subject.

Broadly speaking, verses 11–12 are instructions and verses 13–14 are support for what is said. But what is the precise relationship between 11–12 and 13–14? Are verses 13–14 put forward (1) as theological reasons for Paul's position; (2) as demonstrating the reasonableness of what Paul says; or (3) as a supporting illustration? Are verses 13–14 intended to support verse 11 or verse 12 or both? It is hard to be sure, because Paul does not fully spell out his reasoning, and he leaves one or more ideas to be understood.

Verse 13 says: 'For Adam was formed first, then Eve.' What point is the reader intended to understand from this? Paul does not explain the relevance of Adam being formed first. Traditionalists, no less than contemporary complementarians and egalitarians, have struggled to understand Paul's reasoning here. Calvin in his *Commentary on 1 Timothy* was candid about his own puzzlement:

> Yet the reason Paul assigns, that woman was second in order of creation, appears
> not to be a very strong argument in favour of her subjection; for John the Baptist
> was before Christ in the order of time, and yet was greatly inferior in rank.

Is it perhaps about Adam having the ancient rights of the firstborn male? But patriarchal customs of primogeniture are not mentioned in the story of Adam being formed in Genesis 2, and anyway why would Paul think that they set a suitable precedent for relationships in the church, which is called to live as a new creation in Christ? Perhaps verse 13 is not about subordination, but, if it is not, then what is it about? Is it something to do with Adam being Eve's source, as in 1 Corinthians 11:8? But Paul's point is about timing ('Adam was formed first'), not source (he does not say that Eve was formed from Adam).

Verse 14 says: 'and Adam was not deceived, but the woman having been deceived came into transgression.' What point is Paul making here? Neither complementarians nor egalitarians can agree even among themselves what Paul's reasoning is. Many conflicting theories are proposed on both sides of the debate:

- Was he laying the blame for human sin and death specifically on Eve's shoulders? But that would not fit with Romans 5, where Paul's reasoning is based on Adam's transgression.
- Was he thinking of the consequence of Eve's behaviour as seen in Genesis 3:16, namely, the man's rule over the woman? Perhaps, but the Genesis narrative does not directly connect that consequence to the idea that the woman was deceived and he was not.

- Is he citing Eve's deception as showing women's gullibility, or perhaps even as causing it? Complementarians who once put forward such a view have usually withdrawn it, in the face of the rather obvious retorts that men cannot be proved to be less gullible than women, and that Paul regarded both as susceptible to deception (2 Cor. 11:3). If Paul had really thought women were disqualified from teaching because unduly gullible, he would hardly have instructed elsewhere that women should teach (Titus 2:3).
- Is it that Eve usurped Adam's leadership role, for which she was unsuited? But there is no express statement or even hint of this in Paul's text. Paul highlights the fact that she was deceived, not that she attempted to act outside her proper station. The serpent's deception had nothing to do with Eve's position with respect to Adam; the deception was about the desirability of eating the fruit, contrary to God's command.
- Is Paul illustrating what happens when a woman is deceived, and in turn deceives a man? But Paul states that Adam was not deceived.
- If Adam sinned without being deceived, he sinned with his eyes fully open to what he was doing. On the face of it this makes no sense as a reason for a rule that men rather than women should teach and assume authority, whether temporarily or permanently. As Hurley pointedly puts it: 'Would you rather be led by an innocent but deceived person, or by a deliberate rebel?'[12]
- Does Paul then mean, as some suggest, that Adam was not deceived directly by the serpent but indirectly via Eve?[13] But Genesis 3:6 does not describe any deception of Adam, and in Genesis 3:12 Adam does not say that he was deceived.

Moo candidly remarks: 'These verses [13–14] offer assertions about both the creation and the fall, but it is not clear how they support the commands in vv. 11–12.'[14] So it is widely considered that some further reasoning is implied in verses 13–14 although not expressed, but there is no consensus on what it is.

The compressed nature of Paul's writing in this passage would not have been a problem for Timothy, who as one of Paul's co-workers was familiar with Paul's thought, and who knew the full details of the situation in Ephesus, but it presents a challenge to subsequent readers who lack Timothy's knowledge.

---

12. Hurley 1981, 215. See also *WITC*, 213 (Schreiner).
13. See *M&W*, 407–409.
14. Moo 1980, 68.

Some difficulties for egalitarian interpretations

Egalitarians say that Paul's restriction in 1 Timothy 2:12 was a response to a specific problem that was occurring in the Ephesian church, and so his restriction on women should be taken to be limited to this one problem.[15] Accordingly, what they need to do is (1) identify what the problem was and (2) show how it fits into Paul's train of reasoning. Many speculative suggestions have been made. But it is hard to identify a problem which can be positively shown to have existed in the Ephesian church and which also fits into Paul's exact reasoning in 1 Timothy 2.

The difficulties for an egalitarian case can be illustrated by considering three examples.

Our first example is the Kroegers' theory that in verses 13–14 Paul is contradicting Gnostic myths about Eve being formed first and gaining true knowledge (*gnōsis*) by eating the fruit.[16] This is conceivable, because it would fit verses 13–14. But it is hard to see how contradicting such myths would justify what Paul says in verses 11–12. A greater difficulty is that this reconstruction of what Paul had in mind is speculative and unprovable, because there is no firm evidence that such myths were circulating in Ephesus in the first century.[17]

Our second example is the theory that the specific problem which Paul had in mind was uneducated women.[18] This theory arises from three considerations. The first is that Paul specifically commands in verse 11 that a woman should learn. The second is the background feature of ancient Mediterranean culture that education was mainly reserved for men. Few women were educated to any significant extent. Thus many names survive from Ephesus of students, rhetors, sophists and doctors, and not one of them is a woman's name.[19] The third

---

15. There is a different view proposed by a few writers, which is that throughout chapter 2 Paul's concern is limited to the relations of wives and their husbands (Hugenberger 1992; Westfall 2016, 289, 293, 311). But this view cannot be made to fit what Paul writes in chapter 2. This is addressed by Grudem in *EFBT*, 296–299; by Schreiner in *WITC*, 177–180; and by Belleville in *DBE*, 208–209.
16. Kroeger 1992. See also *M&W*, 298, 405.
17. *WITC*, 169 (Schreiner); see also Kelly 1963, 10–12. There is also a question mark over whether the known second-century myths have been accurately understood by the Kroegers. Perriman 1998, 146–148, interprets them differently.
18. See Keener 1993, 591; *EFBT*, 288–289.
19. *WITC*, 58 (Baugh).

consideration is the background feature that in the relevant culture at least some learners would normally be expected to go on to become teachers (see Heb. 6:12). This egalitarian theory then holds that Paul was restricting women from teaching until they were properly educated.

However, the theory of a lack of women's education collides with contrary evidence. Historical sources show that high-class urban women, including in Ephesus, were an exception to the general rule of women's lack of education: they received private education to fit them for (among other things) their duties in managing a large household.[20] And the women whom Paul had particularly in mind when he wrote 1 Timothy 2 were very rich women. Other women would not need to be told not to adorn themselves in the manner that he describes in 2:9, because they would have no possibility of doing so even if they wanted to. The words he uses – gold, pearls, expensive clothes – suggest very considerable wealth.[21] Accordingly, we cannot conclude that the problem was a lack in the relevant women's general education. It would have to be a lack of specifically Christian education, perhaps because the women Paul had in view were recent converts.

But if the problem in Ephesus was a lack of specifically Christian education, it would not explain what Paul writes. If the problem was the women's lack of such education, they should not be teaching and assuming authority over either men or women, so why in verse 12 does Paul say specifically that men should not be the subject of those activities by a woman? No satisfactory answer has been given.

Moreover, the lack of education theory sits ill with Paul's reference to the creation and fall, since there is no indication either in 1 Timothy 2 or in Genesis 2 – 3 that the reason for Eve's deception was a lack of education; on the contrary, she had been taught that the fruit was forbidden.[22]

---

20. *WITC*, 59 (Baugh). In addition, Grudem in *EFBT*, 290–291, cites evidence that women also served on occasion as gymnasiarch – in effect, superintendent of education. If this is correct, they must have been educated themselves. In Ephesus, as elsewhere, gymnasia were centres for intellectual pursuits as well as physical exercise. The students were men. Paul alludes to the physical training at the gymnasium in 1 Tim. 4:8.

21. Pearls were very valuable items: *M&W*, 313. The clothes are *poluteles*, which indicates great worth, as in Mark 14:3 (more than 300 days' wages; see 14:5). On the realities of life for women of the lower classes, see Capper 2005, 120–121.

22. Grudem enlarges on this aspect of the difficulties in *EFBT*, 293–295.

Our third example is Payne's theory. He presents one of the most careful, coherent and detailed evangelical egalitarian interpretations of 1 Timothy 2. He infers that the false teachers' message, especially forbidding marriage, banning certain foods and regarding the resurrection as already past, had a particular appeal to women and little appeal to men. He says that women were both deceived by the false teaching and passing it on to others. So what Paul was doing was banning women from teaching until they were properly authorized.[23] This fits neatly with Paul's mention of Eve's deception in verse 14, as a salutary example showing the danger of being deceived (although v. 13 – 'Adam was formed first' – is harder to explain[24]). Complementarians accept part of his reasoning: they agree (because of 1 Tim. 2:14 and 2 Tim. 3:6–7) that women were deceived by the false teaching. Let us assume it can also be shown that women were passing false teaching on to others. But how would Payne's theory explain Paul's restriction? Consider the following four questions, which are problematic for most theories which suggest that Paul's restriction related to a temporary situation of false teaching:

1. On the basis that Paul's letter is concerned with combating false teaching, why in verses 8–15 does he restrict false teaching only *by women*, and not by men? Shouldn't male false teachers also be stopped?
2. Why does Paul restrict the female false teachers from teaching and assuming authority specifically *over men*, and not also over women? Don't women also need protection from false teaching?
3. If it is right that the false teaching *mainly appealed to women* rather than men, how does that square with Paul restricting women from teaching and assuming authority *over men*? If there is to be a distinction between men and women here, should we not expect the opposite, namely, a restriction on delivering false teaching to women?
4. If the problem is female false teachers, why does Paul apparently restrict *all women* in verse 12 and not specifically the false teachers?

Payne's theory does not seem to me to provide a set of satisfying answers to these tough questions. In chapter 13 we will reassess his theory and find more substantial answers.

---

23. *M&W*, 291–444, in particular 299–304, 443–444.
24. Payne cross-refers to 1 Cor. 11 and proposes the idea of respect for one's source: *M&W*, 402–404.

Some difficulties for complementarian interpretations

Complementarian interpreters seem to have the advantage here. They would respond to the four tough questions by saying that question 1 is posed on a wrong basis: Paul's concern in verse 12 is not false teaching. Instead, his concern is women's proper role in the church in submission to male leadership. Questions 2 to 4 are then easily answered. In general, women may teach; Paul's concern here is that women should not deliver authoritative teaching to men in the church.[25]

However, the objections which complementarians have to overcome in order to establish their limitation on Paul's meaning, or anything close to it, are at least as severe as those which face the egalitarian theories. We will here review four of them, in ascending order of difficulty.

1. Why only 'I am not permitting'?

The first difficulty arises from Paul's particular choice of language in verse 12, where he uses the phrase *ouk epitrepō*, which translates as 'I am not permitting' or 'I do not permit'. Complementarians would have a stronger case if they provided a convincing explanation of why, if Paul intended an enduring rule, he chose this unusual form of words.

Before focusing on the real difficulty, we must clear out of the way any idea that this is merely an expression of a personal preference. It is right to say that in the course of the letter Paul presents his instructions, warnings and advice with differing degrees of emphasis, ranging from 'if you do this you will be a good servant of Christ Jesus' (4:6) through 'I want/desire' (2:8), 'I urge/request' (1:3; 2:1) and 'it is necessary' (3:2) to 'I charge you before God' (6:13–14).[26] In chapter 2, with only one exception, Paul chooses not to use the language of command. The only outright command in this chapter is that a woman must learn quietly and in all submission (v. 11). Nevertheless, we can readily recognize from the context that, while verse 12 is not a direct instruction, Paul is quite definite in what he writes and he expects Timothy to act in line with it. Perhaps he expresses himself in the way that he does because he is conscious of Timothy's relative weakness (1:18; 5:23; 2 Tim. 1:7), as if he were saying to Timothy: 'you may be tempted not to intervene, but I am not permitting this behaviour.'

---

25. *EFBT*, 65–78; *WITC*, 175–176, 190–192 (Schreiner); Smith 2012, 29.
26. Köstenberger agrees that different forms of exhortation have more or less potency. See *WITC*, 155.

This is the only place in his letters where Paul uses the expression *ouk epitrepō*. It contrasts with the more direct expressions used elsewhere in this letter. There is a particular contrast with the direct command of verse 11 (within the same Greek sentence). Paul positively commands that a woman should learn. Why does Paul make such a strong verbal contrast between this command and his next statement, that he is not permitting a woman to teach and assume authority over a man? Does this not rather create the impression that his restriction on women's teaching is only a statement of his current approach to a current problem? He could have written 'Women must never teach' or some similar expression, but did not. The phrase which he uses seems a counter-intuitive choice of words to express a rule which Paul intends shall apply to all worship assemblies of the church in all times and places.

Accordingly, the first question here is whether these words convey an instruction for a particular situation or a rule which is general in scope (for all Christian assemblies everywhere) and enduring in time (until the Lord returns).

Moo makes a comparison with Paul's use of *epitrepō* in 1 Corinthians 16:7 ('I hope to remain some time with you if the Lord permits'). But this does not help. The fact that God is the subject of the word 'permit' in 1 Corinthians 16:7 does not determine the intended force of the word in the different context of 1 Timothy 2. Moo further says the present tense of the verb 'can have almost a gnomic timeless force', thus 'any limitation will have to be inferred from the context'.[27] It is indeed possible for the present tense to be used in a timeless way (as in 2 Cor. 9:7 – 'God loves a cheerful giver'). And whether it is used timelessly must indeed be determined by attending to the context to determine the writer's intention. But it does not seem very likely on the face of it that a church leader who is getting on in years and conscious of his mortality (1 Tim. 6:16) is thinking of his own current withholding of a permission as something timeless.[28]

Complementarians say that 'a woman' in verse 12 refers generically to all women.[29] But how can that be? In a context which does not involve the use

---

27. Moo 1980, 65. Schreiner agrees that context must decide: *WITC*, 190.

28. There is one other possibly relevant use of the verb 'permit', which is in the phrase 'it is not permitted' in 1 Cor. 14:34–35. This is of uncertain significance and doubtful authenticity: see chapters 9 and 10. There is no example elsewhere in the whole of the Bible where an enduring or general rule is expressed by the phrase 'I do not permit'.

29. *WITC*, 184 (Schreiner). We will consider this argument further in chapters 12 and 13.

of physical force, the expression 'I do not permit' only makes sense within a range of jurisdiction. Discussing the meanings of 'permit', Tom Schreiner gives the examples of saying to his daughter that she is not permitted to go into the street or is not permitted to drive his car at one hundred miles per hour.[30] These statements make sense because he has jurisdiction over his daughter and his car. But he has no jurisdiction over other people's daughters or cars. If he were to say that he does not permit 'a girl' to go into the street or to drive too fast, such a statement could not be taken to mean that he was laying down the law for all girls in all times and places. If, like Philip (Acts 21:9), he had four daughters, his words would be taken to apply to them. In the same way, Paul's words must be for particular people over whom he has jurisdiction, as the apostle who built up their Christian community. There is nothing in the text to suggest that he is here meaning to claim jurisdiction over future generations everywhere.

Thus Paul's words express a particular restriction. He is not directly laying down the law for all women.

The second question is whether a principle of general application should nonetheless be inferred from this particular restriction. Drawing an inference of this kind is a perfectly normal procedure. So, for example, Paul's instructions on prayer in verses 1–2 are directed to particular people in a particular situation, but this does not prevent them being taken as appropriate guidance for all believers everywhere. His reasoning in verses 3–6 supports such an extrapolation of his remarks about prayer. Similarly, complementarians say that there is good reason to generalize from verse 12 to guide all believers everywhere. Their primary reason is that in verse 13 Paul bases his restriction on a creation principle. By its very nature, a creation principle applies to everyone.[31]

---

30. *WITC*, 190.

31. Their secondary reason is that v. 14, by referring to how Adam and Eve fell, could be intended as more than an illustration; it could be meant as a general justification which has something to do with the differing nature or differing roles of men and women. Such theories are problematic for various reasons, not least that they lack solid support in Genesis (see chapter 5 above), and hence imply that Paul drew something from Genesis that is not really there. Ray Ortlund states: 'Paul in 1 Timothy 2:14 cites the woman's deception as warrant for male headship to be translated from the home into the church.' But he candidly adds, 'Please note that I am not interpreting the logic of the apostle in his making this connection, which logic I am not satisfied that I clearly understand' (*RBMW*, 95, 103). He is right to acknowledge the difficulty.

The complementarian interpretation therefore depends on whether this understanding of verse 13 is correct. But this understanding of verse 13 generates the fourth and severest difficulty, which we will come to after we have considered the second and third.

2. Exclusively male leadership?

The next difficulty lies in establishing Paul's belief in a universal rule of exclusively male leadership authority in the local churches.

We know that he believed in the equal spiritual status of men and women (Gal. 3:26–29) and in the Spirit's distribution of gifts to all believers, and that these gifts included teaching and governing (1 Cor. 12; 14; Rom. 12:3–6). From these beliefs it would follow that suitably gifted women may teach and govern as leaders. So, to establish that he nonetheless believed in exclusively male leadership in the churches, we need to find a clear statement to that effect.

If a clear statement of Paul's belief in male-only leadership were to be found anywhere, the most likely place would be in what he writes about the qualifications for local church elders.[32] We will take a close look at those in chapter 15. For the present, it is sufficient to note that there are prominent complementarian scholars who candidly acknowledge that Paul does not express the qualifications in a way that clearly excludes women.[33] This is distinctly odd if he believed that only men could qualify.

In the absence of a clear statement in the qualifications for elders that only men may become elders of the church, we are left with 1 Timothy 2:12 as the primary scripture for establishing that Paul believed in exclusively male leadership.

But if Paul is concerned to preserve male leadership authority, why in verse 12 does he apparently ban *teaching* by women of men without also banning *prophecy* by women to men? Paul's numbered list in 1 Corinthians 12:28–29 does not show teachers to be more authoritative than prophets. He mentions prophets before teachers not only in that list but also in Romans 12:6–7 and Ephesians 4:11. In the context of the New Testament churches, the correct exercise of a gift of prophecy can be at least as authoritative in its own way as the correct exercise of a gift of teaching. And women are permitted to prophesy to men (1 Cor. 11:2–16). Grudem's answers to this objection largely miss the

---

32. 1 Tim. 3:1–7; Titus 1:6–9.

33. Moo 1981, 211; Schreiner 2010, 35. This feature is a substantial difficulty for the view argued in Blomberg 2014.

point.[34] His only relevant answer is that prophesying did not carry the same authority as teaching. But he offers no convincing justification for this.[35]

Schreiner acknowledges the difficulty. He rejects Grudem's explanation that New Testament prophecy was less authoritative than New Testament teaching. His proposal is that 'women can exercise the gift of prophecy without overturning male headship, whereas 1 Timothy 2:11–15 demonstrates that women cannot regularly teach men without doing so'. But this is not an explanation or justification, for all it does is assert the proposition that Schreiner seeks to establish.[36]

We are left with an unresolved puzzle.

3. Authoritative teaching as a special category?

Complementarians interpret Paul's meaning in verse 12 as something on the lines of 'I do not permit any woman to teach Christian doctrine authoritatively to men, or to exercise authority over men'. They base this on the twin propositions that (1) the word 'teach' in the Pastoral Epistles always has a restricted sense of 'authoritative doctrinal instruction' and (2) authority to teach resides in qualified males (if not apostles, then elders and pastors).[37] These propositions are in harmony with strong traditions concerning church

---

34. He says that (1) prophecy and teaching are separate gifts; (2) prophecy is reporting something that God spontaneously brings to mind while teaching is explaining the apostles' teachings; (3) the fact that people could learn from prophecies does not mean that prophets were the same as teachers; (4) prophecy, like other spiritual gifts, was to be subject to the teaching authority of the elders; and (5) even those who believe that New Testament prophecy was the same as canonical Old Testament prophecy still see a difference between prophecy and Bible teaching. We may readily grant that prophecy and teaching are different gifts (1 Cor. 12:28–31; 14:1–5, 22–33; Acts 11:28; 21:11), and that both must be subject to checks on whether they are being exercised correctly (1 Cor. 14:29; 1 Tim. 1:3). But none of these points meets the objection that genuine prophecy appears to have been as authoritative in the New Testament churches as teaching, and that women are permitted to prophesy to men.

35. Within *EFBT*, 227–232, this is 'Answer 7.3c'.

36. *WITC*, 193–194. Further, his qualification 'regularly' is inconsistent with his own reasoning elsewhere. On 190 he rejects the suggestion that v. 12 is banning frequent teaching while accepting infrequent teaching.

37. *RBMW*, 176–188, especially 181–182 (Moo); *EFBT*, 274–275; *WITC*, 149 (Köstenberger).

leadership in some parts of the church, but there are at least nine factors which raise concerns about whether this perspective can be correct.

1. The immediate context in 1 Timothy 2 does not imply the suggested restrictive meaning for verse 12; there is no indication, in what leads up to verse 12, that Paul's topic is how authority may or may not be properly exercised.

2. This proposal concerning the proper exercise of legitimate authority provides no explanation for Paul's deployment of the very unusual verb *authenteō* in verse 12.

3. As we have seen, Paul's concept of teaching is not restricted in the way that is suggested in the first of the twin propositions, even if we arbitrarily limit our consideration to the Pastoral Epistles. In Titus 2:3–5 the older women are to be teachers of what is good, encouraging the young women to love their husbands. This is teaching, and it is commended in the Pastoral Epistles, but it is not authoritative doctrinal instruction delivered by male elders.[38]

4. We have seen above that Paul appears to expect women to teach in the assembly (Col. 3:16); that in 1 Corinthians 14:26 the men's or women's teaching is not different in kind from the teaching which Paul would deliver in the assembly (1 Cor. 14:6); and that the same word describes also the teaching that Timothy should do (2 Tim. 4:2), or that elders must hold on to (Titus 1:9), without any contextual requirement of a different meaning.

5. The concept that there are two kinds of teaching activity, one being 'authoritative doctrinal instruction' and the other being some other kind of Christian teaching activity, is not explicit in Paul's writings or anywhere else in the New Testament.[39] This distinction, which was invented later, would likely

---

38. Moo 1980, 65–66, had earlier argued from 1 Tim. 3:2; 5:17; Titus 1:9 that the teaching gift was restricted to elders, supported by the fact that Paul and Timothy were teachers. This argument lacked merit. None of the texts cited by Moo states that the gift is restricted in this way. The fact that Paul and Timothy were teachers does not tell us to what other men or women the teaching gift was given. Moo 1981, 200–201, subsequently clarified his statement about the teaching gift being restricted to elders as applying only to the Pastoral Epistles. Given the absence of the stated restriction in the Pastoral Epistles, and the explicit evidence that the teaching gift was not so restricted (for example, Titus 2:3), this clarification did not rescue the argument.

39. That is, unless one adopts the minority view that Paul's expression in 1 Cor. 7:25 ('I have no command from the Lord') indicates non-authoritative teaching, despite his phrase, in the same verse, 'one who has been shown by the Lord's mercy to be faithful' and despite 7:40 ('I consider myself to have the Spirit of God'). This would

have puzzled him; in the New Testament, teaching is generally either true or false: either faithful to the apostolic message or not.[40]

6. We have also seen that the apostolic tradition, which Paul calls the 'pattern of sound words' and the 'good deposit' (2 Tim. 1:13–14), and which includes how to live a godly life as a Christian, is not passed on solely by words spoken in a meeting but also by godly example across the whole of life (see 1 Tim. 4:11–16 and other references discussed above). This makes it even more difficult to imagine Paul thinking in terms of a special category of teaching activity which constitutes authoritative verbal doctrinal instruction, as contrasted with all other legitimate forms of teaching. We would need some clear evidence of Paul making the supposed distinction somewhere in his writings. But the distinction is an artificial one, which Paul does not make.[41]

7. If the ban were on women delivering authoritative teaching, it should ban women both from authoritative teaching of men and from authoritative teaching of women. For if women teachers are not called and equipped by God to convey accurate Christian teaching, other women need protection from their substandard teaching as much as men do. To meet this objection a complementarian may say that the problem is not in the teaching itself but in the fact that the proper relation between men and women should be observed. But that is to give up the idea of there being a particular mode of teaching that counts as authoritative. The argument is then simply that women should never teach men. But that sits ill with Acts 18:26; 1 Corinthians 14:26; Colossians 3:16.

8. If Paul's concern is that authoritative teaching must only be delivered by a particular group of qualified males, why does he not say so? What he says in verses 11–14 is cast in terms of 'a man' and 'a woman'. His choice of words does not point to teaching authority residing specifically in a particular group of qualified men. Nor is it said anywhere else in the New Testament that the task of handing on the authoritative apostolic message resides exclusively in

---

(note 39 *cont.*) mean a distinction between some apostolic teaching that was authoritative and other apostolic teaching that was not. This is not the distinction that complementarians propose.

40. There are also things that are matters of indifference, being neither commanded nor forbidden. These do not impact on the present discussion, which is about an explicit restriction.

41. Of course, teaching delivered by a person who is in a recognized position, whether eldership or some other position, will thereby tend to carry more 'authority' than teaching delivered by someone who is not in such a position. But that is a different point.

such a group. This notion, though widely held, is not biblical. It rests on a confusion. Some elders have a ministry of teaching (1 Tim. 5:17). And the elders
as a group are responsible for guarding the flock against false teaching (Acts
20.28–31; 1 Pet. 5:2). This means that they are responsible to ensure that what
is taught is in line with the apostolic teaching, so that the apostolic message is
handed on. But it does not mean that they must do all of the teaching themselves, silencing the gifts of those (whether men or women) whom the Lord
has equipped with ability to teach.

9. The example of Priscilla's teaching of Apollos is about as authoritative as
one may imagine. As we have seen, with her husband, as co-host of the local
congregation in Ephesus (1 Cor. 16:8, 19), she corrects the doctrinal understanding of one of the chief teachers of the church. If authoritative teaching
is a special category, Priscilla is doing it.[42]

The New Testament does not portray authoritative doctrinal instruction by
qualified males as a special sub-category of Christian teaching.

4. A creation principle?

In verse 13 Paul appeals to the order of creation of man and woman before the
fall. This is said to show that we should infer from verse 12 an enduring rule,
which is rooted in creation and 'transcends cultures and societies', not merely a
temporary restriction applicable to a particular situation.[43] It is often considered
that Paul's appeal to creation is the trump card in favour of the complementarian
view of 1 Timothy 2. But in reality Paul's appeal to Genesis raises one of the most
serious objections to the coherence of the complementarian interpretation.

The problem is that the argument proves too much.[44] If it is really the case
that Paul understood the order of creation of Adam and Eve as establishing a

---

42. In addition, hypothetically, if there had been in New Testament times a distinction
    between authoritative teaching by qualified men and non-authoritative teaching by
    others, there would be a difficulty in applying this distinction to the situation today.
    Evangelical Christians recognize the Bible as the primary authority for faith and
    practice. Doctrinal authority under God does not reside in the teacher, but in the
    text. Today, if we were to make a distinction between authoritative teaching and
    other teaching, it would be a distinction between the Bible and human teachers.
    See further Tidball 2012, 267, citing J. I. Packer.

43. *EFBT*, 69.

44. An argument 'proves too much' when it proves not only the desired conclusion
    but also a further conclusion which is evidently false. This shows that the argument
    is unsound.

principle that men are created to be the authoritative leaders of women, then there is no justifiable basis for restricting the application of this creation principle to leadership in the churches; rather, it should apply across the whole of human life. It would follow that women should not be leaders with authority in public or political life or civil society, or in education, science, commerce or the arts, or anywhere else where men are to be found. In substance, this was the traditional view (see chapter 1), though it is now rejected by egalitarians and most complementarians as not truly justified from Scripture. The idea that verse 13 established a universal creation principle of male leadership has had to be abandoned, because the six Greek words which constitute that verse could not bear the weight that was placed on them. Here the fragility of the complementarian position on church ministry comes into sharp focus, as an uncomfortable half-way house between the traditional view and full affirmation of women's participation in leadership.

The standard answer to this objection is that the New Testament only applies the creation principle of authoritative male headship to marriage and to church leadership, so there is no scriptural warrant for applying it to the whole of life.[45] But this is not a sufficient answer, for it fails to grapple with the incoherence of the complementarian understanding of the nature of Paul's reliance on Genesis in verse 13.

Genesis 2 is itself authoritative Scripture. If Paul genuinely considers that there is a creation principle of exclusively male leadership in Genesis 2, its application cannot be limited to marriage, on the basis that Adam and Eve were husband and wife, because Paul himself applies the principle beyond that sphere (namely, to church leadership). On this basis we have to regard Adam and Eve not merely as husband and wife but also as representative of humanity more generally. Accordingly, this creation principle ought to be applied consistently to the relations of created men and women in general. If there is really a creation principle of authoritative male leadership, which ought to apply across the whole of created human life, this conflicts with the modern complementarian position, in which the only definite places for exclusively male leadership are marriage and church. Thus the argument from verse 13 proves too much; it leads to a conclusion which modern complementarians say is wrong.

---

45. *EFBT*, 392–393. Similarly, Sandom 2012, 177–197, argues that the only definite restrictions on women's roles are in marriage and church. See also Smith 2012, 64–65. But sometimes a less crisp view is expressed. In *RBMW*, 37–43 (Piper) and 80 (Piper and Grudem) there are expressions of uncertainty about whether women should refrain from certain occupations.

Moreover, if there were a creation principle of authoritative male leadership, the most likely place for there to be an exception to it would not be in society at large. It would be in the church, where creation is being overtaken by new creation in Christ. In the church, the effects of the fall, including the male rule of Genesis 3:16, are being healed and put right. In the church, men and women are full partners in God's work (Rom. 12:1–8; 16:1–16). In the church, men and women receive the same full inheritance in Christ (Gal. 3:26–29).

How can the difficulty be resolved? The obvious answer is to say that Paul's appeal to Genesis should be understood as a supporting illustration, not as reliance upon a creation principle. This would also have the advantage of removing the clash with what we see in the Old Testament, where God called Deborah to a position of authoritative leadership over men (see chapter 5).

But once we accept that Paul is not relying on a creation principle, how can we say that his reference to Genesis justifies an enduring and universal rule rather than only a temporary and local restriction? On this alternative basis the argument from verse 13 proves too little; it seems that egalitarians have after all a valid point about the nature of Paul's appeal to Genesis.

The severity of this difficulty for the complementarian position on women's ministry is hard to overstate. In one way or another it keeps rearing its head in complementarian discussions of 1 Timothy 2. For example:

- In *WITC* Tom Schreiner discusses 1 Timothy 2:9–15 over more than sixty pages without offering an answer to it. Instead, he magnifies it by making clear that there is no real basis for restricting the application of the principle of male leadership to church and marriage. He states explicitly that Paul 'inferred from the order of creation in Genesis 2 that women should not teach or exercise authority over men'. He adds: 'role differences were common in ancient societies. The original readers would have understood Paul, then, to be defending such role differences and to be doing so on the basis of the created order.'[46] If the creation order places men in authority over women, such a principle must apply across all human society. The standard complementarian position contradicts this, because it applies exclusively male leadership only to marriage and church and not elsewhere. The complementarian analysis of Paul's reasoning is incoherent.
- Similarly, Douglas Moo states: 'Women are not to teach men nor to have authority over men because such activity would violate the structure of created sexual relationships and would involve the woman in something

---

46. *WITC*, 163–225 (201, 204).

for which she is not suited.'[47] If this is so, it means that all women are subject to all men, and this should apply in every area of life. But most complementarians, including Moo,[48] reject this conclusion.

Is there perhaps another way out of the difficulty? Is it possible that Paul sees Adam and Eve as standing not only for husband and wife in a human family but also as standing for the leaders and the led in the new family of the church? This idea seems to lie behind some complementarian expositions, even if only by implication.[49] But this is not a viable solution for understanding how Paul views the Genesis account. No-one seriously suggests that Paul reads Genesis 2 allegorically as being really about church life under the new covenant, with Adam standing for male elders and Eve standing for church members; it is truly about what it appears to be about – God's creation of man and woman – and Paul so reads it. Any solution which tries to read across from Genesis to church leadership ends up distorting the usual scriptural analogies of God's people as a family. Instead of God as the parent and God's people as the children (John 1:12–13), or Jesus as the firstborn and believers as his brothers (Rom. 8:29), it becomes necessary to see Adam (the husband) as corresponding to authoritative male teaching elders and Eve (the wife) as corresponding to the other men of the church plus the women and children. No such analogy is drawn anywhere in Scripture. Believers are God's family, not the elders' family.

We are given no satisfactory explanation of how it can be that Paul sees in Genesis a creation principle of men's authority over women, which is sufficiently general that it extends beyond the relation of husband and wife, but which nonetheless is to be applied nowhere else except in the least likely setting: the community of God's redeemed people where in Christ a new creation has begun (2 Cor. 5:17).

Making a fresh start

The debate is at an impasse.

Among egalitarians, there is a wide range of conflicting suggestions on how to interpret 1 Timothy 2; there is no consensus, and tough questions remain unanswered.

---

47. Moo 1980, 82.
48. *RBMW*, 182–183.
49. *EFBT*, 80–81; *RBMW*, 237–250 (Poythress).

Some complementarians fair-mindedly acknowledge, either expressly or by implication, that their reading of 1 Timothy 2, which they mistakenly term 'traditional', is ripe for review. Al Wolters states that there are certainly difficulties that justify a reconsideration. Robert Yarbrough says that Bible-believing Christians of all persuasions must realize that 1 Timothy 2:12 presents an interpretive challenge.[50]

When two sides are locked in a disagreement over something that ought to be resolvable, sometimes a fresh start is needed. Experience teaches that, when a dead end has been reached, this may be because both sides share an incorrect perspective. Identifying and correcting such a perspective can open up a new path to a better understanding. Might that be the case here?

The debate has taken place largely on the basis that Paul's focus in chapter 2 is on the conduct of the public worship assemblies of the church. This is a regular feature of both complementarian and egalitarian expositions.[51] It is of particular importance in most complementarian analyses, because limiting Paul's words in verse 12 to the public assemblies of the church enables them to accommodate the example of Priscilla: even if her teaching of Apollos was authoritative doctrinal instruction, it was certainly not delivered in the public assembly (Acts 18:26).

But is it correct that in 1 Timothy 2 Paul is giving instructions specifically for the conduct of the public assemblies of the church? Is this perspective supported by the context?

1 Timothy 2 and the public assemblies of the church

When we examine the context closely, there are numerous features which suggest that this common perspective may be mistaken. There are no contextual features which establish a specific focus on the public assembly. Some features are definitely not limited to the public assembly. Some suggest that Paul's focus is not the public assembly.

1. The context leading up to chapter 2 is chapter 1. This chapter contains no specific reference to public assemblies and is certainly not limited to them.

---

50. *EFBT*, 647 (Wolters), 655–656 (Yarbrough). Their reading is in fact novel, not traditional. The traditional reading involves a male leadership principle applicable across all human society.

51. For example, complementarian: Hurley 1981, 200; *EFBT*, 65–66; Sandom 2012, 155; *WITC*, 175–176, 190–191 (Schreiner); Smith 2012, 45–46; Yarbrough 2018, 144, 161–185; and egalitarian: Perriman 1998, 141, 166–167; *DBE*, 206 (Belleville), 376 (Fee); Towner 2006, 190; *M&W*, 326; Tidball 2012, 256–257.

2. In 2:1–7 Paul urges prayers for a quiet and godly life, to facilitate the effective spread of the gospel. Such prayers could be offered individually or corporately and, when corporately, in small groups or in large, in private or in public. Paul gives no indication that he envisages the public assembly of the church as the only situation in which they are offered; no such limitation is stated or even hinted at in verses 1–7. (Compare Eph. 6:18.)

3. The most prominent driver of the conventional view is verse 8. Paul desires that the men lift holy hands in prayer without quarrelling. The possibility of quarrelling indicates a group context. The conventional view draws an inference that Paul's focus is the public worship assembly.[52] But this inference is not warranted. He says that this mode of prayer is to be 'in every place' (*en panti topō*).[53] The phrase *en panti topō* is not limited to the public assemblies of the gathered church; it extends to any and every location where men pray together, presumably meaning at least all such locations in Ephesus. There is a possibility that Paul is here echoing Malachi 1:11, where Malachi foretells a time when there will be pure worship of God in every place (Septuagint: *en panti topō*).[54] So the phrase *en panti topō* could refer more widely, not just to all the various places where men pray in Ephesus, but to every place in the world where there are people who have accepted the Christian message. Either way, the focus of the phrase is on every location where men are praying, not specifically on the gathered assembly of the men and women of the church.

Moreover, in New Testament times men and women were not separated in the assembly of the gathered church.[55] Paul's separate instructions for 'the men'

---

52. So, for example, *EFBT*, 65; Smith 2012, 27.

53. Some have seen an allusion to the Jewish temple here, because in a few instances in the Gospels and Acts the temple is referred to by the word *topos* (Matt. 24:15; John 11:48; Acts 6:13–14; 21:28). Such an allusion is conceivable, but *topos* is a very common word, and the phrase *en panti topō* is a quite different usage.

54. Certainly, for Paul the universality of the spread of true godliness through the gospel is an important idea: see 1 Cor. 1:2 (God's people *en panti topō*); 2 Cor. 2:14 (the knowledge of Christ *en panti topō*); 1 Thess. 1:8 (the Lord's message and faith known *en panti topō*). See also the references in 1 Tim. 2:1, 4 and 6 to 'all people', which lead up to v. 8.

55. See Chrysostom, Homily 73 on Matt. 23:14. He refers to the partitions used in the church in his time (late fourth century). He says that, as he hears from the elders, 'of old' there were no such partitions, and in Paul's time 'both men and women were together'. But he considers the partitions are justified in his own day as a remedy against wantonness ('the men are in no better state than frantic horses').

and for 'women' provide no positive support for the view that he is thinking specifically of the assembly of the gathered church.

4. In verses 9–10 he gives women instructions about adornment. It is not reasonable to read these instructions for women as focused specifically on the public assembly, since Paul says that, instead of adorning themselves with gold and the like, women should adorn themselves with good works (v. 10). It cannot seriously be suggested that he intended their good works to be done specifically and only, or even primarily, in the meetings of the assembled church. He is mainly thinking of the good works that women do, or should do, away from the assembly.

5. Verses 11–14 are concerned with learning and with teaching. There is no indication by Paul of a change of context from verse 10, and there is no justification in the text for reading these verses as focused specifically on the assembly or as limited to the assembly. The public assembly is just one of a variety of situations where learning and teaching may take place. When in Ephesus, Paul taught both 'in public and from house to house' (Acts 20:20, ESV). A meeting in a house could be private or open, with one person or many. Teaching may take place in groups of any size, formal or informal. As we have seen, teaching by example takes place across the whole of life. Schreiner tries to limit verses 11–14 to the public assembly by arguing that 'teaching' in the Pastoral Epistles refers only to 'the transmission of tradition in congregational contexts, not to informal sharing'.[56] But this is not borne out by what Paul writes. For example, it cannot seriously be suggested that Paul's instruction in Titus 2:3–5 to the older women to teach the younger women to love their husbands and children, to be good household managers, and so on, is to be implemented specifically and solely by teaching them in the public assembly where men and women gather together to worship the Lord. Are the men supposed to stop their ears while the women deliver this teaching in the assembly? Similarly, once we have understood Paul's holistic view of teaching, it is difficult to read 2 Timothy 2:2 as limited exclusively to transmission of tradition by formal verbal teaching of an assembled congregation. Neither Paul's concept of teaching nor the Greek words for teaching are so narrow. (And see 2 Tim. 2:3 – can it sensibly be proposed that Paul's mind is on the public assembly?) But in any event the mode and setting of teaching which Paul has in mind in 1 Timothy 2:12 must be determined from its own context, such as the adjacent reference to doing good works.

---

56. *WITC*, 175 (Schreiner).

6. For verses 11–12 Paul switches from the plural ('women' – vv. 9–10) to the singular ('a woman should learn'). The shift makes advance preparation for his references to Adam and Eve in verses 13–14.[57] But he could have said the same things about Adam and Eve without making this shift in advance. In verse 12 he is not allowing 'a woman' to do something to 'a man'. This does not sound like something done in the public assembly. It sounds like something done by one individual to another. The transition to the singular at this point would be a confusing and counter-intuitive move if his focus were on the public assembly of men and women.

7. Paul's supporting material in verses 13–14 is from the story of the creation and fall of Adam and Eve. This is not set in anything even remotely analogous to a public assembly of the church, nor is there anything in the story that indicates its application specifically to public worship. It is about transgressive behaviour by one woman and one man.

8. In verse 15 Paul says that 'she' will be saved through the childbearing, if 'they' remain in faith and love and holiness, with self-control. We will consider in chapter 13 what Paul intends by his reference to childbearing. In whatever way it is interpreted, we may say with a high degree of confidence that Paul was not thinking of the childbearing taking place in the public assemblies of the church. And the qualities of faith, love, holiness and self-control, like the good works instructed in verse 10, are to be exhibited across the whole of life. These remarks are not focused on the public assembly.

9. Looking at how the context continues after chapter 2, Paul moves on to the qualifications for elders and deacons. The qualities which Paul lists as requirements for elders and deacons are qualities which apply across a wide range of life circumstances. And there is nothing in 3:1–13 or anywhere else to show that the duties of elders or deacons are limited to what occurs in the public assembly of the church. Verses 1–13 are not focused on the public assembly, which is not mentioned. (On *ekklēsia* in 3:5, see below.)

10. In 3:14–15 Paul restates the general reason for his instructions to Timothy, which is that until Paul's own arrival back in Ephesus Timothy should know how to behave in the household of God, the church (*ekklēsia*), which functions as a pillar of the truth. This should not be read anachronistically, as if Paul had in mind what we might call 'being in church'. In 3:15, as also in 3:5 and 5:16, he uses *ekklēsia* in the sense of the people whom God has called into a new family. As we see throughout the letter, the steps which Timothy is to take relate to a wide range of aspects of the life of God's people. Paul is

---

57. Köstenberger concurs: *WITC*, 155.

certainly not limiting Timothy's actions to things done in the church's public assemblies.[58]

In sum, the supposed limitation of chapter 2 to the public worship assembly does not fit what Paul writes. There is no specific mention of the public assembly in chapters 1–3. The supposed limitation is supported neither by the preceding context (chapter 1) nor by the succeeding context (chapter 3). It is in sharp conflict with the references to good works, faith, love, holiness and childbearing. These show that Paul is not focusing on the public assembly.[59]

'Do your best to present yourself to God as one approved, a worker who does not need to be ashamed and who correctly handles the word of truth' (2 Tim. 2:15, NIV). The kinds of difficulties we have seen in the present chapter, which are faced by egalitarian and complementarian interpretations, may suggest that the word of truth is not yet being correctly handled. Viewing 1 Timothy 2 through the specific lens of assembled public worship has made it hard to understand; it is like trying to get a better view by looking through the wrong end of a telescope.

Having identified this misunderstanding, we can lay it aside and make a fresh start.

Summary of chapter 11

1. The purpose of Paul's instructions in 1 Timothy is to combat false teaching and ungodliness and promote right teaching and godliness in Christ.

---

58. If, contrary to the more natural interpretation of the Greek, 3:14–15 is read as meaning that Paul is writing to tell Timothy how the church should behave, rather than how Timothy himself should behave in order to guide the church, this makes no material difference. The instructions concerning how God's people should behave are not limited to what occurs in the public assemblies, as we have seen in 1 Tim. 1 – 2, and as is apparent also from 1 Tim. 3 – 6.

59. This point is also made by J. M. Holmes: see *WITC*, 175–176, n. 58 (Schreiner). Hugenberger 1992 and Westfall 2016, 286–289, 297, both concur that the public assembly is not in view (but their interpretation that Paul is speaking narrowly of husband and wife has not proven widely persuasive; see above). Knight 1992, 131, acknowledges that the context of vv. 9–15 is not limited to worship services. But in contradiction of this, he interprets Paul's remarks in vv. 11–14 largely as if they were so limited: 139, 141 ('the edification of the service', 'women's learning in public instruction', 'in the midst of the assembled people of God', 'publicly teaching men, and thus teaching the church').

2. There is a debate about the meaning of Paul's restriction on women in 1 Timothy 2:11–15. Major difficulties which all interpreters must deal with include (a) the incompleteness of our information about the circumstances in Ephesus; (b) the uncertainty over the meaning of the rare verb *authenteō* in verse 12; and (c) Paul's compressed style of writing in the critical passage.

3. The debate about the meaning of Paul's restriction is not a contest between an absolute and universal interpretation and a contingent and limited interpretation. Both sides recognize that Paul's intention must be limited in some way, in order to be consistent with his affirmations of teaching by women. The disagreement is about the nature of his intended limitation.

4. Egalitarians have suggested that Paul's restriction in verse 12 is limited to remedying a particular temporary problem in Ephesus. But they have struggled to find an explanation of Paul's meaning which both fits the available evidence about what was actually occurring at Ephesus and fits with the details of what Paul writes. I have drawn attention to four tough questions which egalitarian interpretations have difficulty in answering (see 219).

5. Complementarians contend that in verse 12 Paul is concerned with who delivers authoritative teaching in the church. But there are severe difficulties with this. They include the following:

- 'I do not permit' / 'I am not permitting' would be a strange choice of expression for stating an enduring rule applicable to all public assemblies of the church in all times and places. Paul's restriction applies to particular people over whom he has jurisdiction. This form of expression is not used anywhere else in the Bible for laying down an enduring rule. Inferring a principle of general application is dependent upon understanding verse 13 as Paul's appeal to a creation principle.
- There is no clear statement by Paul that local church leadership must be exclusively male. If Paul meant in verse 12 to preserve male leadership authority, he should also have banned women from prophesying to men, but in 1 Corinthians he permitted it.
- Scripture does not explicitly recognize a special activity of authoritative teaching that is different from other Christian teaching activities and that is allocated to a specific group of men.
- If Paul really considers (as complementarians assert) that Genesis 2 teaches a creation principle of authoritative male leadership, which applies to the church, this principle should apply across the whole of life. But complementarians contradict this by their reluctance to apply it so widely. Their analysis does not provide a coherent explanation of Paul's reliance on Genesis.

6. The debate has reached an impasse. A fresh start is needed. Most commentators on both sides have proceeded on the basis that in 1 Timothy 2 Paul is giving instructions specifically for the conduct of the public assemblies of the church. But this does not fit the details of what Paul writes. To break the impasse, the first step is to recognize that chapter 2 is not focused on the public assembly.

Questions to consider

1. Under the heading 'The nature of the disagreement' there are seven bullet points. Do you regard any of these as controversial? If so, which ones? Why?
2. What is your view of the context of verse 12? Is chapter 2 dealing specifically with public worship assemblies or not? If you are unsure of the answer, what are your doubts?
3. Are there any ideas in chapter 11 which are new to you? What are they, and what do you think of them? In what ways are they relevant to your life?

12. TEACHING AND 1 TIMOTHY 2: CONTEXTUAL KEYS

How can a young person stay on the path of purity?
By living according to your word.

(Ps. 119:9, NIV)

Opening the doors into 1 Timothy 2

In the last chapter we looked at some severe difficulties with both egalitarian and complementarian interpretations of 1 Timothy 2. This passage of Paul's writings seems like a locked room. Interpreters peer through the keyholes of different doors, but without getting a full view of what is inside. So they cannot agree on what they are seeing.

We have identified the shared misconception that the context is limited to or focused on the public assemblies of the church. The removal of this misconception frees us to move forward. In this chapter I identify four keys which unlock the doors. Over the next two chapters these will enable us to enter the room. In different ways, all of the keys are concerned with the use of context to help us understand what Paul means. When we use these four keys, we find an understanding of Paul's text as a clear and continuous train of connected thought.

Before identifying the four keys it is necessary to sketch out more fully the historical context of chapter 2.

Because of the controversy over the meaning of *authenteō* in verse 12 I will initially use its Greek root *authent-* as if it were an English word, without translation.

The historical context

To help us to understand what Paul writes to Timothy in chapter 2 of his first letter we may make judicious use of background information from Paul's ministry in Ephesus as recounted in Acts (from 52 to 55), his farewell to the Ephesian elders at Miletus (57), his subsequent letter to the Ephesians (about 57–59), the wider situation in Ephesus, the whole of his first letter to Timothy (63 or 64), the nature of the false teachings and the nature of Paul's relationship with Timothy.[1]

We may also make careful use of 2 Timothy, since this is widely believed, on strong grounds, to have been written not long after the first letter.[2] Paul's letter to Titus, written near the same time, may be used as evidence of Paul's own thinking, but should not be treated as a reliable source of information about false teaching current in Ephesus, because Titus was working in Crete, not in Ephesus.

Paul describes Timothy as his co-worker, his brother, and his beloved son in the faith.[3] Timothy was already a believer when Paul first met him (Acts 16:1–2). The description 'son' probably reflects the difference in their ages (1 Tim. 4:12) and the nature of their relationship as mentor and apprentice. Paul circumcised him, so that (paradoxically) he could take Timothy with him when delivering the apostles' and elders' ruling that circumcision was not required (Acts 15:1 – 16:4), and probably so that Timothy could accompany him when he was preaching in synagogues (Acts 17:1–4, 11–14).[4] Timothy was a companion of Paul during the events described in Acts 16:3 – 17:15; 18:5 – 19:22; and 20:3–12. This means he was present for part of Paul's ministry in Ephesus. Luke does

---

1. Dates in this paragraph are taken from Mosse 2007, 298–301. See also Acts 19:10; 20:31.

2. Mosse 2007, 311, 313, dates 1 Timothy in 63–64 and 2 Timothy in 67–68. Knight 1992, 54, suggests 61–63 for 1 Timothy and 64–67 for 2 Timothy.

3. See Rom. 16:21; 1 Cor. 4:17; 2 Cor. 1:1; Phil. 2:22; 1 Thess. 3:2; 1 Tim. 1:2, 18; 2 Tim. 1:2.

4. This seemingly paradoxical action by Paul shows the lengths he was prepared to go, to defend and advance the gospel. He had very recently taken a firm stand of insisting that circumcision was not necessary to salvation (Acts 15), having written to the Galatians that, if they let themselves be circumcised, Christ would be of no benefit to them (Gal. 5:2). The principle having been established, there was no inconsistency in asking Timothy to accept the personal cost of being circumcised in order to facilitate their mission.

not say for how long after Acts 20:12 Timothy continued to travel with Paul. However, we may infer that Timothy was very familiar with Paul's teaching and outlook, and that in their partnership Paul was the one who supplied the leadership by example and instruction.

Priscilla and Aquila were prominent in the work at Ephesus. Paul's close partnership with them had commenced at Corinth (Acts 18:1–3) and they travelled with him to Ephesus, where he left them in situ (18:18–21). The church met in their house (1 Cor. 16:8, 19). It was while Paul was away that they took Apollos aside and explained to him the way of God more accurately (Acts 18:24–26). During Paul's years in Ephesus he overcame evil spirits in the name of Jesus (19:11–16), while some Jewish exorcists who tried to do the same were overpowered by the person who was under the influence of the evil spirit. This became well known. Some of the Ephesians who became believers were practitioners of magic (sorcery). As a result of what happened to the Jewish exorcists, and presumably also Paul's teaching, these believers disclosed their magical practices (*praxis*),[5] brought their books of magic arts (*periergos*)[6] and burned them. The value of the books was estimated at 50,000 pieces of silver (Acts 19:19). Evidently there were wealthy people at Ephesus who were deeply involved in the occult.[7] For God's people, sorcery was forbidden knowledge. It was strictly prohibited in the Law and was condemned in the Prophets (for example, Exod. 22:18; Deut. 18:9–13; Mal. 3:5). This setting probably explains why Paul's subsequent letter to the Ephesians contains his longest passage of instruction concerning effective warfare against the spiritual forces of evil (Eph. 6:10–18). A book known to Paul called the Wisdom of Solomon condemned sorcery (Wis. 12:4), and it appears that when he wrote to the Ephesians Paul drew from this book for his vivid description of the Christian's spiritual armour.[8]

---

5. One of the meanings given for this word in LSJ is 'magical operation, spell'.

6. This word refers to the practice of magic, not to the books.

7. Arnold 2010, 34, suggests that Luke's choice of words in v. 18 (*pepisteukotōn* – 'having believed') shows the strong pull that magical practices and the like continued to have even on some who had become believers. This may be reading too much into Luke's choice of words on its own, since the meaning could simply be 'when they believed'. However, the suggestion seems true to life and does not conflict with the context.

8. Paul draws on the Wisdom of Solomon in several of his letters. Well-known examples are Rom. 1:19–32 (Wis. 13 – 14) and 9:21 (Wis. 15:7). For the Christian's spiritual armour, Paul appears to draw the helmet of salvation from Isa. 59:17; the breastplate of righteousness from Isa. 59:17 and Wis. 5:18; the 'whole armour' from

Ephesus was famous for its vast temple of Artemis. The impact of the gospel on participation in the cult of the goddess led to a major public disturbance, instigated by a silversmith concerned at the loss of trade and the denigration of the goddess (Acts 19:23 – 20:1). The riot was defused only by skilful intervention on the part of the town clerk (19:35–41). This event suggests that the impact of the gospel was mainly upon pagans, although it seems there were also Jews who responded (see 19:8–10, 33–34). Paul saw his time there as a wonderful opportunity, albeit with many fierce adversaries (*antikeimai*) (1 Cor. 15:32; 16:9). This was par for the course: 'all who want to live a godly [*eusebos*] life in Christ Jesus will be persecuted' (2 Tim. 3:12).

Historical background information confirms and fills out the setting of these events. Ephesus was the leading city of the richest region of the Roman Empire. The temple of Artemis was known as the greatest of the Seven Wonders of the ancient world. In first-century Ephesus Artemis seems to have been something of a combination: a traditional Asian deity with the Greek huntress-goddess myth superimposed. In the Greek myth, shortly after Artemis was born, she helped her own mother through childbirth. Worshippers of this idol sought her help for safety in childbearing. She was depicted with the astrological signs of the Zodiac around her neck (indicating that she was lord over the cosmic powers), and was also directly linked with magical practices. Magic included manipulation of the spirit world. Ephesus was such a well-known centre for magic that written magic spells (magic words) were known as 'Ephesian letters'. These were supposed to ward off or drive out demons. Astrology was not the same as magic, but it was closely connected, because magic offered the possibility of altering fate by manipulating astral powers. Exorcism was in some cases linked to the planets. Inscriptional evidence indicates that the cult of Artemis included the performance of 'mysteries'. The pagan mystery religions supported astrology, and even first-century Judaism was influenced by astrological beliefs.[9] Christians regarded magic and astrology together as demonic,

Wis. 5:17; and perhaps also the belt of truth from Isa. 11:5 and the shield and the sword from Wis. 5:19–20. (Wisdom dates from the first century BC. It is included in Roman Catholic editions of the Bible.)

9. Arnold 1993a, 249; Arnold 1989, 20–29; Antipater of Sidon, *Greek Anthology* 9.58. As to safety in childbearing, see Glahn 2015. For additional details on Artemis, astrology and magic, see Arnold 2010, 31–36. An online search for images of 'Artemis of the Ephesians' will find statues of Artemis with the signs of the Zodiac around her neck and bulbous objects hanging on her front, which are now thought to be little bags of magic spells.

and astrology was associated with heresy in the minds of early Christian writers.[10] Practitioners of magic could be either men or women.[11] Chapter 3 of the *Didache* (about 60–100) says: 'Do not be an enchanter or an astrologer or a magician. Moreover, have no wish to observe or heed such practices, for all this breeds idolatry.'

There are numerous implied cross-links between the text of 1 Timothy and the known religious life of Ephesus. God the Saviour (1:1; 2:3–4) and Jesus the Lord (1:2, 12; compare 1:15) stand in contrast to Artemis, who was acclaimed by her devotees as Saviour (*sōteira*) and Lord (*kuria*).[12] Deacons are required to hold to the mystery of the faith (3:9), not to the mysteries of Artemis and other pagan deities who were worshipped in Ephesus. Ephesians loudly claimed that Artemis was *megas* ('great' – Acts 19:27–28, 34–35), but Paul affirms that Jesus Christ, who embodied the mystery of godliness, is *megas* (1 Tim. 3:16). The believers are the congregation of 'a living god' (3:15) not of a lifeless idol. In 4:7–10 there is an implied contrast of true godliness with false teachings and devotion to Artemis ('we have put our hope in a living god, who is a saviour of all people').[13]

When Paul met with the elders of the Ephesian church at Miletus, he reminded them of his ministry among them, especially his example of serving the Lord with humility, tears, trials and hard work, and teaching publicly and from house to house (Acts 20:19–21, 31–35). He warned them that savage wolves would come into the flock and some even from among their own number would teach falsely to draw disciples after them (Acts 20:29–30). There are indications in his subsequent letter to the Ephesians that there may have been an influx of new converts subsequent to his period of ministry in Ephesus (Eph. 1:15; 3:2–4; 4:21). His letter warned the Ephesians again about the danger of false teaching (4:14; 5:6).

Subsequent events showed that his concern was well justified. It appears that a crisis of false teaching overtook his expectation in Acts 20:25 that he would never see the Ephesian elders again. It caused him to change his previous plan

---

10. Hegedus 2007, 139, 146. Augustine later expressed this in typically pithy fashion, stating that 'heretics and astrologers' came from the serpent: *Literal Commentary on Genesis* 2.17.35.

11. Cartwright 2016.

12. Although salvation is a common theme in Paul's letters, it is only in this letter (with the letter to Titus, written around the same time) that Paul, apparently provoked by beliefs about Artemis, describes God as Saviour.

13. Compare Paul's similar contrast with idols in Acts 14:15; 2 Cor. 6:16; 1 Thess. 1:9.

of heading west from Rome (Rom. 15:23–28).[14] Instead, upon release from his first Roman imprisonment, he went to Asia, including to Ephesus, where he excluded two false teachers from the church (1 Tim. 1:19–20). First Timothy was written to continue the task of combating false teaching in Ephesus.

We shall make use of this background information as we seek to understand what Paul writes to Timothy.

Four contextual keys

Four keys will unlock an interpretation which does full justice to Paul's words. Each key opens a different door into the room. Each way in leads towards the same conclusion as to the meaning of verse 12.

These are the keys:

- The first key is to ensure that we read 2:9–15 genuinely in the context of 1:1 – 2:8, because that is the context which leads up to the disputed passage.
- The second key is to use 5:3–16 to aid our understanding of the historical situation in chapter 2.
- The third key is to ascertain the meaning of *authenteō* provisionally from the context of what Paul writes, and then check it against the range of possible meanings. (This is appropriate in the current circumstances where scholars differ sharply over the meaning of this word, both here and in other texts where it appears; there is no sufficient consensus from which to begin. Some commentators have proceeded in the opposite direction of first selecting a meaning from the range, and then shoehorning the passage into an interpretation that is consistent with the selected meaning; this is a faulty method.)
- The fourth key is to pay attention to the signposts which Paul provides in 2:15.

I chose the first and third keys at the outset of my study of this passage, on the basis that they embody sound methods of interpretation in the applicable circumstances. I only became aware of the second and fourth keys while examining the context.

---

14. Mosse 2007, 221.

The basis of the second key

The basis of the second key requires explanation.

There are two extended passages in the letter where Paul focuses particularly on women: 2:9–15, which is the focus of our inquiry, and 5:3–16, where Paul gives instructions about widows. To arrive at an interpretation which is fully grounded in the historical context we may place 2:9–15 and 5:3–16 together and allow them to be mutually interpretive.

But is this a legitimate step? How would the first readers of 2:9–15 know what is coming three chapters later? Is it realistic to imagine that they would understand Paul's words in the first passage in the light of the situation which he mentions in the second passage?

We can give a confident 'yes' to this question. It is a legitimate step. More than that, it is a necessary step.

Paul's first reader is Timothy. Timothy is present in Ephesus and actively engaged in ministry there (1:3; 4:11–16). He necessarily has close knowledge of the situation. Paul has previously given his instructions to Timothy in person (1:3). He is writing to reinforce them, and perhaps add to them. Accordingly, we can be confident that Paul's first reader, when reading what we call 2:9–15, already knows every piece of factual information that can be derived from what we call 5:3–16. We can also be confident that Paul is aware, when writing, that his reader has this knowledge. We should therefore take it into account when seeking to ascertain Paul's intended meaning.

His instructions in chapter 5 concerning widows are extraordinarily long. Why is this? We noted in chapter 3 that the average age of marriage for girls was around fourteen and their husbands were typically ten years older. If women survived childbearing, many of them would become widows (see also Acts 6:1; 9:39, 41). But the number of widows does not fully explain the length of Paul's instructions here. There is very little mention of widows in any other New Testament letter (only 1 Cor. 7:8, 39–40; Jas 2:27). We shall see that an important reason for the length of the instructions is Paul's concern about the ungodly activities of some of the widows at Ephesus.

When we take into account the information found in 5:3–16 in order to help us understand 2:9–15 we are putting ourselves more closely into the situation of Paul's first reader. We shall see that there are more practical and verbal links between the women of chapter 2 and the widows of chapter 5 than can plausibly be explained as mere chance coincidences.

Using the first key: reading 2:9–10 in the context of 1:1 – 2:8

The first key is to make sure that we read the controversial verses in the context of 1:1 – 2:8. We saw in chapter 11 that the context here is not specifically the public assemblies of the church; it is much broader.

Smith writes: 'Paul's instructions appear to have been written to correct an actual problem in an actual church.'[15] We have already identified the actual problem as being false teaching, expressed in word and in manner of life. Timothy's primary task, which Paul identifies in chapter 1, is to combat false teaching and promote godly lives of love and goodness in Christ. We have also noted that chapter 2 starts with 'therefore' (*oun*), which tells us that the instructions which it contains relate to that task.

Lest there be any doubt, Paul ties in his remarks to this topic again by another 'therefore' (*oun*) in verse 8. Accordingly, we should read chapter 2 as a connected train of thought concerned with this task. The unity of subject matter in chapter 2 is further confirmed by the fact that the topic of living a saved life is in view at the beginning of the chapter (vv. 1–4) and still in view at the end (v. 15).

Paul's instruction to pray (2:1) is 'first of all'. This comes first because combating false teaching and advancing God's salvation is a spiritual battle – a 'good fight' (1:18). It is a battle which will not be won without prayer (Eph. 6:16–20). Paul urges, specifically, prayer for lives which are quiet (*hēsuchios*) and lived in all godliness (*eusebia*) (vv. 1–2). Such lives embody sound teaching rather than false teaching. He urges prayer for 'all people'. This includes the false teachers mentioned in 1:3–7 and the two men mentioned in 1:20, at least one of whom had been caught up in the famous riot at Ephesus (Acts 19:33–34). There is particular resonance in Paul's urging prayer for the governing authorities (v. 2) and for a quietness that would facilitate the further acceptance of the gospel of salvation through Christ Jesus (vv. 3–7). One of the authorities to be prayed for would be the town clerk. It was the town clerk, or his predecessor, who had quelled the riot which had threatened the progress of the gospel in Ephesus. Prayer and gospel ministry produce knowledge (*epignōsis*) of the truth (2:4). This is in contrast with what is falsely called knowledge (*gnōsis*), from which Timothy must turn away (6:20).

In verses 8–15 Paul continues his instructions. The further instructions are divided between those addressed to the men (v. 8) and those addressed to women (vv. 9–15). These should not be read as indicating that he thinks men

---

15. Smith 2012, 44.

and women should behave differently as Christian believers. His instruction to men to pray (v. 8) does not imply that prayer is not an activity for women, for verse 1 urges prayer by all (see also Eph. 6:18). His instruction to women to dress decently and do good works (vv. 9–10) does not imply that men may dress indecently or are excused from good works (4:12; 5:25; 6:11, 18; Eph. 2:10). The likely reason for his different instructions to men and women is that false teaching has affected men and women differently. In particular, false teaching is influencing women to a greater extent than the men, since Paul gives only brief attention to the men (a mere fifteen words) and says much more about women (eighty-four words).

The men must stop getting involved in angry arguments and must get on with praying in a way that is holy (v. 8).[16] False teaching is generating controversy and disputes (6:4–5). Just as the collision between the gospel and devotion to Artemis had resulted in a riot, so also within the church the collision between truth and false teaching is producing quarrelling. Perhaps the men have been disputing with the false teachers and getting angry. Instead of the men arguing with them, it will be Timothy's task to deal appropriately with the remaining false teachers (1:3, 18; 4:6–16; 6:20).

Verse 9 starts with *hōsautōs*, meaning 'in the same way'. This may simply emphasize the holiness which should be displayed in the matters of behaviour which Timothy needs to address with some of the women, or it may also indicate that Paul wants women to pray (following the urging of v. 1) in a way that is holy.[17]

From the instructions which Paul gives, we can infer how the wealthy women who have been affected by false teachings have been behaving. They have to be advised to dress decently, and not with braided hair and gold, pearls or expensive clothes (v. 9).[18] These are the fashions worn by wealthy courtesans, which were also adopted by some other fashionable women.[19] They have been influenced

---

16. There is some debate about how to translate *dialogismos* in v. 8. Knight 1992, 129–130, surveys the options and concludes that it here means 'disputes'. ESV renders it as 'quarrelling'.

17. In the Greek text v. 9 does not have a main verb: it is grammatically dependent on the reader supplying one or more verbs from v. 8; see *M&W*, 311; *RBMW*, 178 (Moo).

18. The text refers to braided hair *and* (*kai*) gold *or* (*ē*) pearls *or* expensive clothes, indicating that it is not the braiding of hair on its own which is Paul's target, but the addition of gold or pearls and the extravagant display. See *M&W*, 312–313.

19. Chrysostom, Homily 8 on 1 Tim. 2:8–10 ('Imitate not therefore the courtesans'); Hurley 1981, 199; Knight 1992, 135 ('the mode of dress of courtesans'). Note that

by immorality and turning away (*ektrepō*) from conscience (1:10, 19), and by love for material possessions (see also 6:5, 17). Some of them may have been toying with sexual adventure (1:10), like the 'new women' who arose in Roman culture from the first century BC and into the next century, neglecting their household duties, engaging in illicit liaisons and avoiding childbearing.[20] Seneca (brother of Paul's judge, Gallio, in Acts 18) praised his own mother for not adopting the use of jewels and pearls and fashionable see-through clothes which 'exposed no greater nakedness by being removed', as well as for not terminating her pregnancies by abortion.[21] The women need to dress not only with decency (*aidōs*) but also with *sōphrosunē*, meaning 'propriety' or 'self-control'. They profess reverence for God (*theosebeia* – related to *eusebeia*), but have evidently not been living accordingly. They have to be told that the way to show real reverence for God is by means of (*dia*) the doing of good (*agathos*) works (*ergon*) (2:10).

---

dressing up in a public religious gathering was a way for marriageable girls to be put on display to attract a suitor: *WITC*, 57 (Baugh). Thus Hoag 2015, relying on *Ephesiaca*, argues that Paul's description of the women's appearance is not like courtesans but like young virgins dressed for a procession in devotion to Artemis. But this is unconvincing. It is right that *Ephesiaca*'s young heroine, Anthia, is expensively costumed for the procession, with her hair partly braided, but there is no indication that her dress was indecent. Moreover, it is uncertain when *Ephesiaca* was written, and the author leaves the intended date of its dramatic setting undefined, making use of both classical and Hellenic elements (see Tagliabue 2011).

20. Winter 2000.
21. Seneca the Younger, *ad Helviam* 16.3–5, cited by Winter 2004. Winter adds that the whole of Seneca's letter is enlightening because it shows the social pressure that was on Seneca's mother and other married women of his day to dress and live as the 'new' woman did. Questions have been raised about whether Ephesus was directly affected by this Roman trend: see *WITC*, 172 (Schreiner). Ephesus was an important hub city in the Roman Empire, so it seems unlikely that it was immune from it. Women's hair fashions appear to have come from Rome: *WITC*, 55 (Baugh). However, whether Rome was or was not the source of the fashion for immodest dress in Ephesus makes little difference to our understanding of the letter, because the pressing issue presented by Ephesian lifestyle choices of immodesty, rejection of childbearing and living for pleasure is readily apparent from 2:9, 15; 5:6, 14. Schreiner agrees it is likely that Paul's words on adornment 'contain a polemic against seductive and enticing clothing': *WITC*, 182.

Paul does not identify the particular settings in which the wealthy women were wearing clothing which was considered indecent.[22] There is no specific reference here to the public assemblies of the church. Perhaps the most likely setting for such clothing would be high-class social occasions.

Using the second key to aid understanding of 2:9–10

When we use the second key, we find that chapter 5 fills out the picture of these wealthy women that we get from 2:9–10. It confirms that Paul's allusions to their bad behaviour were not merely theoretical or precautionary. Paul contrasts the widow who devotes herself to prayer (5:5) with 'she who lives for pleasure' (5:6).[23] He contrasts those who do good (*kalos* or *agathos*) works (*ergon*) (5:10) with those who are idle (*argos*) (5:13). He says the latter women grow wanton (*katastrēniaō*), that is, become filled with sexual desires drawing them away from Christ, and incur condemnation for abandoning their former faith (5:11–12).[24] They are man-hunters, looking for new partners (5:11). This provides a motive for their fashionable and immodest mode of dress, and their display of their wealth, which is alluded to in 2:9.

---

22. What modes of dress are considered indecent varies from culture to culture and from one social setting to another. Intention is an important element. By imitating courtesans, these fashions were deliberately out of step with the general view of what constituted decent attire for respectable women.

23. Although some women are dressing in the fashion of courtesans, the suggestion that Paul here means that some of them are actually employed as courtesans (for sources, see Kelly 1963, 114; Stott 1996, 131) goes beyond the evidence.

24. This need not mean that they have stopped believing; rather, they are not living obediently to the faith. Winter 2003, 132–133, considers that the word *katastrēniaō* indicates a promiscuous lifestyle. NIV translates 5:12 with 'they have broken their first pledge'. This translation seems to imply that a widow had to pledge not to remarry in order to qualify for financial support from the church. But this is doubtful. Such a policy would increase the long-term financial burden on the church to no good purpose, contrary to the approach seen in 5:3–4, 8, 15.
The word 'pledge' here translates *pistis*, the ordinary word for faith. See ESV. There is also a debate over whether in v. 11 Paul may be thinking of marriage to an unbeliever: see Yarbrough 2018, 278.

Using the first key again: reading 2:11–12 in context

Paul turns next to the only direct command in chapter 2 and its accompanying restriction:

> A woman should learn [*manthanō*] in quietness [*hēsuchia*] in all submission [*hupotagē*] and [*de*] I am not permitting a woman to teach and *authent* a man [*anēr*], but [*alla*] to be in quietness [*hēsuchia*].' (vv. 11–12)

To reflect Paul's text accurately, verses 11–12 should be considered together as a unit.[25]

Four questions may be asked about this unit. The method by which we answer them will crucially affect our interpretation. We must make use of the first key again. Since Paul has not signalled any change of topic,[26] we should answer them on the basis that verses 11–12 form part of Paul's connected train of thought, continuing smoothly on from verses 1–10:

- *For whom are this command and this restriction intended?* For the women who are in view in the context, namely, those who need to be given the instructions in verses 9–10. The singular expression 'a woman' is generic in the sense of representing a group. But the context does not suggest that the genus is all women in all times and throughout the world. Rather, the group which Paul is concerned with is the wealthy women whose ungodly conduct evokes his strictures in verses 9–10 and over whom he is exercising his jurisdiction as an apostle.[27] We will see in chapter 13 how this fits in with the subsequent reference to Eve and is confirmed by what is said in verse 15. He is

---

25. Köstenberger agrees: *WITC*, 155–156. The two verses are joined in one sentence by the conjunction *de*, meaning (according to context) 'and' or 'but'. Even with the meaning 'but', *de* is a weaker contrast than *alla*, which is used later in the same sentence. ESV and NIV unhelpfully divide v. 12 off from v. 11 and omit the conjunction. Moo suggests that the connection between v. 12 and v. 11 can be brought out by paraphrasing the beginning of v. 12 as 'full submission means also that I do not permit . . .' (*RBMW*, 180).
26. See further appendix 6.
27. In *WITC*, 184, Schreiner asserts that the genus is 'all women', but without giving a reason. His discussion of vv. 11–12 from 184 to 199 does not pay attention to the flow of Paul's thought in context.

not forbidding Priscilla, or anyone like her, to teach or to have influence over men.[28]

- *What should a woman learn in quietness?* At least, from the immediate context, to live a quiet and godly life (v. 2), that is, to pray in a holy manner and not to dress indecently or with an extravagant display of wealth (v. 9), to exercise self-control (v. 9) and to show true reverence for God by doing good works (v. 10). This way of life contrasts with false teaching. False teaching involves quarrelling (1:4; 2:8; 6:4–5) (opposite to quietness and holy prayer); it involves immorality and rejection of conscience (opposite to godliness); and it involves idleness (opposite to good works). Paul is not saying that women should be silent, as some translations have it.[29] This misses the point. Paul has in mind the contrast between false teaching, expressed in an argumentative and irreverent manner of life, and true teaching, expressed in a quiet and reverent manner of life.

- *To what or whom should she be in full submission?* From the context, to God. The women have been professing (*epangellō*) reverence for God (*theosebeia* – v. 10). Instead of a partly false claim, this must become a full reality.[30]

---

28. We do not know whether Priscilla had returned to Ephesus from Rome at the time this letter was written (see Rom. 16:3; 2 Tim. 4:19). She was a devoted co-worker with Paul, who had even risked her life for him; her influence over Apollos had been important for the advance of the gospel (Rom. 16:4; Acts 18:18–26). Paul greets her again in 2 Tim. 4:19. While she and her husband were of sufficient means to be able to host a church in Ephesus (1 Cor. 16:8, 19) and in Rome (Rom. 16:5), as tentmakers (Acts 18:2–3) they were not among the idle rich. Given the scale of wealth apparent from 1 Tim. 2:9, we may infer that the misbehaving wealthy women were probably few in number, perhaps as few as two or three.

29. Schreiner agrees that silence is not in view here: see *WTC*, 186–187. See also *M&W*, 314–315.

30. The word for submission (*hupotage*) is a noun related to the verb *hupotassō* which we saw in chapter 3 refers not to a submissive personality but to a choice of how to live, that is, adopting a lower position. esv 'with all submissiveness' could be misunderstood in the former sense. For uses of *hupotage* see also 2 Cor. 9:13 (where the sense of choice is clear) and Gal. 2:5 (where Paul refuses to make that choice, as in the circumstances it would be wrong to do so). Paul's use in 1 Tim. 2:10–11 of two different words pointing to the one behaviour of reverent submission to God (*theosebeia, hupotage*) is analogous to his use in Eph. 5:24, 33 of two words pointing to the one behaviour of submission to husband (*hupotassō, phobeō*).

Most discussions of this question arrive at a conclusion which is unsupported by the context, because they approach verse 11 as if Paul were turning to a different topic, and hence miss the relevance of verse 10 to verse 11.[31] The proposal that Paul is concerned here with authority structures in which women must submit to men fails because of the context, which is not about authority structures, and because Paul simply does not say here that women should submit to men.

- *What does 'but to be in quietness' refer to?* Paul has already told us. It refers to living a 'quiet' life in all godliness (*eusebia*) and dignity (v. 2), without anger or argument (v. 8) and with reverence for God (*theosebia*) (v. 10). Paul emphasizes the kind of quietness (*hēsuchia*) which should characterize the Christian life not only here but also in 1 Thessalonians 4:11 (*hēsuchazō* – to be quiet) and in 2 Thessalonians 3:12 (*hēsuchia*). This quality is not something applicable only to women. The implied contrast here is not between vocal men and silent women but between the behaviour of these wealthy women and the appropriate behaviour for Christian believers. This is not 'a quiet life' in the colloquial sense, which Paul himself certainly did not live. It is a life characterized by reverence for God and self-control.

Using the second key to aid understanding of 2:11–12

For more help in understanding the historical context of 2:11–12 we turn to chapter 5 and deploy the second key again. In 5:13–15 (ESV) Paul writes:

[13]Besides that [*hama*], they learn [*manthanō*] to be idlers [*argos*], going about [*perierchomai*] from house to house [*oikia*], and not only idlers [*argos*], but also gossips [*phluaros*] and busybodies [*periergos*], saying [*laleō*] what they should not. [14]So I would have younger widows marry, bear children [*teknogoneō*], manage their households [*oikodespoteō*], and give the adversary [*antikeimai*] no occasion for slander. [15]For some have already strayed after Satan [*ho satanas*].

---

31. Differing views on what the woman is to submit to are discussed in *WITC*, 187. Schreiner, like many others, ignores the relevance of v. 10 to v. 11. Köstenberger rightly states that the passage from v. 8 to v. 15 is 'characterized by considerable cohesion' and that there is a 'close connection' between v. 11 and v. 10, but still misses the relevance of v. 10 for understanding v. 11: *WITC*, 155, 158. Payne also seems to me to miss the full relevance of v. 10 to this question: *M&W*, 315–316, but see 317.

The first word, *hama*, means 'at the same time'. This is what translators mean by 'besides'. It confirms that Paul has in mind the younger women whose sexual desires are driving them, in conflict with their dedication to the Messiah, to want a new partner (5:11–12).[32] If the forbidding of marriage in 4:3 is a form of asceticism, this element is not attractive to these women.[33] They are looking for someone who will satisfy their desires. Paul's remedy is that they should marry (v. 14), but instead of living for their own pleasure (v. 6) they should bear children (*teknogoneō*) and attend to governing their households (*oikodespoteō*).[34] This is notably different advice from the general preference that Paul expressed in 1 Corinthians 7:8, 34, 40 that widows should not remarry. The general advice which he gave in the Corinthian letter would not be suitable for the sexually charged women that he has in mind here. He applies to them what he wrote in 1 Corinthians 7:9: 'but if they do not have self-control, let them marry.'

32. While both the word *hama* and the wider context suggest that he still has the younger widows mainly in mind, he also allows for his remarks to be more widely applied by aiming his instructions in 5:14 at what he calls *neōteras* (feminine plural, 'younger ones'), which is how he described younger females generally in 5:2. There may also be an ambiguity in 5:11 over whether the women are wanting to marry (*gameō*) or wanting to take a lover, since *gameō* can be used in either sense (see LSJ). The latter is not impossible, since it would fit not only with 5:11–12 but also with 1:10 (fornicators), 2:9 (indecent fashions), 2:15 (emphasis on holiness), 3:2 (elders must be chaste), 4:3 (if marriage is forbidden, taking a lover is an alternative), 5:6 (living for pleasure) and 5:14 (Paul's advice that they should marry).

33. Since Hymenaeus believed that the general resurrection had already taken place, it was logical for him to teach that there should be no marriage (1 Tim. 1:20; 4:3; 2 Tim. 2:17–18; compare Luke 20:34–36). But he or others may also have drawn the conclusion that sexual licence was therefore acceptable, thus opposing marriage in order to justify sexual promiscuity, free of commitments (1 Tim. 1:10). This would fit with later evidence that the practices of the Nicolaitans were known at Ephesus (Rev. 2:6). The Nicolaitans apparently encouraged sexual promiscuity (Rev. 2:14–15). Clement of Alexandria (about 190) states that they abandoned themselves to lives of pleasure 'like goats': *Miscellanies* (*Stromata*) 2.20.

34. Although these women may be looking to remarry (5:11), there may nevertheless be a link between the possible asceticism of 4:3 and the women's neglect of childbearing and governing households which is implied by 5:14. As Moo points out, the false teaching appears to downgrade marriage and childbearing (*RBMW*, 177–178).

The godly behaviour that Paul has said that women should learn and live out (2:1–2, 9–12) is markedly different from what these women are in fact learning and doing, as stated in 5:13. Most English versions of 5:13 are influenced more by cultural prejudice than by context. They paint a stock picture of gossipy women, poking their noses into other people's business. A translation more sensitive to the literary and historical context would reveal that worse things are going on. These young, wealthy widows are engaged in practising and promoting elements of false teaching which involves magic, astrology and the influence of the evil one. The following eight considerations help to make this clear:

1. Paul says the women are *phluaros*. This adjective is usually translated here as 'gossips'. But this translation is not derived from the context.[35] Nor is there any clear instance in ancient Greek literature where *phluaros* means 'gossips' or 'gossipy'. It normally refers to talking nonsense. The traditional mistranslation was corrected in NIV 2011. 'Talking nonsense' corresponds with the description of false teaching in 1:6 as 'meaningless talk' (NIV) or 'vain discussion' (ESV) and as profane empty utterances in 6:20 and 2 Timothy 2:16. This is what the women are saying.[36] Back in 2:10 Paul was concerned that when the women were professing or proclaiming (*epangellō*) reverence for God, this was in part a false claim. Paul uses the same term again in a linked way in 6:20–21, warning Timothy to beware of the false teaching which some had professed (*epangellō*). It seems that the women's Christian profession is mixed with false teaching.

---

35. There is no reference to gossip in 1 Timothy. The word *diabolos* in 3:11 refers not to gossips but to those who make false accusations.

36. LSJ does not list 'gossip' as a possible meaning for *phluaros*. See further *M&W*, 301–302. Grudem (*EFBT*, 282–283) relies on the BDAG lexicon as giving the meaning 'gossipy', but this does not advance the discussion because it simply repeats the mistake. He shows awareness of the meaning 'talker of nonsense' but does not connect it with Paul's descriptions of the false teaching in 1:6 and 6:20. There is no other use of this word in the New Testament, but the related verb (*phluareō*) is used in 3 John 10, where translations refer to talking 'nonsense' (see ESV and NIV, in which the adjective 'wicked' or 'malicious' represents additional Greek words). The word *phluaros* is also used of women by the first-century astrologer Dorotheus, where he says that if a couple marry in Pisces, this makes the wife warlike and *phluaros*. See Kartzow 2009, 59–60, referring to *Fragmenta Graeca* 392.21. Whatever Dorotheus means by this (talker of nonsense? grandiloquent?), the association with 'warlike' (which reminds us of the quarrelling of 1 Tim. 1:4; 2:8; 6:4–5) makes it unlikely that he means 'gossipy'. The Vulgate translates *phluaros* as Latin *verbosus* – 'full of words'.

2. He says that as they go around they are saying (*laleō*) 'what they should not'. There is nowhere else in this letter which gives any indication that the speaking which Paul is concerned about is women's gossip. In the context, the likely meaning is that they are saying things which express or put into practice false teachings. Some scholars deny this on the ground that in 1 Timothy 5:13 Paul uses the more general word *laleō* (say/speak) rather than the more specific word *didaskō* (teach), but both the immediate context and the overarching theme of the letter suggest that the speaking includes false teaching. False teachers say what they should not. This seems to correspond with Paul's description of the false teachers in Crete as teaching 'what they should not' (Titus 1:11).[37] Schreiner fairly acknowledges that Paul uses *laleō* and *didaskō* to refer to the same activity in at least one instance in the Pastoral Epistles (Titus 2:1, 15).[38]

3. Paul describes the women not only as *phluaros* but also as *periergos*. Again there is a translation issue. This is a highly unusual word in the context of Christian instruction. Having corrected the translation of *phluaros* to 'talkers of nonsense', it seems strange that between 'talkers of nonsense' and 'saying what they should not' Paul sandwiches the description 'busybodies'. Because this is such an odd sequence of thought, NIV changes Paul's order, to make the women 'busybodies who talk nonsense, saying things they ought not to'. But there is no other mention of 'busybodies' in Paul's letter, and with a different translation of *periergos* there would be no oddity needing to be smoothed out. This term means 'meddler' and refers more specifically to meddling by means of magic arts (sorcery). The only other use of this word in the New Testament is in Acts 19:19, where some of those who practised *periergos* brought their very expensive books of magic and superstitions to be burned. This was at Ephesus, the very place that Paul is concerned about in 1 Timothy. There is no justification for ignoring this background. In the Ephesian context the natural meaning is that the women were dabbling in sorcery.[39] Among the things which they ought not to say (*laleō*) are their magical incantations.

---

37. *M&W*, 304.

38. *WITC*, 173. On 205 he also acknowledges as a possibility that some of the women were teaching falsely. See also 1 Pet. 4:11, where Peter uses *laleō* of gifted speaking, without specifying the particular form that it takes (prophecy, teaching or otherwise). Moo's view, that there is no evidence in the Pastoral Epistles that women were spreading false teaching (*RMBW*, 185), depends on the traditional English translation of 1 Tim. 5:13.

39. Towner 2006, 354, acknowledges the meaning 'dabbling in magic', but asserts (without saying why) that this 'is not in view here'. Knight 1992, 48–52, 227, argues

Thus *didaskō* would have been too narrow a word for Paul to use. All three descriptions, *phluaros*, *periergos* and 'saying [*laleō*] what they should not', are focused on the women's activities as false teachers.

4. Paul says the women are going about (*perierchomai*) the houses (*oikia*). There is a triple allusion here:

- At Ephesus Paul had gone from house to house (*oikos*) teaching the truth (Acts 20:20). These women are also going from house to house in Ephesus but teaching falsely.
- During Paul's time in Ephesus Jewish exorcists had gone about (*perierchomai*) trying to meddle with evil spirits, and had been overpowered, and this story had been often told and retold (Acts 19:13–17). The exorcists would have invoked the name of Jesus as part of their magical rite.[40] These women are also going about (*perierchomai*) meddling with occult powers through their magic, and claiming to be followers of Jesus. Involvement in the occult opens a person to contact with deceitful spirits and teachings of demons (1 Tim. 4:1), which in serious cases may require the kind of deliverance that Paul effected at Ephesus (Acts 19:11). Some have gone the whole way and turned aside (*ektrepō*) to the satan (1 Tim. 5:15).[41] In 2 Timothy 2:25–26, in similar vein, Paul describes false teachers as having been captured by the devil in a trap.
- Progress from house to house was a key idea in ancient astrology. There were understood to be twelve 'places' or 'houses' (*topos*, used in the sense of *oikia*), each representing a different stage or aspect of a person's life.[42] Paul's choice of words here suggests that, along with magic, the women are involved in astrology. As we shall see, this is confirmed by a number of further allusions to astrological ideas.

---

impressively for Luke's influence on Paul's vocabulary in this letter but does not consider the possibility that Paul is here using *periergos* in Luke's sense. In 2 Thess. 3:11 Paul refers to certain people as behaving as busybodies; but he there uses a different word (*periergazomai*), and there is no specific reference to women.

40. Arnold 1993b, 582.

41. 'The satan' is not a personal name; it means 'the accuser' or 'the adversary'.

42. Pingree 1979, 222. Further discussion of the houses can be found on astrological websites, such as <www.astrology-x-files.com/houses> and <www.hellenisticastrology.com>.

5. Magical or astrological beliefs are appropriately called useless speculations (1:4), myths and old wives' tales (1:4; 4:7). The last of these descriptions is particularly pointed polemic when they are promoted by young widows. We have noted that Artemis was depicted with the astrological signs of the Zodiac around her neck, and was also directly linked with magical practices. It is therefore unsurprising that Paul makes allusions to the practice of magic and astrology in Ephesus.

6. The verb *oikodespoteō* is used nowhere else in the New Testament. But linked to the idea of astrological houses was the belief that a heavenly body could 'take control of the house' (verb: *oikodespoteō*; noun: *oikodespoteia*). For example, a passage in Ptolemy's *Tetrabiblos* reads: 'Saturn, therefore, once he has taken sole house-control [*oikodespoteia*] of the soul and has gained mastery [*authenteō*] . . . of Mercury and the moon . . . makes people lovers of the body.'[43] With a spirited rhetorical flourish, Paul picks up this conventional astrological language and throws it back in the direction of the misbehaving women, drawing a contrast between their bad behaviour in verse 13 and what they should be doing in verse 14. He wants the wealthy widows to take proper control of their households (*oikodespoteō*) (v. 14).

7. The same astrological passage says that under the influence of Saturn people become 'lovers of the body, . . . dictatorial, . . . lovers of property, avaricious, . . . amassing treasure'.[44] This sounds rather like the wealthy women who live for pleasure (5:6), who care for their bodies by having their hair braided and adorning their bodies with displays of their wealth (2:9), who want to get a man to satisfy their sexual desires (5:11) and who, as false teachers, want to dictate to others how they should live (1:7). If they are avaricious, this further chimes with chapter 6, where the false teachers are people who see godliness (*eusebia*) as a means of increasing their wealth (6:3–10).[45] Paul's instructions to

---

43. The *Tetrabiblos* is a second-century AD astrological treatise concerning the influence of the heavenly bodies. The quoted translation is of *Tetrabiblos* 3.13.10, by Al Wolters in *WITC*, 78, where a misprint gives an incorrect reference. Ptolemy was an Alexandrian scholar who was born around 85–100 and died about 165–170.

44. Translation in Clark 2006. These words are rendered identically in the translation reproduced in *M&W*, 381.

45. The Greek word for the false teachers who are referred to in 6:5 and 6:9 is the gender-neutral term *anthrōpos* (man in the sense of person, human being), so there is no implication that the false teachers must be men. To mix magic with Christian teaching could provide a source of income, since people paid for magic spells.

the rich in 6:17–19 reinforce and expand his instructions for the women in 2:10 – they are to be rich in good works.[46]

8. Paul says in verse 13 what the women are learning (*manthanō*). The first thing he says they are learning is to be *argos* (idle, or useless). He uses a barbed idiom which accuses them of qualifying to be idlers.[47] This idleness contrasts with the good works that he commends in 2:10 and 5:10. He is therefore contrasting what they are actually learning with what they ought to be learning (2:10–11). The use of *argos* to refer to particular people as 'idle' is unusual in Christian instruction.[48] Why does Paul emphasize this word *argos* so strongly, not only by using the barbed idiom but also by repeating this word twice in the same sentence? It is another allusion to astrological learning. The word *argos* is the name of the eighth of the twelve astrological 'houses', known as the idle house or house of death.[49] Paul would certainly have regarded this learning as a myth and a useless speculation (1:4), as something falsely called knowledge (6:20) and as leading to death rather than salvation.

I have here cited Ptolemy's *Tetrabiblos* as evidence of conventional astrological terms and beliefs in first-century Ephesus, even though it was not written until the second century. This requires explanation. *Tetrabiblos* provides relevant evidence because Ptolemy was an anthologist, collating astrological lore from a

---

46. 'The rich' in 6:17 does not have a gender-specific meaning. Paul's instructions in 6:17–19 are not limited to the women in their application, but they are particularly apt for these women.

47. Kelly 1963, 118: 'In the Greek the feminine adjective "idle" (*argai*) and the verb "they learn" (*manthanousin*) are simply juxtaposed. . . . [T]he verb *manthanein* ("to learn") with a substantive denoting a profession or occupation was an idiomatic construction signifying "to qualify as such and such" (e.g. a doctor, wrestler, etc.).' Note the behaviour of v. 13 does not look like that of *poor* widows.

48. Paul's only other use of it is in a quoted proverb (Titus 1:12). It is used of people in a fictional parable (Matt. 20:1–16). James and Peter each use it once in the sense of dead or barren (Jas 2:20; 2 Pet. 1:8).

49. This sense of *argos* is given in LSJ, citing Ptolemy's *Tetrabiblos* '128'. I have not been able to verify this reference, but LSJ also gives three other astrological references, including to Paulus Alexandrinus, who refers to the eighth house as the idle house or house of death. The website <www.astrology-x-files.com/houses/idle-place.html> gives a source for this as Paulus Alexandrinus, *Introductory Matters*, trans. Robert Schmidt, ed. Robert Hand (1993), 53. See also Brennan 2013. It is possible that Paul also employs a word-play alluding to astrological houses in 1 Tim. 2:8 (men should pray in every *topos*, that is, in every aspect or stage of life).

wide range of earlier sources known in the Hellenic world.[50] The women who were promoting astrological speculations must have been familiar with traditional astrological lore in order to do so. We should also expect Paul and Timothy to have been acquainted with the beliefs that they were combating, particularly in view of their personal experience of life in Ephesus.

Paul's second letter to Timothy confirms that false teaching circulating in Ephesus included sorcery.[51] It should also be noted that the false teachers' promotion of magic is consistent with an interest in the Jewish law (1 Tim. 1:7), since we have evidence from Acts of a Jew who was a sorcerer and false prophet (Bar-Jesus/Elymas, Acts 13:6–10; compare 8:9–24).[52]

The wealthy women as false teachers

Without some understanding of the context, many of Paul's remarks in chapter 5 strike the reader as bizarre generalizations. For example, is it true of

---

50. Clark 2006: 'Ptolemy was first and foremost an anthologist. This knowledge came to him from Egypt, Greece, Chaldea, Babylonia and beyond. More to the point, he was in the enviable position of being in Alexandria during the peak of its eminence. . . . Ptolemy is clearly drawing from a wide range of sources in *Tetrabiblos*.' For example, when Ptolemy assigned Judaea to Aries, he was relying on sources contemporaneous with the reign of Herod the Great: van Kooten 2015, 25.

51. After mentioning Hymenaeus and Philetus in 2 Tim. 2:17, in 3:5–9 Paul compares these two, perhaps impliedly along with other active false teachers, with Jannes and Jambres, the sorcerers who opposed Moses: Exod. 7:8–12, 19–22. (The names of the sorcerers are not stated in Exod. 7, but were known from tradition.) This comparison is a strong indication that the false teachings include the practice of magic arts. Paul may be referring to false teachers as sorcerers again in 2 Tim. 3:13, where he uses the Greek word *goēs* (used nowhere else in the New Testament), which has a primary meaning of sorcerer. This word can also be used more loosely to mean a cheat or charlatan, and many English versions therefore translate it as 'imposter'. This is a plausible translation in view of 3:5 ('having a form of godliness but having said no to its power'). But the meaning 'sorcerer' (as translated in TPT) fits both the immediate context of Paul's comparison with Jannes and Jambres and the wider context of the practice of magic at Ephesus which we see in Acts 19 and 1 Tim. 5. Such people resist God's power, as Jannes and Jambres tried to do.

52. The genealogies mentioned in 1 Tim. 1:4 may also have been Jewish. Compare Titus 3:9.

young widows in general that they are idle, and go from house to house talking nonsense and saying things they should not say? Plainly not. Paul must have in mind the actual behaviour of particular women, whom Timothy needs to deal with.

How then, in summary, does chapter 5 fill out the picture of the women Paul has in mind in chapter 2? We may reasonably conclude that the women are false teachers. Several wealthy younger widows, who live for pleasure, are going from house to house, passing on false and unprofitable myths involving magic arts and astrology, while showing off their wealth, dressed immodestly, and each looking for a man who will satisfy her sexual desires.[53]

Complementarian scholars argue that women are only clearly portrayed as being influenced by false teaching, rather than as being its purveyors.[54] However, there was no firm cultural obstacle in Ephesus to women being teachers.[55] Moo now grants it is likely that the false teaching gives rise to Paul's instructions in 2:9–15; and Schreiner acknowledges, 'Paul almost certainly issued the prohibition against women teaching because some women had indeed begun to teach men.'[56] As we have seen, 5:13 and 5:15 provide positive support for understanding some women to be purveyors of false teaching.

The point is also made that all the false teachers whose names are given in the letters to Timothy are men (1 Tim. 1:20; 2 Tim. 2:17–18; see also 2 Tim. 4:14). This is correct, but it does not tell us that there were no women false teachers. Paul regularly refers to opponents in the church, as in 1:3, as 'certain

---

53. We are not told the precise circumstances. It is not hard to imagine the women, dressed in the manner alluded to in 2:9, attending what we might call high-class dinner parties with other socially elite members of the Ephesian church, where they peddle their confused version of Christian truth (1:3–7), provide diversion with their astrology and magic, and exchange magic spells for payment. A comparison with nineteenth-century séances suggests itself.

54. *WITC*, 173 (Schreiner); *EFBT*, 281–284. Grudem additionally relies on Paul's prediction of male false teachers in his farewell to the Ephesian elders (Acts 20:30), but this does not affect the present question. If Paul foresaw that at some time there would be male false teachers this does not tell us whether or not at the time 1 Timothy was written there were female false teachers.

55. We saw in chapter 11 that Baugh demonstrates that wealthy women were educated, and that Grudem cites evidence that women served on occasion as superintendents of education.

56. *RBMW*, 184 (Moo); *WITC*, 173. Schreiner's point is that they were teaching, not that they were teaching falsely.

persons' (*tis*), without naming them.[57] There are at least five possible reasons why Paul does not name any of the misbehaving wealthy women in the letter:

- It is unnecessary for Paul to name them because the false teachers have already been discussed between Paul and Timothy before Paul wrote the letter (1:3).
- Although they are members of the fellowship they have not been formally or publicly recognized as elders or teachers.
- Paul may consider that naming them in the letter would grant them too much recognition as teachers.
- Paul has a pastoral heart. They are young. He does not criticize any named person within the fellowship, because this would expose them to the most acute shame when his letter is shared with the church. He does not want to be more confrontational than is necessary. Rather, he wants Timothy to deal with them firmly but gently, with a view to leading them to repentance without having to employ the more drastic remedy of exclusion (see also Paul's later commendation of this kind of strategy in 2 Tim. 2:24–26).
- As wealthy women, they are socially well connected. It may be wise not to commit their names to writing in case Paul's letter falls into the wrong hands or to avoid unnecessary scandal and conflict.[58]

The opponents named by Paul in 1 Timothy as false teachers are those whom he has excluded. Paul says he delivered Hymenaeus and Alexander to the satan (1:19–20), from which we should infer that he has excluded them from the church fellowship in the hope that this will lead them to repentance.[59] Having been excluded, they are now outside his and Timothy's jurisdiction. Paul cannot instruct them further, or ask Timothy to do so. There is nothing more Paul can do, except provide a warning by naming them openly, and pray.

---

57. Yarbrough 2018, 282–283. Beyond the present letter, see 1 Cor. 4:18; 15:12, 34; 2 Cor. 3:1. Compare also Rev. 2:20, where the name of the female false teacher (Jezebel) is probably symbolic, rather than her real name (see 1 Kgs 16:31; 18:4; 19:2; 21:23–25; 2 Kgs 9:22).

58. This consideration sheds additional light on the prayers of 2:1–2. Paul's criticism of the wealthy women could provoke a strong negative reaction from powerful people in Ephesus, who could use their power against the church.

59. For more on this procedure, see chapter 6, 113.

Throughout the letter, Paul refers to the false teachers gender-neutrally as *tis* (1:3, 6, 8, 19; 4:1; 6:3, 21). We may infer from 5:13 that in 1:3 he at least had several women in mind as false teachers whom Timothy should next deal with. We may therefore ask: is there any evidence that Paul also had in mind in 1:3 some men who were within the Ephesian church? There is not. There is no positive indication anywhere in 1 Timothy that Paul had in mind men who were promoting false teaching and who still remained within the fellowship at the time when he was writing his letter.

This is not contradicted by the additional information that we can glean from Paul's second letter to Timothy. We hear of Hymenaeus again, upsetting the faith of some (2 Tim. 2:16–18). Having already been excluded, he is probably doing this from outside the fellowship. Another false teacher, Philetus, is named alongside him. We have no evidence that Philetus was within the fellowship and teaching falsely at the time of the first letter. Paul warns Timothy to have nothing to do with them (3:5; in contrast with the milder strategy of 2:24–26). It appears that at the time of the second letter they are worming their way into people's homes and taking advantage of immature women (3:2–9).[60] The fact that Hymenaeus is targeting women (2:17; 3:6) suggests a likelihood that he may have done so previously. This may explain why, at the time of the first letter, women had been more affected by false teaching than had men.

In the first letter Paul's remedial actions for the false teachers who remain in the fellowship are noticeably different from the steps that he has already taken with Hymenaeus and Alexander. Timothy is not to exclude them; instead, he is to instruct them not to teach falsely and not to occupy themselves with myths and the like (1 Tim. 1:3–4). Encouragements are offered. If God can save Paul, who was a blasphemer and persecutor, he can save also these false teachers (1:15–16), for God wants everyone to be saved and to come to a knowledge of the truth (2:4).

---

60. Many English versions, reflecting traditional cultural bias, characterize these women as 'silly' or 'weak-willed' or some similar expression. There is no such word in the text. The Greek is *gunaikarion*. This is a diminutive of the ordinary word for a woman. Use of the diminutive often connotes affection (as in Mark 5:23; 7:25 – 'little daughter'; and Matt. 15:26–27; Mark 7:27–28 – 'little doggies'). Paul's reference is to the women's youth and immaturity. His heart goes out to them. The context shows he is expressing not contempt but concern, because their immaturity makes them vulnerable. The reason they are 'always learning and never being able to come to a knowledge of the truth' is because they are under the sway of the false teachers.

Paul's difference in approach must reflect some material distinction between the men who had been teaching falsely, and had been excluded, and the false teachers who remain. This is consistent with those who remain being the women described in 5:13. It is likely that Hymenaeus and Alexander had been elders in the Ephesian church before Paul excluded them. This fits with Alexander having been put forward as a spokesman at the time of the riot (Acts 19:33) and with Paul's warning that male false teachers would arise from among the Ephesian elders (Acts 20:30).[61] In contrast, it appears that the false teachers who remain are aspiring to positions as teaching elders but are not yet in such positions (1:7; 3:1), so they can be dealt with in a less severe manner by setting them straight and ensuring that they do not become elders in the church, or even deacons, until they have proved themselves to be reliable.[62]

If the wealthy women are false teachers, further connections between 1:1 – 2:8 and 2:9–12 are apparent. Paul describes his and Timothy's aims for the false teachers as including a pure heart and 'faith without hypocrisy' (1:5). The women are not noted for their purity (5:11). Timothy must deal with their hypocrisy. They profess reverence for God but are living inconsistently (2:9–10). What the women need to learn (2:11) includes understanding the law and using it legitimately (1:7–8). 'How can a young person stay on the path of purity? By living according to your word' (Ps. 119:9, NIV).

That the wealthy women are the remaining false teachers is consistent with the otherwise puzzling contrast in Paul's use of the article in 2:8–9. He uses the definite article in verse 8 ('the men') but no article in verse 9 ('women'; see ESV). His instructions in verse 8 are for all of the men in the church. His instructions in verses 9–15 are not directed at all of the women but at those who are involved in the false teaching.[63]

---

61. It also fits with the fact that Alexander was a Jew (Acts 19:34): see further the nature of the false teachings as involving genealogies, dietary restrictions and misuse of the Jewish law as seen in 1 Tim. 1:4–8 and 4:3.
62. We will look at the qualifications for elders and deacons in chapter 15. Perhaps the women of 5:15, in distinction from those described in 5:13 who remain, have left the church along with Hymenaeus and Alexander.
63. Use or absence of the article in Greek is not always easy to understand. The explanations of it in Wallace 1996, 206–290, run to eighty-five pages, and Paul's use here does not fit neatly into any of Wallace's categories. G. J. Dannenberg, a Bible translator and exegete for more than forty years, states: 'I think the word for "men" has an article because Paul means "all the men in the church at Ephesus", whereas

At this point in our investigation we cannot say with certainty that when Paul wrote 1 Timothy the only false teachers within the Ephesian church, whom he had in view for Timothy to deal with, were several wealthy women. But it appears probable. We can treat this probability as a working hypothesis. When we move on to the third and fourth contextual keys, we can see whether this hypothesis helps us towards a coherent understanding of what Paul writes in 2:9–15.

Summary of chapter 12

1. Four keys open the way to an interpretation of 2:9–15 which is fully grounded in the literary and historical context. The first is to ensure that we read those verses genuinely in the context of 1:1 – 2:8. The second is to consider together the two extended passages about women in 1 Timothy. By seeing what can be gathered from 5:3–16 concerning the historical context, we put ourselves more closely into Timothy's position as the first reader of the letter. This adds considerably to our understanding of 2:9–15. The third key will be to ascertain the meaning of *authenteō* provisionally from the context, and then check it against the range of possible meanings. The fourth key will be to pay attention to the signposts which Paul provides in verse 15.

2. Information about the historical background of the Ephesian church reveals a milieu in which magic arts and astrology were practised. In his letter Paul makes allusions to magic and to astrological lore. False teaching circulating in Ephesus includes sorcery and astrology. Resisting these influences is a spiritual battle against the unseen forces of evil.

3. Paul's concern in verses 11–12 is with certain wealthy women whose ungodly conduct evokes his strictures in verses 9–10. They are idle. They dress indecently and with extravagant display. They are going from house to house, each looking for a man who will satisfy her sexual desires, and promoting false teaching. Instead, these women should learn to do good works, in full submission to God, living a quiet and godly life. These women are influenced by the evil one. It appears that these are the false teachers remaining in the church, whom Timothy is charged to deal with. He must set them straight and ensure that none of them takes up a position as an elder or deacon in the church until she has proved her reformed life and character.

---

the word for "women" does not have an article because Paul does not want to imply that *all* the women in the church at Ephesus are braiding their hair and flaunting expensive clothes' (personal communication, 1 January 2018).

Questions to consider

1. What are your thoughts on the first key?
2. What are your thoughts on the second key?
3. What practical lessons do you draw from the instructions which Paul gives to Timothy on how to deal with the false teachers?

> Sanctify them to live in accordance with the truth; your word is
> truth.   (John 17:17, NIV margin)

Using the third key: the meaning of *authenteō* from the context, including Paul's reasoning in 2:13–14

Our working hypothesis is that, when Paul wrote 1 Timothy, the false teachers remaining within the Ephesian church, whom he had in view for Timothy to deal with, were the misbehaving wealthy women described in chapters 2 and 5.

Our third key for unlocking the room of chapter 2 is to ascertain the meaning of *authenteō* provisionally from the context, and then check it against the range of possible meanings.

In 2:12 Paul has in mind the danger that such a woman may teach and *authent* a man. What is Paul concerned may happen? From the context, Paul is concerned that a wealthy man-hunting widow, influenced by the wiles of the satan, may lead a man astray with her false teaching. Paul is strengthening Timothy's hand for dealing with these women by stating in his letter that he is not permitting this. His declaration of this restriction as an apostle and a prayerful man of God is part of the spiritual battle against false teaching and the demons that lurk behind it (4:1).[1] Timothy is a combatant in this fight (1:18; 6:12).

---

1. There may be an echo here of Matt. 18:18.

With this understanding of the context, it makes excellent sense that Paul goes on to underline what he says in verses 11–12 by referring back to the first spiritual battle recounted in Scripture, where a young woman, deceived by the satan, taught and *authent*ed a man, with dire results (vv. 13–14). To support what he is saying, he appeals to the story of Adam and Eve: 'For [*gar*]² Adam was formed first, then Eve, and Adam was not deceived, but the woman having been deceived came into transgression' (2:13–14).

We do not need to consider what in the Genesis account is literal and what is symbolic.³ What Paul writes is brief, but is sufficient for Timothy to get the point, for Timothy has been trained in the Hebrew scriptures (2 Tim. 1:5; 3:15). Paul does not need to spell out for him the full story from the forming of Adam to Eve's transgression. Adam was formed first (Gen. 2:7) and was given the command not to take the fruit of the tree of the knowledge of good and evil (2:16–17). Eve was formed later (2:21–22). Eve knew of the command not to take the fruit, that is, not to obtain the forbidden knowledge (3:2–3). But, being deceived, she did not behave in full submission to God. She took the fruit. She also gave some to her husband, who was with her, and he ate it (3:6). Having obtained the forbidden knowledge, they experienced shame (2:25; 3:7). Their disobedience incurred God's judgment (3:8–24).⁴

The analogy with the situation in Ephesus is clear. Before the woman was formed Adam lived in obedience to God, and he continued doing so until the

---

2. Scholars have argued over the force of *gar* here. It can introduce supporting material of various kinds, including reasons, explanations, complementary ideas and illustrations. The precise nature of the connection must be determined from the context. The arguments advanced about it are often flawed and artificial. Schreiner's discussion illustrates the point: 'When Paul gives a command elsewhere *in the Pastoral Epistles*, the [*gar*] that follows *almost invariably* states the reason for the command' (*WITC*, 200, emphases added). If it 'almost invariably' states the reason, this means that it does not always state the reason, so whether it does so or not will have to be determined from the context. And suppose Paul's usage elsewhere in the Pastoral Epistles had happened to be invariable, what would that have told us? There would be no basis for restricting Paul to using *gar* in 1 Tim. 2 only in ways in which he happened to use it elsewhere in three short letters. It is an ordinary word in common use, not a technical term. He can use it in any intelligible way that he chooses. See also *M&W*, 399–402.

3. See the remarks on this in the Preface.

4. For Paul, use of Old Testament illustrations was a normal teaching method (1 Cor. 10:1–14). He had used part of this particular illustration before: see 2 Cor. 11:3.

woman, having been deceived by the satan's promise of knowledge (Gen. 3:5),[5] transgressed. The nature of her transgression was not only taking the fruit of forbidden knowledge herself but also causing Adam to participate in it along with her. Paul does not want this scenario repeated in the Ephesian church. At the point when Paul is writing, the men in the fellowship have not been much affected by false teaching. Their situation compares with that of Adam before he fell, because at the time of writing they have not accepted the false teaching. But the wealthy women are actively sampling and passing on the forbidden fruit of teachings which falsely promise 'knowledge' (1 Tim. 6:20). He does not want these women to be instruments of the satan, causing any man – particularly the men who are in their sights as potential partners – to participate with them.[6]

Paul is concerned even for Timothy himself as possibly being in jeopardy. As Paul's delegate, he will mix not only with the poor but also with the elite in the church. He is young (4:12), and the widows are young, rich, sensual and alluring. Paul expressly warns Timothy to exhort the younger women with all purity (5:2; see also 5:22), to shun the false teachers' love of riches and to pursue godliness (6:5–11), to remain spotless and irreproachable (6:14), and to turn away from the false knowledge (6:20).[7]

The critical point for understanding the meaning of *authenteō* within Paul's train of thought is his explicit emphasis that Adam, in distinction from Eve, was not deceived. This comes directly from the text of Genesis 3, where the woman admits to God that the serpent deceived her (3:13, reflecting 3:1–6) but the man makes no excuse about being deceived. Instead the man says that the woman gave him the fruit and that he ate it (3:12, reflecting 3:6). God states that Adam listened to his wife and broke God's command (3:17). In other words, Adam followed her false teaching rather than holding fast to God's right teaching.

---

5. Septuagint: 'knowing [*ginōskō*] good and evil' (3:5); 'they knew [*ginōskō*] they were naked' (3:7); *ginōskō* is the verb related to the nouns *gnōsis* and *epignōsis*.

6. The analogy gains additional traction if Timothy and other readers are aware of the traditional belief that years passed between the creation of Adam and his fall. Jubilees 3:17 (second century BC) retells the story with additional details, placing the temptation in the eighth year. The Ephesian church was formed some years before the writing of this letter.

7. Paul's concern that Timothy should not be led astray is apparent also in his second letter: 2 Tim. 2:4–7, 15–19, 22–23; 3:13–14; 4:14–15.

Some scholars object that there is nothing in Genesis 3 about Eve teaching Adam.[8] But there is, in 3:17 (ESV, 'you have listened to the voice of your wife'). Perhaps they are looking for a narrow, Westernized concept of teaching. The word for teach (*didaskō*) used in 1 Timothy 2:12 is not limited to what is usually called 'doctrine' but extends to instructing someone what to do or say (see Matt. 28:15). As we saw in chapter 11, teaching, for Paul, includes saying things, setting an example, and getting someone to behave in a particular way.

So, what is Paul's analysis of what went wrong between Eve and Adam? Paul views Adam's failure not as falling prey to a deception, but as a failure of the will.[9] Eve was not only a bad example to Adam; she also verbally encouraged him to eat the fruit (3:17) and took the direct step of giving it to him. Her teaching led him into doing what he knew was wrong. In other words, her influence overbore his will; her bad teaching overpowered him. That appears to be the contextual meaning of *authenteō*.

Why does Paul use the rare word *authenteō*?

The word *authenteō* is very unusual. Paul does not use it in any other letter. It is not found anywhere else in the Bible. It is relatively rare in surviving Greek writings as a whole.[10] Why does Paul choose such a distinctive word?

The context has shown us that the false teachings included astrological ideas and that Paul makes a number of astrological allusions. The reason for Paul's choice of this word is not difficult to find: it is a term used in astrological lore. We have seen that in chapter 5 Paul picks up the conventional astrological language and uses it to challenge the women's behaviour. He is doing something similar in chapter 2 when telling Timothy that he is not permitting a woman to *authent* a man.

In connection with 1 Timothy 5:11–16 I cited Al Wolters' translation of *Tetrabiblos* 3.13.10. I did this because of the correspondences between this astrological lore and Paul's descriptions of the wealthy women in his letter. Wolters provides this very passage from *Tetrabiblos* as an example of the use of *authenteō*. It is one of a small handful of examples of the use of this word close

---

8. *RBMW*, 185 (Moo); *WITC*, 211 (Schreiner).

9. Knight 1992, 144 ('he sinned willfully, not as a result of deception').

10. Scholars have presented detailed studies of how *authenteō* was used in other writings and of the syntax within which Paul uses it in v. 12. For assessments of the results of these studies, see appendices 3 and 4.

to Paul's time. It is one of only two extant examples where *authenteō* is used with the same grammatical construction as in 1 Timothy 2:12 (that is, the verb is followed by a genitive of a person).[11]

In this example, Wolters' translation of *authenteō* is 'gained mastery'. In another English translation of the same astrological text, it is similarly rendered as 'dominates'.[12] This well-attested meaning fits readily into 1 Timothy 2:12, where we have seen that the context suggests the meaning 'overpower'.

Paul's choice of the astrological term *authenteō* looks deliberate. Paul could have used another word for 'gain mastery', 'dominate' or 'overpower' (Luke uses two other such words in Acts 19:16), but we may reasonably infer that *authenteō* was in Paul's mind as a particularly appropriate word because of its use in the false traditions of astrology. This becomes apparent when we set his choice of this word, unique in the Bible, alongside relevant features of the context and the available information in 1 Timothy about the nature of false teachings at Ephesus. We may note especially (1) Paul's use of vocabulary in 1 Timothy 5:13–14 that is quite unusual in the context of Christian instruction (*argos, periergos, oikodespoteō*), sounding multiple echoes of the language of astrology and magic; (2) the association of Ephesian Artemis with both astrology and magic; (3) the known history from Acts 19 of demons, magic and the burning of books of forbidden knowledge in Ephesus; and (4) Paul's instructions in Ephesians 6 about spiritual warfare against the unseen forces of evil.[13]

Making it doubly appropriate, this word was also associated with sorcery and death. The noun *authentēs* meant (among other things) a murderer, a self-murderer (suicide) or the perpetrator of a murder.[14] Eve's teaching of Adam,

---

11. Wolters explains that in astrological literature the heavenly bodies, such as Mercury, are treated as if they were persons: *WITC*, 78–79.

12. *EFBT*, 676. So also in the translation edited by Clark 2006, and in the translation reproduced in *M&W*, 381. Wolters' translation in *WITC*, 78, tries to bring out a possible implication of the aorist tense which is used.

13. One of the main arguments deployed by scholars against the authenticity of 1 and 2 Timothy is the use of distinctive vocabulary which is not used in those letters of Paul which they accept as genuine. Some of this vocabulary (including *goēs* in 2 Tim. 3:13) is readily explained by the distinctive situation which he and Timothy faced in Ephesus.

14. *M&W*, 364, 372. For an example shortly after Paul's time, see Josephus, *The Jewish War* 1.30. Referring to the murder of Herod's brother, Pheroras, Thackeray's translation reads: 'But retribution was now, in turn, descending upon the real

and their breaking of God's command, led to her and Adam's 'death' (Gen. 2:17; 3:23–24; compare Eph. 2:1–2; Rom. 6:23). We have seen that the Wisdom of Solomon appears to have been one of Paul's sources for writing about spiritual warfare. The very passage in the Wisdom of Solomon which uses the word *authentēs* to condemn people for being murderers also speaks of God's hostility towards the same people because they engaged in sorcery (Wis. 12:4–6; see RSV).

Understanding verse 15

So far, our consideration of chapter 2 has only reached verse 14. One verse remains. In verse 15 Paul writes: 'But she will be saved [*sōzō*] by means of [*dia*] the childbearing [*teknogonia*], if they remain in faith and love and holiness, with self-control/propriety [*sōphrosunē*].'

Verse 15 is usually regarded as a problem. There is considerable uncertainty as to what Paul means. English versions contain a wide range of interpretations:

1. Some commentators see here a promise of mothers' physical safety during childbirth. This is reflected in NASB: 'But women will be preserved through the bearing of children if they continue in faith and love and sanctity with self-restraint.'
2. Some say that childbearing is an attendant circumstance during which women will experience their spiritual salvation. This is reflected in EHV: 'But she will be saved – while bearing children – if they remain in faith and love and sanctification with self-control.'
3. Some say that women will be saved by means of childbearing because this means they are adhering to their God-ordained domestic role. This

---

(note 14 *cont.*) perpetrator [*authentēs*] of that crime, Antipater; this retribution arose out of the death of Pheroras. For certain freedmen of the deceased came, in dejection, to the king and informed him that his brother had been carried off by poison.' (Greek text available at <http://www.perseus.tufts.edu/hopper/text?doc= Perseus:text:1999.01.0147:book=1:section=582&highlight=au%29qe%2Fnthn>.) Wolters may class this use as the neutral meaning 'originator', but examples show the typical use to be of the originator of a murder or some related crime. Wolters also discusses a scholion of uncertain date, possibly around the turn of the era from BC to AD, which uses the verb *authenteō* to mean 'murder' (*WITC*, 81–83). See further *M&W*, 362. (A scholion is a comment on an earlier text.)

is reflected in NABRE: 'But she will be saved through motherhood, provided women persevere in faith and love and holiness, with self-control.'

4. Some say that 'the childbearing' refers to the birth of Christ, which brings salvation. This is reflected in DLNT: 'But she will be saved by The Childbearing, if they continue in faith and love and holiness with sound-mindedness.'[15]

The root cause of this uncertainty is the common misconception of the context. If in chapter 2 Paul is writing about how to conduct the public assemblies of the church, verse 15 is indeed baffling, because it has no connection, or at best only a tangential connection, with the subject matter. But this is not what he is writing about. He is continuing on the same topic that he has been addressing throughout chapters 1 and 2: combating false teaching and living saved lives. He is therefore still writing about living a saved and godly life through Christ, in contrast to a life that embodies and promotes false teachings.

In verse 15 he refers to faith, love, holiness and self-control or propriety. These are all qualities to which he has already drawn attention as characteristic of the saved life of love and goodness: see faith in 1:4–5, 12, 14, 19; 2:7; love in 1:5, 14; holiness/purity/godliness in 1:5; 2:2, 8, 10; and self-control in 2:9. He has been writing about the misbehaving women who have been led astray in false knowledge and he has been prohibiting them from leading a man astray. Now he draws this part of his discussion to a fitting conclusion by insisting that they can be saved and live godly lives.

Accordingly, it is the fourth interpretation of verse 15 which is in accordance with Paul's intent. As usual, Paul's thinking is Christ-centred. In context, 'the childbearing' is naturally understood to refer to the Saviour coming into the world through a woman. Although Eve transgressed, she was also the ancestor of the Saviour. Therefore there is hope of salvation. In line with Paul's own experience of God's mercy (1:13–16), even the misbehaving wealthy women will be saved through the Messiah if they show their repentance by their changed lives. Contrary to the behaviour mentioned in 5:11–12, they must continue in faith.[16]

---

15. For (1), see also AMP, CEB, CJB, DARBY, NET, NMB, NTE, PHILLIPS, TLV, VOICE. For (2), see also NKJV. For (3), see also CEV, WYC. For (4), see also GW, ISV, NOG.

16. The condition 'if they continue . . .' is a regular element in Paul's thinking. Compare Rom. 11:22; 1 Cor. 15:2; 2 Cor. 13:5; Col. 1:22–23; 1 Tim. 4:16.

This Christ-centred interpretation of verse 15 is confirmed and rounded out by the following:

- The use of the definite article, *the* childbearing, indicates a particular event.
- Paul's concern in chapters 1 and 2 is with salvation through God's Messiah (1:1, 15–17; 2:3–7) in express contrast to the effect of false teachings and in implied contrast with the Ephesian belief in Artemis as saviour.
- A man (*anthrōpos* – born a real human being, unlike the mythical Artemis), Christ Jesus, has come into the world as the true saviour, which has been witnessed to 'in its own times' (*kairiois idiois*; 2:5–6; also 1:15). This is a recent, real event, not an ancient legend.
- In the previous verse (2:14) Paul has referred to Eve's transgression, in accordance with Genesis 3:13 (ESV): 'The woman said, "The serpent deceived me, and I ate."' The fall is the reason why salvation is needed.
- Timothy must know how the story continued. In Genesis 3:15 God announces to the serpent (ESV):

> I will put enmity between you and the woman,
>   and between your offspring and her offspring;
> he shall bruise your head,
>   and you shall bruise his heel.

This is the first promise that a deliverer will be born, a descendant of Eve, who will tread on the satan's head and suffer in doing so.[17] The promise in Genesis 3:15 is a clear reference to salvation in the Genesis account of the fall, so this is an obvious allusion for Paul to make. It is fulfilled in the 'man' who has come (1 Tim. 2:5).

- Timothy is well aware that the next verse (Gen. 3:16) refers to women's pain in childbirth. Paul casts a sidelong glance at the Artemis cult's belief that the goddess would keep mothers safe during childbearing. In Paul's gospel there is an even more important kind of safety for women, by means of a particular event of childbearing, which is the salvation found in following Christ with faith, love, holiness and self-control.[18]

---

17. See further Luke 3:23, 38; 10:19; Rom. 16:20; Col. 2:15; Rev. 12:9.
18. An additional argument is often advanced that in v. 15 Paul uses his regular word for 'save' (*sōzō*), and if this does not mean 'save' in his regular sense of salvation

Having read verses 11–14 in the context of 1:1 – 2:10, verse 15 no longer looks like a tangential digression. It is exactly on topic. In appendix 5 I assess the challenges that have been made to the Christ-centred interpretation of verse 15 and give further reasons for rejecting the competing interpretations.

Using the fourth key: Paul's signposts in verse 15

Verse 15 now proves to be a fourth key for understanding the disputed passage.

The contents of this verse call into question a critical feature of complementarian analysis. There are said to be no 'contextual cues' which limit the application of verse 12 to the particular circumstances in Ephesus at the time of writing.[19] This is one of the primary justifications for the complementarian insistence that verse 12 should be applied to all women in all public assemblies of the church in all times and places. But verse 15 provides two such cues, or signposts.

The first signpost readily catches the eye. In verse 15 Paul starts with the singular 'she', then jumps to the plural 'they', still within the same sentence, and without an intervening identification of the plural subject. This mixing of the singular 'she' and the plural 'they' is highly unusual and very striking. What is he doing here?

The structure of Paul's discussion is plain. He gives instructions for the misbehaving women in the plural in verses 9–10, switches to the singular in verses 11–15a for his Adam and Eve illustration, then switches back to the plural at 15b, part way through his sentence.

The 'she' in verse 15 refers to 'the woman' of verse 14.[20] This woman is Eve, who taught Adam once falsely, and whose conduct illustrates the importance of the instructions which Paul provides for the 'woman' of verses 11–12.

---

through the Messiah, this would be an improbable sole example of the meaning 'deliver' in the whole of his writings: *M&W*, 418–420; *WITC*, 217–218 (Schreiner). This argument should not be pressed too far. Usage of a word in one of its senses in different contexts elsewhere does not conclusively determine its meaning in the context under consideration. Note also that in Phil. 1:19 Paul uses the related noun *sōtēria* to refer to both practical deliverance and spiritual salvation: see Phil. 1:19–23.

19. Köstenberger 1994, 270 ('neither are there any contextual cues limiting the application of 1 Tim. 2:12 to the circumstances at hand'). We saw in chapter 11 that this is an overstatement, even from v. 12 on its own, since the phrase 'I am not permitting' presupposes a particular range of jurisdiction.

20. In the Greek there is no separate word for 'she' in v. 15 but the effect is the same.

If we track back from verse 15, looking for a plural referent for 'they', we find it in the 'women' of verses 9–10, who are not to dress expensively and indecently but who instead are to adorn themselves with good works. These are exactly the women who need to be advised to live a saved life of faith and love and holiness, with self-control/propriety (v. 15), and to learn in quietness and full submission and not to teach and overpower a man (vv. 11–12).

By his unusual use of grammar, Paul forcefully brings to the reader's attention that he is equating 'she' and 'they'. In other words, *he is equating 'woman' in verses 11–12 (singular) with 'women' in verses 9–10 (plural)*. This confirms that Paul's instruction in verses 11–12 concerning 'a woman' is not a move to a new topic but is aimed at the 'women' of verses 9–10. These are particular rich women in the Ephesian church, not every female believer in the world.

To bring out the meaning of the compressed format which Paul adopts in verse 15, the appropriate expansion is: 'But a woman who misbehaves like Eve will be saved through the Childbearing, as will all the women I am writing about who are being tempted into misbehaviour, if instead they remain in faith and love and holiness, with self-control/propriety.'

The second signpost in verse 15 is Paul's use of the word *teknogonia* (childbearing).

We must keep in mind that Paul is a thoughtful writer and an accomplished wordsmith.[21] As we have repeatedly seen, plays on words and allusions to ideas are part of his stock in trade. His hope that the women will continue in faith (2:15) in contrast to abandoning the faith (5:11–12) is not the only link between 2:15 and chapter 5. Paul makes a conspicuous verbal link by using *teknogonia* in 2:15 and *teknogoneō* in 5:14. These are very unusual words in the context of Christian instruction. They are not found elsewhere in Paul's letters, or indeed anywhere in the New Testament. Thus this appears as a deliberate link, which should not fail to strike the reader.

This link provides further confirmation that the reader should use Paul's remarks about women in chapter 5 to get a better contextual understanding of what he writes about women in chapter 2. It is Paul himself who makes this link between the two passages. This confirms the reader's understanding of the identity of the women whom Paul is writing about in 2:9–15.

When Paul writes of *teknogonia* in 2:15, while his primary reference is to the birth of the Messiah, he is laying the ground for what he will say in chapter 5.

---

21. I do not mean that Paul's letters are polished literary creations. They show evidence of dictation without revision (for example, the unnecessary repetition of *kalos* in 1 Cor. 7:26 and the elliptical relationship between Eph. 3:1 and 3:2).

Prior to this point in chapter 2 his programme for the idle, wealthy widows has been that they should learn true reverence, self-restraint and good works. Now he plants the seed of the idea that childbearing is honourable and worthwhile – after all, it was the means through which the man came who is the true saviour. In chapter 5 Paul will say it is better that these women should marry and, instead of being idle, devote themselves to worthwhile activities, including bearing children (*teknogoneō*; 5:14). This can be one of their good works (2:10; 5:10). When Timothy reads out Paul's letter, the allusion from 5:14 back to 2:15 will be apparent to thoughtful listeners.

These two signposts in verse 15 are conspicuous in the Greek text. Why have they often been missed? Probably because of the common misconception, held by many egalitarian and complementarian scholars, that in chapter 2 Paul is focusing specifically on the public assemblies of the church. This has made verse 15 hard to understand. With this misconception out of the way, the signposts can be read.

The link to chapter 3

We complete our examination of context by looking at how chapter 2 leads into chapter 3.

The first phrase of chapter 3 is *pistos ho logos* ('faithful is the word'; ESV: 'The saying is trustworthy'). Paul uses this expression five times in the Pastoral Epistles. Unless the present instance is an exception, the saying to which he refers is always a saying about salvation. The expression *pistos ho logos* may either precede the saying about salvation (as in 1 Tim. 1:15 and 2 Tim. 2:11–13) or may follow it (as in Titus 3:6–8).

There has been an ongoing debate among commentators over whether this phrase refers back to 2:15 or forward to 3:1b.

Understanding that 2:15 is about the salvation of the female false teachers resolves this debate. Here, *pistos ho logos* reads naturally as an emphatic confirmation of Paul's statement about salvation in 2:15. It refers back to it. The positioning of the division between chapter 2 and chapter 3 is unhelpful.[22]

But two objections have been made to understanding *pistos ho logos* as referring back to 2:15 rather than forward to 3:1b. One is that 'the childbearing' in 2:15 does not refer to Christ. I deal with this in appendix 5. For the reasons given in

---

22. Chrysostom, even though he did not adopt the Christ-centred interpretation of 2:15, understood *pistos ho logos* as referring back to 2:15: Homily 9 on 1 Tim. 2:11–15.

the appendix, I believe we can have confidence that the Christ-centred interpretation of 2:15 is correct.

The other objection, which is maintained even by scholars who accept the Christ-centred interpretation, is that 3:1b ('If someone aspires to being an overseer, they desire a good work') 'seems much too abrupt an introduction to the verses that follow'.[23] In other words, the change from what Paul has been writing about in chapter 2 to the specific topic of eldership seems rather sudden. They see 3:1a as a way of signalling that a new topic is beginning.

However, once we recognize Paul's train of thought, there is no suddenness involved. The wealthy women who are teaching falsely are at the forefront of his mind. At 1:3 he tells Timothy to instruct them not to teach 'differently'. At 1:7 he refers to their desire to become teachers of the law in the church, despite their defective grasp of Christian truth. In 1:12–16, using the emphatic expression *pistos ho logos*, he points to his own experience of salvation and of being appointed to God's service, despite his former ignorance and misdeeds. He does this in order to encourage them that they may be saved and appointed to God's service despite their defective understanding and misbehaviour. By his more general remarks at 2:4–6, he further encourages both them and others concerning salvation. At 2:9–14 he gives instructions for the women to follow, including that they should do good works. Then at 2:15 he directly mirrors what he has said about his own experience of salvation at 1:15–16 by stating explicitly that the women may be saved through the childbearing, and adding the same emphasis again, namely, *pistos ho logos*. Then he immediately addresses their aspiration to become recognized teachers in the church (3:1b). This would be a good work (3:1b). But they would not be eligible while continuing to live in the way alluded to in 2:9 and further described in 5:6, 11–13. Their aspiration can only become a real possibility if they first prove themselves by living in the way described in 2:10, 15; 3:2–7.[24]

Accordingly, there is no sudden change of topic. Rather, there is a continuous train of thought from what we call chapter 2 into what we call chapter 3.

Paul's heartfelt pastoral objective for the rich, young women, and for men whom they may influence, is in line with the prayer of Jesus for his followers: 'Sanctify them to live in accordance with the truth; your word is truth' (John 17:17, NIV margin). Paul's meaning in 2:12 (with vv. 9–11) is:

23. Knight 1992, 153.
24. See further the discussion in chapter 15 of the qualifications for elders.

I am not permitting a woman false teacher with expensive and immodest dress, lacking decency and self-control, to teach and overpower a man: she is to be quiet and reverent and learn how to behave in accordance with the truth, in full submission to God.

What if I am wrong about the nature of the false teaching?

The circumstances that give rise to Paul's instructions are referred to in 1:1 – 2:10, especially 1:3 and 2:9–10, and in other places in the letter where the nature of the false teachings can be seen. My understanding that the women are involved in magic and astrology has been derived mainly from the text, with modest assistance from some basic background information. Nevertheless, what if this view of the false teachings is incorrect? What if *periergos* in 5:13 means merely a meddler and not someone practising magic? What if the apparent multiple allusions to Paul's battle in Ephesus against magic arts and evil spirits, to the association of Artemis with magic and astrology, to the astrological houses such as the idle house and to other astrological lore (*oikodespoteia, authenteō*) are not real allusions but are all mere coincidences, without significance? What if Paul's illustration using the magicians Jannes and Jambres in 2 Timothy was chosen merely as a random illustration of opposition, unrelated to the nature of actual false teaching circulating in Ephesus? What if *goēs* in 2 Timothy 3:13 means merely a charlatan and not a sorcerer?

If I am wrong on all these points, the understanding of 1 Timothy 2:8–15 which I have set out above remains substantially unaltered. The subject matter of chapter 2 remains the same. The evidence in Paul's letter that young wealthy widows were misbehaving, going from house to house spreading nonsensical false teaching and looking for a partner, remains largely unaltered; the only substantial difference would be to our understanding of the nature of the false teaching.

Reassessing current interpretations of 1 Timothy 2

In chapter 11 I enumerated some major difficulties facing complementarian interpretations of 1 Timothy 2. There is more to say. To my mind, the decisive consideration is that they are not sufficiently grounded in the context. I expand this assessment in appendix 6, where I provide a more detailed critique of the reasoning presented in *WITC, EFBT* and elsewhere.

If complementarian readings of verse 12 must be rejected because they do not fit the context, how does Payne's egalitarian reading fare?

For the purpose of interpreting 1 Timothy 2:12 Payne rightly pays considerable attention to the context, which he sketches out over some fifteen pages. He has also studied the meaning of *authenteō* elsewhere. He says 'probably the single most important document illuminating the use' of this word in verse 12 is a letter written by a man who assumed authority over someone else's slave, compelling the slave to agree to pay the proper fare to a ferryman. His proposal is that the relevant meaning of this word in verse 12 is 'assume authority', in the sense of seizing authority illegitimately.[25] Thus Paul does not want women to teach men in the public assemblies of the church until they have first learned properly (v. 11) and have been granted authorization to teach (v. 12).[26]

The meaning of the letter about the slave and the ferryman is much disputed. It is not necessary to adjudicate on this dispute because there are other issues to consider.[27]

Our first concern is Payne's focus on *the assembled church*. We have seen that this is not Paul's focus in chapter 2. In addition, if we keep an open mind about the possible meanings of the word *authenteō*, in the absence of Payne's translation of it, where in 1:1 – 2:15 does Paul indicate that his concern is an issue about *who is exercising authority over whom* in the assembled church? Payne's book is thoroughly researched and generally well reasoned, but it does not contain satisfying answers to these two crucial points.

Moreover, if the focus of Paul's concern is to prohibit unauthorized women from teaching in the assembly, why does he state in verse 12 that they are not to assume authority over 'a man'? There would also be women in the assembly. To teach and exercise authority over women would be even more damaging,

---

25. *Me&W*, 295–310, 365–370, 385–397.

26. *Me&W*, 314 ('not assume for themselves authority to teach men . . . which would be in public worship'); 326 ('probably . . . the context of the verse refers to a public worship setting'); 394 (Paul's restriction 'most obviously applies to teaching in public assemblies of the church'); 443 ('Paul prohibited women from . . . assuming authority to teach in church assemblies'); Payne 2014, 26 ('Paul was prohibiting women from . . . assuming authority without authorization to teach the assembled church').

27. The meaning 'overpower' would nonetheless fit reasonably well into Payne's general understanding of the episode which the letter describes. Similarly, Grudem states in *EFBT*, 680, that the meaning 'compel' seems appropriate in the context. See further appendix 3.

if (as Payne says) women in Ephesus found the false teachings more appealing than men did. The appropriate restriction for Paul to lay down would be a ban on the unauthorized women from teaching anyone, and especially other women.

Payne sees these difficulties, and offers three answers to them.[28] But they are not sufficiently persuasive.

The first two answers are that the public assembly is (1) the place where the most people would be influenced and (2) the public face of the church before the watching world. But the public assembly consists of both men and women, so if this were Paul's thinking he would have no reason to express himself in the way that he does in verse 12, namely, restricting women's activities specifically in relation to 'a man'.[29]

Payne's third answer is that Paul does not establish a rule that would be impossible for Timothy to monitor, namely, a ban on teaching by unauthorized women of other women when no men were present. This also fails to convince. Paul gives other instructions that Timothy has to pass on to the congregation and which Timothy will not be able to monitor directly. Timothy's task is to teach and urge godly behaviour, by word and example.[30] He will not be able to accompany each wealthy widow from house to house checking up on what she is saying (5:13). He will not be able to monitor directly whether slaves are behaving well in every house (6:1–2). This third reason does not convincingly explain why Paul's restriction is limited in the way that it is.

In sum, Payne's proposal of 'assume authority' for *authenteō* does not explain Paul's wording or his train of thought in a satisfying manner.[31]

Payne rightly recognizes that the false teaching is of such central concern to Paul that nearly all of the letter relates to it. He also rightly acknowledges

---

28. *M&W*, 394–395.

29. To be clear, because men and women were together in the public assembly, preventing a deceived woman from seizing authority to teach men in the assembly would incidentally protect women also. But if Paul's intention were to prohibit such a woman from teaching *men and women*, it is very strange that he says that the prohibition is on what is done to '*a man*'.

30. See, for example, 1:3, 18; 3:15; 4:6, 11–16; 5:21–22; 6:2, 11–14, 17, 20.

31. Moreover, Payne's proposal for Paul's thought process in v. 13 is that Paul has in mind an idea of respect for one's source, as in 1 Cor. 11:9 (*M&W*, 402–404). This is conceivable, but Paul's explicit point in v. 13 is not a point about source (he does not say that Eve was formed from Adam) but a point about timing (he says Adam was formed first).

that there are reasons for taking *authenteō* in verse 12 to mean 'dominate'. He even cites Chrysostom's understanding that Eve taught Adam once badly. But he judges that Paul's appeal to Eve's deception does not support the choice of 'dominate' as the correct meaning in verse 12.[32] His reasoning depends upon his interpretation of Paul's wording in verse 14, which proposes that 'Adam was not deceived' is consistent with Adam being in some sense deceived. I would suggest that Paul's wording in this respect should be taken at face value and that more attention needs to be given to the features that Adam did not fall before he came under Eve's influence (vv. 13–14), and that Eve's conduct led to his fall.

It is right to say that Paul does not spell out to Timothy that Eve's conduct led to Adam's transgression. But Paul's style here is compressed. Timothy must know the story well. And verse 12 itself makes clear to Timothy that Paul is concerned with *what is done by a woman to a man*. Timothy must be aware of the importance of the fall of Adam in Paul's understanding of salvation through the Messiah (Rom. 5:12–21; 1 Cor. 15:21–22, 42–50), a salvation which Paul refers to in the very next verse (v. 15).

When Adam was called to account, his explanation was: 'The woman whom you gave to be with me, she gave me fruit of the tree, and I ate' (Gen. 3:12, ESV). This was not the whole truth; it looks like an attempt to shift blame. But as a statement it was true as far as it went. Adam fell not because Eve illegitimately assumed authority over him but because she overpowered him with her false teaching. Even if Adam was to some extent deceived, the critical point for Paul's illustration is that Adam's behaviour resulted from the false instructions given by Eve (Gen. 3:17, ESV: 'Because you have listened to the voice of your wife'). As Payne himself says, in Genesis 3:17 God identifies Eve's words 'as decisive in influencing Adam'.[33] Precisely so.

---

32. *M&W*, 296, 380–385, 391–392. Chrysostom in Homily 9 on 1 Tim. 2:11–15 states, '[T]he woman taught the man once, and made him guilty of disobedience, and wrought our ruin. . . . [S]he made a bad use of her power over the man . . . he transgressed, not captivated by appetite, but merely from the persuasion of his wife. The woman taught once, and ruined all.' Payne cites in 391–392 an additional passage from Chrysostom which, if *authenteō* means 'dominate' or 'overpower', is to the same effect. Inserting *authent* into Payne's translation, it reads, '"I am not permitting a woman to teach." Why? She taught Adam once wickedly. "Nor to *authent* a man." Just why? She *authent*ed once wickedly.'

33. *M&W*, 407.

The four tough questions

In chapter 11 our consideration of the difficulties faced by egalitarian analyses concluded with four questions about 1 Timothy 2:12 to which those analyses generally cannot provide satisfactory answers. The complementarian responses to these questions (see chapter 11) also cannot be sustained, because they do not give proper recognition to the context of what Paul writes (see appendix 6).

The third and fourth keys have confirmed our working hypothesis that when Paul wrote 1 Timothy the false teachers within the Ephesian church, whom he had in view for Timothy to deal with, were women. On that basis we have arrived at a coherent understanding of Paul's remarks.

The four questions may now be slightly rephrased, taking into account the contextual meaning of *authenteō*, and readily answered:

Q1: On the basis that Paul's letter is concerned with combating false teaching, why in verses 8–15 does he restrict false teaching only *by women*, and not by men? Shouldn't male false teachers also be stopped?

> Answer 1: The male false teachers have already been excluded (1:20).
> At the time of Paul's first letter to Timothy, it is certain women in the
> fellowship who remain to be dealt with.

Q2: Why does he restrict the female false teachers from teaching and overpowering specifically *a man* by their false teaching, and not also restrict them from teaching women? Don't women also need protection from false teaching?

> Answer 2: In verse 12 Paul does not have specifically in mind the public
> assembly, where there are both men and women. He is concerned about
> the wealthy women going from house to house, dressed in the indecent
> fashions of courtesans, each looking for a man who will satisfy her sexual
> desires, and whom she may overpower with her false teaching.

Q3: If the false teaching *mainly affected women* rather than men, how does that square with Paul restricting women from teaching and overpowering *men*? If there is to be a distinction between men and women here, should we not expect the opposite, namely, a restriction on delivering false teaching to women?

> Answer 3: The answer is the same as Answer 2. These wealthy female false
> teachers have men in their sights.

Q4: If the problem is female false teachers, why does Paul apparently restrict *all women* and not specifically the false teachers?

> Answer 4: Rightly understood, Paul is indeed restricting specifically the
> false teachers. This is confirmed by the signposts which he provides in
> verse 15. He has in view in verse 12 the wealthy women whose conduct
> makes it necessary for him to give the instructions in verses 9–11 and 15.
> Being well aware of the practical issue which he had to deal with, and
> knowing the people involved, Timothy had no reason to think that Paul
> was proposing a ban applicable to all women.

Our interpretation is confirmed by the fact that the four tough questions now have ready answers.

But isn't this interpretation entirely new?

In chapters 12 and 13 I have offered an interpretation of 1 Timothy 2 of which I was wholly ignorant when I began writing, and to which the context has led.

It may be objected that this interpretation is new. If it is correct, why has it not been advanced before? Several answers may be given.

First, at most, it is only partly new. For example, one element of it is to understand the conduct alluded to in verse 9 to involve dressing like courtesans; Chrysostom also understood verse 9 in this sense. Another element is an understanding of Paul's reasoning in verses 13–14 as an illustration which is based on Eve's bad teaching of Adam. This is not new; Chrysostom understood verses 13–14 as referring to this.[34]

Second, I strongly doubt that it contains any element that is really new. There is a massive literature on 1 Timothy 2. I have read only some of it. I have arrived at this interpretation from study of the context. This makes it likely that every element in it has been mentioned before by someone.[35] What I have done is to put the pieces of the jigsaw together. The hypothesis that Paul had dealt with

---

34. See respectively Chrysostom's Homily 8 on 1 Tim. 2:8–10 and Homily 9 on 1 Tim.
    2:11–15, each cited above (246, 280). In addition, some elements are similar to views
    expressed in *DBE*, 376–377, 380 (Fee).
35. For example, after drafting chapters 12 and 13, I became aware that understanding the
    women of 5:13 to be involved in magic has a long history. See Kelly 1963, 118, 234;
    Hanson 1982, 99, 175; Kroeger 1992, 62–63.

the male false teachers, and Timothy must next deal with the women false teachers, coheres fully with the context and with the wording of Paul's instructions. All the pieces can now be fitted in to complete the picture.

Third, it was only relatively recently that the church came to see that the traditional understanding of the relations of men and women as presented in Scripture was driven more by patriarchal culture than by the words of the Bible text. Both egalitarians and complementarians have agreed that a fresh assessment was required (see chapter 1). The present book is part of that process, which is not yet complete.

Practical consequences of how verse 12 is understood

I have offered a contextual understanding of 1 Timothy 2, and in particular of the true meaning and intent of Paul's restriction on the activities of women in verse 12. How do we move on from interpretation to application?

I touch on methods of application in appendix 1. It has not been necessary to explore these in detail for the purpose of assessing the principal competing evangelical positions, because Grudem and Payne do not materially differ in their approach to this kind of question.

Many apostolic instructions in the New Testament were given because of local and temporary circumstances. This does not mean that faithful Christians are free to ignore them. The usual procedure is to see what principles were involved, and to seek to live consistently with those principles in the different circumstances which we face.

Read in its context, the restriction which Paul laid out for Timothy to implement was a restriction on certain women who were spreading false teaching and who had men in their sights. Paul uses the Genesis story as an apt illustration rather than as an appeal to a creation principle concerning the relations of men and women. The objective of the restriction is to restrain the false teaching and to forestall its impact. His words do not justify a general prohibition on women teaching men in the church, or on exercising authority in the church.

The complementarian interpretation of verse 12 has given rise to much uncertainty and anxiety in its application, some of the complexity of which can be seen from Grudem's very lengthy and detailed discussion of how it might apply.[36] Should gifted women be banned from all Christian teaching of males?

---

36. *EFBT*, 84–101. See also Byrd 2016, 153–157.

If so, should this apply even to male children? If not, what should the age limit be, and how is the limit to be decided? Should women be permitted to write and publish Bible commentaries and theological books? If they do, should men read them? May women teach in seminaries? Should they be allowed to speak at Christian conferences where men are present? If so, does it make a difference, and in what way, if the occasion at which they speak is a worship occasion rather than a lecture? Does it make a difference, and in what way, if their address is inspirational rather than expository? May they lead parachurch organizations? May they lead mixed Bible studies in the local church? May they teach informally in the worship assembly of the local church but not preach? Are they permitted to preach the gospel to men or to lead missions? May they preach in the local worship assembly provided that they do so under the authority of male elders, submitting a script for advance scrutiny? May they fill teaching positions as lay workers or assistant pastors, provided that the senior pastor is a man? None of these questions has an agreed answer among complementarians. This is not altogether surprising, since the principal basis for any ban is a single short verse, interpreted without full attention to its context.

The impact of the complementarian interpretation is not confined to women's use of their teaching gifts. The unbiblical notion that there is a particular kind of teaching in the local church which is regarded as authoritative, and may only be delivered by male elders and male pastors, often silences also the teaching or preaching gifts of men who are not serving in those capacities, contrary to the principles set out by Peter in 1 Peter 4:10–11 and by Paul in 1 Corinthians 12 – 14 and Romans 12:3–8. Paul did not instruct Timothy to limit the activities of teaching and preaching to male elders, whether in the assembled congregation or at all.

At least two principles underlie what Paul says in 1 Timothy 1 – 2. One is that dealing with false teaching is a spiritual battle, which needs to be fought in a manner that is calibrated to the particular situation. Here, Paul does not advise Timothy to exclude the women; he urges him to encourage much prayer, and to instruct them not to continue with the false teaching.

Another principle is that a particular situation may justify temporary restrictions on Christian liberty, to promote the larger purposes of the gospel. As we have seen, there was not in normal circumstances a ban on women teaching, but the inappropriate conduct of particular women required that their activities be restricted. There may be other sorts of circumstances in churches today which would justify some kinds of restrictions, in the greater interests of advancing the gospel.

For example, where a church is functioning in a culture where public leadership by women is considered a scandalous example of Western decadence, the church will have to decide whether in the particular circumstances the gospel is best advanced by freely demonstrating the equal status of Christian women or by accepting temporary restrictions in order to avoid giving unnecessary offence which prevents the gospel being heard. Or in a Western culture where some churches have become over-feminized, and have a disproportion of women over men, a church or group of churches may have to decide whether a temporary policy favouring male public leadership may bring dividends.[37]

This is not to suggest that denying women the opportunity to minister in either culture would not be a great cost, but Paul and Timothy showed the way by accepting the cost of severe restrictions on their own freedoms for the sake of the gospel when the situation demanded (1 Cor. 9:1–23; Acts 16:3).

Summary of chapter 13

1. Using the third key, in the context of 1 Timothy 2:9–12 *authenteō* appears to mean 'overpower'. The nature of Paul's concern is: 'I am not permitting a woman false teacher with expensive and immodest dress, lacking decency and self-control, to teach and overpower a man: she is to be quiet and reverent and learn how to behave in accordance with the truth, in full submission to God.'
2. This interpretation facilitates ready explanation of Paul's reasoning by reference to Genesis in verses 13–14. Paul is underlining what he says in verses 11–12 by referring back to the first spiritual battle recounted in Scripture, where a woman was deceived by the satan into receiving forbidden knowledge, and falsely taught and overpowered a man, with dire results.
3. Paul chooses this rare word because of its use in the same sense in astrological lore, which forms part of the false teaching which the wealthy women are promoting. It is also associated with sorcery and with death, the opposite of salvation.
4. This line of interpretation illuminates the meaning of verse 15, traditionally regarded as a difficult verse. It refers to salvation brought about through the birth of the Messiah, with a sidelong glance at the beliefs of the Artemis cult.
5. Using the fourth key, we find that Paul provides two signposts in verse 15. He signals to the reader that he is equating 'woman' in verses 11–12 ('she' in

---

37. See the concerns expressed by Sandom 2012, 14, cited in *WITC*, 247 (Yarbrough). In some countries, anti-discrimination laws may contain legal constraints which would have to be taken into account in the formulation of such a policy.

v. 15) with 'women' in verses 9–10 ('they' in v. 15). This confirms that Paul's instruction in verses 11–12 is intended to relate to the women of verses 9–10. He also uses unusual vocabulary to construct a conspicuous verbal and thematic link between 2:15 (*teknogonia*) and 5:14 (*teknogoneō*). This is further confirmation that readers may get a better contextual understanding by reading his remarks about women in chapter 2 alongside his remarks about women in chapter 5.

6. The above interpretation fits into Paul's continuous, connected train of thought which starts in chapter 1 and proceeds through the letter. It shows how chapter 2 leads into chapter 3. It also resolves the four tough questions about 2:12 to which I drew attention in chapter 11 above.

7. First Timothy 2 does not justify a general ban on teaching by women in the church, or on the exercise of authority by women in the church.

Questions to consider

1. What are your thoughts on the third and fourth keys?
2. Paul's outlook is that combating false teaching and advancing God's salvation is a spiritual battle. To what extent does that coincide with your own habits of thought and your own experiences?
3. Does the section headed 'Practical consequences of how verse 12 is understood' raise any concerns in your mind? What are they?

[M]any . . . believed in Him because of the word of the woman who
testified. (John 4:39, NASB)

Should church leadership by women be restricted?

We see in the New Testament that, as local churches were established and grew,
elders or overseers were appointed to govern them (Acts 14:23; 20:17, 28; Phil.
1:1; 1 Tim. 3:2; 5:17; Titus 1:5, 7; Jas 5:14; 1 Pet. 5:1).[1]

Egalitarians see no biblical restriction on the ministry roles which women
may fulfil in God's church. On the basis of the same biblical data, complementarians believe that roles of governing and authoritative teaching in the
church should be restricted to men. This means in practice that in complementarian churches women are not permitted to be elders or pastors.

Formerly, the view that women may not fulfil these leadership roles rested
on a belief that women were in a subordinate position and inherently unfit for
leadership, either because this was how God created them or because of the fall.
This belief is no longer regarded as consistent with Scripture (see chapter 1).
While there are differences between individual evangelical complementarian

---

1. The terms 'elder' (*presbuteros*) and 'overseer' (*episkopos*) are generally understood
   as used synonymously in the context of the New Testament churches. Possibly the
   two should be distinguished, while also overlapping: Kruse 1993, 603–604. This
   possibility does not directly impact on our subject of interest so is not further
   discussed here.

scholars, broadly speaking the restriction on women's leadership now appears to rest on one or more of six pillars:

1. the restriction on women's speaking in 1 Corinthians 14:34–35;
2. Paul's restriction on women in 1 Timothy 2:11–15, in particular verse 12;
3. Jesus' choice of twelve male apostles;
4. only men were permitted to be Old Testament priests of the Lord;
5. a view of male headship derived from Genesis 2, interpreted in the light of certain New Testament texts, especially 1 Corinthians 11:3;
6. the qualifications for elders set out in 1 Timothy 3:1–7 and Titus 1:6–9.[2]

This chapter reviews the first five of these and introduces the sixth.

Pillar 1: 1 Corinthians 14:34–35

We saw in chapters 9 and 10 that 1 Corinthians 14:34–35 could not properly be used to reach conclusions about the acceptable scope of women's ministry, for two reasons. First, no solution has been found for harmonizing those verses with what Paul writes elsewhere. The interpretive puzzle of what they mean, and hence their application, remains uncertain. Second, the best explanation of the available textual evidence is that those two verses are not authentic.

Pillar 2: 1 Timothy 2:11–15

We saw in chapters 11 to 13 (with appendices 3–6) that the meaning of 1 Timothy 2:12 is much debated, but that the complementarian interpretation of it does not fit the context. Paul is addressing a particular situation, not laying down a general ban on women's teaching in the assembled church. Nor is he saying anything in 1 Timothy 2 about whether in general women may or may not be in positions which involve the exercise of authority over men in the church.

It appears that when Paul was writing this letter some wealthy women in the Ephesian church were wanting to be teachers or elders, but were spreading false

---

2. There is a further set of contested issues, concerning 'ordination' to be a 'priest' or 'bishop'. These are matters of church tradition and order, which are not prescribed in the New Testament, and which I do not address in this book.

teaching (1 Tim. 1:3, 7; 2:12; 3:1; 5:13). Even if this is wrong, and even if, contrary to what we have seen in chapters 11 to 13, 2:12 should be read as an enduring ban on women teaching in the assembly, this would not of itself rule out a woman being appointed as an elder. The reason for this (as we shall see in more detail below) is that not all elders undertook teaching of the word in the assembly (5:17).

Even if we were to use the complementarian understanding of verse 12, Paul's use of the singular ('a woman', 'a man') does not say what might or might not be appropriate in the context of leadership by a group of elders. The development of the role of elder into that of a 'priest' exercising sole authority over a congregation, or the role of a leading overseer into a separate office held by one person in a particular district (a 'bishop'), only emerged after the New Testament period, so Paul was not addressing it.[3] Even when translated as in the ESV, Paul's wording falls short of clearly ruling out the possibility that a woman may be appointed as a member of a group of elders exercising collective authority, especially if men act as the principal spokesmen of the group.

Pillar 3: twelve male apostles

When Jesus appointed twelve Jewish males as his first apostles, this signalled the founding of a new community of God's people, growing out of the Israelite community which was descended from the twelve patriarchs.

Complementarians say: 'the maleness of the apostles established a permanent position for male leadership in the church.'[4] This proposition is derived from Matthew 19:28 ('Jesus said to them, "Truly, I say to you, in the new world, when the Son of Man will sit on his glorious throne, you who have followed me will also sit on twelve thrones, judging the twelve tribes of Israel', ESV) and Revelation 21:14 ('And the wall of the city had twelve foundations, and on them were the twelve names of the twelve apostles of the Lamb', ESV).

For a full understanding of Matthew 19:28 it would be necessary to explore Jesus' fulfilment of Daniel 7 and how all his disciples share his kingship (see

---

3. See Kelly 1963, 13–16.

4. *EFBT*, 172–173. Because the present work focuses on seeking to understand the teaching of Scripture in its original context, I do not discuss the view that only a male 'priest' may represent Christ at the 'altar', which is based on tradition.

Rom. 5:17; 1 Cor. 4:8; 6:2–3; Eph. 2:6–7; Rev. 20:4). But our question is about the leadership of the new communities of God's people which would gather in different places when the gospel message spread out from Jerusalem. Jesus does not address this question in Matthew 19:28.

Likewise, John's vision of the names of the apostles on the foundations of the new city reflects the unique role of the primary founding apostles; it is not saying anything about how local churches should be led.

Piper and Grudem are therefore being realistic when they write: 'We would not argue that merely because Jesus chose twelve men to be His authoritative apostles, Jesus must have favored an eldership of only men in the church.'[5]

The role of the Twelve spanned a unique period of transition from the old covenant to the new. Their mission was initially restricted to Jews only (Matt. 10:5–6). Before Pentecost, Judas was replaced in order to keep the number at twelve (Acts 1:15–26). But this pattern was not maintained after Pentecost, when the Spirit was poured out on the whole company of disciples (Acts 2:1–18). After the apostle James was martyred, there is no indication that he was specifically replaced (Acts 12:1–2). Nevertheless, it appears that the number of authoritative primary apostles increased. By God's call, it appears that Paul and James, the Lord's brother, were accorded authority equal with the Twelve.[6] And local leadership, which did not carry the same degree of authority, was provided from a broader base.

The maleness of the original group of twelve apostles does not of itself prescribe the nature of the subsequent local leadership.

Sometimes it is said that if Jesus had intended to establish a new order, in which women and men were to be equal in leadership, he would have chosen six men and six women to be his first apostles.[7] This argument is not persuasive. Consider the parallel case of including Gentiles in leadership. No-one argues that, if Jesus had intended to establish a new order in which Gentiles would be equal partners with Jews, he would have chosen six Jews and six Gentiles to be his first apostles. The absence of Gentiles from the Twelve does not mean that Gentiles are not eligible to be elders of a church. Similarly, the absence of women from the Twelve does not mean that women are not eligible to be elders.

---

5. *RBMW*, 62. For further discussion of the Twelve, see *DBE*, 136 (Spencer).

6. See Acts 12:17; 15:13; 21:18; 1 Cor. 9:1–2; 15:7–10; 2 Cor. 10:8; 13:10; Gal. 1:1, 11–12, 19; 2:9, 11.

7. Pawson 1988, 41.

Pillar 3 does not justify a conclusion from the Bible that local church leaders must be men.[8]

Pillar 4: Old Testament priests and teaching

We saw in chapter 5 that the Old Testament does not substantiate a universal principle that women may never lead men or exercise authority over them. We must now consider the more specific arguments against women's leadership which are based on the Old Testament priesthood.

Grudem says that the role of teaching the people was reserved for male priests, and that there is a similar situation in the New Testament.[9]

The proposition that the role of teaching the people was reserved for male priests is not supported by any scripture which stipulates such a reservation, and the Old Testament contradicts it. Certainly, priests were expected to teach (Lev. 10:11; Ezra 7:1–10; Mal. 2:6–7), but that does not mean that no-one else was permitted to do so. King David was not a priest but his role as a teacher can be glimpsed in Psalm 51:13 ('I will teach transgressors your ways', NIV, ESV). He taught the people at least through his psalms (Ps. 34:11). Others who were not priests also taught the people. For example, King Jehoshaphat sent out royal officials to teach, accompanied by Levites and priests (2 Chr. 17:7–9). In Nehemiah 8:7–8 there is a list of thirteen men who taught the law to the people; while all these men were Levites, not all of them were priests (see Neh. 10:1–13).

For the purposes of his argument Grudem insists on a rigid distinction between Old Testament teachers and Old Testament prophets, but this is artificial. The prophet Samuel taught the people (1 Sam. 12:23–25). The prophet Isaiah taught the people (Isa. 1:10; contrast 9:15–16).[10] The prophet Jeremiah was seen as a teacher, alongside the priests (Jer. 18:18).

Schreiner says that the pattern of male-only priests is 'suggestive', and carries over to the New Testament. In *RBMW* he says it is 'instructive to note' that women were Old Testament prophets but never priests; this is said to

---

8. Whether pillar 3 has any implications for 'popes', 'archbishops' or 'apostles' in denominations which have a centralized structure is not something that I address in this book.

9. *EFBT*, 137.

10. Isa. 1:10 is addressed to Judah ('Sodom' and 'Gomorrah' are not meant literally); see 1:1–31 for the context.

show that the gift of prophecy in the New Testament is not as authoritative as the gift of teaching. But how it shows this is entirely unclear, and he casts doubt on this view in more recent writing.[11] We noted in chapter 11 that 1 Corinthians 12:28 does not show teachers to be more authoritative than prophets.

The FIEC Women in Ministry Statement says: 'What we see in the New Testament is, as we would expect, a reflection of patterns laid down in the Old Testament.... [P]riests . . . were men.' It does not explain why we should expect this Old Testament pattern to be reflected in the New. In view of the inauguration of the new covenant and the new creation, the fulfilment of the Old Testament priesthood in Christ and the priesthood of all believers, and in the light of what Paul says in Galatians 3:26–29 and Peter in 1 Peter 2:9, a more scripturally accurate expectation would be that the pattern of priesthood under the old covenant has been left behind.

The fatal flaw in arguments based on the Old Testament priesthood is the New Testament teaching that this priesthood has come to an end, being replaced by Jesus Christ, and priesthood has passed to all believers in him under the new covenant, both men and women (Heb. 2 – 10; 1 Pet. 2:9; Rev. 1:6; 5:10).[12] We see in the New Testament that the function of teaching the people is not restricted to a particular group (Col. 3:16; 1 Cor. 12; 14:26) and that some women fulfilled prominent roles (see below). If priesthood is to be equated with leadership or with a teaching role, leadership and teaching roles are now potentially open to all God's people without gender distinction.

Pillar 5: headship

Some complementarian writers understand biblical notions of male headship as meaning that men have unilateral authority over women. This is based on Genesis 1 – 3, read together with certain New Testament texts: 1 Corinthians 11:3; Ephesians 5:22–23 with Colossians 3:18 and Titus 2:5; 1 Peter 3:1–6; 1 Timothy 2:11–15.

---

11. Schreiner 2010, 34; *RBMW*, 217–218; *WITC*, 193. Note also that the proposition that in the Old Testament men could be priests, while women could not, requires refinement; most men, even most Levites, could not be priests; the priesthood was reserved specifically for healthy males of the house of Aaron (Exod. 29:44; Lev. 8 – 9; 21:16–23).

12. See further *DBE*, 272–286 (Grenz).

Considering each of these references in turn:

- We saw in chapter 5 that Genesis 1 – 3 does not provide explicit support for this understanding of headship.
- We looked at the significance of 1 Corinthians 11:3 for male headship in chapters 7 and 8. Paul does not place any restriction on the scope of women's ministry in 1 Corinthians 11.
- We looked at Ephesians 5, Colossians 3:18 and Titus 2:5 in chapters 3 and 4. Paul does not say that husbands are in authority over their wives or should exercise authority over them. In marriage we found not unilateral authority, but equality, mutual submission and a headship of the husband which reflects the Messiah's role as saviour, not as lord. We looked at 1 Peter 3 in chapter 6, and found a view of equality and mutual honour in marriage very much like Paul's. Even if these interpretations are not accepted, the fact remains that none of these passages is about church leadership.
- We saw in chapters 11 to 13 that 1 Timothy 2 is not concerned with the authority structures of church leadership. Moreover, in 1 Timothy 2:11–15 Paul does not use the term 'head' or explicitly explore any concept of headship. This passage does not establish pillar 5.

So, notions of headship do not provide adequate support for restrictions on women's leadership in the church.

Setting the scene for considering pillar 6

The final pillar in the arguments for exclusively male leadership in the local church consists of the lists of qualifications for elders set out in 1 Timothy 3:1–7 and Titus 1:6–9. To set the scene for considering those lists, we first need to look at:

- the distinction between governing and teaching;
- the degree of women's prominence in the young churches, and the need for care in drawing conclusions about the roles of particular women;
- the openness of the New Testament evidence on whether women served as elders; and
- what would be assumed about who could be elders, in the absence of explicit guidance from the apostles.

The distinction between governing and teaching

Elders as a group are assigned a range of functions. They shepherd, guide, teach, admonish and keep watch over the flock (Acts 20:28; 1 Tim. 3:5; 5:17; 1 Pet. 5:2; see also 1 Thess. 5:12 and Heb. 13:17). This includes guarding against false teachers (Acts 20:28–31). They are to set a good example (1 Pet. 5:3) and to pray for healing of the sick (Jas 5:14–15). They are also involved in prophecy and in the laying on of hands to impart spiritual gifts (1 Tim. 4:14).

Sometimes the question about governing in the church is treated as if it were the same as the question about teaching in the church. Biblically, it is not the same question.

It is right to say that in Titus 1:9 there is a general assumption that elders will teach and in 1 Timothy 3:2 Paul says that an elder must be able to teach.[13] All elders will necessarily be teachers to the extent that they set an example to the flock. But it seems that Paul does not view teaching by word as an essential role of an elder in all cases, for in 1 Timothy 5:17 he writes: 'The elders who govern well should be considered worthy of double honour, especially those who labour in the word and teaching.' This suggests that, in Paul's view, not all elders will be directly involved in teaching the word by the use of speaking gifts. We may easily imagine, for example, that a respected Christian householder in whose house a church met might be an elder, and an example to the flock, but not necessarily a gifted speaker.

Moreover, even if elders were always teachers, there is no indication in the New Testament that teachers were always elders. The activity of Christian teaching was not restricted to elders (see 1 Cor. 14:26; Col. 3:16; Titus 2:3). This should not be a surprise, in view of God's varied distribution of spiritual gifts (1 Cor. 12:1–31). To be a teacher (*didaskalos*, 12:28) and to govern (*kubernēsis*, 12:28; or *proiestēmi*, Rom. 12:8; 1 Thess. 5:12; 1 Tim. 5:17), though they may overlap, are different activities and different giftings.

It follows that scriptures addressing whether or in what circumstances women may or may not teach the word cannot definitively resolve the question whether women may be elders. Even though we have seen in chapters 11 to 13 that women may teach, and are not subject to a general ban on teaching men, this does not establish that women may be elders.

---

13. Mowczko 2015b argues for translating *didaktikos* in 1 Tim. 3:2 in the passive sense of 'teachable'. But the context (1:3, 6–7; 2:12; 3:1) favours the usual translation in the active sense of 'able to teach'.

Women's prominence in the young churches

On the Day of Pentecost, the men and women are all together (Acts 1:14; 2:1). Peter announces that an outpouring of God's Spirit is occurring upon both men and women:

> [T]his is what was uttered through the prophet Joel:
>
> > 'And in the last days it shall be, God declares,
> > that I will pour out my Spirit on all flesh,
> > and your sons and your daughters shall prophesy,
> > > and your young men shall see visions,
> > > and your old men shall dream dreams;
> > even on my male servants and female servants
> > > in those days I will pour out my Spirit, and they shall prophesy.'
> > > > (Acts 2:16–18, ESV)

In line with Peter's declaration, we see that women are gifted as prophets (Acts 21:9; 1 Cor. 11:5; compare Eph. 2:20).

While details remain in dispute, it is not controversial to say that women made prominent contributions to the life of the early churches. Women who were wealthy householders with substantial houses hosted assemblies of believers (for example, Nympha – Col. 4:15; and probably Lydia – Acts 16:14–15, 40[14]). Whether any of the prominent women had a recognized governing or leadership position is a separate question.

As the early church grew, so did opposition and hostility. When hostile authorities and rival groups want to oppose a new movement, they usually pay most attention to those who are seen as significant actors in it. Before he met Jesus on the Damascus Road, Saul (Paul) abducted both men and women and had them jailed (Acts 8:3; 9:2; 22:4). Later he writes of Priscilla (Prisca) as someone who risked her neck for him (Rom. 16:4). Junia was imprisoned with him (Rom. 16:7).

These facts show that women were perceived by outsiders to be significant participants in the early church whose activities needed to be stopped.[15] But this does not tell us specifically whether women were appointed to recognized positions of leadership in local churches.

---

14. The fact that Lydia was a dealer in purple cloth suggests that she was a wealthy businesswoman.

15. For a modern-day comparison, see *WITC*, 276 (Yarbrough).

More detailed statements about women's participation require great care in handling the evidence. Partisan interpretations have a tendency either to claim for women more than is justified from the text or to unduly minimize what we see in the text. As a warning to be cautious, we will take an example of each.

First, making too much of Phoebe.

Egalitarian writers often claim, from Romans 16:1–2, that Phoebe held a formal office of church leadership.[16] Paul describes her in verse 1 as being a servant (*diakonos*) of the church in Cenchreae. It is possible that she was appointed as a deacon (same word – *diakonos*), because of the phrase 'of the church in Cenchreae', and because elsewhere in the New Testament we see this as a recognized role (Phil. 1:1; 1 Tim. 3:8–13; possibly Acts 6:1–6). But in Paul's letter to the Romans there is no clear use of the word *diakonos* in this sense. So Phoebe may have been formally appointed as a deacon, but we cannot be sure.[17] If she was formally a deacon, this appears to have been a role subsidiary to that of the elders, so it would not show that she was appointed to a governing position.[18] Egalitarians point to the further uses of the same term in Romans 13:4 (rulers are God's servants) and 15:8 (Christ became a servant of the Jews), but these are not relevant, because there Paul is using the term *diakonos* to make points about service, not about the office of deacon.

In Romans 16:2 Paul writes that Phoebe had been a *prostatis* to many, including to himself. What Paul says about Phoebe is too brief for us to be able to get the exact meaning from the context alone, and this is the only use of the word *prostatis* in the New Testament. So we have to do the best we can to understand it from how this noun and related words are used elsewhere. It is related to the verb *proiestēmi*, meaning 'govern'. It is the feminine form of the masculine term *prostates*. In the Septuagint, the masculine term is used of superintendents of works (1 Chr. 29:6; 2 Chr. 8:10) and of an officer of the chief priest (2 Chr. 24:11). Outside the Bible, the masculine term is used of presidents of associations and of patrons and protectors, and there is evidence of the feminine form being used to mean a female patron.[19]

---

16. For example, *M&W*, 61–63.

17. This has often been noted. For example, Karssen 1985, 194–197: '*Wir wissen nicht, ob Phöbe ein regelrechtes Amt innehatte (z.B. eine Diakonisse war) oder ihren Dienst "inoffiziel" tat.*' My translation: 'We do not know whether Phoebe held a regular office (for example, she was a deaconess) or whether her service was done "unofficially".'

18. The view of the diaconate as a training ground for priesthood did not emerge clearly until after New Testament times, so is not considered in this book.

19. Horsley 1987, 241–244.

Egalitarian writers can reasonably express concern about the opaque nature of translations like NIV 1984 and NASB, which describe Phoebe as a 'help' or 'helper'. But the egalitarian claim that Paul is using *prostatis* to mean a female president or leader of a church cannot be proved. He does not say she was the *prostatis* of a particular assembly. To say that she had been a 'president' or 'leader' to many, including to him, would be an odd thing for the apostle to say. It therefore appears more likely, and makes better sense, that she was a patron to many, including to him. The ESV is justified in translating what Paul says about her as 'she has been a patron of many and of myself as well'.

The patronage system of Paul's world is unfamiliar to many contemporary Western Bible readers. David deSilva explains:

> For everyday needs there was the market, in which buying and selling provided access to daily necessaries. For anything outside of the ordinary, the person sought out the individual who possessed or controlled access to what the person needed and received it as a favor. . . . The greater part of the property, wealth and power was concentrated in the hands of the few, and access to these goods was through personal connection. . . . The kinds of benefits sought . . . might include plots of land or distributions of money . . . protection, debt relief or an appointment to some office or position in government. . . . If the patron granted the petition, the petitioner would become the client of the patron and a potentially long-term relationship would begin.[20]

On the basis that 'patron' is a more likely meaning than 'leader', what does Romans 16:2 tell us? Phoebe was a wealthy and influential person, of high standing in society; she was a patron who provided substantial benefits to many believers, including Paul. In the social structure of the day, he and these other believers were her clients. This would have made her influential in the church, but it does not tell us whether she was recognized as a governing elder in the church.[21]

---

20. deSilva 2000, 96–97. The patronage system is well attested in both Roman and Greek cultures: deSilva 2000, 102.

21. Paul must have had confidence in her godly character and good judgment, since acceptance of her patronage would create a social obligation of loyalty to her, which it would have been painful to have to break if she tried to command him. Theodoret of Cyrrhus (Cyrus) (died about 458) in his commentary on Rom. 16:1–2 explained her patronage as involving giving protection and hospitality. There was also a specialized form of patronage in which someone obtained for non-citizens the benefits of citizenship. This is not relevant here, for Paul was a Roman citizen

Verses 1–2 also tell us something else about Phoebe. She is from Cenchreae, a port a few miles from Corinth which Paul had visited (Acts 18:18). He informs his readers that she is going to Rome. Paul is commending her to the recipients of his letter and asking them to give her an appropriate welcome and any help she may need. The natural inference is that she was the person deputed to carry his letter to Rome.

To understand the nature of this task, we should keep in mind that the method of writing was for words to be run together as a continuous string of capital letters, and punctuation in Paul's original letters would have been minimal, if there was any at all. Based on evidence of historical practice, Ben Witherington has vividly described how people communicated in these circumstances:

> The notion that Paul would just send letters off to be deciphered afresh by bewildered semi-literate converts is a nonsense. This is not how ancient literary texts were normally treated. To the contrary, it is far more likely that Paul had someone take the text his scribe had written, already knowing its contents, and then orally deliver the text at the destination, with full ability to comment on and explain the text. Otherwise, it was just a bewildering maze of letters that could be parsed in various ways. Texts in an oral culture do not function like texts in our world.
>
> Texts that are worthwhile or important would not merely be read out once, but repeatedly read, repeatedly digested, and in part would be memorized, and the first person to do this would be the lector, tasked with delivering the text orally at the destination. Notice for example the distinction made between 'the reader' (singular) in Rev. 1:3 and the hearers (plural) to whom he would speak. The reader is not the audience! The reader is the emissary of John of Patmos, sent to orally deliver his apocalypse not just once, but to seven different churches.[22]

The procedure of reading out the letter to the assembled believers is mentioned in Colossians 4:16 and 1 Thessalonians 5:26–27. Phoebe is not the only person named in a Pauline letter as apparently being the letter carrier (see Tychicus in Eph. 6:21–22 and Col. 4:7–9; Zenas and Apollos in Titus 3:13). Judging from Romans 16:1–2, Phoebe was probably the first person to read out and explain Paul's letter to the Romans. If so, this might suggest that she was an able teacher,

---

(note 21 *cont.*) by birth (Acts 22:28), so he did not require patronage in this specialized sense. Against Barrett (see Payne 2015, 9, n. 16), this specialized meaning is not a reason for rejecting a meaning referring to a patron in the ordinary sense.

22. Witherington 2011. Head 2012 contests that the letter carrier read out the letter but agrees that the letter carrier would have explained it.

otherwise Paul would not have chosen her for the task. But that would still not justify any egalitarian claim that she was a church leader with a governing role, whether in Cenchreae or anywhere else.[23]

Next, making too little of Junia. This remarkable woman stands as a caution against the converse error of unduly minimizing what we see in the text.

From Romans 16:3 onwards, Paul sends greetings to people he knows in the Roman church. Verse 7 says: 'Greet Andronicus and Junia, my relatives and fellow prisoners, who are notable [*episēmos*] among the apostles, and who became in Christ before me.'

The natural reading of this is that Andronicus and Junia were relatives of Paul, that at some period they had been imprisoned with him, that they were notable apostles and that they had started to follow Christ before Paul did. This is how the verse was understood by native speakers of Greek for hundreds of years.

Chrysostom studied rhetoric and was famed for his facility with words. He was a prominent church leader and Bible commentator and has been read with profit ever since his own time. Calvin praised his skills as an expositor.[24] Although Chrysostom firmly opposed women's leadership in the church in his own day, he commented on this verse (about 390):

> 'Who are of note among the apostles.' And indeed to be apostles at all is a great thing. But to be even amongst these of note, just consider what a great encomium this is! But they were of note owing to their works, to their achievements. Oh! How great is the devotion . . . of this woman, that she should be even counted worthy of the appellation of apostle![25]

This is unambiguous. Chrysostom regarded Junia as a woman apostle, whose achievements were outstanding.

That Junia was a woman apostle should not cause undue surprise. In the New Testament the term 'apostle' (*apostolos*) is not only used to refer to the primary

---

23. Even if we take into account the statement by Theodoret in his commentary on Rom. 16:1–2 about the wealth of her accomplishments, and that she was known by the Romans, the Greeks and the barbarians, this still does not tell us whether she became an elder of a church.

24. Calvin wrote that Chrysostom was the best patristic interpreter of the New Testament, and he quoted Chrysostom in his New Testament commentaries more than any other patristic author: Huijgen 2011, 121.

25. Homily 31 on Romans.

founding apostles; in Acts and in Paul's letters it also extends more widely to travelling evangelists and church planters, such as Barnabas (Acts 14:14; see also 1 Cor. 9:3–6), Apollos (1 Cor. 3:5–6; 4:6–9) and Silas (1 Thess. 1:1; 2:2, 6–7; with Acts 16:19–40).[26] Paul was himself an apostle in this broader sense, albeit he was also accorded authority comparable with the Twelve and James, as noted above. It therefore appears that Andronicus and Junia were within this wider category of what we may call pioneer missionaries or missionary apostles. Calvin took the same view as Chrysostom, describing them as apostles in the sense of people who planted churches by carrying here and there the doctrine of salvation.[27] Their apostolic activities were probably the reason why at one time they were imprisoned with Paul.

Accordingly, the natural reading of Romans 16:7 tells us that Junia, with Andronicus, had a leading role as a missionary apostle, though this does not of itself imply a settled position in ongoing local church government. This is fully in line with Chrysostom's understanding of early Christian history, that in apostolic times (unlike his own time) women were preachers or teachers of the word.[28]

Complementarian writers are unable to accept that a woman could be an apostle. They say that (1) Andronicus and Junia were only messengers, not apostles; or (2) Junia was actually a man; or (3) she and Andronicus were not 'notable among' the apostles but were merely 'well known to' the apostles.[29]

---

26. Silas (Silvanus) also had some kind of governing (*hēgeomai*) role, with Judas Barsabbas (Acts 15:22).

27. Calvin, *Commentary on Romans*, 16:7. From the available information, they may also have been eyewitnesses to the risen Jesus (1 Cor. 15:6–7), but we cannot be sure of this. See the judicious discussion in Shaw 2013, 113–116.

28. In Homily 73 on Matthew 23:14 he contrasts the women of his own day with New Testament women who, without bringing evil report upon themselves, 'went about with the apostles, having taken unto themselves manly courage, Priscilla, Persis, and the rest; . . . even travelling into far countries. . . . [T]he business of those women was to spread the word.'

29. (1), (2) and (3) are discussed in *RBMW*, 72–74, 84 (Piper and Grudem), 215, 221 (Schreiner); *EFBT*, 223–227, 526. It has also been said that Junia was merely a companion to her husband, Andronicus, not an apostle herself. The analogy is drawn with unnamed wives of apostles, who travelled with their husbands (see 1 Cor. 9:5). It is likely, although we cannot be sure, that Junia was Andronicus's wife. (Conceivably, she could have been a blood relative.) But what Paul says about Andronicus and Junia in Rom. 16:7 is said equally about both of them. There is no justification in the text for regarding Andronicus, but not Junia, as a missionary apostle.

The first complementarian proposal, that Junia and Andronicus were only messengers, is based on a third sense of *apostolos* as referring to a courier, which is found in 2 Corinthians 8:23 ('apostles of the churches') and Philippians 2:25 ('your apostle'). In each instance there is a specific task of carrying money from one place to another. In 2 Corinthians 8:23 the term refers to some brothers delegated to receive and transport some funds collected by the Corinthians for the relief of poor believers. In Philippians 2:25 it refers to Epaphroditus as a messenger sent by the Philippians to Paul with a financial gift for his needs.[30]

But this would be an odd sense in Romans 16:7. There is no evidence that being a money-carrying messenger was a definite or enduring calling or office in the early church, so there are no grounds for regarding such occasional couriers as a known group, among whom Andronicus and Junia could be outstanding. And this task offered perhaps limited scope for being outstanding: if the messengers faithfully delivered the money to the correct destination, their job was done.

If this had been a realistic interpretation, we might have expected it to have been adopted or at least mentioned by Chrysostom, who was firmly opposed to women's leadership in his own day. But his remarks do not fit this sense.

The second proposal is that Junia was really a man.

This proposal is made even though Chrysostom regarded her as a woman, as did Ambrosiaster (fourth century), Jerome (died about 420), Theodoret (died about 458) and subsequent commentators for hundreds of years. Furthermore, the Greek Orthodox Church has always regarded her as a woman, and has traditions about her ministry and mission, including the locations where she worked, and about her ultimate martyrdom.[31] Nonetheless, various attempts have been made to reassign her gender:

- Some writers rely on a citation from a Latin translation of a Greek text by Origen, where Junia's name is masculine. But complementarian scholars acknowledge: 'Origen seems to cite the name once as masculine

---

30. Epaphroditus and Epaphras are usually understood as being two different people. If they were the same person, the nature of the argument is not materially affected, since the evangelist Epaphras could have acted as a courier on the occasion mentioned.

31. They also believe her to have been among the seventy or seventy-two sent out in Luke 10:1. Nicholas Calligraphos believed, as a result of a dream, that he discovered her relics, with those of Andronicus, at Constantinople in the fifth century: McGuckin 2011, 'Newly Revealed Saints'. Some commentators suggest possible identification with Joanna (Luke 8:3; 24:10); see Bauckham 2002, 184–186; Bauckham 2006, 298.

and once as feminine, though the masculine is most likely a later corruption of his text.'[32]

• Others rely on a sentence in a work sometimes attributed to Epiphanius, bishop of Salamis in Cyprus, who was a contemporary of Chrysostom. The writer's grammar shows that he thought Junia was a man, who became an *episkopos* (overseer/elder/bishop) of Apameia in Syria. But the previous sentence refers to Priscilla (Prisca) as a man who became an *episkopos* of Colophon.[33] Even a cursory glance at what is said about Priscilla in Scripture is sufficient to show that she was certainly a woman (see Rom. 16:3; Acts 18:2, 18, 26; 1 Cor. 16:19; 2 Tim. 4:19). This writing is therefore not reliable testimony on the sex of the persons mentioned. Epiphanius had a reputation for scholarship and it is very unlikely that he made such an elementary mistake about Priscilla. The attribution of this work to Epiphanius rests on slender evidence. It may be better dated in the eighth century.[34] Whoever wrote it had some information about Priscilla and Junia being bishops or elders in the stated locations. The cultural belief that women could not be leaders in churches, coupled with a lack of accurate knowledge of the Bible, may have led the writer to infer that they must have been men. There is no reasonable justification for relying on this work as evidence that Junia was a man.[35]

32. Burer 2001 (republished with some editorial changes as Wallace 2001c). *Origen's Commentary on Romans*, in J. P. Migne, *Patrologia Graeca*, vol. 14, col. 1280–1281, 1289.

33. *Index Discipulorum* 125: '*Xg. Priscas, ou kai autou ho Paulos memnētai, episkopos Kolophōnos egeneto. Xd. Junias, ou kai autou ho Paulos memnētai, episkopos Apameias tēs Surias egeneto.*' My translation: '63. Priscas, whom Paul also mentions, became an overseer of Colophon. 64. Junias, whom Paul also mentions, became an overseer of Apameia of Syria.'

34. See Schermann 1907, xxxv; Bauckham 2002, 166–167, n. 242; Huttner 2013, 195. I have not located an argument supporting the attribution to Epiphanius.

35. Despite its egregious error concerning Priscilla, Anonymous 2007 relies on this work and suggests that, in contrast, Chrysostom may have mistaken Junia's name as that of a woman because he was writing 'at a time when the knowledge of Greek was on the decline in the West'. But Chrysostom (who became an archbishop in the Eastern church) was a native Greek speaker who used Greek throughout his life. He was educated in the Greek classics and was widely regarded as the foremost Greek Christian orator of his generation. The decline of Western knowledge of Greek is of no conceivable relevance. If a factual conclusion were to be inferred from this patchy testimony, it would be that at some period of their lives Junia served as an elder in Apameia and Priscilla in Colophon.

- The third attempt at turning Junia into a man involves a claim that Junia is a very rare name because (so it is said) it only occurs a handful of times in ancient Greek literature, so there is very little evidence for us to go on, and the name could possibly be that of a man. But this is an artificial argument. Junia is living in Rome (Rom. 16:7) and has a name that is well known in Latin. So we should also be looking at Latin sources for this name. In Latin there are at least several hundred examples from antiquity of the female name 'Junia'. There is no shortage of evidence.[36]
- The fourth attempt to make her a man is a variation of the third. It is said that, simply from the spelling in verse 7, where the name is in the accusative case, the name could be Junias (masculine), as rendered in ASV, NASB and at least thirteen other English versions. (Such a Greek name would be unrelated to the common Latin man's name 'Junius'.[37]) We need to ask whether there are examples of such a male name from antiquity. Except for Pseudo-Epiphanius's misstatement, and the probably corrupted Latin translation of Origen, there is not one known example of the male name 'Junias' in inscriptions or ancient literature, compared with the hundreds of examples of the female name 'Junia'.
- A fifth attempt at making her a man is to say that the name could be a contraction of a male name such as 'Junianus' or some similar known name. However, not one piece of evidence has ever been found of Junianus or a similar name being shortened to Junias.[38]

The most interesting proposal for contending that Junia was not an apostle is to translate verse 7 as 'Greet Andronicus and Junia, my kinsmen

---

36. In *EFBT*, 226, Grudem, correcting his earlier view, fairly acknowledges the weight of the evidence from Latin names.

37. Rendering 'Junius' into Greek would not result in the accusative form seen in Paul's letter: Shaw 2013, 109.

38. There is a dispute between scholars over whether the first reliably documented reference to Junia being masculinized (other than Epiphanius's mistake and the corrupt Latin version of Origen) is seen in the accenting added to some ninth-century Greek manuscripts or is in about the late thirteenth century. Assuming the former to be correct, it is no more evidence of her gender than Luther's popularization of her as a man in his German translation. We may note that similar attempts at gender reassignment were made upon Nympha by scribes who 'found Nympha's evident leadership role so scandalous that she was turned into a man (Nymphas) in parts of the textual tradition': Capper 2005, 114.

and my fellow prisoners. They are *well known to* the apostles' (ESV, emphasis added).

A translation on these lines was strenuously advocated in articles published in 2001.[39] Instead of the emphasized phrase being in praise of Andronicus and Junia, as Chrysostom and other native Greek speakers thought, this translation turns it into an item of incidental information about them, that is, that they are known to the apostles. This translation has been strongly contested. The details of the technical linguistic arguments need not concern us here, as there are larger issues to consider.[40] Three factors make the new translation improbable:

1. After Paul identifies Andronicus and Junia by name and as his relatives (meaning possibly fellow Jews, possibly much closer relations), his first commendation of them is that they were in prison with him, and his final commendation is that they have been Christians for even longer than he has. So we would expect his intermediate statement to be also *a point of praise*. But it 'is unlike Paul to make something like acquaintance with the apostles a matter of praise'.[41] And if it is not a point of praise but only a passing comment, it would produce an odd sequence of thought. It is not easy to see why Paul would sandwich between the two commendations an incidental comment that they are well known to the apostles. When dictating letters, Paul did not willingly waste words. But if Paul means that they are outstanding apostles, this makes sense as a commendation like the other two points.

What is said about Andronicus and Junia is admittedly only a brief greeting, rather than part of a sustained discourse where we could have more confidence about the precise flow of Paul's thought. However, there are two weightier factors.

2. As far as the evidence goes, until about the sixteenth century no-one had ever thought that Paul's phrase could be translated in the way proposed in the 2001 articles. It occurred to no-one while New Testament Greek was either a living language or a recent memory. Given his firm opposition to women's leadership,

---

39. Burer 2001 and Wallace 2001c. The authors say that Beza and Grotius (sixteenth to seventeenth centuries) support their translation, but without identifying sources. A variant of this translation is to say that Andronicus and Junia were 'outstanding in the eyes of the apostles'. Schreiner regards this as 'possible': *RBMW*, 221.

40. For the technical arguments, see *M&W*, 66; *DBE*, 117–120 (Belleville); Shaw 2013, 111–113.

41. Hurley 1981, 121.

if Chrysostom had known any tradition of understanding the scripture about Andronicus and Junia in the sense of 'well known to the apostles', or if it had occurred to him that this was even a possible way to read it, he would have been likely to mention it. Instead he read it, without any qualification or uncertainty, in a sense which confirmed that a woman was an apostle. The alternative translation theory asks us to believe an improbable scenario:

- For 1,500 years commentators familiar with Greek failed to see the true meaning of what Paul wrote, even as a possibility; instead, they misunderstood him as definitely commending Junia's apostleship.
- This happened even though those commentators included native Greek speakers in the early centuries after Paul.
- This happened even though those commentators were strongly opposed to women holding any position of leadership, so had a strong motive to notice a different interpretation if the text so allowed.

Viewed dispassionately, such a counter-cultural, universal and long-enduring failure by commentators appears very unlikely.

3. On the traditional interpretation, while Paul's text in Romans 16:7 says that Andronicus and Junia were outstanding among the apostles, it does not say why or in what respects. Was it because of Christlike character, or exceptional giftedness, or the way they endured suffering, or the fruitfulness of their ministry, or something else? But Chrysostom provides a specific explanation. They were notable because of 'their works, . . . their achievements'. Either this was free-floating speculation or he knew something about their apostleship independently of Paul's text. Given the general quality of Chrysostom's expositions of Scripture, and given his reservations about women's leadership, it is unlikely that he was indulging in speculation. We therefore infer that he had independent information about their apostleship. This would also provide a reason why he did not read Romans 16:7 in the sense now proposed by complementarian scholars, if a native speaker could have read it in that way.

This is consistent with the fact that the Greek church has traditions about the nature and locations of their ministry. The Orthodox Church in America summarizes: 'Through the efforts of Saints Andronicus and Junia the Church of Christ was strengthened, pagans were converted to the knowledge of God, many pagan temples closed, and in their place Christian churches were built.'[42]

---

42. Orthodox Church in America 2016.

Whether the details of the traditions as currently held are accurate is beside the point. The point is that the Greek church, in which Chrysostom served, retained a memory of them as fulfilling an apostolic missionary role, with considerable practical impact.

In sum, there are two possibilities. (1) The newly proposed meaning did not appear to native speakers to be linguistically viable. In that case it is improbable that Paul, as a fluent Greek speaker from childhood and a reader of Greek literature, intended this meaning.[43] (2) If the new meaning appeared to native speakers to be linguistically viable, nonetheless they did not consider it to be a realistic option because of what they knew about Andronicus and Junia independently of Paul's letter.

The attempts to minimize Junia's significance are unpersuasive. On the available evidence we can say with a high degree of confidence that she and Andronicus were outstanding among the missionary apostles. Junia was a worthy successor to the woman of Samaria, of whom it was said: 'many . . . believed in Him because of the word of the woman who testified' (John 4:39, NASB).

In so far as what Junia did or said carried authority, we may perhaps compare her with Barnabas, Silas or Apollos. But could someone like Junia become an elder, participating in the government of a local church? We will see that the general answer must depend on whether there was a ban on women's eldership.

The openness of the New Testament evidence on whether women served as elders

If we look in the New Testament for general evidence that women did or did not serve as elders, what do we find?

Some have seen evidence of an exclusively male eldership in the glimpse of the elders of the Ephesian church in Acts 20:17–38, where Luke gives a vivid account of Paul's farewell speech to them.

Paul warns them: 'from among your own selves will arise men [*anēr*] speaking twisted things, to draw away the disciples after them' (20:30, ESV). The primary sense of *anēr* is a male adult, although it is sometimes used more broadly to refer to adults, whether men or women. There is no clear indication that Paul means the broader sense in 20:30, so he may have been foreseeing that male

---

43. Paul's training in Jerusalem (Acts 22:3) was not his only education. His own explanation for his fluency in Greek was that he was from Tarsus (21:37–39), where he was born (22:3). Tarsus was a centre of Hellenic culture. His education in Greek literature is illustrated by Acts 17:28; 1 Cor. 15:33; Titus 1:12.

false teachers would arise from among them. Some therefore deduce from this passage that the Ephesian elders at that time were all men.[44] But this does not follow. If the elders were a mixed-sex group, could Paul have said that men teaching falsely would arise from among them? Yes, he could. And even if we somehow knew that all the Ephesian elders at that time were in fact male, this would not tell us whether this was the result of a gender requirement or of men being called to this role more readily than women.

Some have referred to Paul's use of a specifically feminine form of the word for an elder in 1 Timothy 5:2 (*presbuteras*). While this could refer to female elders, this cannot be definitely proved from the context. The adjacent reference to younger women suggests that the meaning here is more likely to be older women, rather than church elders who are women; the question therefore remains open.[45]

Moving on from general evidence to searching for individual women elders, what do we find?

There is an immediate difficulty here, arising from the limitations of the evidence. Given the social conditions of the time, if there were women in leadership, we might expect them to be relatively few in number, compared with the number of men. And in the context of the New Testament documents eldership is not a high-profile position like being an apostle or pioneer missionary. So we cannot reasonably expect to find much direct evidence of individually identifiable women elders, even if they existed.

Nevertheless, the point is sometimes made that there is no named woman in the New Testament who can with certainty be identified as serving as an elder of a church, and this fact is said to be significant for the debate over whether women may be elders.

Is it right that not one named woman elder can definitely be identified, and, if so, is this truly of significance?

---

44. *EFBT*, 363.

45. The view that *presbuteras* in 5:2 should be translated 'women elders' is argued by Bailey 2000, 4–5. The essence of his argument is that in the inverted parallelism of Paul's rhetorical structure 5:1–2 belongs with 4:12–16 (which refers in 4:14 to the council of elders), and the section comprising 4:12 – 5:2 corresponds to the section comprising 5:17–20 (which refers to elders); therefore 5:1–2 is about elders, with a reference to younger people thrown in, as in 4:12 (and as also in 1 Pet. 5:5). Conversely, Paul's use of the masculine word *presbuteros* in 1 Tim. 5:19 does not mean that elders were necessarily men. Male terms could be used either specifically for men or generically for men and women, as I explain in more detail below.

We will see in the next chapter that one element in Paul's list of qualifications for eldership is a track record as a reputable householder. In the culture of the day, it would make sense for householders, including women householders, to serve as elders of the churches which they hosted. We should not imagine this situation as it would be if a group of believers met in a home in the modern Western world. 'The conventions of reciprocity and hospitality would have been broken if women householders were denied authority in the gatherings which took place in their own homes.'[46] The social requirement for householders to retain authority over what occurred in their houses makes it a probability that householders were appointed in this capacity. In turn, this would point to a probability that hosts such as Nympha became elders.[47]

But, as Grudem points out, this falls short of definitive proof that women householders such as Nympha were in fact appointed as elders.[48] If we were to find that there was an apostolic ban on women elders, the apparent probability of Nympha's eldership, on the ground that she was a householder host, would disappear.

Was Priscilla an elder? Elders were responsible for ensuring the accuracy of Christian teaching delivered under their oversight. The information in the New Testament about Priscilla appears to show a woman who, with her husband, carried out a similar role. Contrary to custom, Priscilla's name is four times mentioned before Aquila's, which suggests that she was the more prominent of the two of them.[49] She co-hosted a church in her house at Ephesus (1 Cor. 16:8, 19; see also Acts 18:18–19). Paul appears to have left the two of them to oversee the work while he was away from Ephesus. When Apollos arrived and started preaching in the synagogue, they evaluated his teaching. Finding it wanting, they took Apollos aside and explained to him the way of God more accurately (Acts 18:24–26). At another period they were in Rome, hosting a church. But these facts fall short of definitive proof that Priscilla and Aquila were formally appointed as elders.

---

46. Capper 2005, 128, referring to Phoebe. While there is a reasonable likelihood that the church in Cenchreae may have met in Phoebe's house, we do not have any clear statement to that effect; it may have met in someone else's house. But the New Testament evidence that Nympha hosted a church is explicit (Col. 4:15).

47. For an example of the householder's social responsibility to the community for the conduct of those received into the house, see Acts 17:5–7.

48. *EFBT*, 261–262.

49. See Acts 18:18, 26; Rom. 16:3; 2 Tim. 4:19; contrast 1 Cor. 16:19; Acts 18:2.

It is right to say that there is no *certain* identification of an individual woman elder in the New Testament. However, this observation is of limited significance. For comparison, the number of named men in the New Testament who can be identified with practical certainty as serving as an elder is very small. There are just two, both of whom are special cases: the apostle Peter calls himself an elder in 1 Peter 5:1, and the John who wrote 2 John and 3 John (probably the apostle John) also describes himself as an elder (2 John 1; 3 John 1). These men had wider roles which were the cause of their eldership being mentioned in the New Testament writings. We have no certain example of a named man who was a local church elder without such a wider role.

If we expand our search for named male elders from certainties to probabilities, we can add Hymenaeus and Alexander (1 Tim. 1:20), who were probably elders in the church at Ephesus before Paul excluded them, as we saw in chapter 12. But if we are accepting names on the basis of probability, we should accept also Nympha, Priscilla and other women named as church hosts, unless there was an apostolic ban on women elders.[50]

What would be assumed about whether women could be elders?

Let us imagine for a moment that we are in the early days of the New Testament church. Let us imagine also that no definite rule has yet been laid down concerning who may or may not be suitable for appointment as elders of a local assembly of believers. In this situation, in the absence of specific guidance, would there be a general assumption that only men could be elders, or not?

Twelve points, all taken from the historical and cultural context of New Testament thought and life, can help us to answer this question.

1. From the Old Testament background, it could not be assumed that God would never call women to lead. There are Old Testament examples of women who were called by God to take leading roles, as we saw in chapter 5.

2. Jesus contravened cultural conventions in his dealings with women (see chapter 1). He showed that men and women could relate to each other directly, and could do so without a family connection, a chaperone or an introduction (John 4:27). He valued women as disciples. When he was raised from death, he revealed himself first to a woman (Mary Magdalene), whom he chose to be the first person to announce his resurrection, and he trusted her to make this

---

50. Capper 2005, 124–131, has presented a sustained argument for concluding that Lydia, Phoebe and Nympha were elders. If *Index Discipulorum* (see above) is correct in what it says about Priscilla and Junia except as to their sex, they both became formally recognized as elders. But the provenance of *Index Discipulorum* is unclear.

announcement to his male disciples (John 20:14–18). He thereby rejected the prevailing view that women's testimony was of little value and demonstrated that women were to be trusted with important tasks in his service.

3. At Pentecost the Spirit was given to both men and women, in fulfilment of prophecy to that effect (Acts 2:16–18).

4. Women heard and responded to the preaching of the gospel (Acts 5:14; 8:12; 17:34), and those responding sometimes included leading women of high standing (Acts 17:4, 12).

5. The apostles taught the equality of men and women in Christ (Gal. 3:26–29; 1 Pet. 3:7). As we saw in chapter 2, Paul departed from the prevailing cultural assessment of the relations between men and women by envisaging complete equality in personal relations (1 Cor. 7:1–16, 25–28, 32–40).

6. The apostles' conduct after Pentecost appears to have been predicated on the equality of women with men. For example, when Paul first entered Europe with the gospel, against convention he began his evangelistic work among a group of women (Acts 16:9–15). This was a remarkable action in ancient society. It affirms the value of women in the new Christian movement. Unless, improbably, he knew in advance that every woman present at the place of prayer in Philippi was not currently married, it also shows that Paul rejected the common view that married women should relate to wider society only through their husbands.[51] His conduct was perhaps all the more remarkable given the vision which he had received of a man of Macedonia calling for help (Acts 16:9–10), and given that Philippi was a leading city (Acts 16:12), so it is unlikely that there was a shortage of men to preach to. Even if there was no Jewish synagogue in Philippi, culturally speaking it remains remarkable that Paul began his work among a group of women. Similarly, in Romans 16 Paul commends a number of women for their work, including Phoebe, Mary (of Rome), Tryphaena, Tryphosa and Persis. The way he related to women followed the lead given by Jesus.

7. After Pentecost, the apostles taught that ministry was gift-based, and that spiritual gifts were distributed among God's people (Rom. 12:3–8; 1 Cor. 12:1–30; Eph. 4:11–13; 1 Pet. 4:10–11). There is no statement in the New Testament that certain gifts were reserved for men.

---

51. See Plutarch, *Moralia*, 'Advice to Bride and Groom', 31–32, quoted in chapter 9, 177. Paul may also have been emboldened to relate directly to the women, without contravening his principle of not giving unnecessary offence (1 Cor. 10:32–33), because Hellenic culture in Macedonia was less restrictive of women than Hellenic culture in the province of Asia. As to Macedonia, see Keener 1993, 589–590; Perriman 1998, 62.

8. We have seen above that women played a prominent part in the life of the early church, even to the extent that Junia was a missionary apostle.

9. Paul describes various prominent men as his co-workers (*sunergos*). The men include Timothy (Rom. 16:21; 2 Cor. 1:24; 1 Thess. 3:2), Apollos (1 Cor. 3:9), Silvanus (2 Cor. 1:24) and Titus (2 Cor. 8:23). He applies the same description to women, such as Euodia and Syntyche, who struggled alongside him in the gospel (Phil. 4:2–3), and Priscilla (Rom. 16:3–5).

10. As we saw above, when a church met in someone's house, the householder retained control of the house and was likely to be held responsible for what took place. Some churches were hosted by female householders.

11. As we have seen, Priscilla, as a church host and a teacher, appears to have carried out an oversight function.

12. While first-century cultures regarded leadership by men as the general norm, we should not make the mistake of thinking that this was an inflexible rule. In wider society the prevailing cultural assumptions about leadership by men alone were far from absolute at any level. There were women who were exceptions to the usual practice. Women were leaders of local organizations, of provinces and even of empires. To name a few examples approximately contemporary with Paul:

- In Pompeii, Eumachia was a public figure, as priestess of Venus and possibly patroness of the fullers' guild. Other women were also patronesses of guilds.[52]
- King Agrippa shared power with his sister, Bernice (Acts 25:13).
- The Kandake was the female ruler of the Ethiopians (Acts 8:27).
- When the youthful Nero first became emperor of Rome, it was his mother, Agrippina, who was in charge, as is shown by the way in which they were depicted together on Roman coinage.[53]

---

52. *DBE*, 114 (Belleville). Hemelrijk 2015, 198, 283. Hemelrijk affirms that wealthy high-ranking women were patronesses of guilds, but challenges the commonly held view that Eumachia was herself a patroness of the fullers' guild at the time when her statue was erected.

53. See coin R.6509 in British Museum 2017. The curator states: 'Agrippina's dominant influence is shown by the fact that her portrait shares the obverse with the emperor (her son) and her title alone appears on the obverse.' Even in remote eastern Britain a woman, Boudicca, was a queen and war leader. Her famous revolt against Roman rule was provoked in part by Seneca (brother of Gallio, Acts 18:12) calling in large loans made to the British: Cassius Dio, *Roman History* 62.

At this point our question is whether, in the absence of specific guidance, there would be a general assumption in the young churches that only men could be elders and that no woman could ever, in any circumstances, be called by God to eldership. In the light of the twelve factors enumerated above, such an assumption would be unlikely. If there were already exceptions to men's leadership in the Old Testament, and if there were already exceptions in wider society, and if Jesus' and the apostles' attitude to women was more positive than prevailing culture, and if women received and exercised the gifts of the Spirit, then there was no basis for simply assuming that leadership in the churches was forbidden to women.

Accordingly, if the apostles intended that no women should ever be involved in church leadership and serve as elders, they could not safely rely on people assuming that women's leadership was never to be allowed. To ban all women from leadership they needed to say so with clarity, in order to guide the church for the future. They could have done this either directly or through their associates.

When the apostles or their associates wrote about leadership in the churches, they did not take the opportunity to lay down such a ban:

- Acts 14:23 briefly relates how Paul and Barnabas appointed elders. While Luke's account does not say positively that women may be appointed, neither does it indicate a restriction to men.
- Peter writes about eldership in 1 Peter 5:1–5. Like Luke, while he does not say positively that women may be appointed, neither does he indicate a restriction to men.
- Hebrews 13:17 instructs believers to 'obey' (ESV) or 'have confidence in' (NIV) their leaders. Again there is no clear indication that restricts leadership to men.[54]

First Corinthians 11 and 1 Timothy 2 are also sometimes relied on as impliedly excluding women from eldership, but we have seen that these texts do not specifically mention eldership or church leadership.

The only remaining texts which are possible candidates for a clear statement prohibiting women elders are Paul's two lists of qualifications for eldership. Having set the scene, we turn to these in the next chapter.

---

54. RSV and NIV 1984 specify that the leaders are 'men'. If this is supposed to mean 'males', it is not justified by the Greek text, which does not contain any word with that meaning.

Summary of chapter 14

1. A rule of male-only church leadership is not justified by 1 Corinthians 14:34–35 or by 1 Timothy 2:11–15.

2. Jesus' choice of twelve Jewish male apostles does not determine the qualifications for local church leadership.

3. In the Old Testament much, but not all, teaching was done by priests. The priestly function has been brought to fulfilment by Jesus; and in Christ all believers are 'priests'. If priesthood is to be equated with leadership or with a teaching role, leadership and teaching roles are now potentially open to all God's people without gender distinction.

4. We considered ideas of 'headship' in chapters 4, 5, 7 and 8. Ephesians 5, Genesis 1 – 3 and 1 Corinthians 11 do not support restrictions on women's ministry.

5. Governing the church and teaching in the church may overlap, but they are distinct activities. A prohibition on women's teaching would not prove that women may not become elders. Conversely, permission for women to teach does not prove that they may become elders.

6. Women fulfilled prominent roles in the early church. They were significant participants and were so perceived by outsiders. But this does not tell us specifically whether women were appointed to recognized positions of leadership in local churches.

7. Care is needed not to make either too much or too little of the New Testament evidence concerning women's activities and roles. For example, it cannot be shown that Phoebe held a governing role in a church; conversely, we can say with a high degree of confidence that Junia was an outstanding missionary apostle.

8. We do not find in the New Testament any named women who can with practical certainty be identified as elders. But the same is true of men, except for special cases (Peter and John). If we expand our search to probabilities, we can identify both men and women, unless there was a definite ban on women's eldership.

9. In the historical and cultural context of New Testament thought and life, there would not have been a general assumption that only men could be elders. If the apostles intended that no women should ever be involved in church leadership and serve as elders, they needed to say so with clarity, in order to guide the church for the future. But passages dealing with elders or leaders, such as Acts 14:23; 1 Peter 5:1–5; Hebrews 13:17, do not contain statements limiting eldership or leadership to men.

Questions to consider

1. Does chapter 14 contain some things that are new to you? What are they?
2. Chapter 14 describes five of the pillars on which the restriction on women's church leadership rests. In your view, which is the strongest of these, and which the weakest? Why?
3. For your own life, what is the practical significance of the teaching that in Christ all believers are 'priests'?

[T]his is what was spoken by the prophet Joel:
'. . . on my servants, both men and women,
   I will pour out my Spirit.'
             (Acts 2:16–18, NIV)

Qualifications for elders

The principal list of qualifications for elders is in 1 Timothy 3:1–7, with a parallel passage in Titus 1:5–9. These provide the fullest available scriptural guidance on the appointment of elders.

Why are these instructions contained in these particular letters? It appears that Paul wrote to Titus about appointing elders in the churches in Crete because those churches were newly planted (Titus 1:5). However, the church in Ephesus had been in existence for a decade. The existing elders had been unsuccessful in guarding the flock against false teaching and Paul had had to exclude two false teachers from the church, who were probably elders (1 Tim. 1:3, 20; Acts 19:33). So he is giving instructions about filling the vacancies and strengthening the eldership. This will help the church to fulfil its role of being the pillar and foundation of the truth (1 Tim. 3:15). It is also important for him to give appropriate guidance to ensure that the misbehaving women whose conduct we considered in chapters 12 and 13 cannot fulfil their aspiration to teach from a recognized position unless they first give evidence of repentance and a changed life.

If Paul believed that only men should be considered for eldership, and that women were automatically excluded simply because they were women, here was a prime opportunity for him to say so with clarity.

316

WOMEN ELDERS?

Do Paul's requirements include or exclude women?

Does Paul stipulate in 1 Timothy 3 that elders must be men? The short answer is: no, he does not. The textual situation regarding the qualifications for elders can be stated crisply: *In nearly all English versions it appears that only men may qualify as elders; in the Greek text this is not so.* For users of English versions, this needs a considerable amount of explanation.

The list of qualifications is introduced in verse 2 by *dei* ('it is necessary') *oun* ('therefore'). But what are the reasons to which 'therefore' refers, and do Paul's requirements include or exclude women? Twelve points may usefully be made.

1. Paul's instructions about elders do not come suddenly out of left field, apropos of nothing. The immediate context of 1 Timothy 3 is 1 Timothy 1 – 2, which we looked at in chapters 11 to 13. In chapter 1 he has expressed his concern about false teachers who desire to become teachers of the law but do not understand what they are talking about (1:3, 7). In chapter 2 he has set out instructions related to this problem of false teaching (2:1 'therefore . . .'; 2:8 'therefore . . .'). His instructions are first for everyone (2:1–7), next for men (2:8) and then for women (2:9–15). He immediately goes on to the qualifications for elders, who should be able to teach (3:2). Eldership is a good work (3:1), which therefore (*oun*) requires (*dei*) people who will teach and behave quite differently from those he has referred to, whether men (1:19–20) or women (2:9, with 1:3, 7).

2. Does the juxtaposition of 2:15 (women) with 3:1 (elders) indicate that Paul is thinking about women as potential elders? It does. We saw in chapter 12 that *tis* is a gender-neutral pronoun, applying to men and/or women without distinction. By writing about women (2:9–15), and then commencing 'If someone [*tis*] aspires to be an overseer' (3:1), he indicates that women, as well as men, may aspire to eldership. Thus he is here giving positive encouragement for women to aspire to eldership.[1]

---

1. Paul's use of *tis* echoes the way he has previously referred to the false teachers. In 1:3 Timothy was to command *tis* (ESV 'certain persons') not to teach falsely. In 1:6–7 these same *tis* (ESV 'certain persons') were wanting to become teachers of the law but did not correctly understand it. *Tis* is translated opaquely in many English versions of 3:1 as 'a man' or 'any man'. ESV correctly uses 'anyone'. NIV correctly uses 'whoever'. Yarbrough 2018, 192, prefers for *tis* in 3:1 the rendering: 'if a certain person'.

3. To exclude the misbehaving women from eldership, Paul needed only to say that women are not permitted to be elders, who must be men. But he does not here exclude them on the ground of their sex. Instead, he excludes them by listing characteristics and behaviours for an elder which contrast with the characteristics and behaviours of these women. They dress indecently and lack self-control (2:9), but an elder must have self-control, be above reproach and respectable, and should have a good testimony from outsiders (3:2, 7). They are talkers of nonsense, saying what they should not (5:13), but an elder must be a skilful teacher (3:2). They are keen on gold, pearls and expensive clothes (2:9), but an elder should not be a lover of money (3:3). They are neglecting to rule their households (5:14), but an elder should be a good household manager (3:4). They are conceited, thinking that they are qualified to teach even though they are not (1:7; compare 6:3–4), but an elder should not be conceited (3:6).

4. The impression that women may become elders is strengthened because, having just said that the wealthy Ephesian women, instead of misbehaving (2:9), should do good works (2:10), Paul uses a similar expression to refer to eldership: if someone aspires to eldership, they desire a good work (3:1). Eldership is a good work that these women could properly aspire to if they were to qualify for it, instead of qualifying as idlers (5:13).[2]

5. Nearly all English versions use masculine pronouns ('he') and possessives ('his') in 1 Timothy 3:1–7. For example, the NIV uses 'he' seven times in those verses and 'his' four times. But in the Greek text (UBS) all the verbs are generically expressed, capable of application to either gender, and there are no masculine pronouns or possessives. Paul chooses to use gender-neutral pronouns (*tis*, in vv. 1, 5), and he avoids using masculine possessives. Again, it seems he is giving positive encouragement for women to aspire to eldership.[3]

---

2. In 2:10 'good' is *agathos*. In 3:1 it is *kalos*. Paul makes the same equation of these two descriptions of good works again when he writes of the good elderly widow in 5:10: 'in good works [*en ergois kalois*] . . . every good work [*panti ergō agathō*]'.

3. If one were back-translating the ESV of v. 4 and v. 5 into Greek, the expression 'his own household' (ESV) would become literally 'the own household of him'. But Paul's choice of words is 'the own household'. And the expression 'keeping his children submissive' would become literally 'having children of him in subjection'. But Paul's choice of words is 'having children in subjection'. This is not the only example of Paul choosing his words to make inclusivity clearer: see his addition of 'and daughters' to his Old Testament citation at 2 Cor. 6:18.

The upshot of points 1–5 is that, if Paul intended to lay down a rule that only men could be elders, he could hardly have worded his letter to Timothy more misleadingly. His choice of words creates the opposite impression.

6. In the parallel passage about appointment of elders in Titus, Paul again uses the introductory gender-neutral expression 'if someone . . .' (Titus 1:6). Again, as in the list sent to Timothy, all the verbs used in Titus 1:6–9 are generically expressed. Again, there are no masculine pronouns. Again, there are no masculine possessives. Where the NIV says 'a man whose children believe', the Greek text says 'having believing children' (1:6).[4]

7. With one apparent exception, all the behaviours and criteria set out are capable of being true of women. Whether instinctively or deliberately, Paul reinforces the message that women may have the necessary qualifications for eldership. He does this by using the same or similar Greek words and ideas when he writes elsewhere in 1 Timothy and Titus about women. Running through the list in 1 Timothy:

- Eldership is a good work (3:1); Paul expects women to do good work (5:10).
- Elders must be above reproach (3:2); Paul expects women to be irreproachable (5:7).
- Elders must be temperate (3:2); Paul expects women to be temperate (3:11).
- Elders must be self-controlled (3:2); Paul expects women to be self-controlled (2:9, 15).
- Elders must be respectable (3:2); Paul expects women to be respectable (2:9).
- Elders must be hospitable (3:2); Paul expects women to be hospitable (5:10).
- Elders must be able to teach (3:2); Paul expects women to be teachers of what is good (Titus 2:3).
- Elders must not be drunkards (3:3); Paul expects women not to be drunkards (Titus 2:3).
- Elders must not be lovers of money (3:3); Paul expects women to avoid adornment with gold, pearls and expensive clothes (2:9).

---

4. Note that CEB translates both 1 Tim. 3:1–7 and Titus 1:6–9 generically.

- Elders must be good managers of their households (3:4); Paul expects women to rule their households (5:14).[5]
- Elders must show dignity in the way they keep their children under control (3:4); Paul expects women to show dignity (3:11).
- Elders must not be new converts, falling into condemnation on account of pride (3:6); Paul expects women to be humble and not under condemnation (5:10, 12).
- Elders must have a good testimony from outsiders (3:7); Paul expects women to have a good testimony from others (5:7, 10).[6]

Paul also includes a group of further qualifications: gentle, not violent (compare 1:13!), and not quarrelsome (3:3). It is uncontroversial that these may be found in women. Thus Paul has listed at least sixteen qualities or behaviours which may certainly be found in both men and women. He appears to regard women as capable of satisfying the qualifications.

8. The one apparent exception is not a real exception. In 1 Timothy 3:2 and Titus 1:6 Paul writes that an elder must be a *mias gunaikos andra* – a 'one-woman man'.[7] We will come to the exact meaning of this distinctive expression in our next point. First, we need to understand that, taken in context, because of

---

5. Vern Poythress in *RBMW*, 237–250, relies on Paul's reference to good rule of households in arguing for exclusively male leadership in the church essentially on the basis of an analogy between a human family and the church family (see also *EFBT*, 80–81). He seems to be aware that Paul regarded women as capable of ruling their households but considers that leadership in the family is necessarily the domain of the father. This is not borne out by Deut. 6:4–9; Prov. 1:8; 6:20; 31:10–31; Eph. 5:21 – 6:4; Col. 3:20; 1 Tim. 5:14; see the discussions in chapters 4 and 5. He does not address the further problem for his argument that the Greek text of 1 Tim. 3 does not establish that elders must be male.

6. Payne, drawing attention to these comparisons in *M&W*, 449–451, works out that the chance of these verbal similarities occurring randomly in a single passage is approximately five in one trillion. This statistic does not provide a meaningful comparison. No-one argues that Paul used words randomly when writing his letters. This statistic should not be allowed to distract from the better point that, as we would expect of Paul, he uses words advisedly. He reveals his view of women's competence by describing women's potential qualities and behaviours in similar terms to those in the list of qualifications for eldership.

7. *Andra* is the accusative form of *anēr*.

the way the Greek language works, this expression should be understood generically.

Where a Greek writer wishes to refer to both men and women, a standard way of doing so is to use an appropriate noun for males. For example, the Greek for 'brothers' (which differs in form from the Greek for 'sisters') can be used to refer either to men alone or to both men and women.[8] Similarly, the primary meaning of *anēr* is a male adult, but in Acts 17:22 Paul uses the plural expression *andres athēnaioi* ('men of Athens') to address a mixed audience at the Areopagus, for in verse 34 Luke reports that a woman named Damaris was among the *andres* ('men', plural of *anēr*) who believed Paul's message. This kind of gender-neutral usage can also apply to singular nouns.[9] So, here, Paul's expression 'a one-woman man' could either refer specifically to a one-woman man or encompass also a one-man woman. The presence of this expression does not establish that Paul is stipulating that only men may be elders, or even that he is assuming that elders will be men.

Greek writers are of course well aware of the ambiguity when they use a noun which carries a specifically male sense: it could be intended to refer to men alone or to both men and women. A thoughtful writer should therefore ensure that there are sufficient clues in the surrounding context to guide the reader's understanding. Here, the clues point to a gender-neutral sense. As we have seen, in 1 Timothy the list immediately follows a discussion of women (2:9–15), and it is introduced by the gender-neutral term 'someone' (3:1; similarly in Titus 1:6). Moreover the expression 'one-woman man' is in a long list of other qualities, not one of which specifically pertains to men; every other quality

---

8. Payne 2015, 7, contains a short discussion of this convention. For *adelphos* used generically, see 1 Tim. 4:6; 2 Tim. 4:21. This convention is much like modern French where, if a mixed group contains even just one man, a noun or pronoun which refers to the group is expressed in the form appropriate for males rather than females: for example, ten friends, nine of whom are women, are *ils* (they, masculine) rather than *elles* (they, feminine) and *amis* (male friends) rather than *amies* (female friends). At the time of writing there is a debate going on in France about whether to change this convention.

9. For examples, see Jas 1:8 (*anēr*), 9 (*adelphos*), 12 (*anēr*), 20 (*anēr*). For the gender-neutral context, see 1:5 (*tis*), 7 (*anthrōpos*). For further examples of *anēr* as referring to both men and women, see Luke 11:31–32; Acts 1:13–16. As a matter of language, the references to the Areopagus (Acts 17:19, 22) could refer either to the Council called by that name or to the location (Gempf 1993, 52). The context suggests that they refer to the location.

listed can be true of both men and women. The same is true of the list in Titus. These features provide ample pointers that Paul intends the expression 'one-woman man' generically, so as to include also 'one-man woman'.[10]

9. What does the expression 'one-woman man' mean? Two other Pauline texts shed useful light on this.

First, 1 Timothy 5:9. This is part of the list of qualifications which enable a widow to be placed on a church roll for financial support. In this verse Paul uses the corresponding female version of the same expression. The relevant qualification is that the widow has been a 'one-man woman'.

This female version is not a generic expression. By linguistic convention, a specifically female noun normally refers in Greek to women only. (Although 'brothers' is capable of meaning 'brothers and sisters', 'sisters' is not normally capable of meaning 'sisters and brothers'.) The context is instructions about widows, which provides additional confirmation that the female expression is not used generically in 5:9.

Nevertheless, although the female version is not used gender-neutrally, it provides useful pointers to what Paul has in mind.

For what purpose does he include in his list of requirements for enrolling widows the expression 'one-man woman'? Evidently, his purpose is not to lay down a requirement that the widow has been and still is a woman, for a widow is by definition a woman. Evidently also, his purpose is not to lay down a requirement that the widow must have been married, for a widow necessarily has been married. Rather, his purpose is to lay down a requirement that she has proved herself to be chaste, and remains so. In other words, she was faithful to her husband while he lived, and she is not having sexual relations with anyone else. The Christian sexual ethic is that sexual intercourse is intended by God only within a monogamous marriage of one man and one woman, as depicted in Genesis 2:24 and endorsed by Jesus (Matt. 19:4–5; Mark 10:6–8) and by Paul (1 Cor. 6:13 – 7:2). Paul has in mind this Christian standard of chastity.[11]

---

10. It might be objected that a generic understanding of the expression 'one-woman man' is contrary to the convention that only male nouns may be used gender-neutrally, because this expression includes 'one-woman'. But the convention is not truly contravened, for 'one-woman' is here used as an adjectival phrase, qualifying the male noun.

11. Patristic writers understood 5:9 on similar lines. For example, Theodore of Mopsuestia (died 428/9) wrote: 'If she has lived in chastity with her husband, no matter whether she has had only one, or whether she was married a second time.' See *M&W*, 451. To have remarried after earlier widowhood would not indicate a character defect.

Thus the expression 'one-man woman' in 5:9 is a requirement of chastity, not a requirement that the widow be female and that she has been married. This points towards an understanding of the expression 'one-woman man' in 3:2 as a similar requirement of chastity, rather than a requirement of being male and married.

The second helpful text is 1 Corinthians 7. In that chapter Paul writes about the spiritual advantages of the gift of singleness for both men and women (1 Cor. 7:7–8, 32–35). Timothy would have been well aware of Paul's views on this topic, since he was Paul's co-worker and had a long association with him (see chapter 12). Timothy would therefore have understood that Paul was not intending to ban the unmarried from eldership, since some unmarried people would be particularly suitable.

With this understanding, we may now ask: for what purpose does Paul include in the list of requirements for eldership his idiomatic expression 'one-woman man'? Evidently, his purpose is not to lay down a requirement that the candidate be a man; for he has already indicated that eldership is open to anyone (3:1, *tis*). Evidently also, his purpose is not to lay down a requirement that the candidate be married; for Timothy knows that Paul views those with a gift of singleness as even better placed than married people for serving God. Rather, his purpose is to lay down a requirement that the candidate for eldership be chaste. In other words, in conformity with the Christian sexual ethic, if someone lives a sexually immoral life, or is a polygamist, they cannot be an elder.[12]

The alternative interpretation, namely, that Paul is laying down that an elder must be male and married, is not plausible. It takes insufficient account of the context, of the way the Greek language works, of 1 Timothy 5:9 and of 1 Corinthians 7. On this alternative, even Paul would not qualify for eldership, because he was single (1 Cor. 7:7–8), nor even the chief shepherd, Christ Jesus himself (1 Pet. 5:4). Protestant churches which appoint elders – including churches which are complementarian – therefore read this requirement in an exclusionary rather than a positive sense, and they accept unmarried men as elders. The reasoning underlying their position is that this criterion is intended as an exclusion of the sexually immoral and polygamists from eldership, not as a positive requirement that an elder must necessarily be a married man.

---

12. Some commentators consider that the expression is directed only against polygamy and not also against sexual immorality. This is unlikely. The corresponding expression in 1 Tim. 5:9 cannot be directed only or even principally against polyandry (one woman having several husbands), since polyandry was not practised in Roman, Greek or Jewish society.

This approach to interpretation is further confirmed by considering other requirements in the list. For example, Paul writes that an elder must have children in subjection (v. 4). This is also properly to be read as an exclusionary criterion. In other words, if a person has children who are wild and rebellious, this disqualifies that person from eldership. If this statement were read as a positive criterion, it would require that no-one can be an elder unless they have at least two children, who are well behaved. This would be an unlikely interpretation. I am not aware of any churches making it a condition of becoming an elder or pastor that a candidate must have at least two children.

This understanding of Paul's intent is consistent with what he writes in verse 5: 'But if someone does not know how to lead their own household, how will they care for God's church?' Paul adds this explanatory comment to make his reasoning more explicit. He spells out his exclusionary rationale. If it is apparent from someone's mismanagement of their own household that they cannot lead well, they are not suitable for eldership. The exclusionary interpretation is to be preferred.[13]

10. As noted above, Paul uses the same expression (one-woman man) in the corresponding list in Titus 1:5–9. In that list he adds that the person's children should be believers, not under any accusation of debauchery or insubordination (v. 6). If read as a positive requirement, this would rule out not only unmarried men, but also all childless men and all men whose children are young. For the reasons given above, this is not the most reasonable interpretation and is not a policy generally adopted by complementarian or other churches. The reasonable understanding of this requirement is that it is exclusionary. It is intended to bar candidates if they have children who have grown up to reject the faith and are known for wild living. This further supports the exclusionary reading of the requirement that a candidate be a one-woman man: that is, it is intended to rule out people whose sexual conduct makes them unsuitable. It is not a requirement that a person be married or male.

Grudem disagrees. His discussion in *EFBT* makes no reference to the convention in Greek that nouns for males may be used to refer to both men and women. Nor does he mention the multiple indications in the context that Paul

---

13. A reader of this chapter in draft raised the question: if these requirements are read as exclusionary, does that mean logically that even children and young persons could qualify as elders? It does not. Children and young persons by definition are not 'elders'. While the word used in 3:2 is 'overseer' (*episkopos*), the word used synonymously in 5:17, 19 is 'elder' (*presbuteros*).

has both men and women in view. He interprets 'one-woman man' as an exclusionary requirement, for he says that the expression which Paul uses is not intended to rule out a single man or a divorcee. At the same time, inconsistently, he reads 1 Timothy 3:2 and Titus 1:6 as laying down a positive requirement that elders be men.[14] Payne reasonably comments:

> If Grudem is permitted to dismember 'one woman man' and arbitrarily designate one word of it out of context as a new requirement, what is to keep one from isolating 'one's own house' from 'ruling one's own house well' (3:4–5) and designate home ownership or rule of a household as a new requirement for overseers?[15]

In *RBMW* both Piper and Grudem seem to accept that Paul's lists of qualifications for elders do not clearly exclude women. In order to prohibit women's leadership in the church they rely on different texts, without mentioning 1 Timothy 3:2 or Titus 1:6.[16]

Complementarian Douglas Moo agrees that the phrase 'one-woman man' does not require that elders be male. This expression

> may mean . . . that the male elder/overseer must be faithful to his wife, without excluding unmarried men or females from the office. . . . [I]t would be going too far to argue that the phrase clearly excludes women.[17]

Some complementarians, while accepting that Paul's list of qualifications does not explicitly teach that elders have to be male, draw comfort from what is said to be an *assumption* in the list that elders are male.[18] On this approach Paul would also be assuming that all elders are married and have at least two children, which is improbable. And in any event we have seen that Paul's list does not assume that elders are male.

---

14. *EFBT*, 80.
15. *M&W*, 447.
16. See *RBMW*, 56 ('Where in the Bible do you get the idea that only men should be the pastors and elders of the church? The most explicit texts relating directly to the leadership of men in the church are 1 Timothy 2:11–15; 1 Corinthians 14:34–36; 11:2–16').
17. Moo 1981, 211. Moo rests the complementarian restriction of women's ministry principally on 1 Tim. 2:12.
18. See the FIEC 'Women in Ministry Statement'.

11. Some writers have drawn attention to a contrast with the requirements for deacons in 1 Timothy 3:8–13. Within those requirements, at verse 11, Paul refers specifically to 'women' (*gunaikas*, plural of *gunē*). It is said that verse 11 refers to women deacons, and that the absence of a corresponding verse in the midst of the requirements for elders suggests that Paul expects elders to be men.

There is much debate about the meaning of verse 11. The usual objection to the suggestion that it refers to women deacons appears quite strong. If Paul is here introducing women deacons as a new category, that would appear to mean that verses 8–10 and 12–13 apply to male deacons only. But why would Paul interrupt his qualifications for male deacons by inserting brief qualifications for women deacons half way through, before resuming his longer list of qualifications for male deacons? This does not seem to make any sense as a train of thought, whether in terms of order (why oscillate between men and women deacons?) or in terms of content (why so much shorter for women?).

The other proposals for verse 11 are that it refers to (a) women generally, (b) the wives of deacons, (c) the wives of both deacons and elders, or (d) deacon-esses, whose responsibilities are said to differ from those of male deacons. The issue is much debated, without any resolution, because these suggestions similarly run into strong objections.[19] We may add that, irrespective of how verse 11 is interpreted, it is certainly not an explicit prohibition of women elders.

But the issue over the meaning of verse 11 appears in a new light once we have appreciated how Paul has used language generically in the qualifications for elders. Having completed his discussion of the qualifications for elders in verse 7, he moves on, dictating to his scribe what we call verses 8–10. These three verses begin to lay out the qualifications for deacons. He commences with the ordinary word for deacons, which is *diakonous* (masculine plural), and all the qualifications in these three verses are grammatically masculine. Unlike in

---

19. Kelly 1963, 83–84; Hurley 1981, 229–233; *EFBT*, 265–266; *RBMW*, 214–215, 220 (Schreiner); *DBE*, 122 (Belleville); *M&W*, 453–459. The objections to the four rival proposals are: (a) Why would Paul insert a comment about women in general into the middle of a list of qualifications for church office? This makes no sense. (b) When writers are using *gunē* in the more particular sense of 'wife', rather than 'woman', they usually give a verbal clue to make this sense clear (see chapter 7, 138). Paul gives no such verbal clue here. (c) Not only is the needed verbal clue absent, but why would Paul place a comment about the wives of elders and deacons in the midst of a discussion of deacons alone? (d) There is no other New Testament evidence of a separate order of deaconesses. (They cannot be identified with enrolled widows, for Paul states the separate requirements for them in chapter 5.)

the passage about elders, these three verses contain no verbal or contextual indications that he is thinking of women as well as men. Before he goes too far, he needs to give a positive indication that, as in the case of elders, women are as eligible as men, provided that their character and behaviour are suitable, unlike that of the women false teachers. This is what he does in verse 11, which crisply covers the same points that he has stated more fully in verses 8–10. Having made clear that he means women as much as men, so that the qualifications for deacons should be understood as applying to both sexes, he can go on to complete the list of qualifications. He does this in verses 12–13, which are to be understood in that way (including the expression 'one-woman men' in v. 12).[20]

The objection to reading verse 11 as referring to women deacons now falls away. Verse 11 is not an interruption. It is a clarification that qualified women may be deacons, which is followed by the completion of what Paul wants to say about deacons, who, like elders, may be either men or women.

The result is that verse 11 does not cast any doubt on Paul's intent that the qualifications for eldership are applicable to both men and women.

12. We must recall the backdrop of New Testament life and thought explained in chapter 14 ('What would be assumed about whether women could be elders?'). Against that backdrop, if Paul intended to ban women from eldership, he needed to say so explicitly, and perhaps with an accompanying theological rationale to justify it. He does not make any such statement in 1 Timothy 3 or in Titus 1. In the absence of a theological reason for banning women, their eligibility makes good practical sense. The inclusion of women is likely to enhance the quality of the eldership both because it enables appointments to be made from a wider pool of candidates and because it should deliver benefits of complementarity.

Like Moo, complementarian Tom Schreiner fairly acknowledges, 'The requirements for elders in 1 Tim. 3:1–7 and Titus 1:6–9, including the statement that they are to be one-woman men, does not in and of itself preclude women from serving as elders.'[21]

---

20. If before conversion to Christ a person had entered into a form of marriage which was inconsistent with the Christian sexual ethic, presumably they would be welcomed into the fellowship of the church but not appointed as a deacon or elder.

21. Schreiner 2010, 35. (Similarly, the Danvers Statement does not place explicit reliance on 1 Tim. 3:1–7 or Titus 1:6–9 for its ban on women elders.) Yarbrough 2018, 195 and n. 384, disagrees, under the misapprehension that New Testament Greek never uses the word *anēr* (1 Tim. 3:2; Titus 1:6) to refer to women.

This conclusion is not egalitarian special pleading. It is a sober assessment by reputable complementarian scholars, which is compelled by the Greek text.[22]

Conclusion on women's eldership

None of the six pillars supports a definite ban on women's eldership.

If we are looking for absolute certainty, the New Testament evidence of what women actually did falls short of definitive proof that women were appointed as elders, but the probabilities are in favour. The evidence certainly shows women in a variety of prominent roles.

In the context of New Testament thought and life, it would be surprising if there were a general assumption that only men could ever be elders. Therefore, if the apostles intended to ban women from leadership they could not rely on such an assumption but needed to express the prohibition with clarity, in order to guide the church for the future. There is no such statement of prohibition in the New Testament. Nor is there any text in the New Testament where elders are specifically said to be all men.

Paul provides two specific lists of the qualifications for eldership. These lists do not contain a clear and explicit ban on women's eldership. On the contrary, they contain positive indications that women may qualify. The conclusion to be drawn from the lists of qualifications, especially the list in 1 Timothy 3, is that eldership was open to women.

---

22. Egalitarians rely additionally on the absence of any equivalent to 1 Tim. 2:11–15 (the restriction on women's teaching etc.) in the parallel passage regarding elders in Titus. They point out that there is no material in the letter to Titus from which any restriction to men could be inferred: so we should not infer any restriction in the letter to Timothy. See *M&W*, 453. However, this argument is not persuasive. It can be deduced from Paul's letters that he and Titus worked together, on and off, for a considerable number of years (for details, see Mosse 2007, 296, 298–299, 301, 304–307, 312–313). Titus would have known Paul's views on most topics. Paul had already given him directions in person about appointing elders (Titus 1:5). So we cannot draw any conclusions from what was *not* said in the letter to Titus. Nevertheless, the weakness of this egalitarian argument does not affect the overall conclusion that the list of requirements for eldership is written gender-neutrally and appears designed to include women.

Elders as guardians

Alastair Roberts has strongly challenged the conclusion that women may serve
as pastoral leaders. In his view 'a masculine priesthood is essential'. He offers a
different perspective from books such as *RBMW* and *EFBT*. He derives his
view from 'scripturally-informed reason and reflection upon reality and society'.
He believes 'the human race is pre-wired for male dominance in power' and
'the biblical pattern, from Genesis 2 onwards, is that the task of establishing
and guarding the foundations is particularly entrusted to men and is something
that they are apt for in a way that women aren't'. He links the description of
Adam's responsibilities for the garden in Genesis 2:15 with the similar language
used of the Levites' duties to serve and guard the tabernacle (see Num. 1:53;
3:7–8; 8:26; 18:5–6). Thus he sees Adam as 'the priestly guardian' of the garden,
this being a different vocation from Eve's. This view of men's and women's
vocations and aptitudes leads him to the belief that 'priests' in the church must
be men. This is because he considers the church leader to have not only a
nurturing role but also a combat role. The combat function requires alpha-male
characteristics to guard against the assaults of wolves upon the flock (1 Cor.
4:21; 2 Cor. 10:1–6; 11:2–3; 13:2–4).[23]

Roberts's emphasis on the need for backbone in church leadership is laudable.
He writes:

> The shepherd who loves his sheep and tenderly carries them in his bosom must be
> prepared and equipped mercilessly to fight the wolves, the bandits, the thieves, the bears,
> and the lions. He must be prepared to lay down his life in their defence. Those who
> perform this calling are servants of the sheep, not lords over them. The shepherd must
> put his life in jeopardy for the sake of the lives of his sheep, valuing them above himself.

Roberts has provided a fascinating and spirited defence of exclusively male
priesthood in the church. But his conclusions do not appear to be adequately
supported. At least a dozen issues appear to arise.[24]

1. As regards his reflections on 'reality and society', he says that his claims rest
not upon universals but upon 'general differences in tendencies, preferences and
capacities'. Accordingly, if his claims are correct, the effect should not be to bar
women from leadership as pastors or elders; the effect should only be that

---

23. Roberts 2014a, 2014b.

24. I say 'appear to', because I may not have fully understood his views from short blog
    pieces. As I write, his book on theology of the sexes has yet to be published.

proportionately fewer women than men would qualify as suitable for these ministries, because proportionately fewer women would have the needed qualities.

2. His own summary of the basis of his theory – 'scripturally-informed reason and reflection upon reality and society' – is a warning that his theory may not be sufficiently based on explicit scriptural teaching. As we saw in chapter 5, church history teaches the need for great caution in using implications from Scripture to establish Christian doctrine; it can be hazardous to go beyond what is written.

3. Roberts's references to 'priests' and 'priesthood' in the church do not correspond with the use of these terms in the New Testament, where our high priest is the Lord Jesus Christ and in him all believers constitute the priesthood (Heb. 2 – 10; 1 Pet. 2:9; Rev. 1:6; 5:10).

4. Assuming Roberts is right to see Adam as the 'priestly' guardian of the garden, what justification is there for reading across from this to church leadership in the New Testament? This is not a connection that Scripture itself makes. If he is using the term 'priest' to denote an elder (*presbuteros*) in its original New Testament sense, this role or office is different from and unconnected with the priests or Levites of the Old Testament.[25] If he is using the term 'priest' to denote someone in holy orders as subsequently understood in some church traditions, this raises other questions, which Scripture does not address.

5. If, contrary to the above, he is right to read across from Genesis 2 to church leadership, the text of Genesis is equally consistent with a conclusion which is the opposite of the one that he draws. It says that the woman is created to be the man's helper, a helper corresponding to him (Gen. 2:18). According to the presentation of the story in Genesis 2, helper in what tasks? At least in the task of guarding and tending the garden. So, if it were correct to draw conclusions from this for church leadership, it may be inferred that women should be men's powerful allies in that task, not excluded from it. If women are to be men's equal helpers ('corresponding to' them), there is no sufficient ground for saying that women must fill only junior positions.[26]

---

25. Gen. 1 can be seen as presenting the heavens and the earth as the temple of the creator God, where he sets up his image and rests (1:27; 2:2–3; see Isa. 66:1–2). See also Walton 2009. The calling to be God's image on the earth, and to 'fill' and 'subdue' it, is given to mankind, both male and female (1:27–28). This provides some support for seeing a temple/tabernacle allusion in 2:15 but not for Roberts's view of church leadership.

26. The idea of a junior assistant is not contained in the Hebrew word for 'helper'. See chapter 5, 76–77.

6. Courage is not an exclusively male quality. In the New Testament those who risk their lives for the gospel are both men and women (Acts 8:3; 9:1–2; Rom. 16:3, 7). Priscilla risks her neck to save Paul's life (Rom. 16:4). Likewise, the Old Testament shows women acting courageously to protect God's people (for example, Moses' sister in Exod. 2:3–7; Jael in Judg. 4:18–22; Esther in Esth. 4:10 – 5:2).

7. It is right to say that the task of elders is like that of shepherds who protect and nurture (1 Pet. 5:2). But in the Bible both men and women are shepherds: Genesis 29:9; Exodus 2:16–17. Where is the solid scriptural justification for tying this comparison so strongly to combative alpha males? This does not sound like the kind of leadership which Jesus commended (Mark 10:42–44).

8. If Roberts regards providing leadership to churches as a task that is fulfilled largely by male or masculine qualities, this is out of step with Scripture. When Paul wrote about his, Silas's and Timothy's ministry among the Thessalonians, he said: 'we were gentle among you, like a nursing mother taking care of her own children' (1 Thess. 2:7, ESV).

9. If Roberts is right, Paul's advice to Timothy misses the target. Paul describes what is 'necessary' (1 Tim. 3:2) for eldership. He lists at least sixteen qualities and behaviours which are found in both women and men. (The seventeenth is 'one-woman man', which should be understood as a generic requirement of chastity.) The same feature runs through the corresponding list in Titus 1:5–9. If Roberts's view is that eldership is an essentially or distinctively masculine task, this is radically different from Paul's.

10. Roberts makes comparison with the deadly violence of the Levites and of Phinehas (Exod. 32:27–28; Num. 25:6–8) and allows the metaphor of fighting wolves to obscure the social reality of what is required to protect the church. While it is true that more men than women are suited to physical combat, this is not the kind of combat that is required in church leadership. Protection is likely to require strength of character and clarity of thought concerning God's truth. Women are capable of this (for example, Priscilla, or in the fourth century Marcella and Paula). What may be termed social strength may be used in this task, when such strength is yielded to the cause of Christ.[27]

---

27. Selina, Countess of Huntingdon is a fine example of this from the eighteenth century: although she was not herself an ordained minister, she was a patron who helped George Whitefield and installed many evangelical ministers in churches (compare Nympha and Lydia; and compare Paul's own use of the social strength derived from his Roman citizenship in Acts 16:37–39; 21:30 – 22:1, 23–30; 23:23–35; 25:10–12). The Countess's story is vividly retold in Rinehart 2013, 57–83, 168.

11. Paul never instructs the appointment of a sole elder to oversee a local church; in the New Testament, leadership is plural. The task of church leadership requires a range of qualities, found in varying proportions in men and women. If we are to be guided by reflection upon reality and society, it is reasonable to suppose that the twin tasks of nurture and protection may be more effectively undertaken by a mixture of men and women than by a single-sex group.[28]

12. It seems that Roberts's reasoning is based squarely on creation and the life of the flesh, when it ought to take account of new creation and the life of the Spirit. What is the church? God is creating for himself a new family, which will endure into the age to come. This family is a new creation in Christ (2 Cor. 5:17). The battle of 2 Corinthians 10:1–6, to which Roberts refers, is a spiritual battle, conducted with spiritual weapons. It does not depend upon human physical strength or, in particular, upon the deployment of natural abilities found only or mainly in men. The power at work in the church should not be merely the power of humanity as created beings but also the power of the Holy Spirit – resurrection power (2 Cor. 1:9, 22; 3:3, 18; 4:7–14; 5:5; 6:6–7; 13:4, 14; Eph. 1:19–20), a power that is made perfect in human weakness (2 Cor. 12:9–10). The redeemed life of the church looks forward to completion in Christ, not backward to Genesis 2. Even if everything Roberts says about creation were correct, it would not follow that the life of the church should embody a model constrained by the original creation. Women participate in the life of the Spirit as much as men. A woman may be gifted as an apostle (Rom. 16:7), a prophet (Acts 21:9) or a teacher (Acts 18:26). There is no statement in the New Testament that spiritual gifts for leadership are given only to men.

---

28. It is not evident that past insistence on male-only leadership has had great success in protecting the church from false teaching and in preserving unity of doctrine. Before the Reformation, it allowed many unbiblical ideas to be absorbed into Christian doctrine, not least the theory that the purchase of indulgences would shorten a soul's time in purgatory. After the Reformation, male leaders in Protestant groups, who regarded their own particular version of 'truth' as more important than the preservation of relationships, were responsible for split after split, often over small points of disagreement on secondary matters. This is not in itself a reason for including women in leadership, since we cannot know for certain whether including women would have made a positive difference, but it is a reminder not to credit speculative claims about the effectiveness, and hence the necessity, of male leadership.

I am not proposing that we can simply ignore the fact that the church lives in the midst of the old creation. This fact has considerable practical impact. We have already noted that there is no evidence of a substantial proportion of church leaders in the New Testament being women rather than men. This is so, despite the equality of men and women being well understood and taken on board by the early churches, as we have seen illustrated in the emphases of Paul's instructions to wives (see chapter 3) and in the prominent roles sometimes taken by women (see chapter 14). For as long as this present life remains, there will be an overlap between the 'now' and the 'not yet' of God's kingdom. But the continuing reality of the old creation does not justify denying women's participation in ministries of the Spirit, including ministries of leadership. Such participation models the unity and equal status of men and women in God's new creation.

Moreover, there are likely to be practical benefits from women's full involvement alongside men, as Roberts himself appears to affirm. It is often the case that men and women have differing perspectives and insights. Paul worked closely with many women co-workers, as we see from the extensive list in Romans 16, and no doubt he benefited from doing so. Wayne Grudem has wisely written: 'God has given much insight and wisdom to women . . . and . . . any church leaders who neglect to draw on the wisdom that women have are really acting foolishly.'[29] In order to realize the full benefits of the complementarity of women and men, women should participate in leadership, not be excluded from it.

Women as leaders

Since women's involvement in church leadership is nowhere expressly forbidden in Scripture, it seems unwise for the church to insist on maintaining a general rule that forbids it. If this is correct, those who strongly believe in the complementary nature of men and women should be able to put their belief into practice by ensuring that their church leadership teams include women. Many evangelical Christians, whether complementarian or egalitarian, hold this belief.

Some egalitarians may say that it does not matter whether a church is led by men or by women. But, if men and women are complementary, it does matter. The contributions of both are needed. Others may say that there ought to be

---

29. Grudem 1994, 944.

equal numbers of men and women in church leadership. But this may also be incorrect. To the extent that Roberts is right about general differences between men and women, it may perhaps follow that more men than women should become pastors and elders. Irrespective of whether he is right or wrong about this, since leadership in the church is a spiritual gift (Rom. 12:8; 1 Cor. 12:28; Eph. 4:11), if we are to be guided by Scripture, we may say that women's participation in church leadership should depend upon God's call and God's gifts to individuals and church communities in the particular and varied circumstances of their lives and host cultures. 'This is what was spoken by the prophet Joel: "... on my servants, both men and women, I will pour out my Spirit"' (Acts 2:16–18, NIV). In view of the fulfilment of this promise we might reasonably expect many women to be both gifted and called to be leaders.

Postscript to chapters 11 to 15: a threefold test

In the courtroom, as in science, medicine or history, the best explanation takes into account all of the available data which bears on the question under consideration. For reasons of probability, the best explanation is likely to exhibit an appropriate degree of simplicity.[30] And if an explanation which accounts for all the data with appropriate simplicity also sheds light on areas outside the immediate focus of the inquiry, that will further increase our confidence in it.

This threefold test is a useful check to apply to interpretations of Scripture. The best explanation should account for all of the available data, which are the words of Scripture and information about its historical and cultural context. The explanation should have a simplicity that does not require reliance on unevidenced speculations. And if the explanation sheds light on scriptures outside the immediate focus of the inquiry, we can have all the more confidence

---

30. This is an application of the principle known as Ockham's razor (*'pluralitas non est ponenda sine necessitate'* – my translation: 'plurality is not to be posited without necessity'). This is a principle of reasoning. The simplest explanation, requiring the fewest inferences or assumptions, is generally most likely to be correct. For example, if I throw a brick out of my house window into the garden, and a moment later hear a thud which sounds like a brick landing on a patio, it is possible that my brick fell silently upon soft earth and that someone in the garden happened at the same moment to throw another brick onto the patio. But it is more likely that the sound which I heard was from the brick which I threw.

in it. To apply this test is an example of what the Westminster Confession (1647) calls 'a due use of the ordinary means'.

This book has proposed an explanation of the meaning of chapters 2 and 3 of 1 Timothy, as regards women's teaching and eldership, which takes into account the available New Testament data and information about the historical and cultural context.

In essence, the explanation is simple, and it contains no unevidenced speculations. At the point when 1 Timothy is written, there is a crisis of false teaching in Ephesus, as Paul had anticipated would occur. He has excluded two male elders who have been involved in this. It remains necessary for Timothy to deal with a small number of wealthy widows who are caught up in magic and astrology, which they are promoting from house to house. They are aspiring to eldership, wanting to become recognized teachers. They are also dressing expensively and provocatively, each seeking to attract a man who will satisfy her desires. These circumstances provide an explanation both for what Paul writes in 2:9–15 (his instructions for setting right the conduct of these women) and for what he writes in 3:1–7 (his instructions for appointing new elders).[31]

Does this understanding also shed light on other areas, outside the immediate focus of our inquiry? It does. Here are three examples.

1. When Paul writes that he has been appointed a teacher of the Gentiles in faith and truth, why does he add 'I am telling the truth, I am not lying' (2:7)? Without understanding Paul's train of thought from the context, this sounds a strange thing for him to write to a close colleague. From years of experience Timothy must know perfectly well that Paul is telling the truth. And Paul's credentials are well known in Ephesus (Acts 19:15–17). Can Paul seriously be thinking that Timothy, or anyone who hears the letter read out, will suspect him of lying about this? What is going on?

---

31. It may also help explain the differences between the lists of qualifications in 1 Tim. 3 and in Titus 1. In the letter to Timothy, Paul adds that the candidate must be respectable, having a good reputation with outsiders (3:2, 7), and must not be a recent convert (3:6). The wealthy Ephesian women do not dress in a respectable fashion and will therefore not have a good reputation with outsiders; and it is possible that they are also recent converts. This is not contradicted by Paul's statement about their abandoning their former faith (1 Tim. 5:12, ESV), since they may have been converted only a relatively short time before Paul's letter. However, he may have been unable to apply the latter requirement (not recent converts) in Crete because the churches were newer there than in Ephesus (Titus 1:5).

Paul is reminding Timothy of how incredible his own story is: a story that could scarcely be believed if Timothy did not know it to be really true. Paul wants his own transformation, from misguided chief persecutor to faithful teacher, to encourage Timothy to believe that the misguided false teachers can be similarly turned around. Paul had gone from house to house destroying the church; but God the Saviour was merciful to him (Acts 8:3; 1 Tim. 1:12–16). So when Paul came to Ephesus he went from house to house teaching what was helpful (Acts 20:20; 1 Tim. 2:7). Now the women false teachers in Ephesus are going from house to house, damaging the church by spreading futile nonsense (1 Tim. 1:3–7; 5:13; 6:20). Despite their great wealth, even they need a 'mediator' if they are to have access to salvation.[32] Through Christ Jesus the mediator, God can fully save them also (2:3–6, 15). Potentially, they can even be appointed as elders and recognized as faithful teachers of the truth (3:1–2). This perspective helps us to see the full weight of the 'therefore' with which 2:8 begins. Because through Christ God can save and transform – yes, and even appoint to his service as a teacher the chief persecutor of the church (2:7) – therefore the problem of the false teachers is resolvable through the steps which Paul instructs.[33]

2. Without understanding of the context, if only men may be elders, the transition of subject matter from 5:11–16 (widows) to 5:17–22 (elders) is abrupt.

But in reality there is a close connection. In 5:11–16 Paul has in mind the wealthy young widows who want to become teaching elders, though currently unsuitable. This topic leads on naturally, by way of contrast, to 5:17–18 (elders who do a good job, especially those who teach the word) and, by way of similarity, to 5:19–20 (elders who misbehave).

3. In 5:21–22 Paul instructs Timothy to do 'nothing from partiality. Do not be hasty in the laying on of hands, nor take part in the sins of others; keep yourself pure' (ESV). Considered without understanding of the context, this appears to be an extraordinary collocation of ideas. What is the connection between

32. In the patronage system, a 'mediator' was a patron who granted access to another powerful person who would provide the needed benefit: deSilva 2000, 97–98.
33. Note that in 2:7 Paul describes himself not only as an apostle but specifically as a 'teacher of Gentiles in faith and truth', in contrast to his former ignorance and lack of faith (1:13). He is not defending his apostleship. He is comparing himself, as an example (1:16), with those who wish to be teachers of Gentiles but who are currently somewhat lacking in faith and truth (1:4, 7).

partiality, hasty commissioning of an elder by laying on of hands, taking part in other people's sins and not keeping himself pure?

We saw in chapter 13 that Paul is concerned even for Timothy himself as possibly being in jeopardy from these young, rich, socially powerful, racily dressed widows. Timothy must not allow himself to be overpowered by one of these women so as to give any room for any of their false teaching. Therefore, he is not to defer to their wishes because of their social position or be hasty in appointing any of them as an elder, and he must make sure he remains wholly unaffected by their alluring conduct. In this historical context, the ideas in verses 21–22 belong closely together.

These additional insights may reassure us that our interpretation of Paul's concerns in 1 Timothy genuinely fits the context.

Summary of chapter 15

1. The fullest guidance about the appointment of church elders is found in Paul's lists of qualifications for eldership (1 Tim. 3:1–7; Titus 1:5–9). Contrary to the impression given in most English versions, in the Greek text Paul's lists of qualifications for elders do not contain a clear exclusion of women. Prominent complementarian scholars acknowledge that this is so. These passages (especially 1 Tim. 3) contain positive indications that women may qualify as 'elders', in the sense in which that term is used in the New Testament.
2. Paul's idiomatic expression 'one-woman man' in 1 Timothy 3:2 and Titus 1:6 is directed at faithfulness to the Christian sexual ethic and should be understood generically so as to encompass also 'one-man woman'.
3. A vital aspect of elders' or pastors' duties is to be guardians of the flock. It does not follow from this that only men should be elders or pastors. When we understand 'one-woman man' generically, all seventeen qualifications listed by Paul in 1 Timothy 3:1–7 are qualities and behaviours which are found in both men and women. The same feature runs through the corresponding list in Titus 1:5–9.
4. In conclusion, Scripture does not support a general ban on women becoming church elders. Nor is there a ban on women fulfilling any other function in the local church. The complementarity of men and women suggests that it is advantageous to have both men and women in leadership.
5. In chapters 11 to 15 I have offered an explanation of the meaning of 1 Timothy 2 – 3 as regards women's teaching and eldership. This explanation takes into account the available New Testament data and information about the historical and cultural context, has a simplicity that does not require reliance

on unevidenced speculations, and sheds light on other areas, outside the immediate focus of our inquiry. These three features provide grounds for confidence in it.

Questions to consider

1. Does chapter 15 contain some things that are new to you? What questions do you have about them?
2. 'There are likely to be practical benefits from women's full involvement alongside men.' In what respects do you agree or disagree? Why?
3. To what extent are the spiritual gifts of women appropriately affirmed and exercised in your church?

16. TAKING STOCK AND MOVING CLOSER TOGETHER

> The hand of God was on the people to give them unity of mind ..., following the word of the LORD. (2 Chr. 30:12, NIV)

Pulling some threads together

The story of this book may be stated in a few words:

> After it became clear that the traditional view of women's innate inferiority was out of step with Scripture, there began a reformation in the Christian understanding of what the Bible teaches about men and women. New interpretations have been advanced. We have tested these against the words of Scripture, read in context. Fresh light is still emerging. Complementarian interpretations have not taken the reformation far enough, because they still retain unjustified restrictions on women's ministry in the church, and some still depict marriage as a hierarchical relationship. Egalitarian interpretations of Christian marriage seem to have taken the reformation too far, since they deny any definite differentiation of responsibilities of husband and wife beyond the biological. The labels 'complementarian' and 'egalitarian' are unhelpfully restrictive, because they over-simplify the task of interpretation. It is time to move beyond them. Faithfulness to God and his word requires a revitalized conversation in which we will strive for unity of relationship and of understanding, in order to please the Lord and be a blessing to his world.

The purpose of this final chapter is threefold: first, to take stock of where we have arrived on the issues which divide; second, to reflect on some wider themes connected with our study; and third, to encourage progress towards healing the division.

Where we have arrived

To recap:

- Men and women are created by God to be different (Gen. 2). The woman is to be the man's powerful ally. Husbands are not called to be rulers of their wives. The only explicit statement in the Bible about the rule of man over woman is in Genesis 3:16, which presents this as a negative consequence of the fall. There is no statement anywhere in the Bible that husbands ought to exercise unilateral authority over their wives. Christian husbands are called to a special responsibility of self-sacrificial service to their wives, in demonstration of the self-sacrificial love of Christ for his bride, the church (Eph. 5).
- Although God's design does not make husbands masters over their wives, wives are nevertheless called to submit to their husbands. This is for several reasons, particularly to imitate the humility of Christ (Eph. 5; 1 Pet. 2 – 3). But both partners are called to humility and love. In the marriage relationship husband and wife have equal authority and are called to yield to one another (1 Cor. 7:3–5).
- In the New Testament, most prominent roles in the church are fulfilled by men. But the question at issue is whether there is a general biblical ban on women's involvement in church leadership. There is not. Women and men are united in Christ on an equal footing. Ministry is gift-based, not gender-based (Rom. 12:3–8; 16:7; 1 Cor. 12:1–30; Eph. 4:11–13; 1 Pet. 4:10–11). More particularly:
  - 1 Corinthians 11 shows both men and women praying and prophesying. It does not address the question of women's leadership or place any restriction on the scope of women's participation.
  - No-one has been able to find a satisfactory contextual understanding of 1 Corinthians 14:34–35. The best explanation of the manuscript evidence is that these two discordant verses, which require women to be silent in the assembly, are not original to Paul.

- When 1 Timothy 2 is understood in its context (which is not focused specifically on the assembled church), it does not contain a general ban on women's teaching or leadership.
- Nor does 1 Timothy 3 or Titus 1 contain such a ban. The complementarity of men and women suggests that it is advantageous to have both men and women in church leadership.

Wider themes

It is worthwhile to reflect briefly on four wider themes which are connected with our study. We will consider (1) the paradox of equality and humility; (2) the balance of creation and new creation; (3) what it means to be male or female; and (4) raising expectations of Scripture.

Additionally, in appendix 7 I draw together the translation issues that have arisen in the course of examining the texts.

1. The paradox of equality and humility

A major obstacle to understanding the Bible's teaching on marriage arises from an instinctive resistance to the concept of submission.

In some egalitarian thinking, a full-blooded idea of submission seems to come under pressure from the implicit concept of the autonomous individual with full freedom to make their own choices. Submission is watered down to no more than being considerate and thoughtful.[1]

To some complementarians, who welcome full submission on the part of wives, submission is anathema when enjoined on husbands. To those who think of the husband–wife relationship as hierarchical, 'mutual submission' raises an alarming spectre of wives issuing commands for husbands to obey. Some confine the biblical instruction (Eph. 5:21), saying that it does not apply to husbands.

But submission is at the heart of Christ-centred gospel living. We noted in chapters 3 and 4 that to be imitators of Christ (Eph. 5:1–2), believers are called not to rule over other people but to be the 'slave' of all. This is what Jesus taught and lived, both in his ministry and supremely at the cross (Mark 10:42–45; John 13:1–17; 15:12–17; Phil. 2:5–8). Submission, in the sense of humbly ranking others as more important than oneself, is a vital element of godliness.

---

1. Grudem discusses this, with references, in *EFBT*, 189–192.

In the New Testament this humility is combined with an understanding that all God's people are equal inheritors of his abundant grace. The result is that we keep finding a seeming paradox of equality and humility.

Thus in Ephesians 5 the husband is to love his wife as himself (equality: vv. 28, 33) and also to treat her as more important by giving himself up for her (humility: v. 25). In 1 Peter 3:7 husbands are to pay honour to their wives (humility) as co-heirs of the grace of life (equality). In Romans 12:10 believers are to love one another with brotherly love (equality) and also to prefer one another in honour (humility). In Philippians 2:2–3 believers, as those who are joined in soul, are to have the same love for each other (equality), while valuing others more than themselves (humility). While this combination is paradoxical it is not contradictory, for neither element is based on rights, whether one's own or the rights of the other person; both are based on love and on reverence for God.

Humility is therefore a deeply Christian calling. In marriage, where husband and wife are equal, some writers insist that there must be a tie-breaker to resolve disagreements, and this tie-breaker is the supposed unilateral authority of the husband, who must exercise authoritative leadership. But to insist on the need for a tie-breaker is to abandon the aspiration of husband and wife living under the authority of the living Lord Jesus Christ in the humble and loving way that is depicted in Ephesians 5:21–22, 25. As Paul might say: 'Rather than being deflected from living in a truly Christlike manner, why not rather be wronged?' (see 1 Cor. 6:7).

2. Creation and new creation

Our conclusions about the relations of men and women should be seen in the context of the Bible's overarching story of creation and new creation. Paul's expositions show a careful balance. Because his thinking is Christ-centred, new creation is in the foreground.

Complementarians sometimes express concerns that views which place new creation in the foreground embrace 'an over-realized eschatology that appeals to the consummation of the kingdom to justify what appears to be a disregard for the explicit biblical commands concerning the role of women in pastoral leadership'.[2] In other words, plain instructions are set aside by appealing to how things will be in the age to come. Some expositions of the relevant texts may indeed give rise to such concerns. It is not legitimate to say simplistically that new creation trumps the patterns of the old creation. Grudem is right to say

---

2. Storms 2007, 24.

that the instructions in the New Testament letters are written for believers, in whom new creation has commenced, and the instructions must be taken seriously and interpreted correctly.[3]

While this present life continues, there is necessarily an overlap between the 'now' and the 'not yet' of God's kingdom. In this book I have sometimes criticized complementarian reasoning for paying proportionately too much attention to creation and not enough to new creation. But in order to interpret the relevant scriptures I have not proceeded from any prior assumption about where the balance lies. Nor have I used any general argument from new creation to sideline any particular New Testament instructions. The appropriate way to proceed is to start from the texts in their contexts.

In God's original creation, men and women are created to be both similar and different. Marriage is a creation gift. Women's distinctive task of childbearing is affirmed in Scripture with great emphasis (Gen. 3:15, 20; 1 Tim. 5:14; see also the life stories of Sarah, Ruth, Hannah, Elizabeth, Mary the mother of Jesus, and others). But human marriage is for this life only. It is a temporary arrangement, which looks forward to the consummation of the marriage of the Lamb and the Bride in the new creation (Eph. 5:27, 31–32; Rev. 19:9; 21:2, 5). It is therefore fitting that the relationship of husband and wife as depicted in Ephesians 5 is re-framed in the context of this great hope, functioning as a present demonstration of the sacrificial love of Christ and his redeeming purpose for his church.

Unlike human marriage, the church endures into the age to come (Eph. 2:7). Creation is being overtaken by new creation. The curse of Genesis 3:16 is taken away in Christ. God's great purpose is to bring everything, including men and women, into unity in Christ (1 Cor. 11:11; Gal. 3:26–29; 6:15; Eph. 1:10). In Galatians 3:28 Paul introduces his scriptural quotation from Genesis 1:27 ('male and female') with the remarkable words 'there is not'. In anticipation of this new unity, the Holy Spirit of God is given to men and women alike (Acts 2:17–18). The differentiated biological functions of men and women derived from the original creation are not carried through in the same way into the age to come (Matt. 22:30).[4] It is therefore appropriate that

---

3. *EFBT*, 187.

4. However, we do not fully know how similar or different the new creation will be: 'Now we are children of God, and what we will be has not yet been made known' (1 John 3:2, NIV). For further reflection on the implications of the new creation, see *DBE*, 177–185 (Fee).

relationships in the church are shaped by the new creation. Created gender distinctions remain in existence, but are also transcended. It is fitting that women may be called to leadership alongside men. This models the unity that is to come.

3. What it means to be male or female

The conclusions reached in our study may give rise to questions about gender distinctiveness. If a husband declines to exercise commanding authority over his wife, and if in the fellowship of the church a woman may do anything that a man may do, might this not submerge the differences between the sexes and lead to gender confusion?

In chapter 5 we saw that the Bible presents being male or female as a created fact. Although the new creation has begun in Christ, and in the fullness of the new creation there will not be human marriage or procreation, in the present time we remain in our mortal bodies. These bodies belong in the old creation, and we are by nature male or female. God's calling to live now in ways that are truly Christian in marriage and in the church does not change this fact.

Therefore the inauguration of the new creation should not cause gender confusion. When a husband attends to the example of the perfect man and gives himself up in self-sacrifice for his wife, that is the best possible model of what it means to live as a husband. And there is no reason for women to aspire to stereotypes of masculinity. Hollywood films may portray fantasy action heroines who have exactly the same strengths and abilities as fantasy action heroes, or women CEOs who behave just as if they were stereotypical men. But when a woman is called to church leadership, she is under no obligation to follow these unimaginative models. When a woman becomes a leader in the church, she remains a woman, with her own personal qualities, just as a man who becomes an elder or pastor remains a man, with his. We may rejoice in the diversity and complementarity which God has joyfully created.

4. Raising expectations of Scripture

We have seen interpretations which fall short because the interpreter has had insufficiently high expectations of Scripture. Commentators have missed the mark because they did not expect New Testament letter writers to display a closely reasoned train of thought, or a contextually sensitive use of the Old Testament. For example, complementarians say that the final phrase of Ephesians 5:23 is an irrelevant digression; egalitarians say that 1 Peter 3:6 depends on a contextually inaccurate reading of Genesis 18.

For me, one of the greatest impacts of the writing of this book has been a fresh appreciation of biblical writers.[5] I had not previously paid attention to the careful narrative structure of Genesis 2 – 3. While I already regarded Paul as a thoughtful writer, I had no more than an inkling of his rhetorical skills, the vividness of his allusions and word-plays, and the consistency of his logic. I had missed the careful flow of Peter's argument in 1 Peter 2 – 3 and the brilliance of his illustration at 3:6. We give glory to the Holy Spirit who has spoken through these writers. The experience has sent me back to the biblical texts with raised expectations of finding more riches.

The importance of the divine mandate of unity

In chapter 1 I highlighted how the complementarian–egalitarian divide threatens the unity of the church. How can progress be made towards healing the division?

If churches, groups of churches and other associations claim to be evangelical, this means they accept an obligation to be obedient to what the New Testament says about unity.

The apostle Paul instructs the believers in Ephesus, as one body, to *make every effort* to maintain the unity of the Spirit in the bond of peace (Eph. 4:3–4; and 1 Cor. 1:10–11; 3:17). Jesus prays for the unity of those who will follow him (John 17:11, 20–23), so that the world will know that he was sent by the Father. In a Christ-centred view of the world, this is a vitally important objective.

Writing to the believers in Rome, Paul gives detailed instructions on how to handle disagreements on secondary matters (Rom. 14:1 – 15:13). He says that those who are strong in faith must welcome those who are weak in faith, not despise them; they must be willing to curtail their own liberty so as not to put any stumbling block in others' way; and they must *make every effort* to do what leads to peace and to mutual edification. His keynote statement is: 'Receive one another, as also the Messiah received you, to the glory of God' (15:7).

The obstacles to unity

If we are going to make progress in receiving one another in the spirit of Romans 15:7, we must be realistic about the obstacles which need to be

5. Another has been a new awareness of the awesome force of Eph. 5:25, which it would have been good to appreciate much earlier in forty-four years of married life.

overcome. From what I have read in books and on blogs, the principal obstacles seem to be twofold. First, and obviously, there are continuing disagreements on interpretation of Scripture. In addition, there are misunderstandings of the very nature of the debate. We will consider each of these in turn.

Ongoing disagreements on interpretation of Scripture
Wayne Grudem wrote in 2004:

> I personally think that one reason God has allowed this controversy on manhood and womanhood to come into the church at this time is so that we could correct some mistakes, change some wrongful traditions, and become more faithful to Scripture in treating our wives and all women with dignity and respect.[6]

This is a frank acknowledgment that the church's understanding of the Bible's teaching on men and women was distorted. After the rejection of a misunderstanding of Scripture embedded for many generations, it must inevitably take time for the church to reach substantial agreement on a more accurate understanding. We should not be surprised that there have been disagreements over the precise extent and nature of the needed corrections.

Grudem states in *EFBT* that those who disagree with his complementarian position have failed to win the arguments on the basis of the biblical text. Instead, they 'increasingly deal not with detailed analyses of biblical texts, but with broad generalizations about Scripture, then with arguments from experience or arguments from philosophical concepts like fairness, or from the supposed negative results of the complementarian position'.[7] This may be a fair description of some egalitarian writings, but it does not apply to Philip Payne's subsequent major book (*M&W*), which presents detailed arguments from Scripture. Some complementarians realistically acknowledge that the debate is still ongoing and unresolved. It is not the case that complementarian arguments have substantially carried the day.[8]

---

6. *EFBT*, 28.

7. *EFBT*, 53.

8. For example, Evangelical Alliance 2012. A survey of the views of evangelicals in the UK asked 17,000 people about the statement: 'Women should be eligible for all roles within the church in the same way that men are.' Only 10% disagreed strongly and 10% disagreed a little; 20% agreed a little and 51% agreed strongly.

I have found that there are weaknesses on each side of the partisan debate. Examples include:

- Some complementarians believe, based largely on interpretation of Genesis 2, that the husband has a God-given unilateral authority. But their interpretation of Genesis 2 rests entirely on supposed implications from the text. They need to provide viable explanations of why Paul contradicts their belief in 1 Corinthians 7:3–5, why the Bible nowhere states that a husband should exercise such authority, and how Paul's use of 'but' to connect Ephesians 5:24 with 5:23 fits the context.[9]

- Those egalitarians who deny any special responsibility of the husband in marriage need to explain why in Ephesians 5, to teach how husband and wife should live, Paul uses the asymmetrical metaphor of head and body and the asymmetrical analogy of Christ and the church.[10]

- Those who claim that 1 Corinthians 11:3 establishes authoritative male headship need to tell us what role the third couplet in verse 3 plays in the development of Paul's argument from 11:4 to 11:16. They also need to provide a convincing justification for reversing the meaning of 11:10 by means of a paraphrase which lacks any textual or linguistic support. They need to say where in 11:4–16 Paul clearly mentions any authority other than that of a woman over her head. They need to explain how, on their interpretation, the first phrase of verse 11 stands as a qualification of what is said in verse 10. Certainly this passage says nothing about teaching by women or about restrictions on being a church pastor or elder.[11]

- Those who say that 1 Timothy 2:12 bans all authoritative teaching by women in the public assembly need to explain why their theory limits the application of Paul's words to that particular context. How can that limitation stand with Paul's emphasis on good works in 2:10, his words about childbearing, faith, love and holiness in 2:15, and the lack of any specific mention of the public assembly in chapters 1–3? They need to say how their interpretation is justified by the context visible in 1:1 – 2:7, and to demonstrate why their interpretation of 2:12 is right to ignore the topic which Paul says he is writing about (combating false teaching), and how the context explains Paul's choice of the rare word *authenteō*.

---

9. See chapters 2 to 5 above.
10. See chapter 4.
11. See chapters 7 and 8.

They need to explain how it can be that the creation principle which they say Paul is relying on applies only to marriage and to authority in the church, and not to the whole of life. They also need to explain why they disregard Paul's equation of 'she' and 'they' in verse 15, when 'she' evidently refers back to the woman of verses 11–12, to whom Paul's restriction applies, and 'they' evidently refers back to the misbehaving women in view in verses 9–10.[12]

- Those who claim that 1 Timothy 3:1–7 and Titus 1:5–9 ban all women from New Testament eldership need to explain why they take that view when multiple indications in the text point to the eligibility of women, and prominent complementarian scholars accept that these texts do not justify the exclusion of women. They also need to give a satisfactory explanation of why, to be consistent with their interpretation of these texts so as to ban church leadership by women, they do not also ban single men, childless men and men with only one child.[13]

Neither side in the partisan debate is in a position to claim that it has all the good arguments. In such a situation we may do well to recall Oliver Cromwell's plea in his letter to the General Assembly of the Kirk of Scotland (3 August 1650): 'Is it therefore infallibly agreeable to the Word of God, all that you say? I beseech you, in the bowels of Christ, think it possible you may be mistaken.'[14]

We may suspect that cultural pressures are influencing each side's interpretations. Complementarians have sometimes accused egalitarians of being in thrall to the spirit of the age, and to ideas derived more from the philosophies of the eighteenth-century Enlightenment than from Holy Scripture. A counter-accusation has sometimes been made that complementarians are trying to perpetuate a traditional hierarchical culture, which has always fought tooth and nail against the liberating teachings of Jesus and his apostles in order to preserve male privileges. Such claims and counter-claims have often been overstated and have seldom been edifying. Wayne Grudem and John Piper have judiciously and graciously said:

The history of exegesis does not encourage us that we will have the final word on this issue, and we hope we are not above correction. . . . Whether feminists are more

---

12. See chapters 11 to 13.
13. See chapter 15.
14. The phrase 'in the bowels of Christ' reflects the literal translation of Phil. 1:8 found in the KJV.

influenced by the immense cultural pressure of contemporary egalitarian assumptions, or we are more influenced by centuries of patriarchalism and by our own masculine drives is hard to say.[15]

The present book is a contribution to a debate which needs to be taken further. Others have laboured much longer on this topic. I have come to it lately and have benefited enormously from their work, especially from that of Grudem and Payne. I offer some different perspectives from each of them because they have lifted me up, to stand on their shoulders.[16] And it is reasonable to suppose that there is fuller understanding yet to be gained.

We must turn next to a difficulty which is larger than the disagreements themselves. This difficulty has to do with some inaccurate perceptions, on each side, of what is really going on in this debate.

Egalitarian misunderstanding of the nature and motivations of the debate

Some egalitarian writings, especially on online blogs, see the debate as a moral contest. In this contest, complementarians are placed beyond the pale and egalitarians view themselves as on the moral high ground. Because to them an egalitarian outlook seems obvious, they infer that those who express a different opinion must somehow be insincere or in thrall to base motives. Complementarian writers and preachers are supposedly driven by a lust for power or status, using a claim of adherence to Scripture as a cloak for maintaining male supremacy. Or, if they are women, they hold complementarian views because they are too weak to resist them.

This view ignores inconvenient facts. If this is what is really going on, how is it that, on personal acquaintance, most complementarian writers are kind-hearted, thoughtful, reliable, godly people? The intellectual honesty evident in Tom Schreiner's approach to 1 Timothy 2 is attractive and persuasive. Egalitarians should not ignore or dismiss his conviction that the interpretation of Scripture needs to be intellectually convincing before a new position can be adopted.[17]

---

15. *RBMW*, 76–77.
16. This remark also applies to the work of numerous others, especially Clinton Arnold's research into the historical and cultural context of Ephesians, Al Wolters' study of the usage of *authenteō*, and the discussions of the qualifications for elders by Tom Schreiner and Douglas Moo.
17. See *WITC*, 164; his instinct is towards there being no limitations on women's ministry but the inadequacies of egalitarian interpretations have so far persuaded him otherwise.

And if the real agenda is the maintenance of male power, why are some capable women scholars vigorously advancing complementarian interpretations?

Insinuations of this kind should have no place in the debate. They are neither justified nor constructive. They hinder mutual listening.[18] They should be jettisoned.[19]

How complementarians characterize the debate
On the other side of the debate, complementarian misunderstandings of what is at stake require fuller exposition.

In 1991 John Piper and Wayne Grudem wrote a chapter in *RBMW* entitled 'Charity, Clarity and Hope'. It refers warmly to their sense of kinship with the founders of CBE: 'In profound ways we share a common passion with the members of CBE: a passion to be obedient to Biblical truth.' The chapter includes positive words of hope:

> There is hope because we stand together on the authority of God's Word, the Bible. As agonizing as the impasse may feel, there is reason to believe that while this common ground prevails, new light may yet break forth upon us. . . . He is the Spirit of truth (John 16:13). . . . He is urging and pressing us ever on toward 'the unity of the Spirit' (Ephesians 4:3).[20]

Unfortunately, this approach of acknowledging that evangelical egalitarians are passionate about being obedient to biblical truth quickly faded away. When Piper and Grudem wrote *Fifty Crucial Questions: An Overview of Central Concerns about Manhood and Womanhood* (1992), the Foreword (written by the then President and Executive Director of CBMW) stated: 'This debate is about whether or not the people of God will submit to the Word of God. For this reason the gender issue is not peripheral but central to the advance of the gospel.' This re-characterized the issues contested by complementarians as primary issues of gospel truth. Those who took a different view were now seen not as holding a different interpretation but as refusing to submit to God's Word. Expressing a similar mindset, the FIEC Women in Ministry Statement asserts: 'To ignore

---

18. Egalitarians should read Claire Smith's eloquent and heartfelt protest: Smith 2012, 223–224.
19. I am not saying that no male ministers are ever influenced by a desire to maintain their power. What I am saying is that such people are irrelevant to the interpretive debate.
20. *RBMW*, 406, 418.

the prohibitions of Scripture is not something we can endorse.' This paints those who do not hold to the complementarian position on women's ministry as ignoring Scripture.

This framing of what is at stake has become a repeated refrain. The Gospel Coalition website hosts a video discussion explaining why TGC is complementarian. Those who do not agree with the full complementarian position are 'dodging what the Bible says' (Piper) or 'using hermeneutics to side-step what Scripture clearly, repeatedly and unambiguously says' (Carson).[21] Grudem has also expressed this perspective. He poses a pointed question: 'Will we glorify God through manhood and womanhood according to His Word? Or will we deny His Word and give in to the pressures of modern culture? That is the choice we have to make.'[22]

This mindset has practical consequences. Because they believe the issue to be a question of submission to Scripture, many complementarians have written about the need, as they see it, to define their organizations or denominations by a red line which excludes the holding of egalitarian views. They see egalitarianism as undermining adherence to the Bible.[23] They also see it as a slippery slope: if it is accepted, all sorts of unbiblical outcomes will ensue. According to Albert Mohler, a 'church that ordains women as pastors' is guilty of 'obstinate refusal to be corrected by Scripture'. If a person remains in such a church, at some point 'refusal to separate becomes complicity in the heresy'. This is because 'no faithful believer should remain in a church that refuses to be bound to God's Word'.[24]

Similar views have been expressed in the UK by the National Director of the FIEC. Writing to explain why the FIEC 'has felt it essential to maintain a complementarian position', he argues that 'egalitarianism threatens the ultimate authority of Scripture' and 'undermines historic evangelical convictions'.[25]

This complementarian argument about the need to draw a red line is buttressed by the observation that recent church history demonstrates an observable correlation between egalitarianism and theological liberalism.[26]

---

21. Carson [no date].

22. *EFBT*, 61, summarizing 50–61.

23. *EFBT*, 500–517, 528–532. Also Grudem 2006. Similar views have been expressed by, among others, Denny Burk, Mark Dever, Ligon Duncan and Kevin DeYoung. See Burk 2012.

24. Mohler 2009.

25. Stevens 2012.

26. *EFBT*, 503 ('an egalitarian advocacy of women's ordination goes hand in hand with theological liberalism'). This use of the term 'liberal' has no connection with either

Those who have publicly framed the debate in this way are highly respected as servants of the gospel, and rightly so. But it has to be said that their approach involves a degree of confusion and a lack of realism, as we shall see.

Re-framing the debate

To dispel the confusion, it is necessary to keep in mind the differences between three kinds of arguments which are used to support non-complementarian positions on marriage or on women's ministry:

1. Some arguments are advanced on the basis of theologically liberal presuppositions which reject the authority of Scripture.
2. Some evangelical writers who have advocated the appointment of women to positions of church leadership have claimed to base their position on Scripture but have used arguments which have not been properly thought through, and which in reality are not fully consistent with accepting the authority of Scripture. They advance novel principles of interpretation which give a wide latitude to say that apostolic teaching should not be followed.
3. Some arguments are squarely based on Scripture, understood in accordance with orthodox principles of interpretation.

The first kind of argument is not relevant to the debate which takes place among evangelical believers and on the basis of evangelical presuppositions about adherence to Scripture. It is undoubtedly true that many Western Christians in mainline denominations are egalitarian on the basis of theologically liberal reasoning which rejects the authority of the Bible. It is also true that, if those reasons were accepted as valid, all sorts of unbiblical outcomes would ensue. But correlation is not proof of causation. Where theologically liberal egalitarians reject the authority of Scripture, this flows from their theologically liberal convictions, not from their position on women's leadership in the church.

Everyone really knows that correlation is not causation. The divorce rate in Maine from 2000 to 2009 correlated very closely with the per capita consumption of margarine in the USA. And in the same period the number of civil engineering doctorates awarded correlated with the per capita consumption of mozzarella cheese.[27] Nevertheless we remain sceptical that margarine causes

---

the meaning that has to do with valuing personal freedom or the meaning that has to do with a progressive or left-wing political stance.

27. See Vigen [no date].

marital breakdown. And we are unpersuaded that greater consumption of mozzarella would materially increase the number of well-qualified civil engineers.

Grudem knows that correlation is not causation. He states that he is personally acquainted with egalitarians who are thoroughly committed to the authority of Scripture. He realistically acknowledges that some denominations have approved women's 'ordination' for reasons other than liberalism, such as the Assemblies of God (who have had women pastors since 1914) and the Willow Creek Association.[28] In the late nineteenth and early twentieth century conservative evangelicals were more open to women's ministry and leadership than they later became.[29] In the UK the first major denomination to ordain women was the Salvation Army, in about 1870.[30] The Salvation Army was explicitly evangelical then and remains so today. Any claim that egalitarianism causes theological liberalism would be counter-factual.[31]

Moving on to the second kind of argument, it is certainly true that some evangelical writers have advocated women's ordination or leadership by using novel interpretive arguments which undermine the authority of Scripture. When they have done so, Grudem has been right to call them out

---

28. *EFBT*, 504.

29. See Larsen 2007. A shorter version of Larsen's essay is available at <https://reformedjournal.com/evangelicalisms-strong-history-women-ministry/>.

30. Salvation Army 2018: Catherine Booth 'utilised an interpretation of the Bible which supported equality and challenged the precept that it was unfeminine for women to preach; these ideas were presented in her pamphlet *Female Ministry; or, Woman's right to preach the Gospel* (1859) which was published in defence of a contemporary female preacher, the American revivalist Phoebe Palmer. From 1860 Catherine began preaching herself. She was a successful speaker who won many converts and succeeded in changing William's stance. Subsequently the value of female ministry was proclaimed by The Salvation Army and a statement regarding sexual equality in ministry was published in The Salvation Army's Orders and Regulations.'

31. However, it appears that complementarianism advances the cause of theological liberalism, as an unintended consequence. There is survey evidence that women clergy are disproportionately liberal in their theology: James 2007, 359–360. Because some influential evangelical churches hold complementarian views, many evangelical women are deterred from ordination, or from becoming pastors in churches which do not 'ordain'. If this continues, it may have far-reaching consequences, particularly for denominations with substantial numbers of women pastors.

on it.[32] But, to be fair, distinguishing between legitimate and illegitimate inter-pretations is not always easy. In other words, while the distinction between arguments of the second and third kinds is clear in principle, it can be more difficult to draw in practice. Even when the original meaning is entirely plain, it is still necessary to decide how we should respond. For example, when we read the often-repeated instruction to greet one another with a holy kiss (Rom. 16:16; 1 Cor. 16:20; 2 Cor. 13:12; 1 Thess. 5:26), we have to decide whether we should take this as a reminder to greet our brothers and sisters in a way that is both holy and culturally appropriate, or whether, since no cultural limitation is apparent in the text, we should follow it literally.

The evangelical debate about what the Bible teaches ought to take place on the basis of arguments of the third kind. I have sought to confine the present book to that kind of argument. When the debate takes place on this basis, Grudem's pointed question becomes inappropriate. A Bible-believing egalitarian might wish to turn the question around 180°, asking instead: 'Will we glorify God by being obedient to His Word? Or will we deny the full equality of men and women by insisting on adherence to patriarchal elements of traditional culture? That is the choice we have to make.' Such a question would be equally misplaced, because in the evangelical debate the central issue is not obedience but interpretation.

The analysis which says that egalitarians are simply rejecting, ignoring or disobeying Scripture depends upon the conviction that it is plain to any faithful Bible reader that the full complementarian position is correct. But such a conviction is unrealistic, for the correctness of the complementarian position is far from plain. It faces serious interpretive challenges from fellow believers who hold the same view of Scripture and whose methods of interpretation are orthodox. These challenges assert that complementarianism is not fully faithful to the inspired text.[33]

---

32. I do not mean that he has always chosen the correct targets. For example, his criticism of Gordon Fee's argument as to the inauthenticity of 1 Cor. 14:34–35 is misdirected. In *EFBT*, 235–237 he misunderstands it (see chapter 10 above). He mischaracterizes it as part of 'a pattern of using sophisticated scholarly procedures in order to evade the requirement of submitting to the authority of the Word of God'. On the contrary, for everyone who accepts the authority of Scripture the scholarly discipline of text criticism is essential so that we may have in our hands a Bible that is as close to what was originally written as possible, without alterations introduced during copying.

33. In addition to the substantive chapters of this book, see further appendix 6.

If faithful, evangelical interpreters conclude after careful, serious, diligent study that women are permitted to be elders, this does not mean that they are undermining historic evangelical convictions. On the contrary. One of those historic convictions is that, if a traditional interpretation is judged at the bar of Scripture and found to be faulty, it should be corrected.

It is illegitimate to condemn a position on the grounds that some Christians hold it on the basis of unsatisfactory methods of reasoning, when other Christian scholars (of whom Payne is a prominent example) hold it because of their adherence to the Bible. Payne is explicit in his acceptance of the authority of Scripture.[34] So is the CBE Statement. From Payne's point of view, everyone who adheres to the TGC Confessional Statement, the Danvers Statement, the FIEC Women in Ministry Statement or the Southern Baptist Convention statement of faith is in fact, contrary to their intention, rejecting the teaching of Scripture.

The complementarian insistence on characterizing the position of egalitarian evangelicals as an obstinate refusal to be obedient to Scripture, rather than as a disagreement over interpretation, is out of step with the facts. The insistence on complementarianism as a confessional issue in associations such as The Gospel Coalition lacks proper justification, as complementarian Carl Trueman has pointed out in characteristically lively and lucid terms.[35] The argument that a red line must be drawn as a bulwark against liberalism is particularly puzzling, given that TGC's Confessional Statement (like that of the FIEC) excludes those of theologically liberal convictions. Within the confines of The Gospel Coalition (or the FIEC) there is no realistic possibility that allowing disagreement on

---

34. *M&W*, 27.

35. Trueman 2012. The response in Burk 2012 illustrates the extent of the problem. Burk cites Ligon Duncan: 'The gymnastics required to get from "I do not allow a woman to teach or to exercise authority over a man," in the Bible, to "I do allow a woman to teach and to exercise authority over a man" in the actual practice of the local church, are devastating to the functional authority of the Scripture.' This is misconceived. It simply assumes the unchallengeable correctness of the complementarian position as to what Paul meant, as if the orthodox evangelical reasons to the contrary did not exist, and as if context could have no effect on meaning. It is like criticizing the apostle Paul by saying: 'The gymnastics required to get from "Do not work for food that spoils" (John 6:27) in the teaching of Jesus to "Do work for food that spoils" in the actual practice of the local church (see 1 Thess. 4:11; 2 Thess. 3:10; Titus 3:14), are devastating to the functional authority of Scripture.'

women's ministry on the basis of orthodox arguments would open the door to rejection of the authority of Scripture.

I believe that the present book provides substantial grounds for questioning complementarian interpretations of 1 Timothy 2 and some other passages. I have laid out my presuppositions and methods for the reader to see, and have chosen to study the issues not as an advocate for a pre-selected position but with the judicial mindset of going wherever the texts, evidence and reasons might lead. I have paid close attention to the texts in their contexts and have used only methods of interpretation which are accepted among Bible-believing Christians. For me, this has been a voyage of discovery. The reader will have to judge whether any of the new light, for which Piper and Grudem fervently hope, is breaking forth. Complementarians who read this book will be able to assess whether I am ignoring, sidelining or refusing to obey Scripture, or whether I am merely disagreeing with some of their interpretations. I suggest it is time for complementarians to stop claiming that evangelical disagreement with complementarian interpretations threatens the authority of Scripture or the truth of the gospel.

Next steps

'Make every effort to keep the unity of the Spirit through the bond of peace. There is one body and one Spirit' (Eph. 4:3–4, NIV).

The issue of women in church leadership is challenging. If we are going to make progress towards unity, there needs to be a fresh conversation. And this must take place on a basis of mutual respect, living together graciously with different points of view, and receiving one another as the Lord has received all of us (Rom. 15:7). Whatever position we start from, we need to explore whether we can move closer together on points of difference, and meanwhile refrain from insisting on unnecessary red lines. As I said in chapter 1, I have not ended up where I thought I might when I began writing. So this book is a testament to the possibility of changing one's understanding.[36]

There is some truth in the old quip: 'It is difficult to get a man to understand something, when his salary depends on his not understanding it.'[37] Some theological colleges, particularly in the USA, insist that their faculty sign up to a

---

36. Johnson 2010 and (with a wider perspective) Wood 2017 contain stories of evangelical leaders who changed their minds about women in leadership.
37. A saying of Upton Sinclair, US author and journalist (died 1968).

defined position in the egalitarian–complementarian controversy, which makes open-minded discussion of it a challenging task, to say the least. To be able to listen closely and change one's mind under such constraints must require a maturity of Christlikeness which draws on deep wells of charity, of humility and of courage.

To make progress towards unity it will be necessary for those who have taken up opposing positions in the evangelical debate to acknowledge that this is not a primary gospel issue, to look afresh at the biblical arguments, to take care to use only sound methods of interpretation, and especially to pay closer attention and give more weight to context and to the train of thought in the relevant texts. The labels 'egalitarian' and 'complementarian' are unhelpful, because they squeeze the discussion onto artificial tramlines which can never meet. I suggest it is time to move beyond them. To have a fruitful conversation, participants may need to be willing temporarily to let go of their labels, and be unaligned except for their commitment to God, to his Word, and to their brothers and sisters. Churches with settled traditions concerning forms of church leadership may need to review whether their traditions resolve questions which are matters of indifference so far as Scripture is concerned, or whether any of their traditions are inconsistent with biblical principles.

As we make progress towards unity, I believe we will find that God's design and purpose for men and women, as revealed in the Bible, is far better than any alternative view. Greater unity on these issues will put the church in a better position to be salt and light in wider society, at a time of considerable cultural and ideological confusion on issues of gender and sexuality.

'The hand of God was on the people to give them unity of mind . . . , following the word of the LORD' (2 Chr. 30:12, NIV). May this be true more and more, to the glory of God and to the blessing of the world that he loves, for whom he gave his only Son.

Summary of chapter 16

1. The conclusions reached in chapters 2 to 15 support a view of marriage which is non-hierarchical and partly complementarian, while rejecting any general ban on women's teaching or leadership in churches.
2. The concept of submission should be understood in the context of the Christian paradox of humility and equality. All God's people are equal inheritors of his abundant grace. Because of the example of Jesus Christ, humility is at the heart of Christian living.

3. Our conclusions do not depend on prior assumptions about the relative extent to which creation or new creation should guide believers' behaviour. But they fit well into the context of the presently overlapping relationship of creation (as background) and new creation (as foreground).

4. Husbands are called to serve rather than rule over their wives. Calling women to church leadership is not contrary to Scripture. There is no reason to fear that these callings will lead to gender confusion.

5. Some interpretations fall short because the interpreter has had insufficiently high expectations of Scripture. Close study of the texts should lead to a fresh appreciation of the biblical writers, to the glory of God.

6. If churches, groups of churches and other associations claim to be evangelical, this means they accept an obligation to be obedient to what the New Testament says about unity.

7. There are currently weaknesses on each side of the partisan debate. The disagreements over interpretation require further work in pursuit of unity.

8. Claims by egalitarians that complementarians are driven by base motives should be discarded.

9. Complementarians need to re-frame their understanding of the debate. Egalitarian views on marriage or women's ministry do not cause theological liberalism. Among believers who accept the authority of the Bible, the critical issues are not questions of obedience to Scripture but questions of interpretation, to be settled by using orthodox methods. It is time for complementarians to stop claiming that evangelical disagreement with complementarian interpretations threatens the authority of Scripture or the truth of the gospel.

10. Jesus prays for the unity of those who will follow him (John 17:11, 20–23), so that the world will know that he was sent by the Father. In a Christ-centred view of the world, this is a vitally important objective. The apostolic instruction to make every effort to maintain unity requires a fresh conversation on a basis of mutual respect. Those who have taken up opposing positions on women's leadership or ministry need to recognize that this is not a primary gospel issue, to look afresh at the biblical arguments, to take care to use only sound methods of interpretation, and especially to pay closer attention and give more weight to context and to the train of thought in the relevant passages. Meanwhile we are to receive one another as the Lord has received all of us (Rom. 15:7).

Questions to consider

1. Chapter 16 picks up four wider themes (the paradox of equality and humility, the balance of creation and new creation, what it means to be male or female,

and raising expectations of Scripture). Does any of these strike a chord with you? Why or why not?

2. This book's overall conclusions take a partly complementarian view of marriage while adjudging that there is no general biblical prohibition of women's teaching or leadership in churches. How comfortable or uncomfortable are you with these conclusions? Do you think that the correctness or incorrectness of one or other of these conclusions is an issue which justifies division?

3. Is there anything in your attitude to others, with whom you disagree on women's ministry, that you need to put right? Is there something practical that you can do to promote unity?

APPENDIX 1 (CHAPTER 1)
METHODS OF BIBLICAL INTERPRETATION

The interpretation[1] toolbox

This appendix explains my view of seven tools which help Bible readers to adopt a position of appropriate humility before the text.

1. Primacy of Scripture over tradition

Tradition is entitled to respect. The collective judgment of the church, under the guidance of the Spirit, tells us which books are rightly included in the Bible. The sixteenth-century reformers relied on tradition in support of their criticisms of certain Roman Catholic doctrines and practices. We do not lightly set aside traditions and interpretations held by Christians in former days, who have prayed and worshipped and served God, and have sought to be faithful in interpreting the Bible. But the reformers also insisted that, having settled which books constitute Scripture, then, in the event of conflict with tradition, the words of Scripture must prevail.

---

1. In this book I have tried to avoid using the terms 'exegesis' and 'hermeneutics'. Although these have an appearance of being technical terms, in reality they do not have an agreed, fixed meaning, so can create confusion; compare *DBE*, 355 (Nicole), 364–5 (Fee).

There is a heavy burden of proof on those who seek to overturn a traditional understanding. But if a traditional interpretation of Scripture is convincingly seen to be inaccurate, it must be corrected. This is the reason why both complementarians and egalitarians have rejected the traditional doctrine of women's innate inferiority to men.

2. *Paying appropriate attention to culture*

All interpretation is vulnerable to the impact of culture. Such impact can hardly be overestimated. In the ancient world the institution of slavery was so deeply embedded that it was not widely understood to be inherently wrong. For centuries the church mostly accepted it as ordained by God. In the Southern USA in the nineteenth century devout Christians saw nothing amiss in defending slavery, from texts such as Genesis 9:24–27; 21:9–10; Exodus 20:17; 21:1–6; Leviticus 25:44–46; Ephesians 6:5–8; and they castigated abolitionists as apostates who were abandoning the literal truth of Scripture. Changes in the general culture eventually enabled believers of all persuasions to see that the Bible did not teach divine approval of slavery. A similar process has enabled believers to see that the traditional view of women's innate inferiority lacks sound biblical support.

Paul and Peter were not modern Western thinkers. We must enter into the thought-world of the biblical writers in order to gain an accurate understanding of their meaning, rather than peering at the text through the distorting spectacles of our own times and imposing on it our own concerns. This is very difficult for all of us, because our own culture is so familiar to us that we are often unaware of it.

Sometimes the doctrine of the 'clarity' or 'perspicuity' of Scripture is misunderstood. It began as a slogan for contesting the claim of the late mediaeval Roman Catholic Church hierarchy to be the sole interpreter of Scripture. The original purpose of the slogan was to promote the belief that through Scripture God can reveal himself to anyone, and his way of salvation can be understood by anyone, without the need for authoritative interpretation by a bishop in fellowship with the Pope.[2] But it is often misused. Despite 2 Peter 3:16, where

---

2. The Westminster Confession of Faith (1647) expresses the doctrine of clarity in judiciously limited terms: 'All things in Scripture are not alike plain in themselves, nor alike clear unto all: yet those things which are necessary to be known, believed, and observed for salvation, are so clearly propounded, and opened in some place of Scripture or other, that not only the learned, but the unlearned, in a due use of the ordinary means, may attain unto a sufficient understanding of them.'

the apostle Peter remarks on how hard it is to understand some things in Paul's letters, it is sometimes claimed that the whole of Scripture is clear, and can therefore be accurately understood without any background knowledge of the cultural world of the writers and the first readers. Belief in this kind of clarity is a serious error. It can exclude interpretations which would have seemed obvious to the original writers and their first readers. It can also impose distortions derived from our own culture and worldviews.

To heighten awareness of the potential impact of culture upon interpretation, I have included at the end of this appendix a thought experiment illustrating how easy it is to read Scripture in accordance with the reader's culture.

3. Going back to the source language in context
We generally read the Bible in translation. The impact of culture upon translation is considerable. Translations are affected by translators' own traditions and cultures and by their understanding of the source culture. Translators have to try to imagine themselves within the source culture, since the original meaning has to be understood in order to provide a translation which will convey the author's intention as closely as possible into the target culture. And we read the translation from within our own culture. Because of the very nature of languages, and because each language sits within a different culture, exact translation is an impossibility.

Bible translation has its own strong traditions. Where a verse has been translated in a particular way, there is a marked tendency for subsequent translations to follow, even when there is a mistake.[3] Luke 2:7 provides a notable example. It is well known that at the first Christmas there was no room for Mary and Joseph at the inn, because this verse has said so at least since the preparation of the very influential Latin version known as the Vulgate in the fourth century (*quia non erat eis locus in diversorio*: 'because there was no room for them in the inn'). The first published translation of the New Testament from the original Greek into English was produced by William Tyndale in 1526. Influenced by the Vulgate, he retained the inn ('because ther was no roume for them within in the ynne'). But scholars have long known that no inn is mentioned in Luke's account, and indeed there was probably no inn in Bethlehem at the relevant

---

3. Departure from traditions of translation is a courageous step. As has been said: '*every* translation of the Bible has been condemned by *someone* as soon as it rolled off the press. It is preeminently an act of selfless love that the translator engages in this task at all' (Wallace 2001a; emphases original).

time. The 2011 NIV took the brave step of correcting the unlikely translation. The inn has now reverted to a guest room (*kataluma*), as in Mark 14:14 and Luke 22:11.[4]

The impacts of culture and of translation traditions are particularly powerful upon verses bearing on gender relations, and therefore require special attention to guard against them. In times past it was well known that women could not proclaim a word from God. So Psalm 68:11 was translated in the KJV as 'The Lord gave the word: great was the company of those that published it' (see also RSV, NRSV, NIV 1984). NIV 2011 has corrected this to 'The Lord announces the word, and the women who proclaim it are a mighty throng.' The translated text now reflects the Hebrew, in which the proclaimers are female. The process of making these kinds of corrections is still under way. We cannot assume that English translation traditions are always correct. See further appendix 7.

Where there is uncertainty over translation, we must pay appropriate attention to how the same words are used elsewhere. But it is not enough to study individual words, for usage in other contexts only provides possible meanings; the actual meaning must depend upon the particular context. Examining the context requires mentally removing modern punctuation and chapter and verse divisions, which are not original to the texts. These are sometimes distracting. They also promote a tendency to study verses in isolation rather than attending to a writer's complete train of thought.

While lexicons of Greek are wonderful resources, some caution is needed in using them. The definitions provided for a word tell us how the editor understood the word in a cited context. The editor's reading may be affected by their own cultural viewpoint or by a failure to understand the point the original writer was making. Samuel Johnson, writer of the famous eighteenth-century English dictionary, provided a jocular reminder of how the editor's own viewpoint may intrude when he defined a lexicographer as 'a writer of dictionaries; a harmless drudge'. Subjectivity can be a recurring issue in lexicons dealing primarily with New Testament Greek, where the definitions (explanations) or glosses (English synonyms) tend to reflect the particular religious viewpoint of the editors on matters of controversy. When someone who shares their viewpoint cites the lexicon as evidence to resolve the controversy, this adds nothing; the argument is circular.

---

4. When the Vulgate was written, Bethlehem had been a major destination for Christian monks and tourists for upwards of sixty years, so by then it may have had an inn. The only clear mention of an inn in the Gospels is at Luke 10:34 (*pandocheion*).

Caution is also needed because the important question is not 'what do the individual words mean?' It is 'what did the author intend to convey?'[5] When considering context, we have to take into account the literary context (the surrounding words) and the historical context (the situation on the ground, in so far as we can determine it), as well as the wider cultural context. The Bible should not be read as if it were a police report. We must consider the genre, not reading poetry as if it were prose, or a letter as if it were law, or prophecy as if it were narrative. This makes a real difference. Words are elastic. To determine meaning, context is always king.

4. Coherence

Within any particular passage of Scripture, we should seek a coherent and internally consistent interpretation which accurately accounts for everything said in the passage.

Whilst we acknowledge our human limitations (Rom. 11:33), we recognize that serious writers do not normally contradict themselves, and that they normally have a reason for writing what they do. We should do the biblical writers the honour of attending very closely to what they write, so as to discover their actual reasoning and message.

5. A Christ-centred canonical approach

When considering context, we do not limit our inquiry to the immediate literary context of whatever passage we are considering, or other writings by the same author. Because we believe that the Bible is God's revelation, we also look for appropriate consistency in the wider context of the witness of Scripture as a whole. I qualify this consistency as 'appropriate', because the overall message of the Bible is a story that moves through different stages. It is God's story with the world, a story about the coming of the Messiah.

The canonical approach is an aspect of using context wisely. Context is king not merely because words are flexible but because it is essential for understanding a speaker's or writer's intended meaning. However plain the words used, we must still give full attention to context.

For example, Jesus said: 'Do not work for food that spoils, but for food that endures to eternal life' (John 6:27, NIV). These are utterly plain words. Taken at

---

5. It follows from belief in God's inspiration of Scripture that an early scripture may sometimes be seen, in the light of later scriptures, to have a fuller significance of which the original author may have been unaware. But this possibility does not bear significantly on the present topic of debate.

face value this is a clear and unqualified instruction not to work in order to obtain daily food. A naïve interpreter unfamiliar with Jewish culture might think that the words mean exactly what they say. They might find this meaning confirmed when they see that Jesus took people away from their daily work in order to follow him (Matt. 4:18–22) and told his followers not to worry about getting food and clothes (Matt. 6:25–34). But no serious commentator takes these words at face value, nor would Jesus' first hearers have done so. Part of the historical context is that Jesus and his hearers and followers grew up with the Hebrew scriptures as their guide. These resoundingly affirm the value of daily work (Gen. 1:26–28; 2:15; Exod. 20:9; Prov. 6:6–11). This canonical context helps us to understand that in John 6:27 Jesus is not speaking literally; he is using a rhetorical device involving a vivid contrast, by which he conveys that there is something vastly more important even than the essential and valued task of working for our daily needs, which is to yield all loyalty to him, because he is the life-giving bread of God. This is confirmed when we see that Jesus' followers did not understand him to have contradicted the importance of work to provide for daily needs (1 Thess. 4:11; 2 Thess. 3:10).

I cannot emphasize too strongly the importance of the impact that context (including the historical and cultural context of biblical thought) has upon meaning, *however plain the words*. This is vital in order to understand the meaning which the writer or speaker intends to convey. Over and over again in this book we find interpretations that are unsatisfactory because they do not take proper account of context.

6. Spiritual openness

Hearing new ideas can be a pleasure (Acts 17:21). But being challenged to accept them is a different matter (17:30–32). We prefer to have our existing views confirmed. While writing this book I have had to adjust my views repeatedly. The fact that you are reading this book suggests that you may be willing to consider adjusting yours also.

Paul tells us that, for understanding God's purposes, natural abilities are not sufficient. Spiritual discernment is needed. The source of human understanding of God's ways is God's Spirit (1 Cor. 2:9–16). For Christian leaders and teachers it is an immensely challenging task, even with the utmost effort and prayerfulness, to look with fresh eyes and an open mind at a topic on which they have spent much labour. This applies all the more when they have defended a particular position in public.

There can be deep emotional obstacles to open listening, not least in the present debate. On the egalitarian side, there are many who are passionately committed to equality as a concept. They believe in it with all their hearts, and are instinctively hostile to anything that seems to threaten it. The result can be to give it precedence over the teaching of Scripture. If this distortion is to be overcome, it needs to be brought into the open and realistically acknowledged. On the complementarian side, there is a widespread feeling that historic doctrines and Scripture itself are under attack, so not an inch must be conceded. But those who hold a complementarian position need to come to terms with the fact that there are evangelical egalitarians who in truth disagree because of their commitment to Scripture. I have said more about this in chapter 16.

Above all, we need to keep coming back to the text of the Bible with humility, recognizing that we always have more to learn.

7. Practical wisdom

Appreciation of the other side's point of view is made much more difficult when they deploy weak arguments. Because of their firm belief in their own position, they tend to underestimate the weakness of their poorer arguments. Accordingly, they overlook the negative impact of those arguments, which is to make it hard for the opposite side to hear their better points.

A judge needs to be on the alert when what is served up for consideration is unpersuasive. The fact that someone presents poor arguments does not show that they are in the wrong. Their position may be justified by good reasons which they have not thought of, or which have become obscured among the dross. In the same way, when wrestling with the interpretation of Scripture we must not let the weakness of scholars' poorer arguments distract us from seeing the force of their stronger ones.

Application

Once we have ascertained the meaning of the text, the next step is to consider how it applies to us in our culture and situation, which differ from the culture and situation of the first readers. When we read Paul's instruction that husbands are to love their wives (Eph. 5:25), we infer directly that all Christian husbands should follow this; but when we read his advice to Timothy to take a little wine because of his frequent gastric problems (1 Tim. 5:23), we do not infer that every Christian is under obligation to drink wine for medicinal purposes or whenever the water supply is contaminated. Instead we might conclude that the advice to Timothy illustrates a sound principle that he should use available means to take care of his health in order to facilitate his ministry.

Much has been written on the important question of how one moves from interpretation to application. But the approach to application adopted by

Grudem on one side of the debate is substantially the same as that adopted by Payne on the other. So it has not been necessary to examine this in detail.

I should add that I am not persuaded by those who say that the Bible contradicts itself, or that we need to follow a 'trajectory' that moves decisively beyond it. Nor am I persuaded that the very idea of narrative, poetry and occasional letters being authoritative is incoherent. This is not the place to enter into those debates. It is sufficient to say that Scripture is God's word for us to hear and faithfully to perform. Faithful understanding requires that we keep in mind where we stand in the story, after the resurrection of Christ and the gift of the Spirit at Pentecost, and looking forward to the grand finale that is to come.

Feeling the impact of culture: a thought experiment

In order to illustrate the above discussion concerning the impact of culture on interpretation, I lay out below a thought experiment which shows how easy it is to read Scripture in a way that fits existing cultural expectations. For readers who are not familiar with the debates over the disputed passages, this may make more sense after reading chapters 2 to 15.

Imagine a fictional *female-dominated* world, whose scriptures are uncannily similar to the real thing. The standard understanding that women should always be in charge has come under challenge. You are a woman holding a prominent leadership and teaching position. You have been asked to speak in defence of what everyone should know to be true, that women are the leaders, men merely their junior assistants. Here is your list of points for your presentation:

Genesis 1 – 2: the creation order
Creation is in ascending order of importance, with humans last, and woman last of all (1:3–27; 2:7–23).

The man needs a stronger helper because of his inadequacy (2:18, 20). At marriage he leaves the protection of his father and mother in order to come under the protection of his wife (2:24).

Genesis 3: the fall
The serpent's strategy is to attack the leader, knowing that the man will follow her (v. 1).

After the fall the man, the woman and the serpent are spoken to in ascending order of responsibility (vv. 9–14) and cursed in descending order (vv. 14–19).

The tragic consequence of the fall is to reverse the natural order; the woman's leadership is taken away from her and she is ruled by the man (3:16).

Proverbs 31:10–31
Here is the ideal. The wife is leader and ruler of the family, the sole breadwinner, who provides for her husband and children (vv. 11–25). She is a wise teacher (v. 26). Her husband acknowledges her complete superiority (vv. 28–29), and her accomplishments are recognized by society at large (v. 31).

Prominent women in the early churches
While it took time for women's leadership to be fully restored, already we see examples of a woman who was the host of a church, and therefore in authority over it (Col. 4:15), and of a woman who had to correct a male preacher's defective understanding (Acts 18:24–28 – doubtless her husband helped her to gain insight into the foolishness of men, whether wittingly or unwittingly).

1 Corinthians 11:2–16
A woman ought to have authority over her head (v. 10). Her 'head' is her husband (v. 3).

Ephesians 5
Within the mutual submission of husband and wife (v. 21), the husband's place is lower. He is to serve his wife like a lowly bath attendant (v. 26).

1 Peter 2 – 3
The husband must honour his wife in the same way that he honours the emperor (2:17; 3:7).

1 Timothy 2
There is a crisis of false teaching (1:3). A woman must be allowed to learn in quietness, so that she can go on to teach other women who have been led astray (2:9–11). In this crisis she is not allowed to be distracted by the never-ending task of teaching and exercising authority over a man (2:12). This is emphasized by reference to the order of creation and the woman's position as leader in the story of the creation and fall; the man was so weak that he sinned without even being deceived (2:13–14).

Thus every relevant passage proves that women should be the leaders, and men should be under their authority and protection.

APPENDIX 2 (CHAPTER 4)
ADDITIONAL ARGUMENTS DEPLOYED AGAINST MUTUAL
SUBMISSION

Is Ephesians 5:21 speaking of mutual submission? In chapter 4 we considered and rejected the minority view that Paul envisages submission as being required only of the junior partner in hierarchical relationships. This appendix looks at four further arguments which are deployed against mutual submission.

1. It is said that Paul's call for wives to submit to their husbands indicates one-way-only submission, because he does not repeat the same words in regard to husbands.[1]

This is faulty logic, as can be seen by comparing the general command to submit (v. 21) with the general command to love (vv. 1–2; see also Col. 3:14). Paul's specific instruction to husbands in verse 25 'love your wives' does not imply that wives are exempt from the general command to love, for the command to love in verses 1–2 is addressed to all believers.[2] In the same way, Paul's specific instruction to wives in verse 22 '[submit] to your husbands' does not imply that husbands are exempt from the general command to submit which is found in verse 21, and which is addressed to all believers, like all the previous commands in the same sentence ('And do not become drunk with wine . . . but

---

1. *EFBT*, 191.

2. See also Titus 2:4, where Paul says wives should be 'husband-loving' (*philandros*).

be filled by the Spirit, . . . speaking to one another with psalms, hymns and spiritual songs, singing and making melody in your hearts . . . , giving thanks always').

Of course it is right to say that Paul does not explicitly write in Ephesians 5 that husbands should submit to their own wives. But he does not need to. If husbands are behaving in the way so graphically laid out in verses 25–30, they will also be following the instruction of verse 21 and ranking their wives as more important than themselves. And he has already taught mutual submission of husband and wife in 1 Corinthians 7:3–5, which he wrote while he was ministering in Ephesus (1 Cor. 16:8).

2. It is said that the wife's submission and the husband's loving rule are a restoration of the proper relation of headship before the fall.[3]

This is a mis-step. We consider Genesis 2 in chapter 5. Here we need only notice that this concept of headship as meaning unilateral authority of husband over wife in Christian marriage is in direct conflict with 1 Corinthians 7:3–5, where, as we have seen, Paul indicates that each partner has the same authority.

3. A further argument is that, if Paul had intended his readers to understand husband and wife as under an obligation of mutual submission, this would have been so revolutionary and unexpected that he would have had to make this clear also on the other occasions when he writes about marriage. He writes about wives' submission in Colossians 3:18 and Titus 2:5, and in those contexts it would be understood as one-way only because he does not there mention mutual submission.[4]

This argument is unpersuasive. As we saw in chapter 3, the letters which Paul wrote during his imprisonment were intended for circulation from church to church, so the Ephesian letter would be heard by others also. Tychicus was the bearer of both Colossians and Ephesians. We may be confident that he understood Paul's teaching and appreciated the significance for all, including husbands and wives, of the theme of humility in Colossians 3:12–17, as well as Ephesians 5. He would be expected faithfully to reflect Paul's teaching when explaining the letters to the recipients. In addition, from Colossians 1:7 and 4:7 (with 1:1) Paul makes clear that he, Timothy, Epaphras and Tychicus were to be regarded as 'fellow slaves'. If Paul and his colleagues were not exempt from the obligation to imitate Christ by serving others as slaves, the Colossians certainly

---

3. *EFBT*, 40–41, referring to Col. 3:18–19.

4. *EFBT*, 191, 198–199. It is also said that the same point applies to 1 Pet. 3:1.
   Peter's letter is considered in chapter 6.

had no reason to see Colossians 3:18 as implying that husbands were exempt from treating their wives as if they ranked above themselves.

It is correct that in Titus 2:5 Paul refers to the submission of wife to husband without giving any explicit instructions for husbands. But this letter was written to a long-time co-worker (Gal. 2:1; 2 Cor. 2:13; 8:23; Titus 1:4), who would have been closely aware of Paul's teaching on points not spelled out in the letter.[5]

In sum, Paul would not expect his remarks in Colossians or in his letter to Titus to be misunderstood as teaching one-way-only submission.

4. Although Paul writes in Ephesians 5:21 of submitting to one another (*allēlōn*), Grudem and O'Brien say that it is only some who are lower in a hierarchy (wives, children, slaves) who are required to submit to others who are higher in the relevant hierarchy (husbands, parents, masters). They point to the use of *allēlōn* in other instances, such as Revelation 6:4, where it is used of people killing each other. They say this illustrates that it need only mean that *some* do the stated action to *others*. So also in Ephesians 5 they say this sense of 'some to others' is to be preferred to the 'fully reciprocal' and 'always symmetrical' sense of 'each to each in the same way and at the same time'. Grudem adds to this that in verse 22 Paul does not tell wives to be subject to other people's husbands but only to their own (*idios*) husbands.[6]

But this reasoning is not satisfactory. No-one would say that the often-repeated command to love one another (*allēlōn*) means only that some should love others. Slavery is inherently a one-way relationship, but we would never say that, when Paul tells believers to be slaves of one another (*allēlōn*), he means only that some should serve as slaves of others (Gal. 5:13). In Revelation 6:4, if John had only envisaged men killing others but not themselves being killed, he would not have used the expression 'each other'.[7] There is no example anywhere in English versions of the Bible where *allēlōn* is translated 'some to others'.

In his letter to the Ephesians, when Paul writes that his readers should bear with one another (*allēlōn*) in love (4:2), this applies to all his readers. When he tells them to speak the truth because they are members of one another (*allēlōn*) (4:25), this applies to all. When he instructs them to be kind to one another (*allēlōn*) (4:32), this applies to all. His instructions in 5:1–20 apply to all. The only

---

5. For further evidence about Titus from outside the New Testament, see Mosse 2007, 180. Note also that Titus may have been the bearer of 1 Corinthians, and therefore responsible for explaining 1 Corinthians 7: see Mosse 2007, 298, 304–308.

6. *EFBT*, 190, 196–198; *RBMW*, 172–173 (Grudem); O'Brien 1999, 401–404.

7. *Mc&W*, 280.

reason for the proposal that *allēlōn* should be understood in 5:21 in the unusual sense 'some to others', so that verse 21 is not addressed to all readers, is to make that verse fit into a hierarchical view in which wives are under the unilateral authority of their husbands. But that is not Paul's view, as we have seen.

The extreme 'always symmetrical' meaning ('each to each in the same way and at the same time') is a straw man. Those who accept that mutual submission applies within marriage, who include not only egalitarians but also complementarians such as Piper and Stott, do not put forward this extreme meaning. When Paul says: 'bear one another's [*allēlōn*] burdens' (Gal. 6:2), this is a general obligation upon all, to be fulfilled in a way appropriate to the circumstances; it does not imply that each person must bear burdens in precisely the same way at precisely the same time. The same is true of mutual submission. The ways in which people behave, each with humility towards the other, will vary according to circumstances.[8] Being submissive, in the biblical sense of ranking others as more important than oneself, is an attitude that is adopted, not a fixed set of behaviours. When husband and wife each rank the other as more important than themselves, that does not mean that they will behave in identical ways. They will each bring their own contribution to the marriage, a contribution shaped by their gifts and abilities.

Grudem's additional argument that in verse 22 Paul does not tell wives to be subject to other people's husbands, but only to their own (*idios*) husbands, does not assist his attempt to limit verse 21. Verse 22 uses the words *gunē* and *anēr*. These words primarily mean respectively 'woman' and 'man', but are also used for wife and husband. In the latter event the meaning is made clear by adding a verbal clue.[9] Paul's use of *idios* here is sufficiently explained as giving this clue (*tois idiois andrasin* = 'to the own men' = 'to their husbands').[10] It indicates that in verse 22 Paul is writing about wives and husbands, not women and men generally. Its use does not limit verse 21 by implying that the husband is the *only* fellow believer whom a woman should rank as if above herself.

The command to submission in verse 21 is general. To say that a woman's submission is only to her own husband would be as misguided as saying that 'husbands, love your wives' (v. 25) implies that the only person whom a husband should unselfishly love is his wife, despite the entirely general command in 5:1–2.

---

8. Smith 2012, 146, correctly observes: 'Both inside and outside the Bible, submission is not identically reciprocal, requiring the same response from one to the other.'

9. This is explained more fully in chapter 7, 138.

10. O'Brien 1999, 411, n. 201, confirms that *idios* functions as a possessive.

APPENDIX 3 (CHAPTER 13)
USES OF *AUTHENTEŌ* IN OTHER WRITINGS

The meaning of the word *authenteō* in 1 Timothy 2:12 has been much debated. There is a wide range of different proposals.[1]

This word is not used elsewhere in Scripture, but its use can be seen in other texts. After examination of these texts, complementarian scholars propose the meaning 'exercise authority' or something similar. On the other side of the argument, Payne concludes that there is no established example of *authenteō* as meaning 'exercise authority' from before the time of Paul to three hundred years after.

Scholars have diligently searched for all uses of the verb *authenteō* in surviving ancient writings. Al Wolters lists eight definite or possible uses from the mid-first century BC until Constantine's recognition of Christianity as a lawful religion in 312. Several of these examples depend upon conjectural emendations of obscure or damaged texts, or are otherwise unclear. Wolters fairly points out that the small number of examples close to Paul's time provides a rather slim basis on which to establish the meaning of the verb in 1 Timothy 2:12.[2] This is indeed a problem for the approach taken by a number of scholars, which has

---

1. See *EFBT*, 304–322; *M&W*, 361–380 (Payne); *DBE*, 209–219 (Belleville); *WITC*, 65–115 (Wolters), 194–197 (Schreiner), 279–296 (Burk).
2. *WITC*, 83.

been essentially to select a meaning for the word, and then try to shoehorn the passage into an interpretation that is consistent with the selected meaning, leading different scholars to conflicting interpretations of verse 12. Given the very small number of examples from Paul's time and the sharply conflicting views among scholars over the meaning of *authenteō* both in verse 12 and in the other texts, a more satisfactory procedure, leading to a firmer conclusion, is the procedure we have followed in chapters 12 and 13, namely, to derive the likely meaning first from the context, and then check, by looking at other uses, that the apparent contextual meaning is within the range of possible meanings.

Based on Wolters' discussion in *WITC*, the eight uses can be summarized as follows:

1. Philodemus, *De Rhetorica* 2.133 – The fragment is damaged and it is unclear whether *authenteō* is used at all.
2. Papyrus BGU 1208.38 – This letter certainly uses the word *authenteō*, but the meaning in context is the subject of vigorous dispute. Payne's interpretation and Wolters' interpretation are so different one would hardly know that the same text was under consideration.
3. *Methodus mystica* (*Codicum Parisinorum*) – This is part of an astrological treatise. The meaning is disputed, but does not appear to be 'exercise authority'.[3]
4. Aristonicus Alexandrinus, *On the Signs of the Iliad* 1.694 – The meaning is 'be the originator of'.
5. Ptolemy, *Tetrabiblos* 3.13.10 – The relevant passage is reproduced in chapter 12 (256). Wolters' translation is 'gained mastery'.[4] In this example the word *authenteō* is used grammatically in the same way as in 1 Timothy 2:12 (namely, with a genitive of a person, understanding that a planet is spoken of as if it were a person).
6. Moeris Atticista, *Lexicon Atticum* entry for *autodikēn* – Wolters' translation is 'act on one's own'.
7. Papyrus *P. Tebt.* 276.28 – The text is damaged and therefore unclear.
8. Scholion on Aeschylus, *Eumenides* 42 – The meaning here is 'murder'. Whether this text is really from before 312 is disputed.

---

3. This example uses the same grammatical construction with the genitive of the person as in 1 Tim. 2:12. Depending on how one interprets the text, the expression could seemingly mean 'has full command of' or 'is superior to'. See *WITC*, 76; *EFBT*, 702.

4. Belleville cites a somewhat similar additional example from the astrologer Dorotheus, which she translates with the word 'dominant': *DBE*, 215.

As can be seen, among these eight possible or actual examples, there is not one that is a clear and undisputed use of *authenteō* in the sense 'exercise authority'.

In chapter 13, consideration of the context suggested the meaning 'overpower' for *authenteō*. Is 'overpower' within the range of possible meanings of that word? Because of the example from *Tetrabiblos*, it is plain that this question may be answered affirmatively. Moreover, this particular example uses the same grammatical construction as in 1 Timothy 2:12.

From what we saw in chapters 12 and 13, we can go further. Given the context, the nature of Paul's reasoning, his multiple allusions to the language of astrology and his desire that the activity described by *authenteō* should not take place, it can be stated with reasonable confidence that he had a meaning along these lines in mind.

It is of interest to note that over three hundred years later Chrysostom was aware of, and used, a similar negative meaning of *authenteō*. Despite his firm view that all leadership authority resided in men, in Homily 10 on Colossians 3:18–25, referring to verse 19, he warned husbands not to *authent* their wives. There is no possibility that Chrysostom here intended either the sense 'exercise authority over' or the sense 'assume authority over'. He is expounding Paul's warning to husbands not to act harshly towards their wives. The context therefore indicates that he intends a negative meaning akin to 'overpower' or 'dominate'.[5]

Complementarians argue that the meaning of *authenteō* in *Tetrabiblos* as 'gain mastery' or 'dominate' should be understood as neutral rather than negative.[6] Taking into account the longer context of the relevant passage in *Tetrabiblos*, it is open to argument whether Ptolemy, or whichever earlier astrologer he is drawing from, would have said, if asked, that he was using the word positively, negatively, neutrally, or in a way in which those categories overlap. The astrologers' concern is with the supposed influence of the heavenly bodies, not whether that influence is morally right or wrong. Some effects are said to be beneficent, and others maleficent, but these value judgments do not correspond

---

5. Chrysostom says: 'Do not therefore, because thy wife is subject to thee, act the despot.' See further *M&W*, 381–382. In *WITC*, 100–101, Wolters strenuously tries to save the verb from its negative connotation in this use by Chrysostom and suggests the meaning 'act on one's own', but he yields to the context and fairly acknowledges: 'it would be an example of being harsh. . . . It clearly describes a behavior on the husband's part that Chrysostom forbids.' In current English we could render the meaning suggested by Wolters as 'act autocratically over her'.

6. *WITC*, 78; *EFBT*, 307–308.

with what a follower of Jesus Christ would regard as good or bad. From a Christian point of view the influence described in the passage in question would be harmful. If Saturn really compelled people to be dictatorial, avaricious, and so on, that would undoubtedly be a negative exercise of force, from Paul's point of view.[7]

Al Wolters and Denny Burk refer also to secondary evidence from early translations into Latin and other languages. It is right to consider this further evidence.

Evidence from early versions does not rule out the contextual meaning identified above. For example, the Vulgate translates our word into Latin as *dominari* ('rule', 'dominate'), which can be used positively, neutrally or with a negative connotation, as Wolters acknowledges. The Peshitta (in Syriac) translates *authenteō* with a word that means something like 'lord it over'; this is close to the astrological meaning of 'overpower', 'dominate' or 'gain mastery'.[8]

---

7. Note also Westfall 2014. She argues that a 'basic semantic concept' that accounts for the occurrences of *authenteō* is 'the autonomous use or possession of unrestricted force'. The idea of a word having a single basic semantic concept, as distinguished from a primary (in the sense of most common) meaning, is controversial. Wolters provides some cautionary comments concerning her analytical methodology at *WITC*, 114–115. But the general thrust of her examination of possible meanings does not prevent the meaning 'overpower' in 1 Tim. 2:12, and tends to support it.

8. *WITC*, 84–86 (Wolters proposes a conjectural emendation of the available text of the Peshitta which would remove the negative connotation); *WITC*, 283 (Burk misses Wolters' fair acknowledgment that *dominari* can be used negatively); Bailey 2000, 9. The date of the Peshitta is uncertain. It is variously ascribed to the first to fifth centuries.

APPENDIX 4 (CHAPTER 13)
THE STRUCTURE OF 1 TIMOTHY 2:12

The scholarly discussions

The structure of 1 Timothy 2:12 has generated a substantial scholarly literature. There are potentially at least three ways of reading it. Stating them in order from the narrowest to the widest, the subject matter of Paul's restriction could be:

1. not to teach and (in combination with this) not to *authent* a man;
2. not to teach a man, and also not to *authent* a man;
3. not to teach at all, and also not to *authent* a man.

Analysis 1 sees the two elements as referring to one activity. Analyses 2 and 3 each envisage two separate activities, but the first activity is not the same in each: analysis 2 contains a ban on a woman teaching a man, while analysis 3 contains a complete ban on any teaching by a woman.

The restriction, whatever it is, is contrasted with what is permitted in verse 12, namely, 'but to be in quietness'.

As between analysis 2 and analysis 3, the grammar of the sentence is not decisive. The words for 'to teach' and 'to *authent*' are infinitives (*didaskein*, *authentein*). In Greek, if I teach someone, the word for 'someone' is in the accusative case, which is shown by the form of the word. But if I *authent* someone, the word for 'someone' can be in the genitive case (shown by another word form). In verse 12 the word for 'man' is in the genitive case, which would suggest that it is linked only to *authentein* and not to *didaskein*, and this would favour analysis 3 over analysis 2. But some grammarians say that in Greek a noun governed by two verbs takes the case appropriate to the verb that is closer to it.[1] Even if this is not a recognized exception, writers with a good command of a language occasionally choose to break the ordinary rules of grammar.[2] So grammar alone cannot decide between analysis 3 and analysis 2. On analysis 1 this grammatical question does not arise because only a single activity is in view.

Payne's thesis

Payne argues for analysis 1. The restriction of permission stated by Paul is in the form 'not A and not B but C'. The Greek particles or conjunctions are *ouk* A *oude* B *alla* C, where *ouk* means 'not', *oude* means 'and not', and *alla* means 'but'. The usage of this kind of syntax is discussed at length by Payne. He says it demonstrates that Paul is joining two activities together (A and B) and contrasting them with something else (activity C). Payne's conclusion about the combining effect of the syntax is contested by complementarians.[3]

Köstenberger's thesis

Köstenberger argues, on grounds of grammar, for analysis 3.[4] But his principal interest is in a different question, which is whether the form of syntax consisting of 'not [*ouk*] A and not [*oude*] B' necessitates a particular relation between A and B. He has argued at length, from usage in the New Testament and elsewhere, that A and B must be, in the writer's consideration, either both positive or both negative. He has characterized this conclusion as an 'assured result of biblical scholarship'. His thesis has been widely adopted not only by fellow complementarians but also by some scholars who disagree with the complementarian interpretation of 1 Timothy 2.[5]

---

1. See Moo 1981, 202; *WITC*, 191 (Schreiner). Payne cites a contrary view: *M&W*, 354–355.

2. Because this happens, it has a technical name (anacoluthon). This term also applies if it is done accidentally, rather than deliberately.

3. *M&W*, 337–356; Payne 2014. For disagreement see, for example, Köstenberger in *WITC*, 145–152.

4. *WITC*, 121–122, n. 11.

5. Köstenberger's thesis is argued in *WITC*, 118–145. He states it as an absolute rule: 'it *mandates* that the two activities [in v. 12] *must* be, in Paul's consideration, either both positive or both negative' (121; emphasis added). The reference for the

Assessments

When evaluating the significance of studies of syntax and of usages elsewhere, it is necessary to keep in mind that, unless one is dealing with a precise technical term, these show interpretive possibilities that *could be* in the passage under consideration, not what *is* in the passage under consideration. The reasoning in the scholarly discussions of the structure of verse 12 does not pay sufficient attention to this limitation.

The phrase 'assured result of biblical scholarship' has a chequered history. It brings to mind the many assured results of scholarship published in the nineteenth and twentieth centuries by liberal scholars, which were in reality of no value because they depended on faulty presuppositions. Unfortunately, there is a corresponding defect in Köstenberger's thesis. While his survey is useful work, the idea that there could be an inflexible rule such as he puts forward cannot be supported. The other distinguished scholars who have accepted his thesis have lost sight of the bigger picture. In European languages simple words like 'not' and 'nor' do not function within a straitjacket of narrowly defined rules of this kind.[6]

Let us suppose that I am a first-century Christian historian writing in the Greek language about a military campaign. The winners defeat a foreign army and seize all their supplies. I continue: 'After the battle the foreign warriors who remained alive were not [*ouk*][7] cared for nor [*oude*] were they slaughtered.' According to Köstenberger's thesis, I must necessarily regard merciful care and merciless slaughter both positively or both negatively. As a Christian, I do not. To me, care is positive, slaughter negative. There is no obstacle to expressing this sentence in Greek, and Köstenberger's thesis cannot prevent it from meaning what I intend by it.

The thesis has a second fundamental defect. The syntax in verse 12 is not merely 'not A and not B'; it has the further element 'but C'. From its very nature,

---

(note 5 *cont.*) description as an 'assured result' is provided in *Me&W*, 356, and *WITC*, 282 (Burk). For examples of its adoption, see *EFBT*, 314–316; *WITC*, 198 (Schreiner), 282 (Burk) (complementarians); and *WITC*, 199, n. 164 (reference to Marshall); Padgett 1997, 25; Giles 2000, 153 (egalitarians). But Payne and Belleville disagree with the thesis: *Me&W*, 356–358; *DBE*, 217–218.

6. I qualify this statement as referring only to European languages because I am ignorant of any other languages.

7. This word would not necessarily be written as *ouk*; it could be written alternatively as *ou* or *ouch*, depending on what Greek word follows it.

the principal purpose of a construction in the form 'not A and not B but C' is to contrast both A and B with C.

For example, in 2 Corinthians 7:12 Paul writes: 'Therefore if indeed I wrote to you, it was not [*ouch*] because of the one who did the wrong nor [*oude*] because of the one who was wronged, but [*alla*] in order that your earnestness for us might be revealed to you before God.' Here, two possible reasons why Paul could have written are dismissed, and are contrasted with the actual reason. Paul's point is not whether the first two reasons for writing would have been positive or negative reasons, but that the actual reason was different from both of them.[8]

In my illustration above, I could have written: 'After the battle the foreign warriors who remained alive were not [*ouk*] cared for nor [*oude*] slaughtered but [*alla*] left to fend for themselves.' The contrast would be between two things that did not happen and what actually happened. The existence of the contrast highlights what happened, but the construction does not of itself tell the reader whether A and B are regarded by the writer as both positive, both negative, both neutral or some mixture of these. This depends upon what meaning I intended in the particular context. A different writer, with different values from mine, might have regarded the things which did not happen (care for or slaughter of the remaining warriors) as honourable, and what did happen (ignoring them) as dishonourable. The mere fact that *ouk* and *oude* have been used is of no help for determining the writer's view of the activities.

For these two reasons Köstenberger's thesis concerning syntax constructed with *ouk* and *oude* is misconceived.[9]

The question whether, *in the context*, Paul regarded *didaskein* and/or *authentein* as positive or negative in verse 12 could not be simpler. Paul does not want these things to be done. In Paul's consideration they are both negative in the context that he is concerned with. The extent to which he may regard these activities positively, neutrally or negatively in other contexts is neither here nor there.[10]

---

8. Köstenberger misses the significance of the contrast of A and B with C: *WITC*, 122, n. 13.
9. These fundamental points make it unnecessary to lay out in detail the numerous errors of reasoning in *WITC*, 122–135, which include the artificial and arbitrary nature of the inquiry (122, 124), the instability of the thesis even within the argument (122–123, 125), the drawing of conclusions which do not follow from their premises (130, 133, 134, 135) and the insufficient attention to context (131–135).
10. *M&W*, 358: 'What 1 Tim. 2:12 prohibits, it must regard as negative.'

Köstenberger resists the negative conclusion by constructing a rule that the word for teach is positive unless the context contains a negative qualifier, and reasoning that there is no such qualifier in the context of verse 12.[11] But this rule is artificial. The true rule is simply that meaning depends upon context. Paul's phrase 'I do not permit' makes it unmistakable that the restricted activities are viewed negatively by him.[12]

Payne's thesis is more measured than Köstenberger's, but it does not provide firm support for his interpretation. His thesis is that the overwhelming majority of the uses of *oude* and of the 'not A and not B but C' syntactical construction in the undisputed letters of Paul combine two elements to express a single idea. He usefully shows instances of Paul using the construction 'not A and not B but C', where B means much the same as A or makes it more specific, and both A and B contrast with C (Rom. 2:28; 1 Cor. 2:6–7; Gal. 1:1, 11–12, 16–17; 4:14; Phil. 2:16–17; 1 Thess. 2:3–4). He concludes that to interpret *oude* in verse 12 as separating two different restrictions on women does not conform to Paul's customary use of *oude*.[13]

This is fine as far as it goes, if 'customary' is understood in a qualified sense. But this syntactical argument proves nothing beyond the possibility of the combination meaning. Paul is free to use *oude* differently whenever he wants to. We saw above that in 2 Corinthians 7:12 he uses *oude* to join two contrasting ideas, as Payne fairly recognizes.[14] The relationship between *didaskein* and *authentein* in verse 12 cannot be determined by looking at uses of the word *oude*; it must be determined from considering all the words Paul uses in their full context.

---

11. *WITC*, 159.

12. Compare Matt. 5:19, where the one who teaches relaxation of the commandments will be called least in the kingdom of heaven. Such teaching is viewed negatively by Jesus. See also Titus 1:11. 'Teach' is not an inherently positive or negative concept. To teach truth is good. To teach error is bad. Note also that Paul's progression of thought in v. 12 (*not* to teach *and not* to overpower a man *but* to be in quietness) is not far different from his progression of thought on the same topic of false teaching in 1:3–4 (*not* to teach differently *and not* to pay attention to myths and endless genealogies which promote speculations *rather than* a stewardship of God in faith). The first two of these are viewed negatively, the last positively.

13. For discussion of examples, see *M&W*, 337–338. In some instances there are more than two elements preceding *alla*: 'not A nor B nor C but D'. His conclusion is in *M&W*, 348.

14. *M&W*, 350.

While Köstenberger contests Payne's 'combination' thesis, he demonstrates his intellectual integrity by fairly conceding that the restricted activities in verse 12 are clearly related and overlap to a degree. His analysis is helpful in bringing out a material difference between some of the contentions on each side of the debate. The egalitarian side tends to read the activities as proceeding from the general to the particular (with *didaskein* referring to teaching and *authentein* referring to teaching in a particular bad way);[15] the complementarian side tends to read the two activities as proceeding from the particular to the general (with *didaskein* referring to authoritative teaching and *authentein* meaning 'exercise authority'). Köstenberger acknowledges that the more usual order in such a construction is from the general to the particular, though he argues for the converse in this particular case.[16]

Conclusion

The scholarship concerning the structure of verse 12 does not provide an obstacle to the conclusions reached in chapters 12 and 13 by analysis of the context. The Greek syntax allows the meaning that Paul is not permitting any of the idle, wealthy women to teach, and, explaining his concern more particularly, he is not permitting any of these false teachers to overpower a man, as Eve did, so as to make him disobey God by participating in forbidden knowledge or living in accordance with false teaching. Instead, she must live a quiet and godly life, in full submission to God.

---

15. In Payne's 'combination' view, there is a single activity.

16. *WITC*, 152. To be clear, I do not mean that a 'not A and not B' construction must necessarily move from the general to the particular or vice versa; only that general-to-particular is a frequent usage and that particular-to-general is also one of a number of possible usages, albeit less frequent.

APPENDIX 5 (CHAPTER 13)
INTERPRETATIONS OF 1 TIMOTHY 2:15

In chapter 13 I have offered a Christ-centred interpretation of 1 Timothy 2:15 which follows straightforwardly from, and fits with, the interpretation that I have offered of verses 9–14.

Understanding 'the childbearing' in verse 15 as referring to the birth of the Messiah is not new. Although historically a minority view, it is possibly attested as early as Ignatius of Antioch (died about 107–110), whose native language was Greek. It may be the earliest interpretation.[1]

This appendix answers some objections and discusses competing interpretations.

In verse 15 Paul says: 'she will be saved through [*dia*] the childbearing.' When the preposition *dia* is followed (as here) by a noun in the genitive case, its primary meaning is 'through', in the sense 'by means of'. The Christ-centred interpretation takes it in this sense.[2]

---

1. Knight 1992, 146, refers to Ignatius, Irenaeus and Justin as holding this interpretation. Tradition holds that Ignatius was taught by the apostle John. Giles 2000, 163, refers additionally to Tertullian.
2. For other examples nearby, see 2:10; 4:5, 14.

Schreiner[3] fairly notes that in the history of the church it has often been understood that 'the childbearing' in verse 15 is a reference to the coming of Christ. This interpretation has been advocated in modern times by both egalitarians such as Payne and complementarians such as Knight.[4] Indeed, Schreiner describes the Christ-centred interpretation as 'immensely attractive'.

He raises five objections to it, but they are weak:

- *He says it is obscure.* Certainly it is obscure if Paul's subject in verses 11–14 is the maintenance of proper authority structures in the public assemblies of the church, where women are subordinated to male teachers, as Schreiner proposes. It is indeed hard to see it as connected to that topic. But the obscurity evaporates when we attend closely to the context and follow Paul's train of reasoning through; the whole chapter is concerned with living a saved life in contrast to living out false teachings.
- *It is arbitrary to slide from seeing the subject of 'will be saved' as Eve to seeing the subject as Mary.* But the Christ-centred interpretation does not do this. It is not specifically Mary's salvation that is in view.[5]
- *Paul does not say elsewhere that salvation comes through the incarnation.* But that is exactly what he does say in Galatians 4:4–5.
- *The noun* teknogonia *emphasizes the actual giving birth to a child, not the result or effect of childbirth; it would wrongly imply that salvation is secured as a result of giving birth to Jesus.* But why is this an objection? Salvation was indeed brought about by means of Mary giving birth to Jesus. The angel's message was: 'She will bear a son, and you shall call his name Jesus, for he will save his people from their sins' (Matt. 1:21, ESV).[6]

---

3. *WITC*, 216–224.

4. *M&W*, 417–441; Knight 1992, 144–149.

5. Schreiner compounds this error (219) by saying on 220 that he has eliminated the option that 'Eve or Mary' is the subject of 'will be saved'. Then on 221 he says that the singular verb is accounted for by the reference to Eve, as representing Christian women. So he acknowledges that Eve, as representing other women, is the implied subject of the verb.

6. The objection here may reflect a tendency, in some evangelical circles, to think about Christ's work of salvation in isolation from the incarnation, contrary to Gal. 4:4–5; John 1:9–18; and Heb. 2:9, 14–17.

- *The definite article cannot sustain the Christ-centred interpretation, as it is*
  'notoriously perplexing in Greek'. The use of the definite article is sometimes
  hard to understand, but it may be a useful pointer here,[7] and in any event
  its use is merely one factor. The Christ-centred interpretation principally
  depends not on the use of the definite article but on understanding
  Paul's words in their context.

What about the alternative interpretations of verse 15?

The first option that we identified in chapter 13 was a promise of physical
safety during the painful process of childbirth.[8]

But this interpretation is implausible. It sounds odd that present safety in
childbirth should depend on fulfilment of a future condition ('if they continue . . .'). And it would hardly be a fitting conclusion to this section of Paul's
argument, where he has been expounding how to combat false teaching
and promote a saved life of love and goodness, for him to veer off onto the
subject of physical safety during childbirth. More fundamentally, the New
Testament does not promise the believer a charmed life in which nothing
harmful ever happens. There is nothing else either in Scripture or in practical
experience which suggests that godly women will necessarily be kept safe
during childbirth. Many such women have died during or as a result of
childbirth.

The next alternative is that childbearing is an attendant circumstance
during which women will experience their spiritual salvation. This reads verse
15 as if Paul had written: 'But she will experience her salvation in the course
of childbearing, if they remain in faith and love and holiness, with self-
control.'[9]

But this is some way away from the actual words, including from the primary
meaning of *dia*. It is strained. It does not follow from the previous verses. Paul's
concern is that these women be saved through Christ (see 2:1–7, 10).

Others have said that Paul is referring to motherhood: a woman's task of
rearing children.

But that is not what he writes. Bearing children and rearing children are
not the same thing, and a doctrine that women are saved by rearing children

---

7. This is argued in persuasive detail by Payne in *M&W*, 429–431.
8. For references and discussion, see *WITC*, 217 (Schreiner).
9. This interpretation is argued by Moo in *RBMW*, 187. This and related
   interpretations are further discussed and rightly rejected in *M&W*, 425–429.
   It is also rejected by Schreiner in *WITC*, 220.

would conflict with the central New Testament message of salvation by grace through faith.[10]

Schreiner's own proposal is a refinement of the motherhood idea. He keeps in mind that *dia* (when followed by a genitive) most often denotes 'by means of', and he makes a valiant effort to interpret accordingly. He reasonably suggests that, since the false teachers banned marriage (4:3), they 'probably also criticized bearing children', and says Paul selected childbearing 'as a specific response to the shafts from false teachers'. On the supposition that Paul is using this part of a woman's role to represent the whole of a woman's role, Schreiner argues that women are saved by means of adhering to their ordained domestic role as mothers:

> His [Paul's] purpose is to say that women will not be saved if they do not practice good works. One indication that women are doing good works is if they do not reject bearing children as evil but bear children in accord with their proper role.[11]

Schreiner is right to see that what Paul writes should be understood by reference to the false teachings. He is also right to try to give *dia* its primary meaning. But his interpretation owes more to beliefs about motherhood than to Paul's actual words. Paul says nothing about childbearing standing for the whole of women's domestic role as mothers. Where would childless women fit in? And because this interpretation removes the Saviour from verse 15, it sits ill with the gospel of God's grace (1:15–16; 2:3–6; Eph. 2:8). Schreiner makes understandably heavy weather of trying to explain how his interpretation is consistent with the gospel. The idea that women are saved by means of bearing children is unparalleled anywhere else in the whole of the Bible.

The Christ-centred interpretation of verse 15 is to be preferred because it best fits the context and encounters no persuasive objection.

---

10. Schreiner provides references and rightly rejects this theory in *WITC*, 219–220. See further the detailed discussion of the meaning of *teknogonia* by Payne in *M&W*, 431–434.

11. *WITC*, 221–224. *EFBT*, 73 is to the same effect.

APPENDIX 6 (CHAPTER 13)
SHORTCOMINGS IN COMPLEMENTARIAN ANALYSES
OF 1 TIMOTHY 2

This appendix contains some additional criticisms of complementarian analyses of 1 Timothy 2. I begin with *WITC*, as representing a recent re-examination of the interpretive issues by a group of able complementarian scholars. I wish to say again that nothing I write here is intended as a personal criticism. The mindset with which the contributors have approached the issues, as eloquently described by Schreiner, should attract only praise.[1] My criticisms are of the reasoning.

Chapter 1, by Steve Baugh, is about Ephesus in the first century. It has the express purpose of highlighting points that illuminate the historical background of 1 Timothy 2, in order to assist with a correct understanding of it. After surveying what is known about some aspects of first-century Ephesian life from inscriptions and other historical evidence, Baugh's summary is that Ephesus was in most ways a typical, generally patriarchal, Hellenic society, which preserved its Greek roots in its political and cultural institutions. This conclusion disposes of theories that women were widely dominant in Ephesian culture.[2]

However, the chapter falls short of its expressed purpose, for Baugh tells us little about Ephesian beliefs, other than that the Ephesians worshipped Artemis

---

1. *WITC*, 164.

2. But see the correctives on matters of detail in *DBE*, 219–221 (Belleville).

and were polytheists. His section on childbirth does not mention the belief that Artemis was the protector of women in childbirth. He does not reveal her links with astrology and magic. He says nothing about the likely contents of the books of magic that were burned in Ephesus (Acts 19:18–19). He passes over in silence the pagan mysteries which, for Timothy and other readers in Ephesus, stand in contrast with the mysteries of the true faith and of godliness (1 Tim. 3:9, 16). We are left without any information that might help us have a better understanding of the false teachings which Paul mentions in the letter.

WITC editor Andreas Köstenberger rightly observes in a 1994 article on methodology: 'a general reconstruction of the Ephesian milieu in the first century must not be used indiscriminately in one's reconstruction of the circumstances prevailing in the Ephesian church that occasioned the writing of 1 Timothy.'[3] Based on the finding that Ephesus was in most ways a typical Hellenic society, and without giving any consideration to 1 Timothy 1:1 – 2:8, Baugh concludes that Paul's injunctions throughout 2:9–15 are not temporary measures in a unique social setting but are reminders to the wealthy women not to step outside their divinely ordered role in the new covenant community. This is an unwarranted leap. Baugh does not say how his conclusion about Paul's intent can be derived from his general survey of the political and cultural institutions of the city, without any consideration of the context that Paul himself provides in his letter.[4]

Chapter 2, by Al Wolters, considers the meaning of *authenteō*. His thesis is that in 1 Timothy 2:12 *authenteō* means 'exercise authority'. In support of this, he looks at usage elsewhere, similar words, ancient versions and patristic commentary. But, as Köstenberger rightly notes in his 1994 article, word studies of *authenteō* can only supply 'a range of possible meanings'.[5] And as Moo says: 'good exegesis always takes into consideration the larger context in which a text appears.'[6] Wolters does not look at the larger context. His attention to context is limited to the use of *didaskō* (teach) in the same verse and a reliance on Köstenberger's flawed thesis about the two verbs in the verse both being positive because the conjunction between them is 'and not' (*oude*).[7] The idea that the meaning of a rare and disputed verb in a sentence can be confidently

---

3. Köstenberger 1994, 272.

4. *WITC*, 60, 64.

5. Köstenberger 1994, 265.

6. *RBMW*, 177.

7. *WITC*, 65–66, 113, 83–84, respectively. On Köstenberger's flawed thesis, see appendix 4.

determined by attending to two other words in that sentence, without considering the whole train of reasoning of which the sentence forms part, cannot be defended.

Köstenberger rightly insists in his 1994 article that the process of interpretation should include reconstruction of the historical and cultural background, a survey of the passage's literary context and attention to the flow of the argument.[8] Perhaps because of the structure of the book, in chapter 3 his syntactical examination of verse 12 and his discourse analysis of verses 8–15 pay scant attention to any of these. He dismisses the relevance of the historical and cultural background. His analysis does not acknowledge that Paul expressly states in 1 Timothy 1 what his concern is, namely, combating false teaching and promoting a saved life of love and goodness; nor does it notice that Paul explicitly connects what he writes in 1 Timothy 2 to that concern by starting with 'therefore' (2:1, repeated in 2:8). Attention to context and to the flow of the argument only begins substantially at 2:8, largely ignoring 1:1 – 2:7. Paul's stated concern therefore plays no role in Köstenberger's analysis of verses 8–15. Having ignored the false teaching in his analysis, in his conclusion he summarily dismisses its relevance for understanding Paul's train of thought. These flawed steps enable him to conclude that Paul's concern is not as Paul has stated but is for upholding a proper authority structure.[9]

Chapter 4, by Tom Schreiner, is the heart of the book. Over some sixty-three pages he offers a detailed and comprehensive interpretation of verses 9–15. (I will here include page references.)

He correctly notes:

- Paul's concern in 1 Timothy 1 is to respond to false teaching, and the word 'therefore' in 2:1 and in 2:8 connects Paul's remarks in chapter 2 with this topic (174).
- The appointments of elders and deacons discussed in 3:1–13 are for the purpose of making the church a bulwark against false teaching, as 3:14–15 indicates (179).
- Paul immediately returns to the threat of false teaching and the need to resist it in chapter 4 (179).

One might conclude from these uncontroversial remarks that 2:8–15 is concerned with the topic of resisting false teaching. However, the false teaching

8. Köstenberger 1994, 263.
9. *WITC*, 117–118, 152–161, 159, n. 85.

plays no role in Schreiner's interpretation of verses 9–14 (176–216). He expounds those verses on the only basis which enables him to support the complementarian ban on authoritative teaching by women, namely, by arguing against the relevance of what Paul says he is writing about (205–206, 210–212). But Schreiner then brings Paul's concern about false teaching back in for the purpose of trying to explain 2:15 (221). This inconsistent procedure must lead any dispassionate reader to doubt his exposition.

Chapter 5, by Robert Yarbrough, summarizes a wide range of views on 1 Timothy 2, but does not engage directly with Paul's reasoning.

In chapter 6 Denny Burk surveys English versions of verse 12. His survey omits to mention the ASV's rendering 'have dominion over'. He accepts the views of Wolters and Köstenberger, briefly discusses the grammar of the verse, and concludes in favour of 'exercise authority' or 'have authority'. He can gain comfort from the fact that at least one prominent egalitarian scholar nearly agrees with this meaning, but Burk arrives at his conclusion without any consideration of how this meaning might or might not fit into Paul's train of reasoning in the actual context.[10] Accordingly his conclusion lacks a sound basis.

The weakness of complementarian analyses of 1 Timothy 2 is reflected in the structure of *WITC*. After Baugh's chapter, it proceeds with backwards logic. The meaning of *authenteō* as 'exercise authority' is determined first, without proper attention to the context of Paul's use of this word, and the expositions which follow are then largely fashioned on the basis of this meaning.[11]

Grudem's approach in *EFBT* suffers from corresponding methodological defects. He starts with his beliefs about male–female authority structures, which he sees as implied in Genesis 2, then expounds 1 Timothy 2:11–15 in the light of those beliefs and without looking at what Paul says in 1:1 – 2:7.[12]

Smith's exposition shares a similar flaw. She notes the relevance of false teaching to 2:1–2, but her exposition then makes no mention of it until she reaches verse 15. In similar vein, Sandom starts her exposition of 1 Timothy 2:8–15 with the words 'We should note the context of this passage' but then

---

10. *WITC*, 279–296. Padgett 1997, 25, opts for 'have authority', but with 'a subtle negative connotation'.
11. Another important feature of the reasoning is that submission is understood to be contrasted with the exercise of authority: *WITC*, 135 (Köstenberger), 187–188 (Schreiner). But submission can as easily be understood to be contrasted with domination.
12. *EFBT*, 29–45, 65–74.

ignores the context which leads up to 2:8–15, except for stating that Timothy
has been left in charge of the church at Ephesus. Nothing of 1:1 – 2:7 is
mentioned in her exposition. Poythress, when interpreting 2:8–15, similarly
ignores the immediate context and Paul's train of reasoning from 1:1 to 2:7. He
discusses 2:8–15 without any reference to the false teachings which are Paul's
stated concern.[13]

The central question to which these expositions give rise is: why do these
complementarian scholars believe or assume that verses 11–14 are a digression,
away from Paul's main topic of combating false teaching? Köstenberger
considers that Paul signals a change of topic by starting verse 11 with the word
gunē. This is a weak argument, which ignores Paul's flow of thought. Its weakness
is a symptom of the unsatisfactory method adopted, which is, explicitly, to
ignore the context until after analysis of the syntax.[14] Grudem's justification is
that no Ephesian women were teaching falsely, so verses 11–14 cannot be about
combating false teaching; in substance, this is also Schreiner's view.[15] But in
chapters 12 and 13 we saw the evidence in Paul's letter that some Ephesian
women were indeed teaching falsely, and identified also the features which tie
1 Timothy 2 together as a connected train of thought concerned with combating
false teaching.

Once we see from the context what 1 Timothy 2 is about, the translation of
authentein as 'exercise authority' strikes an evidently discordant note. Paul is not
writing in chapter 2 about who should exercise authority over the church
assembly. He is not writing about this subject anywhere in 1:1 – 2:10, so why
should we suppose a sudden switch to this subject in 2:11–14? He does not say
that the quarrelsome men (2:8) or the immodest wealthy women (vv. 9–10) have
been exercising authority over the public assembly, whether legitimately or
illegitimately. Eve did not exercise authority over Adam (vv. 13–14). The
childbearing (v. 15) has nothing to do with exercising authority over the assembly.
Even when Paul moves on to the subject of elders in chapter 3, he makes no
remarks about elders having or exercising authority over the church, whether

---

13. Smith 2012, 26–40; Sandom 2012, 154–160; *RBMW*, 237–250 (Poythress), especially
    242. Moo (*RBMW*, 176–192) considers some possible content of the false teaching
    but still expounds the critical part of 1 Tim. 2 without identifying how Paul's train
    of thought flows on from his remarks in 1:1 – 2:7.

14. *WITC*, 155, 152–153.

15. *EFBT*, 280–284; *WITC*, 205 (but Schreiner acknowledges, albeit only as a possibility,
    that some of the women may have been teaching falsely).

in the public assembly or otherwise.[16] The exercise of authority is not the issue that he is addressing. The context of chapter 2 shows that Paul is concerned that a woman might teach a man falsely, not that women might authoritatively teach men true doctrine. This context stands, even if the details of the interpretation that I have offered in chapters 12 and 13 are mistaken.

I must suggest that the subject of authority structures for public worship in 1 Timothy 2 is a mirage. It arises from a misreading of chapter 2 as a set of instructions for public assemblies, coupled with a cultural belief in past centuries that men should always be in charge.

WITC has certainly helped to clarify the interpretive issues. I stand in awe of the prodigious labour and erudition that has gone into it. But the reasoning is unsatisfactory. It is grieving to conclude that devout and able scholars have put such great efforts into advancing an interpretation which divorces verses 11–14 from their context.

---

16. We can infer from 3:5 that Paul's view of eldership includes a responsibility to exercise authority, but in this passage his actual description of the elders' task is 'taking care' (*epimeleomai*) of the church. This is the same word as is used of the good Samaritan and the inn-keeper, taking care of the injured traveller (Luke 10:34–35). Paul makes no express mention of the exercise of authority in chapter 3.

APPENDIX 7 (CHAPTER 16)
TAKING STOCK OF TRANSLATION ISSUES

In appendix 1 I suggested that cultural ideas and traditions in Bible translation have had powerful impacts upon verses bearing on a woman's place, and therefore require special attention to guard against them. This is borne out by what we have seen in nearly every chapter. In particular, we have seen the influence of traditional patriarchal culture upon translation choices.

In chapter 2 we saw the obscure translation of 1 Corinthians 7:4 by the NIV 1984, which hid from the reader Paul's statement about a wife's authority over her husband's body.

In chapter 4 we saw that in Ephesians 5:23 both the ESV and the NIV obscure Paul's designation of Christ as head in the sense of saviour. We saw that many English versions do not accurately translate the first word of Ephesians 5:24 ('but'), because they have not grasped Paul's train of thought, which is that he wants wives to submit to their husbands even though their husbands are not in authority over them. We also saw that in 1 Timothy 5:14 Paul wants widows to remarry and be masters over their households. ESV and NIV dilute this to 'manage' and EHV to 'keep house'.

In chapter 5 we saw that English translations of Judges 4:4 do not agree on whether Deborah was 'judging' Israel or 'leading' Israel, but that it is clear both from Judges 2:16–19 and from the book as a whole that the Hebrew word is used to refer to governing, and not only to judging.

In chapter 6 we saw that in 1 Peter 3:7 many versions follow a translation tradition which contains a mistake. The mistake obscures Peter's reasoning that husbands should behave with gentleness towards their wives as the weaker partner, and should pay honour to their wives as co-heirs of salvation.

In chapter 7 we saw many translation issues, mainly arising from a mistaken conception that in 1 Corinthians 11 Paul is writing about veils, supposedly as a symbol of women being under men's authority. We saw that some versions reverse the meaning of verse 10, effectively deleting Paul's words that a woman ought to have authority over her head and replacing them with a creative paraphrase to the effect that a woman ought to have her head covered as a symbol of her subjection to men's authority. We saw translators reversing the meaning of verse 16, changing 'no such custom' to 'no other custom'. We saw that in some instances in this passage the ESV translates *anēr* as 'husband' and *gunē* as 'wife', despite the absence of verbal signals flagging these specific meanings in place of the more general meanings of 'man' and 'woman'.

In chapter 9 we saw that 1 Corinthians 14:33 should not be split into two and partly joined onto verses 34–35 as in some versions. In chapter 10 we saw that, at the least, our Bibles should have a footnote, along the lines of: 'Manuscript evidence indicates that verses 34 and 35 may be an interpolation, not original to Paul, and should be omitted.' Better, verses 34–35 should be placed in italics or in a footnote, together with an explanation that discrepancies in manuscripts suggest that they are of doubtful authenticity.

In chapter 11 we saw that translations of 1 Timothy 1:3 which refer to false 'doctrine' produce an unduly abstract impression of what Paul is concerned about, which extends to behaviour.

In chapter 12 we saw that 1 Timothy 2:12 should not be divided off from verse 11. It should not be translated as many versions have it, along the lines: 'I do not permit a woman to teach or to exercise authority over a man; she is to keep silent.' From the context, a literal rendering would be on the lines of: 'I am not permitting a woman to teach and overpower a man, but to be in quietness.' Moreover, the conventional picture of gossipy women poking their noses into other people's business, as depicted in most English translations of 1 Timothy 5:13, misses the mark. The wealthy young widows are going around from house to house talking nonsense (not gossip) and dabbling in sorcery (not being busybodies). They are abandoning their faith (1 Tim. 5:12, ESV), not breaking their first pledge (NIV). In Paul's subsequent letter the women who are under the sway of false teachers (2 Tim. 3:6) are not 'silly' (as in ASV and eighteen other versions) or 'weak-willed' (as in CJB and OJB). These descriptions reflect the traditional cultural view that women are inherently defective in nature. The Greek text contains no word meaning 'silly' or 'weak-willed'. Paul's attitude to these women is not contempt but concern. They are 'little women', that is, they are immature, and hence vulnerable to false teachers.

In chapter 14 we saw that Phoebe (Rom. 16:2) was not merely 'a great help' (NIV 1984) but almost certainly 'a patron' (ESV). We saw that many versions misrepresent the outstanding missionary apostle Junia (Rom. 16:7) as a man called Junias. We saw that ESV's rendering, making her merely a person 'well known to the apostles', should be rejected with a high degree of confidence.

In chapter 15 we saw that English versions of 1 Timothy 3:1–7 and Titus 1:5–9 exclude women from qualifying as elders, but such exclusion does not reflect the Greek text.

While scholars have direct access to the original languages of the Bible, church ministers and other believers rely heavily on English versions for understanding Scripture. The process of making corrections to translations, which started when contemporary translators became more aware of the distorting impact of patriarchal assumptions, needs to continue if the Bible is to be correctly understood.

REFERENCES

Adams, Edward. 2015. *The Earliest Christian Meeting Places: Almost Exclusively Houses?* Rev. ed. London: T&T Clark.

Anonymous. 2007. 'A Female Apostle?' CBMW. <https://cbmw.org/uncategorized/a-female-apostle/>.

Arnold, Clinton E. 1989. *Ephesians: Power and Magic: The Concept of Power in Ephesians in Light of Its Historical Setting.* Grand Rapids, MI: Baker.

———. 1993a. 'Ephesus.' In *Dictionary of Paul and His Letters*, eds. Gerald F. Hawthorne, Ralph P. Martin and Daniel G. Reid, 249–253. Leicester: Inter-Varsity Press.

———. 1993b. 'Magic.' In *Dictionary of Paul and His Letters*, eds. Gerald F. Hawthorne, Ralph P. Martin and Daniel G. Reid, 580–583. Leicester: Inter-Varsity Press.

———. 1994. 'Jesus Christ: "Head" of the Church (Colossians and Ephesians).' In *Jesus of Nazareth: Lord and Christ: Essays on the Historical Jesus and New Testament Christology*, eds. Joel B. Green and Max Turner, 346–366. Grand Rapids, MI: Eerdmans.

———. 2010. *Ephesians.* Grand Rapids, MI: Zondervan.

Atkinson, David. 1990. *The Message of Genesis 1–11: The Dawn of Creation.* BST. Leicester: Inter-Varsity Press.

Bailey, Kenneth E. 2000. 'Women in the New Testament: A Middle Eastern Cultural View.' *Theology Matters* 6, no. 1: 1–11.

———. 2011. *Paul through Mediterranean Eyes: Cultural Studies in 1 Corinthians.* Downers Grove, IL: InterVarsity Press.

Baron-Cohen, Simon. 2003. *The Essential Difference: The Truth about the Male and Female Brain.* New York: Basic.

Barth, M. 1974. *Ephesians: Translation and Commentary on Chapters 4–6.* New York: Doubleday.

Bauckham, Richard. 2002. *Gospel Women: Studies of the Named Women in the Gospels.* Grand Rapids, MI: Eerdmans.

———. 2006. *Jesus and the Eyewitnesses: The Gospels as Eyewitness Testimony.* Grand Rapids, MI: Eerdmans.

Baum, Armin D. 2014. 'Paul's Conflicting Statements on Female Public Speaking (1 Cor. 11:5) and Silence (1 Cor. 14:34–35): A New Suggestion.' *TynBul* 65, no. 2: 247–274.

Berman, Joshua A. 2008. *Created Equal: How the Bible Broke with Ancient Political Thought.* New York: OUP.

Biggs, Sarah J. 2014. 'The Burden of Writing: Scribes in Medieval Manuscripts.' British Library. <http://blogs.bl.uk/digitisedmanuscripts/2014/06/the-burden-of-writing-scribes-in-medieval-manuscripts.html>.

Bird, Graeme D. 2010. *Multitextuality in the Homeric* Iliad*: The Witness of the Ptolemaic Papyri.* Harvard University, Center for Hellenic Studies. <https://chs.harvard.edu/CHS/article/display/4742>.

Bischoff, Bernhard, and Michael Lapidge, eds. 1994. *Biblical Commentaries from the Canterbury School of Theodore and Hadrian.* Cambridge: CUP.

Blomberg, Craig L. 2005. 'Women in Ministry: A Complementarian Perspective.' In *Two Views on Women in Ministry*, ed. James R. Beck, 121–184. Rev. ed. Grand Rapids, MI: Zondervan.

———. 2014. 'Women in the Pulpit?' <http://www.lionelwindsor.net/wordpress/wp-content/2015/04/women_in_the_pulpit.pdf>.

Blue, B. B. 1993. 'Love Feast.' In *Dictionary of Paul and His Letters*, ed. Gerald F. Hawthorne, Ralph P. Martin and Daniel G. Reid, 578–579. Leicester: Inter-Varsity Press.

Brennan, Chris. 2013. 'The Planetary Joys and the Origins of the Significations of the Houses and Triplicities.' *ISAR International Astrologer* 42, no. 1: 27–42. <http://www.hellenisticastrology.com/the-planetary-joys.pdf>.

British Museum. 2017. 'Coin R.6509.' <http://www.britishmuseum.org/research/collection_online/collection_object_details.aspx?objectId=1216066&partId=1>.

Brookins, Timothy A. 2014. *Corinthian Wisdom, Stoic Philosophy, and the Ancient Economy.* New York: CUP.

Brown, J. G. 2012. 'A Historian Looks at 1 Timothy 2:11–14.' *Priscilla Papers* 26, no. 3: 7–11. <https://www.cbeinternational.org/resources/article/priscilla-papers/historian-looks-1-timothy-211-14>.

Buckland, W. W. 1921. *A Text-Book of Roman Law from Augustus to Justinian.* Cambridge: CUP.

Burer, Michael H., and Daniel B. Wallace. 2001. 'Was Junia Really an Apostle? A Reexamination of Romans 16:7.' *NTS* 47: 76–91.

Burk, Denny. 2012. 'How Important Is Complementarianism? A Response to Carl Trueman.' <http://www.dennyburk.com/how-important-is-complementarianism-a-response-to-carl-trueman/>.

Byrd, Aimee. 2016. *No Little Women: Equipping All Women in the Household of God.* Phillipsburg, NJ: P&R.

Capper, Brian J. 2005. 'To Keep Silent, Ask Husbands at Home, and Not to Have Authority over Men: The Transition from Gathering in Private to Meeting in Public Space in Second Generation Christianity and the Exclusion of Women from Leadership of the Public Assembly.' *ThZ* 61, no. 2: 113–131 (Part 1); and 61, no. 4: 301–319 (Part 2).

Carson, D. A., John Piper and Tim Keller. [no date]. 'Why Is The Gospel Coalition Complementarian?' TGC. <http://resources.thegospelcoalition.org/library/why-is-the-gospel-coalition-complementarian>.

Cartwright, Mark. 2016. 'Magic in Ancient Greece.' *Ancient History Encyclopedia.* <https://www.ancient.eu/article/926/magic-in-ancient-greece/>.

Clark, Elizabeth A. 1983. *Women in the Early Church.* Message of the Fathers of the Church 13. Wilmington, DE: Michael Glazier.

Clark, Peter J., ed. 2006. *Tetrabiblos or the Quadripartite Mathematical Treatise, Four Books of the Influence of the Stars.* By Claudius Ptolemy. Translated from the Greek paraphrase of Proclus by J. M. Ashman (London: Davis and Dickson, 1822). <http://www.astrologiamedieval.com/tabelas/Tetrabiblos.pdf>.

Clarke, Graham. 2001. 'As in All the Churches of the Saints.' *BT* 52, no. 1: 144–147.

Cottrell, Jack. 1997. 'Christ: A Model for Headship and Submission; A Crucial Verse in 1 Corinthians 11 Overturns Egalitarian Interpretations.' *CBMW News* 2, no. 4: 7–8.

deSilva, David A. 2000. *Honor, Patronage, Kinship and Purity: Unlocking New Testament Culture.* Downers Grove, IL: InterVarsity Press.

Evangelical Alliance. 2012. 'Statistics on Women in Ministry.' <http://www.eauk.org/church/research-and-statistics/women-in-ministry.cfm>.

Fee, G. D. 1987. *The First Epistle to the Corinthians.* NICNT. Grand Rapids: Eerdmans.

———. 1994. *God's Empowering Presence: The Holy Spirit in the Letters of Paul.* Peabody, MA: Hendrickson.

Fine, Cordelia. 2010. *Delusions of Gender: How Our Minds, Society and Neurosexism Create Difference.* New York: Norton.

Finney, Mark. 2010. 'Honour, Head-Coverings and Headship: 1 Corinthians 11.2–16 in Its Social Context.' *JSNT* 33, no. 1: 31–58.

Freisenbruch, Annelise. 2010. *Caesars' Wives: Sex, Power and Politics in the Roman Empire.* New York: Free Press.

Gempf, Conrad. 1993. 'Paul at Athens.' In *Dictionary of Paul and His Letters*, eds. Gerald F. Hawthorne, Ralph P. Martin and Daniel G. Reid, 51–54. Leicester: Inter-Varsity Press.

Georges, Jayson. 2017. *The 3D Gospel: Ministry in Guilt, Shame and Fear Cultures.* Rev. ed. Timē Press.

Giles, Kevin. 2000. 'A Critique of the "Novel" Contemporary Interpretation of 1 Timothy 2:9–15 Given in the Book *Women in the Church.*' *EvQ* 72, no. 2: 151–167 (Part 1); *EvQ* 72, no. 3: 195–215 (Part 2).

———. 2017. *The Rise and Fall of the Complementarian Doctrine of the Trinity.* Eugene: Cascade.

Gill, David W. J. 1990. 'The Importance of Roman Portraiture for Head-Coverings in 1 Corinthians 11:2–16.' *TynBul* 41, no. 2: 245–260.

Glahn, Sandra. 2015. 'The Identity of Artemis in First-Century Ephesus.' *DTS Magazine*, 15 July.

Grudem, Wayne. 1994. *Systematic Theology: An Introduction to Biblical Doctrine.* Leicester: Inter-Varsity Press.

———. 2004. *Evangelical Feminism and Biblical Truth: An Analysis of 118 Disputed Questions.* Leicester: Inter-Varsity Press.

———. 2006. *Evangelical Feminism: A New Path to Liberalism?* Wheaton, IL: Crossway.

Gurry, Peter. 2018. 'Preferring a Longer Reading in Ephesians 5.22.' Evangelical Textual Criticism. <http://evangelicaltextualcriticism.blogspot.co.uk/2018/05/preferring-longer-reading-in-ephesians.html>.

Haidt, Jonathan. 2012. *The Righteous Mind: Why Good People Are Divided by Politics and Religion.* London: Penguin.

Hanson, A. T. 1982. *The Pastoral Epistles.* NCBC. London: Marshall, Morgan & Scott.

Head, Peter M. 2012. 'Letter Carriers and the Pauline Tradition: N. T. Wright on Phoebe.' <http://tychichus.blogspot.co.uk/2012/11/nt-wright-on-phoebe.html>.

Hegedus, Tim. 2007. *Early Christianity and Ancient Astrology.* New York: Peter Lang.

Hemelrijk, Emily A. 2015. *Hidden Lives, Public Personae: Women and Civic Life in the Roman West.* Oxford: OUP.

Hensley, Adam D. 2012. 'σιγαω, λαλεω, and ὑποτασσω in 1 Corinthians 14:34 in Their Literary and Rhetorical Context.' *JETS* 55, no. 2: 343–364.

Hoag, Gary C. 2015. *Wealth in Ancient Ephesus and the First Letter to Timothy: Fresh Insights from Ephesiaca by Xenophon of Ephesus.* Bulletin for Biblical Research Supplement 11. Winona Lake, IN: Eisenbrauns.

Horsley, G. H. R. 1987. *New Documents Illustrating Early Christianity: A Review of the Greek Inscriptions and Papyri Published in 1979.* Sydney: Macquarie University.

Hugenberger, Gordon P. 1992. 'Women in Church Office: Hermeneutics or Exegesis? A Survey of Approaches to 1 Tim 2:8–15.' *JETS* 35, no. 3: 341–360.

Huijgen, Arnold. 2011. *Divine Accommodation in John Calvin's Theology: Analysis and Assessment.* Göttingen: Vandenhoek & Ruprecht.

Hurley, James B. 1981. *Man and Woman in Biblical Perspective: A Study in Role Relationships and Authority.* Leicester: Inter-Varsity Press.

Hurtado, Larry. 2017. 'Paul and 1 Corinthians 14:34–35.' Larry Hurtado's Blog. <https://larryhurtado.wordpress.com/2017/09/23/paul-and-1-corinthians-1434-35/>.

Huttner, Ulrich. 2013. *Early Christianity in the Lycus Valley*, trans. David Green. Leiden: Koninklijke Brill.

Ibita, Ma. Marilou S. 2016. 'Food Crises in Corinth? Revisiting the Evidence and Its Possible Implications in Reading 1 Cor 11:17–34.' In *Stones, Bones and the Sacred: Essays on Material Culture and Ancient Religion in Honor of Dennis E. Smith*, ed. Alan H. Cadwallader, 33–53. Atlanta, GA: Society of Biblical Literature.

James, Sharon. 2007. *God's Design for Women: Biblical Womanhood for Today*. Darlington: EP Books.

Johnson, Alan F., ed. 2010. *How I Changed My Mind about Women in Leadership: Compelling Stories from Prominent Evangelicals*. Grand Rapids, MI: Zondervan.

Karssen, G. 1985. *Frauen der Bibel*. Stuttgart: Neuhausen.

Kartzow, Marianne Bjelland. 2009. *Gossip and Gender: Othering of Speech in the Pastoral Epistles*. Berlin: Walter de Gruyter.

Keener, C. S. 1993. 'Man and Woman.' In *Dictionary of Paul and His Letters*, eds. Gerald F. Hawthorne, Ralph P. Martin and Daniel G. Reid, 583–592. Leicester: Inter-Varsity Press.

———. 1996. '"I've Got You Covered": The Cultural Background for Veiling Women.' *Priscilla Papers* 10, no. 1: 7–8.

Kelly, J. N. D. 1963. *A Commentary on the Pastoral Epistles: I Timothy, II Timothy, Titus*. BNTC. London: A&C Black.

Kidd, Thomas. 2012. 'Campus Ministry Conflict: Cru Finds Itself in Debate over Women's Roles in Ministry.' *World Magazine*. <https://world.wng.org/2012/11/campus_ministry_conflict>.

Kloha, J. J. 2006. 'A Textual Commentary on Paul's First Epistle to the Corinthians.' Ph.D. thesis, University of Leeds.

Knight, George W. III. 1992. *The Pastoral Epistles: A Commentary on the Greek Text*. NIGTC. Grand Rapids, MI: Eerdmans.

Kooten, George H. van, and Peter Barthel, eds. 2015. *The Star of Bethlehem and the Magi: Interdisciplinary Perspectives from Experts on the Ancient Near East, the Greco-Roman World, and Modern Astronomy*. Leiden: Koninklijke Brill.

Köstenberger, Andreas J. 1994. 'Gender Passages in the NT: Hermeneutical Fallacies Critiqued.' *Westminster Theological Journal* 56, no. 2: 259–283.

———, and Thomas R. Schreiner, eds. 2016. *Women in the Church: An Interpretation and Application of 1 Timothy 2:9–15*. 3rd ed. Wheaton, IL: Crossway.

Kroeger, Richard Clark and Catherine Clark. 1992. *I Suffer Not a Woman: Rethinking 1 Timothy 2:11–15 in Light of Ancient Evidence*. Grand Rapids, MI: Baker.

Kruse, C. G. 1993. 'Ministry.' In *Dictionary of Paul and His Letters*, eds. Gerald F. Hawthorne, Ralph P. Martin and Daniel G. Reid, 602–608. Leicester: Inter-Varsity Press.

Larsen, Timothy. 2007. 'Women in Public Ministry: A Historic Evangelical Distinctive.'
In *Women, Ministry and the Gospel: Exploring New Paradigms*, ed. Mark Husbands and
Timothy Larsen, 213–236. Downers Grove, IL: InterVarsity Press.

Lausanne Movement. 2011. 'The Cape Town Commitment.' <https://www.lausanne.
org/content/ctc/ctcommitment>.

Lavrinoviča, Alesja. 2017. '1 Cor. 14.34–5 without "In All the Churches of the Saints".'
NTS 63, no. 3: 370–389.

Lewis, C. S. 1960. *The Four Loves*. New York: Harcourt.

Lincoln, A. T. 1990. *Ephesians*. WBC. Dallas, TX: Word Inc.

McGuckin, J. A., ed. 2011. *The Encyclopedia of Eastern Orthodox Christianity*. Oxford:
Wiley-Blackwell.

Middleton, J. Richard. 1994. 'The Liberating Image? Interpreting the Imago Dei
in Context.' *Christian Scholars Review* 24, no. 1: 8–25.

Mohler, Albert R. 2009. 'Should I Stay or Should I Go?' Ligonier Ministries.
<https://www.ligonier.org/learn/articles/should-i-stay-or-should-i go/>.

Moo, Douglas J. 1980. '1 Timothy 2:11–15: Meaning and Significance.' *TrinJ* 1,
New Series: 62–83.

———. 1981. 'The Interpretation of 1 Timothy 2:11–15: A Rejoinder.' *TrinJ* 2,
New Series: 198–222.

Mosse, Martin. 2007. *The Three Gospels: New Testament History Introduced by the Synoptic
Problem*. Milton Keynes: Paternoster.

Mowczko, Marg. 2015a. 'What Eve's Reply to the Serpent Tells Us.' <http://
margmowczko.com/eves-statement-to-the-serpent/>.

———. 2015b. 'What Is Meant by Didaktikos in 1 Timothy 3:2 and 2 Timothy 2:24?'
<http://margmowczko.com/didaktikos-teachable/>.

O'Brien, P. T. 1999. *The Letter to the Ephesians*. PNTC. Grand Rapids, MI: Eerdmans.

Ogden, Daniel. 1996. *Greek Bastardy in the Classical and Hellenistic Periods*. Oxford:
Clarendon.

Orthodox Church in America. 2016. 'St. Junia.' <https://oca.org/saints/lives/2016/
05/17/101406-st-junia>.

Osiek, Carolyn, and David L. Balch. 1997. *Families in the New Testament World: Households
and House Churches*. Louisville, KY: Westminster John Knox.

Padgett, Alan G. 1997. 'The Scholarship of Patriarchy (on 1 Timothy 2:8–15): A Response
to *Women in the Church*.' *Priscilla Papers* 11, no. 1: 24–29.

———. 2011. *As Christ Submits to the Church: A Biblical Understanding of Leadership and
Mutual Submission*. Grand Rapids, MI: Baker.

Pawson, J. David. 1988. *Leadership Is Male: A Challenge to Christian Feminism*.
Crowborough: Highland.

Payne, Philip B. 1995. 'Fuldensis, Sigla for Variants in Vaticanus, and 1 Cor. 14.34–5.'
NTS 41, no. 2: 240–262.

———. 2006. 'Wild Hair and Gender Equality in 1 Corinthians 11:2–16.' *Priscilla Papers* 20, no. 3: 9–18.

———. 2009. *Man and Woman, One in Christ: An Exegetical and Theological Study of Paul's Letters.* Grand Rapids, MI: Zondervan.

———. 2014. 'Οὐδέ Combining Two Elements to Convey a Single Idea and 1 Timothy 2:12: Further Insights.' *Missing Voices: Broadening the Discussion of Men, Women, and Ministry* (special edition journal of CBE International): 24–34.

———. 2015. 'The Bible Teaches the Equal Standing of Man and Woman.' *Priscilla Papers* 29, no. 1: 3–10.

———. 2017a. 'Vaticanus Distigme-obelos Symbols Marking Added Text, Including 1 Corinthians 14.34–5.' *NTS* 63, no. 4: 604–625.

———. 2017b. 'More Positive Reviews of My New Article on Codex Vaticanus in New Testament Studies.' <https://www.pbpayne.com/positive-reviews-new-article-codex-vaticanus-new-testament-studies-2/>.

Pearson, Allison. 2017. 'Only Connect: The TV Quiz Where Men Are No Competition.' *Daily Telegraph*, 12 April 2017; reprinted in *The Week*, 22 April 2017.

Pelikan, Jaroslav, ed. 1958. *Luther's Works*, Vol. 1: *Lectures on Genesis: Chapters 1–5*. St Louis, MO: Concordia.

Perriman, A. 1998. *Speaking of Women: Interpreting Paul.* Leicester: Apollos.

Peterman, G. W. 1999. 'Marriage and Sexual Fidelity in the Papyri, Plutarch and Paul.' *TynBul* 50, no. 2: 163–172.

Peterson, Jordan B. 2018. *12 Rules for Life: An Antidote for Chaos.* London: Allen Lane.

Pierce, Ronald W., and Rebecca Merrill Groothuis, eds. 2005. *Discovering Biblical Equality: Complementarity without Hierarchy.* 2nd ed. Downers Grove, IL: InterVarsity Press.

Pingree, David E. 1979. 'Astrology.' In *The New Encyclopaedia Britannica*, 2:219–223. 15th ed. Chicago, IL: Benton.

Piper, John. 2009. *This Momentary Marriage: A Parable of Permanence.* Wheaton: Crossway.

———, and Wayne Grudem. 1992. *Fifty Crucial Questions: An Overview of Central Concerns about Manhood and Womanhood.* Wheaton, IL: CBMW.

Piper, John, and Wayne Grudem, eds. 1991. *Recovering Biblical Manhood and Womanhood: A Response to Evangelical Feminism.* Wheaton, IL: Crossway.

Prior, David. 1993. *The Message of 1 Corinthians: Life in the Local Church.* BST. 2nd ed. Leicester: Inter-Varsity Press.

Prioreschi, Plinio. 1996. *A History of Medicine*, Vol. 2: *Greek Medicine*. 2nd ed. Omaha, NE: Horatius.

Resnick, Irven M. and Kenneth F. Kitchell, Jr, trans. 2008. *Albert the Great: Questions Concerning Aristotle's* On Animals. Vol. 9 of *The Fathers of the Church: Mediaeval Continuation*. Washington DC: Catholic University of America Press.

Rinehart, John. 2013. *Gospel Patrons: People Whose Generosity Changed the World.* Lexington, KY: Reclaimed Publishing.

Roberts, Alastair. 2014a. 'Feminism, Equality, and Authority.' Alastair's Adversaria.
  <https://alastairadversaria.com/2014/08/28/feminism-equality-and-authority/>.
———. 2014b. 'Why a Masculine Priesthood Is Essential.' Alastair's Adversaria.
  <https://alastairadversaria.com/2014/08/30/why-a-masculine-priesthood-is-
  essential/>.
Robinson, J. Armitage. 1909. *St Paul's Epistle to the Ephesians.* 2nd ed. reprint. London:
  Macmillan.
The Salvation Army. 2018. 'Catherine Booth.' <https://www.salvationarmy.org.uk/
  history-catherine-booth>.
Sandom, Carrie. 2012. *Different by Design: God's Blueprint for Men and Women.* Fearn,
  Ross-shire: Christian Focus.
Scheidel, Walter. 2008. 'Monogamy and Polygyny in Greece, Rome and World History.'
  Paper, Stanford University. <https://www.princeton.edu/~pswpc/pdfs/scheidel/
  060807.pdf>.
Schermann, Theodorus. 1907. *Prophetarum Vitae Fabulosae Indices Apostolorum Discipulorumque
  Domini Dorotheo, Epiphanio, Hippolyto Aliisque Vindicata.* Leipzig: Teubner.
Schmid, U. 2011. 'Conceptualizing "Scribal" Performances: Reader's Notes.' In *The
  Textual History of the Greek New Testament: Changing Views in Contemporary Research*,
  eds. K. Wachtel and M. Holmes, 49–64. Atlanta, GA: Society of Biblical
  Literature.
Schreiner, Thomas R. 2010. 'Philip Payne on Familiar Ground: A Review of Philip
  B. Payne, *Man and Woman, One in Christ.' JBMW* 15, no. 1: 33–46.
———. 2018. *1 Corinthians: An Introduction and Commentary.* TNTC. London: Inter-Varsity
  Press; Downers Grove, IL: InterVarsity Press.
Shack, J. 2014. 'A Text without 1 Corinthians 14.34–35? Not According to the Manuscript
  Evidence.' *JGRChJ* 10: 90–112.
Shaw, David A. 2013. 'Is Junia Also among the Apostles? Romans 16:7 and Recent
  Debates.' *Churchman* 127, no. 2: 105–118.
Smith, Claire. 2012. *God's Good Design: What the Bible Really Says about Men and Women.*
  Kingsford: Matthias Media.
Snapp, James. 2017. 'Fool and Knave! Hebrews 1 in Codex Vaticanus.' The Text of the
  Gospels. <http://www.thetextofthegospels.com/2017/06/fool-and-knave-hebrews-1-
  in-codex.html>.
Stackhouse, John G. 2015. *Partners in Christ: A Conservative Case for Egalitarianism.*
  Downers Grove, IL: InterVarsity Press.
Stark, Rodney. 1996. *The Rise of Christianity: How the Obscure, Marginal Jesus Movement Became
  the Dominant Religious Force in the Western World in a Few Centuries.* Princeton, NJ:
  Princeton University Press.
Stevens, John. 2012. 'FIEC: Why Are We Complementarian?' John-Stevens.com.
  <http://www.john-stevens.com/2012/09/fiec-why-we-are-complementarian.html>.

Storms, Sam. [no date]. 'Men and Women in Ministry: The Meaning of Headship.'
    Sam Storms: Enjoying God. <http://www.samstorms.com/all-articles/post/
    men-and-women-in-ministry:-the-meaning-of-headship>.

———. 2007. 'Women in Ministry in the Vineyard, USA.' *JBMW* 12, no. 2: 20–25.

Stott, John R. W. 1979. *The Message of Ephesians: God's New Society.* BST. Leicester: Inter-
    Varsity Press.

———. 1996. *The Message of 1 Timothy and Titus.* BST. Leicester: Inter-Varsity Press.

Stuttard, David. 2018. *Nemesis: Alcibiades and the Fall of Athens.* Cambridge, MA: Harvard
    University Press.

Tagliabue, Aldo C. F. 2011. 'Commentary on the First Book of the *Ephesiaca* of
    Xenophon of Ephesus.' Ph.D. thesis, Universities of Padua and Swansea. <http://
    paduaresearch.cab.unipd.it/3425/1/PHDDISSERTATIONTAGLIABUE.pdf>.

Tidball, Derek and Dianne. 2012. *The Message of Women: Creation, Grace and Gender.* BST
    Bible Themes. Nottingham: Inter-Varsity Press.

Towner, Philip H. 2006. *The Letters to Timothy and Titus.* NICNT. Grand Rapids, MI:
    Eerdmans.

Trueman, Carl. 2012. 'Confused by Complementarianism? You Probably Should Be.'
    Mortification of Spin. <http://www.alliancenet.org/mos/postcards-from-
    palookaville/confused-by-complementarianism-you-probably-should-be#>.

Vigen, Tyler. [no date]. 'Spurious Correlations.' <http://www.tylervigen.com/spurious-
    correlations>.

Wallace, Daniel B. 1996. *Greek Grammar beyond the Basics: An Exegetical Syntax of the New
    Testament.* Grand Rapids, MI: Zondervan.

———. 2001a. 'From Wycliffe to King James (The Period of Challenge).' Bible.org.
    <https://bible.org/seriespage/1-wycliffe-king-james-period-challenge#>.

———. 2001b. 'From the KJV to the RV (from Elegance to Accuracy).' Bible.org.
    <https://bible.org/seriespage/3-kjv-rv-elegance-accuracy>.

———, and Michael H. Burer. 2001c. 'Was Junia Really an Apostle? A Reexamination
    of Romans 16:7.' *JBMW* 6, no. 2: 4–11.

Walsh, Jerome T. 2001. *Style and Structure in Biblical Hebrew Narrative.* Collegeville, PA:
    Michael Glazier.

Waltke, Bruce K., with Cathi J. Fredricks. 2001. *Genesis: A Commentary.* Grand Rapids, MI:
    Zondervan.

Walton, John H. 2009. *The Lost World of Genesis One.* Downers Grove, IL: InterVarsity
    Press.

Wenham, Gordon J. 1987. *Genesis 1–15.* WBC. Dallas, TX: Word Inc.

Westfall, Cynthia Long. 2014. 'The Meaning of αὐθεντέω in 1 Timothy 2.12.' *JGRChJ* 10:
    138–173.

———. 2016. *Paul and Gender: Reclaiming the Apostle's Vision for Men and Women in Christ.*
    Grand Rapids, MI: Baker.

Winter, Bruce W. 2000. 'The "New" Roman Wife and 1 Timothy 2:9–15: The Search for a *Sitz im Leben.' TynBul* 51, no. 2: 285–294.

———. 2003. *Roman Wives, Roman Widows: The Appearance of New Women and the Pauline Communities.* Grand Rapids, MI: Eerdmans.

———. 2004. 'You Were What You Wore in Roman Law: Deciphering the Dress Codes of 1 Timothy 2:9–15.' *SBL Forum*, n.p. <http://sbl-site.org/Article.aspx?ArticleID=277>.

Witherington, Ben. 2011. 'Ancient Readers and Manuscripts: William A. Johnson's Take.' Beliefnet. <http://www.beliefnet.com/columnists/bibleandculture/2011/01/ancient-readers-and-manuscripts-william-a-johnsons-take.html>.

Wood, Beulah, and contributors. 2017. *How I Changed my Mind about Women in Leadership.* Bangalore: SAIACS Press.

Yarbrough, Robert W. 2018. *The Letters to Timothy and Titus.* PNTC. Grand Rapids, MI: Eerdmans.

INDEX OF NAMES

This index includes names of places, of Christian organizations and of people, whether real (including authors, except as names of books of the Bible) or fictional. Certain names are not included, due to their frequency of appearance: Jesus Christ, Paul, Wayne Grudem and Philip Payne.

Artemis 241–242, 246–247, 256, 269, 272, 277, 285, 386–387
Asia/Asia Minor 34, 130, 243, 310
Assemblies of God 352
Athens 320
Atkinson, David 76
Augustine of Hippo 5, 87, 242
Augustus, Emperor 108

Babylonia 258
Bailey, Kenneth E. 166, 178, 187, 307, 375
Bar-Jesus 258
Barak 94
Barnabas 300, 306, 312
Baron-Cohen, Simon 83
Barrett, C. K. 298
Barth, M. 57
Bauckham, Richard 301–302
Baugh, Steve 39, 128, 217–218, 247, 259, 386–387, 389
Baum, Armin D. 168
Becke, Edmund 111
Belleville, Linda L. 73, 217, 231, 304, 311, 325, 372–373, 378, 386
Bengel, Johann 183–184, 196
Berman, Joshua A. 92
Bernice 311
Bethlehem 361–362
Beza, Theodore 304
Biggs, Sarah J. 182
Bilezikian, G. 69
Bird, Graeme D. 182, 184, 197
Bischoff, Bernhard 183
Bithynia 130
Blomberg, Craig 72, 208, 223
Blue, B. B. 21
Boaz 85
Booth, Catherine 352
Booth, William 352

Boudicca 311
Brennan, Chris 257
Brookins, Timothy A. 167
Brown, J. G. 11
Bruce, F. F. 57
Buckland, W. W. 24, 41, 66
Burer, Michael H. 302, 304
Burk, Denny 350, 354, 372, 375, 378, 389
Byrd, Aimee 89, 283

Caesarea 34
Calligraphos, Nicholas 301
Calvin, John 5–6, 9, 23, 94–95, 207, 215, 299–300
Cape Town (South Africa) 3
Cappadocia 130
Capper, Brian J. 167–168, 194, 218, 303, 308–309
Carson, D. A. 19, 81, 162, 165–166, 169, 175, 177, 190–192, 195–197, 350
Cartwright, Mark 242
Cassius Dio 311
Catiline 166
Cato 177
CBE (Christians for Biblical Equality) 2, 18, 158, 349, 354
CBMW (Council on Biblical Manhood and Womanhood) 2, 18–19, 349
Cenchreae 296, 298–299, 308
Chaldea 258
Chariton 128
Chrysostom, Dio 128
Chrysostom, John 7, 9, 23, 60–61, 77, 162, 165–166, 175, 232, 246, 275, 280, 282, 299–302, 304–306, 374
Cicero 166
Clark, Elizabeth A. 5
Clark, Peter J. 256, 258, 269
Clarke, Adam 7
Clarke, Graham 162

INDEX OF SCRIPTURE REFERENCES

Bold indicates main references where all or most of the chapter is concerned with a particular passage.

426   INDEX OF SCRIPTURE REFERENCES

1 Timothy (*cont.*)

5:15 *248, 255, 259, 262*
5:16 *87–88, 234*
5:17 *225, 227, 287, 289, 294, 323*
5:17–18 *335*
5:17–20 *212, 307*
5:17–22 *335*
5:19 *307, 323*
5:19–20 *335*
5:21 *149, 209*
5:21–22 *279, 335–336*
5:22 *267*
5:23 *211, 220, 365*
5:25 *212, 246*
6:1–2 *41, 212, 279*
6:2 *209, 279*
6:3 *210, 212–213, 261*
6:3–4 *317*
6:3–5 *213*
6:3–10 *256*
6:4–5 *246, 250, 253*
6:5 *212, 213, 247, 256*
6:5–11 *267*
6:6 *212*
6:9 *256*
6:9–10 *212*
6:11 *212, 246*
6:11–14 *209, 212, 279*
6:12 *265*
6:13–14 *209, 220*
6:14 *267*
6:16 *221*
6:17 *247, 257, 279*
6:17–19 *212–213, 257*
6:18 *246*
6:20 *209, 213, 245–246, 253, 257, 267, 279, 335*
6:20–21 *212, 253*
6:21 *261*

2 Timothy

1:2 *239*
1:5 *206, 266*
1:7 *220*
1:13–14 *226*
2:2 *18, 207, 233*
2:3 *233*
2:4–7 *267*
2:11–13 *275*
2:14 *213*
2:15 *205, 235*
2:15–19 *267*
2:16 *253*
2:16–18 *213, 261*
2:17 *258, 261*
2:17–18 *252, 259*
2:17–19 *213*
2:18 *213*
2:22–23 *267*
2:23 *213*
2:24–26 *113, 260, 261*
2:25–26 *213, 255*
3:1–5 *113*
3:2–9 *261*
3:5 *213, 258, 261*
3:5–9 *258*
3:6 *261, 393*
3:6–7 *219*
3:12 *241*
3:13 *258, 269, 277*
3:13–14 *267*
3:13–15 *206*
3:15 *266*
3:16 *xxii*
3:16–17 *xxiii, 210*
4:2 *208, 225*
4:14 *259*
4:14–15 *267*
4:19 *250, 302, 308*
4:21 *320*

Titus

1 *326, 334, 340*
1:1 *210*
1:4 *370*
1:5 *287, 315, 327, 334*
1:5–9 *315, 323, 330, 336, 347, 394*
1:6 *318–320, 323–324, 326, 336*
1:6–9 *223, 288, 293, 318, 326*
1:7 *287*
1:9 *208, 225, 294*
1:11 *254, 380*
1:12 *257, 306*
2:1 *254*
2:1–15 *210*
2:3 *206, 216, 225, 294, 318*
2:3–5 *3, 225, 233*
2:4 *368*
2:4–5 *31, 41*
2:5 *31, 41, 44, 87, 101, 195, 292–293, 369–370*
2:9 *44*
2:9–10 *195*
2:15 *254*
3:2 *101*
3:5 *90, 151*
3:6–8 *275*
3:9 *258*
3:13 *298*
3:14 *354*

Philemon

2 *167*
8–21 *43*
23 *34*

Hebrews

1 *185*
1:2 *144*

INDEX OF SOURCES BEFORE 1900

This index covers all sources before 1900 (except Scripture references), sorted by category, time frame and author, or title where author is unknown.